DIMENSIONS
OF
MAN

EDITED BY

Harold P. Simonson and John B. Magee

DIMENSIONS OF MAN

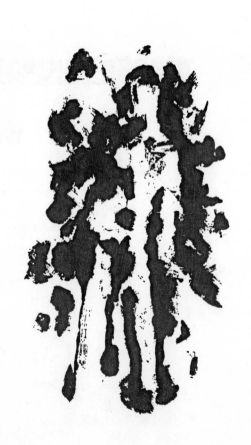

DIMENSIONS OF MAN

Harold P. Simonson
University of Washington

John B. Magee
University of Puget Sound

HARPER & ROW, Publishers
New York, Evanston, San Francisco, London

Sponsoring Editor: *Raleigh S. Wilson, Jr.*

Project Editor: *Alice M. Solomon*

Designer and illustrator: *Frances Torbert Tilley*

Production Supervisor: *Valerie Klima*

DIMENSIONS OF MAN

Library of Congress Cataloging in Publication Data

Simonson, Harold Peter, 1926-   comp.
  Dimensions of man.

  1. Religion—Collections. I. Magee, John
Benjamin, 1917-   joint comp.   II. Title.
BL25.S5   200'.8   73-1037
ISBN 0-06-046177-2

to BOB ALBERTSON

contents

alternate contents

EXPOSITION

classification and analysis

comparison and contrast

detail

definition

argumentation

description

narration

poetry

meditation

introduction

"Whoever you are, I fear you are walking the walks of dreams," writes Walt Whitman in the first selection of this anthology. This book was conceived as a personal address to that growing public of young and old who have again begun to ask ultimate questions about the dimensions of human nature. It is not so much a collection of readings *about* religion; it is directed instead to the themes that give rise to the religious gesture of the human spirit, stirring our intuitions and inviting us to the immemorial speculations about ourselves in relation to what we deem to be of final importance.

The present surge of interest in religion would have been difficult to predict a decade ago except to say that each generation has to come to terms somehow with the ultimate issues of life. The scene is complex—startling renewal in venerable institutions and on the streets; diverse experimentation with consciousness expansion through "high play," hypnosis, methods of meditation, or, following the lead of Aldous Huxley, drugs. There are psychological therapies, practiced at places like Esalen, that aim at "peak experiences," or "human optimums"; there are "underground" or "house" churches, where ancient rites are celebrated informally with high feeling; there is a new, high-paying, well-educated clientele for professional horoscope readers; and there is a revival of interest in the occult. From the East has come an increasing flood of exotic literature that has in turn produced a crop of devotees who practice yoga, work at transcendental meditation, or cast yarrow stalks with the *I Ching* in hand. And this list is far from complete.

It would appear that there is a growing dissatisfaction with the prevailing outlook, which is pragmatic or scientific. It is not hard to see why this has come about. The one-dimensional, prosaic consciousness of our culture has increasingly failed to yield life-supporting values. Under its aegis life for many people has become dreary, anxious, and increasingly devoid of meaning. The prestige of its great ideals has been eroded by the failure of its supporting institutions. Political institutions have failed to curb the growing violence evident in international and domestic affairs. Economic institutions, while exploiting and polluting our common environment, have made little headway with the chronic problems of human rights, the status of minorities, or the development of the nations of the third world. Education, too often equated with schooling, has been disappointing in many ways, but chiefly in its failure to respond to the quest for meaning and to show the way to some dimensions of ecstasy and joy in life. The churches, in possession of mysteries they do not seem to understand, insist on a rigid version of ethics they claim to be sure of and reenact rituals that are no longer vital to their people.

On the positive side, among those exploring new dimensions there have been experiences that are exciting and, in many cases, salutary. Some have discovered new depths of their own existence, found ways of relating more significantly to other people, and, occasionally, found new levels of psychic energy and enthusiasm for life.

It is obvious that this book is not organized around the standard academic disciplines. We have not, for instance, considered the standard problems of philosophy of religion: the problem of evil, the existence of God, and so on. There is a place for that kind of study, but in our opinion it properly comes after one has confronted the fundamental questions and facts of experience—the meaning of selfhood, time, the place of religious experience—that generate the religious attitude toward life. It is out of these that the rationally structured problems of philosophy of religion emerge. We have tried to expose the religious nerve and sometimes, perchance, its heart. Religion is a dimension at the center of man's existing. Whenever he comes to the ultimate issues about his own being—who he is, what his fellow man is, what lies in the human future—he is in the domain of religion.

If this book is used in connection with religion or philosophy of religion courses, the reader will discover there is much here that makes a sharp goad for philosophical reflection. What is the *meaning* of the concepts that are common throughout the selections—religion, God, transcendence, faith, ultimate time, the power of the future, self, the oneness of self and other, and so on? What secular experiences verge on the category of religion—the future, violence, history? Is there an ideal of personality implicit in these essays? Is there an ideal of society implicit here? In the light of the wide interest in the ecstatic aspect of human experience, what is the place of reason in religion? How does transcendence function in experience? What is the nature of the self? What kind of knowledge is self-knowledge? What are the differences in the categories of religion Eastern and Western? What distinguishes a secular stance toward life from a religious one? These are some of the questions that might be pursued.

America has tried hard to be a secular country—the most secular in the world despite its motto, "In God We Trust," engraved upon, of all things, its money. Our confidence has been in material things and material forces. But lacking a sense of some transcendent dimension, a sense of meaning, and a scale of reliable values, we have sickened. A society that "never had it so good" is discovering that affluence is not enough. About ten years ago a poll revealed that a majority of people thought a 30-percent rise in income would solve most of their problems. But since that time most of them have enjoyed such a rise of income, and they are not that much better off, "humanly speaking." It would seem that the more we have the more we need a dimension to life that will give sense to our affluence. We have grown fat but not healthy on a one-dimensional diet.

This doesn't indicate a need for a return to "the good old times" or "the old time religion," if there ever were any. Received faiths are questioned as much as any other parts of the establishment, but this question is itself religious in substance.

In addition to selecting readings that lead the student into the heart of religion itself, we have tried to sample a wide variety of traditions both Eastern and Western; there are selections from Hindu, Buddhist, Jewish, Christian, and Moslem sources, along with a variety of modern commentaries on contemporary experience. There was not space to balance the work with more viewpoints critical of religion. We have had to content ourselves with only a few, such as Freud's relegation of religion to an illusion of immaturity.

Though we have presented many ways of defining human life, we have not aimed at a complete anthology, and certainly not at a balanced collection of statements from the world's religions. There are several such works, and we have not tried to rival them. Our purpose is to give a sampling that will stimulate reflection, and we believe that anyone who carefully examines the contents will be driven at one point or another to consider the dimensions of man.

The main divisions of the work represent themes that structure this search for larger dimensions of being human. Part 1 begins with the *self* and its relations with the Other that constitutes its environment. Part 2 turns to the various expressions of *transcendence* itself—the ways in which man finds this dimension in the world of his experience but pointing somehow beyond the world, at least beyond the world as presently understood and experienced. Part 3 opens up the *future* as a dimension that has come disturbingly into our modern consciousness in the form of "future shock," as one writer puts it. The future is not yet, and still it is present in our every moment. Man is the being that lives toward the future in a way not suffered or enjoyed by any other being we know. We are anxious or burdened by that future. The notion of "future studies" has come recently to the fore, but generally, these studies suffer from being a simple projection of elements already working in the past. The potential human future is more mysterious and frightening than that.

In Part 4 we explore some possible *new directions*. Some of them imply the dehumanization, or what could be called the abolition, of man—a denigration of man to one-dimensional existence. Others suggest different possibilities. We have not passed on the promise of each of these. They belong to the contemporary exploration of man's dimensions. These things—new experiences, new types of communities, new dialogues between old enemies and rivals, and new forms of research—are actually happening. No one can say with complete assurance which of them, if any, contains the promise of man's future.

Part 5 is a short handbook of *religious experiences*. Not since William James have scholars been so interested in the strange varieties of the religious consciousness. Much that once belonged only to scholars is now in the public domain. A modern student would be wise to apprise himself of this material. The selections constitute a wide range of religious experience, from drug experiences and madness to the highest forms of Eastern and Western mysticism.

The purpose of this collection is not to make the student into a scholar of religion but to give him some resources to set him thinking about human experience in this dimension. He may want to compare his own experiences where they seem similar to or different from those of the authors quoted. Or he may find it interesting to discover where his fellow students stand in this strange territory. The great traditions are open to him in the works of the scholars of comparative religion. And, on every hand, there are those proclaiming their own experiences with drugs or with what they claim to be the influence of the Holy Spirit.

All of this has its chief significance when we ask what bearing it has on how to exist as a human being and what it means in our search for humanity, for man as a species. It is not primarily a problem for scholars; it is a problem for everyman. It will be settled, if at all, not in the library but in the cities of living people.

Though we have used these five headings to divide the material, a study of it could proceed in many different ways. Any one of the headings could be used to explore all of the readings. The "Search for the Self" rubric, for instance, could be extended to cover all of the readings, and coherent patterns could be found to answer that inquiry. "The Transcendent Dimension in Human Experience" could be used in the same way. A couple of other overarching themes could be "The Human Future," or "The Meaning of Religion to Man." Any of these would make a significant semester's exploration—as significant, certainly, as any of the major themes now common in our academic life, such as environment or politics. After all, man has been religious since his earliest beginnings. Fifteen thousand years ago he buried his dead in ways suggesting his haunting concern for what lies beyond. Religion is an institution that everywhere and always arises. That most recently, in the midst of the most secular age known to this planet, religious concerns have come again to the fore attests to the perennial nature of our topic. Whatever one's appraisal of these phenomena, their significance cannot be dismissed without serious reflection.

J. B. M.
H. P. S.

introduction to writers

The Alternate Contents indicates the importance given to form as well as to content. That this feature receives special notice should come as no surprise to the practiced writer who already knows that content requires form, that content indeed determines form, and that, finally, the strategy of the one assimilates that of the other. To the student just beginning to grow in effective writing this fact cannot be stressed too much. Whatever he reads should quicken him to its form; whatever he writes should do the same. *Dimensions of Man* brings both matter and manner, content and form, to the surface so that in reading the book the writer will be reminded that *what,* for example, Nietzsche, St. Paul, or Laotzu say owes its effectiveness and to a large extent its meaning to *how* they say it.

Underlying this notion is an assumption worth thinking about. The philosopher would identify it as epistemological. Simply put, it posits different ways of knowing and maintains that these ways largely determine what we know. The knowledge of faith, for example, may be different for Paul Tillich from what it is for a Zen poet because for each of them the way to such knowledge has been different. For the one, it may have come through speculation, art, mythical symbols; for the other, through a flash of insight, feeling, revelation. If such is the case, the former can be expected to write theology, which is a critical and systematic self-examination of faith; the other will write meditations and poems. A dedicated empiricist like B. F. Skinner, who brings an austere scienticism to his way of knowing, can be expected when writing about what he knows to report more dispassionately than, say, Loren Eiseley, whose empiricism leaves room for a good deal of personal feeling and therefore lyricism. It is not without both epistemological and rhetorical significance that Pascal's account of religious experience should explode into sudden flashes of expression, whereas that of Mr. K. Y., a middle-aged Japanese business man, should be a prosaic letter that begins, "Thank you [Dear Nakagawa-roshi] for the happy day I spent at your monastery."

That the way we know influences what we know, and that this in turn influences what we say is the logic underlying the six divisions of the Alternate Contents. It is the same logic that impels any writer's strategy of rhetoric. Somewhere in his creative work he is conscious that the force that drives the word also drives the thought. Hopefully the writing that comes from his having first read *Dimensions of Man* will bear a similar relationship.

The first and longest section of the book concerns Exposition. That this is the case perhaps reveals a Western bias and owes too much to Descartes' credo, "I think, therefore I am." If so, it is worth mentioning at once that what impels the last section of the book comes from the notion that, "We adore, therefore we are." No apology, however, is intended for placing exposition first. To some degree the ideas have already been felt, sensed, experienced; and what our Western mind immediately demands is the understanding of them. Such understanding serves to heighten their significance, not to vitiate it. This opening section, therefore, presupposes both interest in and, to a certain extent, an experience of the subject matter. In conventional but useful ways it presents four classifications under which exposition functions: classification and analysis, comparison and contrast, detail, and definition. In the fact that each serves the overruling function of exposition—to inform, to explain—these four procedures demonstrate the far-ranging usefulness of the expository method.

The second section, on Argumentation, is patently shorter. Even though polemics have typified much philosophical and religious writing through the centuries, the editors of this book found no need to bring to it this kind of weight. The selections do demonstrate, however, both deductive and inductive methods of argument. With St. Paul we have the opening generalization—life with Christ—from which all subsequent issues follow. With Bertrand Russell we have the accumulated evidence leading inductively to his fateful pronouncement, "Brief and powerless is Man's life; on him and all his race the slow, sure doom falls pitiless and dark." In Freud's essay the evidence is speculative and abstract; in Norman O. Brown's it is concrete, even sensuous. Evident in all the essays are strong, central generalizations; issues that grow with supporting evidence; and certain dynamics of personality that bring the overall arguments to life.

In the next four sections the tone of writing changes, suggesting that the prior way of knowing also has changed. Rather than cognitive knowledge from which exposition and argumentation arise, there is a "sensible" knowledge, which expresses itself in imagery of the senses, depends upon emotion, allows for imagination, and creates narrative situations. Its logic can be called aesthetic rather than rational, and its rhetorical aim is to show rather than to explain or prove. Knowledge of this kind flowers into Description such as that which shapes and infuses the Bhagavad-Gita, the horrible ecstacies of Jean-Paul Sartre, and the epiphanies of James Joyce. Through descriptive detail the writer seeks to convey a sense of reality beyond that of understanding and logical proof.

Further dimensions of insight open when imagery combines with the imaginative situation of Narration. No longer are the philosopher's speculations in the forefront. Instead they are incarnated within specific settings, moments, and persons—all interrelated to suggest the world men inhabit: the everyday world of father and son (the Prodigal Son narrative), human values (Tolstoy and Camus), rapt faith (Faulkner), plus such quotidian things as a cup of tea (in Zen tradition) and common stones (Beckett).

When time and place, thought and action, emotion and person, all combine into a single dramatic tension; when this tension is aesthetically unified; and when in it the unity issues in language of imaginative vision, we have something that human beings for ages have called Poetry but have been unable to define except in the most tentative way. Only in comparatively recent times has poetry been held as an end in itself, a self-contained and autotelic entity separate from its author, epoch, and milieu, and also independent of paraphrase. To grant or deny absolute autonomy to poetry need not detain us here; we need only note the danger of reductionism in regarding poetry as a class alone, *sui generis,* its meaning restricted to its own aesthetic terms. Rather than supposing poetry to have its own beingness, we might equally suppose it to share in the fuller world of human beingness—moral, ethical, religious, scientific, aesthetic. Such at least is the reason for including poetry in *Dimensions of Man.* Like other forms of rhetoric, poetry springs from special knowledge and transforms it unto itself, yet pointing beyond itself—pointing towards, for example, the "rough beast" (Yeats) or the "night more lovely than the dawn of light" (St. John of the Cross).

The concluding section, Meditation, does not designate a conventional rhetorical pattern. Nevertheless, a common feature unifies the disparate selections, from "The Crest Jewel of Wisdom" to Solzhenitsyn's vital prayer. This feature has to do with a state of being in which the writers exist or aspire to exist. Conscious of some overwhelming dimension of knowledge, some transcendent truth empowering their existence, they write in a form that they have discovered appropriate to their condition. Meditating upon this condition, Laotzu wrote poetry and Dag Hammarskjöld wrote poetic aphorisms. The transparent language of meditation is like the glass of vision: truth is All and language is little more than accidental. Language itself seems to rest in meditation.

The writer who attends to these six rhetorical forms and to the selections represented in each has a sound basis upon which to pattern his own work. Yet all is not said when he finishes with form and content. Always antecedent to the one is a creator and to the other, a knower. In short, all writing worth the name begins with human personality. Even though various critics have thought otherwise, theories of language that extinguish personality miss a fundamental premise about words. The critic E. M. W. Tillyard came close to stating it when he said that style "suggests the mental pattern of the author, the personality realized in words." He might have gone further to say that language is an event in which personality is rooted. In the well-wrought phrase the writer's clarity of mind and throb of feeling will always inhere.

The theme throughout this book reinforces this point. First and last the subject is man. Whether depicted as one who searches or discovers, hopes or despairs, his fullness is measured by the extent to which he experiences self-realization. Certainly nothing less should be expected of the writer.

H. P. S
J. B. M

PART 1
the self in dialogue

This section begins with Descartes' *Meditations,* in which he gives his famous proof for the existence of his own self. In Western thought since the time of Christ the self has been a central notion, though we are not sure whether this is the "ego" or some wider and more significant kind of "self." The selection from the Chinese folk novel *Monkey* is a humorous critique of the rationality so dear to Descartes and Western man. The Buddha represents a wisdom beyond reason. Tolstoy's Levin suffers from the thinness of the rational diet of Western science, and Zimmer's tale of awakening bespeaks again the Eastern appeal to a deeper reality beneath the ego.

The rest of the section represents variations on these themes from classical and modern writers, some telling us that the self finds its meaning in the One beyond all dualism, and others, like Buber, insisting that all real living is dialogic meeting of the Other, both human and divine. Love becomes an important theme because its ultimate meaning carries us beyond any self-enclosed identity. Similarly, one of the great issues of our age, violence, contains the question of man as a single species and the fratricidal sin of war.

Because of the contrast between the Eastern monistic way of talking about the self (as in the famous Vedantic formula: "Thou—the self—art That—the eternal Brahman"), we have added some passages from the Apostle Paul's letters to illustrate the more complex syntax of Christian talk about the co-inherence of finite selves and the Infinite Self. The Christian way of intending the world is better expressed in the paradoxical formula: "This also is Thou; Neither is this Thou."

The uninitiated reader may find it hard to understand what the world would be like to a nonself, which, as Bankei-Eitaku says, has "never been born," but it should be worth the effort. And he might remember that there is also a strong Western tradition that says quite harsh things about the ego-centered life.

to you

Whoever you are, I fear you are walking the walks of dreams,
I fear these supposed realities are to melt from under your feet and hands,
Even now your features, joys, speech, house, trade, manners, troubles, follies,
  costume, crimes, dissipate away from you,
Your true soul and body appear before me,
They stand forth out of affairs, out of commerce, shops, work, farms, clothes,
  the house, buying, selling, eating, drinking, suffering, dying.

Whoever you are, now I place my hand upon you, that you be my poem,
I whisper with my lips close to your ear,
I have loved many women and men, but I love none better than you.

O I have been dilatory and dumb,
I should have made my way straight to you long ago,
I should have blabb'd nothing but you, I should have chanted nothing but you.

The mockeries are not you.
Underneath them and within them I see you lurk,
I pursue you where none else has pursued you,
Silence, the dusk, the flippant expression, the night, the accustom'd routine, if
  these conceal you from me,
The unshaved face, the unsteady eye, the impure complexion, if these balk
  others they do not balk me,
The pert apparel, the deform'd attitude, drunkenness, greed, premature death,
  all these I part aside.

Whoever you are! claim your own at any hazard!
These shows of the East and West are tame compared to you,
These immense meadows, these interminable rivers, you are immense and inter-
  minable as they.
These furies, elements, storms, motions of Nature, throes of apparent dissolu-
  tion, you are he or she who is master or mistress over them,
Master or mistress in your own right over Nature, elements, pain, passion, disso-
  lution.

The hobbles fall from your ankles, you find an unfailing sufficiency,
Old or young, male or female, rude, low, rejected by the rest, whatever you are
  promulges itself,
Through birth, life, death, burial, the means are provided, nothing is scanted,
Through angers, losses, ambition, ignorance, ennui, what you are picks its way.

meditations on first philosophy _____

Yesterday's Meditation has filled my mind with so many doubts that it is no longer in my power to forget them. Nor do I yet see how I will be able to resolve them; I feel as though I were suddenly thrown into deep water, being so disconcerted that I can neither plant my feet on the bottom nor swim on the surface. I shall nevertheless make every effort to conform precisely to the plan commenced yesterday and put aside every belief in which I could imagine the least doubt, just as though I knew that it was absolutely false. And I shall continue in this manner until I have found something certain, or at least, if I can do nothing else, until I have learned with certainty that there is nothing certain in this world. Archimedes, to move the earth from its orbit and place it in a new position, demanded nothing more than a fixed and immovable fulcrum; in a similar manner I shall have the right to entertain high hopes if I am fortunate enough to find a single truth which is certain and indubitable.

I suppose, accordingly, that everything that I see is false; I convince myself that nothing has existed of all that my deceitful memory recalls to me. I think that I have no senses; and I believe that body, shape, extension, motion, and location are merely inventions of my mind. What then could still be thought true? Perhaps nothing else, unless it is that there is nothing certain in the world.

But how do I know that there is not some entity, of a different nature from what I have just judged uncertain, of which there cannot be the least doubt? Is there not some God or some other power who gives me these thoughts? But I need not think this to be true, for possibly I am able to produce them myself. Then, at the very least, am I not an entity myself? But I have already denied that I had any senses or any body. However, at this point I hesitate, for what follows from that? Am I so dependent upon the body and the senses that I could not exist without them? I have just convinced myself that nothing whatsoever existed in the world, that there was no sky, no earth, no minds, and no bodies; have I not thereby convinced myself that I did not exist? Not at all; without doubt I existed if I was convinced (or even if I thought anything). Even though there may be a deceiver of some sort, very powerful and very tricky, who bends all his efforts to keep me perpetually deceived, there can be no slightest doubt that I exist, since he deceives me; and let him deceive me as much as he will, he can never make me be nothing as long as I think that I am something. Thus, after having thought well on this matter, and after examining all things with care, I must finally conclude and maintain that this proposition: I am, I exist, is necessarily true every time that I pronounce it or conceive it in my mind.

But I do not yet know sufficiently clearly what I am, I who am sure that I exist. So I must henceforth take very great care that I do not incautiously mistake some other thing for myself, and so make an error even in that knowledge which I maintain to be more certain and more evident than all other knowledge (that I previously had). That is why I shall now consider once more what I thought myself to be before I began these last deliberations. Of my former opinions I shall reject all that are rendered even slightly doubtful by the arguments that I have just now offered, so that there will remain just that part alone which is entirely certain and indubitable.

What then have I previously believed myself to be? Clearly, I believed that I was a man. But what is a man? Shall I say a rational animal? Certainly not, for I would have to determine what an "animal" is and what is meant by "rational"; and so, from a single question, I would find myself gradually enmeshed in an infinity of others more difficult (and more inconvenient), and I would not care to waste the little time and leisure remaining to me in disentangling such difficulties. I shall rather pause here to consider the ideas which previously arose naturally and of themselves in my mind whenever I considered what I was. I thought of myself first as having a face, hands, arms, and all this mechanism composed of (bone and flesh and) members, just as it appears in a corpse, and which I designated by the name of "body." In addition, I thought of the fact that I consumed nourishment, that I walked, that I perceived and thought, and I ascribed all these actions to the soul. But either I did not stop to consider what this soul was or else, if I did, I imagined that it was something very rarefied and subtle, such as a wind, a flame, or a very much expanded air which (penetrated into and) was infused throughout my grosser components. As for what body was, I did not realize that there could be any doubt about it, for I thought that I recognized its nature very distinctly. If I had wished to explain it according to the notions that I then entertained, I would have described it somewhat in this way: By "body" I understand all that can be bounded by some figure; that can be located in some place and occupy space in such a way that every other body is excluded from it; that can be perceived by touch or sight or hearing or taste or smell; that can be moved in various ways, not by itself but by some other object by which it is touched (and from which it receives an impulse). For to possess the power to move itself, and also to feel or think, I did not believe at all that these are attributes of corporeal nature; on the contrary, rather, I was astonished to see a few bodies possessing such abilities.

But I, what am I, on the basis of the present hypothesis that there is a certain spirit who is extremely powerful and, if I may dare to say so, malicious (and tricky), and who uses all his abilities and efforts in order to deceive me? Can I be sure that I possess the smallest fraction of all those characteristics which I have just now said belonged to the nature of body? I pause to consider this attentively. I pass and repass in review in my mind each one of all these things—it is not necessary to pause to take the time to list them—and I do not find any one of them which I can pronounce to be part of me. Is it characteristic of me to consume nourishment and to walk? But if it is true that I do not have a body, these also are nothing but figments of the imagination. To perceive? But once more, I cannot perceive without the body, except in the sense that I have thought I perceived various things during sleep, which I recognized upon waking not to have been really perceived. To think? Here I find the answer. Thought is an attribute that belongs to me; it alone is inseparable from my nature.

I am, I exist—that is certain; but for how long do I exist? For as long as I think; for it might perhaps happen, if I totally ceased thinking, that I would at the same time completely cease to be. I am now admitting nothing except what is necessarily true. I am therefore, to speak precisely, only a thinking being, that is to say, a mind, an understanding, or a reasoning being, which are terms whose meaning was previously unknown to me.

I am something real and really existing, but what thing am I? I have already given the answer: a thing which thinks. And what more? I will stimulate my imagination (to see if I am not something else beyond this). I am not this assemblage of members which is called a human body; I am not a rarefied and penetrating air spread throughout all these members; I am not a wind, (a flame,) a breath, a vapor, or anything at all that I can imagine and picture to myself—since I have supposed that all that was nothing, and since, without abandoning this supposition, I find that I do not cease to be certain that I am something.

But perhaps it is true that those same things which I suppose not to exist because I do not know them are really no different from the self which I do know. As to that I cannot decide; I am not discussing that question at the moment, since I can pass judgment only upon those things which are known to me: I know that I exist and I am seeking to discover what I am, that "I" that I know to be. Now it is very certain that this notion (and knowledge of my being), thus precisely understood, does not depend on things whose existence is not yet known to me; and consequently (and even more certainly), it does not depend on any of those things that I (can) picture in my imagination. And even these terms, "picture" and "imagine," warn me of my error. For I would be imagining falsely indeed were I to picture myself as something; since to imagine is nothing else than to contemplate the shape or image of a bodily entity, and I already know both that I certainly exist and that it is altogether possible that all these images, and everything in general which are involved in the nature of body, are only dreams (and illusions). From this I see clearly that there was no more sense in saying that I would stimulate my imagination to learn more distinctly what I am than if I should say: I am now awake, and I see something real and true; but because I do not yet perceive it sufficiently clearly, I will go to sleep on purpose, in order that my dreams will show it to me with more truth and evidence. And thus I know manifestly that nothing of all that I can understand by means of the imagination is pertinent to the knowledge which I have of myself, and that I must remember this and prevent my mind from thinking in this fashion, in order that it may clearly perceive its own nature.

But what then am I? A thinking being. What is a thinking being? It is a being which doubts, which understands, (which conceives,) which affirms, which denies, which wills, which rejects, which imagines also, and which perceives. It is certainly not a trivial matter if all these things belong to my nature. But why should they not belong to it? Am I not that same person who now doubts almost everything, who nevertheless understands (and conceives) certain things, who (is sure of and) affirms the truth of this one thing alone, who denies all the others, who wills and desires to know more about them, who rejects error, who imagines many things, sometimes even against my will, and who also perceives many things, as through the medium of the senses (or the organs of the body)? Is there anything in all that which is not just as true as it is certain that I am and that I exist, even though I were always asleep and though the one who created me directed all his efforts to deluding me? And is there any one of these attributes which can be distinguished from my thinking or which can be said to be separable from my nature? For it is so obvious that it is I who doubt, understand, and desire, that nothing could be added to make it more evident. And I am also certainly the same one who imagines; for once more, even though it could happen that the things I imagine are not true, nevertheless this power of imagining cannot fail to be real, and it is part of my thinking. Finally I am the same being which perceives—that is, which observes certain objects as though by means of the sense organs, because I do really see light, hear noises, and feel heat. Will it be said that these appearances are false and that I am sleeping? (Let it be so; yet at the very least) it is certain that it seems to me that I see light, hear noises, and feel heat. This much cannot be false, and it is this, properly considered, which in my nature is called perceiving, and that, again speaking precisely, is nothing else but thinking.

WU CH'ÊNG-ÊN

the wager _____

"I'll have a wager with you," said Buddha. "If you are really so clever, jump off the palm of my right hand. If you succeed, I'll tell the Jade Emperor to come and live with me in the Western Paradise, and you shall have his throne without more ado. But if you fail, you shall go back to earth and do penance there for many a kalpa before you come to me again with your talk."

"This Buddha," Monkey thought to himself, "is a perfect fool. I can jump a hundred and eight thousand leagues, while his palm cannot be as much as eight inches across. How could I fail to jump clear of it?" "You're sure you are in a position to do this for me?" he asked. "Of course I am," said Buddha.

He stretched out his right hand, which looked about the size of a lotus leaf. Monkey put his cudgel behind his ear, and leapt with all his might. "That's all

From *Monkey,* trans. Arthur Waley. Reprinted by permission of Grove Press, Inc. Copyright © 1943 by The John Day Company, Inc.

right," he said to himself. "I'm right off it now." He was whizzing so fast that he was almost invisible, and Buddha, watching him with the eye of wisdom, saw a mere whirligig shoot along.

Monkey came at last to five pink pillars, sticking up into the air. "This is the end of the World," said Monkey to himself. "All I have got to do is to go back to Buddha and claim my forfeit. The Throne is mine." "Wait a minute," he said presently, "I'd better just leave a record of some kind, in case I have trouble with Buddha." He plucked a hair and blew on it with magic breath, crying "Change!" It changed at once into a writing brush charged with heavy ink, and at the base of the central pillar he wrote, "The Great Sage Equal to Heaven reached this place." Then to mark his disrespect, he relieved nature at the bottom of the first pillar, and somersaulted back to where he had come from. Standing on Buddha's palm, he said, "Well, I've gone and come back. You can go and tell the Jade Emperor to hand over the Palaces of Heaven." "You stinking ape," said Buddha, "you've been on the palm of my hand all the time." "You're quite mistaken," said Monkey. "I got to the end of the World, where I saw five flesh-colored pillars sticking up into the sky. I wrote something on one of them. I'll take you there and show you, if you like." "No need for that," said Buddha. "Just look down." Monkey peered down with his fiery, steely eyes, and there at the base of the middle finger of Buddha's hand he saw written the words "The Great Sage Equal to Heaven reached this place," and from the fork between the thumb and first finger came a smell of Monkey's urine.

LEO TOLSTOY

levin examines his life

Ever since, by his beloved brother's deathbed, Levin had first glanced into the questions of life and death in the light of these new convictions, as he called them, which had during the period from his twentieth to his thirty-fourth year imperceptibly replaced his childish and youthful beliefs—he had been stricken with horror, not so much of death, as of life, without any knowledge of whence, and why, and how, and what it was. The physical organization, its decay, the indestructibility of matter, the law of the conservation of energy, evolution, were the words which usurped the place of his old belief. These words and the ideas associated with them were very well for intellectual purposes. But for life they yielded nothing, and Levin felt suddenly like a man who has changed his warm fur coat for a muslin garment, and going for the first time into the frost is

From *Anna Karenina* by Leo Tolstoy, trans. Constance Garnett, New York, Random House, 1939.

immediately convinced, not by reason, but by his whole nature that he is as good as naked, and that he must infallibly perish miserably.

From that moment, though he did not distinctly face it, and still went on living as before, Levin had never lost this sense of terror at his lack of knowledge.

He vaguely felt, too, that what he called his new convictions were not merely lack of knowledge, but that they were part of a whole order of ideas, in which no knowledge of what he needed was possible.

At first, marriage, with the new joys and duties bound up with it, had completely crowded out these thoughts. But of late, while he was staying in Moscow after his wife's confinement, with nothing to do, the question that clamored for solution had more and more often, more and more insistently, haunted Levin's mind.

The question was summed up for him thus: "If I do not accept the answers Christianity gives to the problems of my life, what answers do I accept?" And in the whole arsenal of his convictions, so far from finding any satisfactory answers, he was utterly unable to find anything at all like an answer.

He was in the position of a man seeking food in toy-shops and tool-shops.

Instinctively, unconsciously, with every book, with every conversation, with every man he met, he was on the lookout for light on these questions and their solution.

What puzzled him and distracted him above everything was that the majority of men his age and circle had, like him, exchanged their old beliefs for the same new convictions, and yet saw nothing to lament in this, and were perfectly satisfied and serene. So that, apart from the principal question, Levin was tortured by other questions too. Were these people sincere? he asked himself, or were they playing a part? or was it that they understood the answers science gave to these problems in some different, clearer sense than he did? And he assiduously studied both these men's opinions and the books which treated of these scientific explanations.

One fact he had found out since these questions had engrossed his mind, was that he had been quite wrong in supposing from the recollections of the circle of his young days at college, that religion had outlived its day, and that it was now practically nonexistent. All the people nearest to him were good in their lives, were believers. The old prince, and Lvov, whom he liked so much, and Sergey Ivanovitch, and all the women believed, and his wife believed as simply as he had believed in his earliest childhood, and ninety-nine hundredths of the Russian people, all the working-people for whose life he felt the deepest respect, believed.

Another fact of which he became convinced, after reading many scientific books, was that the men who shared his views had no other construction to put on them, and that they gave no explanation of the questions which he felt he could not live without answering, but simply ignored their existence and attempted to explain other questions of no possible interest to him, such as the evolution of organisms, the materialistic theory of consciousness, etc.

Moreover, during his wife's confinement, something had happened that seemed extraordinary to him. He, an unbeliever, had fallen into praying, and at the moment he prayed, he believed. But that moment had passed, and he could not make his state of mind at that moment fit into the rest of his life.

He could not admit that at that moment he knew the truth, and that now he was wrong; for as soon as he began thinking calmly about it, it all fell to pieces. He could not admit that he was mistaken then, for his spiritual condition was precious to him, and to admit that it was a proof of weakness would have been to desecrate those moments. He was miserably divided against himself, and strained all his spiritual forces to the utmost to escape from this condition.

These doubts fretted and harassed him, growing weaker or stronger from time to time, but never leaving him. He read and thought, and the more he read and the more he thought, the further he felt from the aim he was pursuing.

Of late in Moscow and in the country, since he had become convinced that he would find no solution in the materialists, he had read and reread thoroughly Plato, Spinoza, Kant, Schelling, Hegel, and Schopenhauer, the philosophers who gave a nonmaterialist explanation of life.

Their ideas seemed to him fruitful when he was reading or was himself seeking arguments to refute other theories, especially those of the materialists; but as soon as he began to read or sought for himself a solution of problems, the same thing always happened. As long as he followed the fixed definition of obscure words such as spirit, will, freedom, essence, purposely letting himself go into the snare of words the philosophers set for him, he seemed to comprehend something. But he had only to forget the artificial train of reasoning, and to turn from life itself to what had satisfied him while thinking in accordance with the fixed definitions, and all this artificial edifice fell to pieces at once like a house of cards, and it became clear that the edifice had been built up out of those transposed words, apart from anything in life more important than reason.

At one time, reading Schopenhauer, he put in place of his will the word love, and for a couple of days this new philosophy charmed him, till he removed a little away from it. But then, when he turned from life itself to glance at it again, it fell away too, and proved to be the same muslin garment with no warmth in it.

. . .

"Without knowing what I am and why I am here, life's impossible; and that I can't know, and so I can't live," Levin said to himself.

"In infinite time, in infinite matter, in infinite space, is formed a bubble-organism, and that bubble lasts a while and bursts, and that bubble is Me."

It was an agonizing error, but it was the sole logical result of ages of human thought in that direction.

This was the ultimate belief on which all the systems elaborated by human thought in almost all their ramifications rested. It was the prevalent conviction, and of all other explanations Levin had unconsciously, not knowing when or how, chosen it, as anyway the clearest, and made it his own.

But it was not merely a falsehood, it was the cruel jeer of some wicked power, some evil, hateful power, to whom one could not submit.

He must escape from this power. And the means of escape every man had in his own hands. He had but to cut short this dependence on evil. And there was one means—death.

And Levin, a happy father and husband, in perfect health, was several times so near suicide that he hid the cord that he might not be tempted to hang himself, and was afraid to go out with his gun for fear of shooting himself.

But Levin did not shoot himself, and did not hang himself; he went on living.

HEINRICH ZIMMER

the roar of awakening

We of the Occident are about to arrive at a crossroads that was reached by the thinkers of India some seven hundred years before Christ. This is the real reason why we become both vexed and stimulated, uneasy yet interested, when confronted with the concepts and images of Oriental wisdom. This crossing is one to which the people of all civilizations come in the typical course of the development of their capacity and requirement for religious experience, and India's teachings force us to realize what its problems are. But we cannot take over the Indian solutions. We must enter the new period our own way and solve its questions for ourselves, because though truth, the radiance of reality, is universally one and the same, it is mirrored variously according to the mediums in which it is reflected. Truth appears differently in different lands and ages according to the living materials out of which its symbols are hewn.

Concepts and words are symbols, just as visions, rituals, and images are; so too are the manners and customs of daily life. Through all of these a transcendent reality is mirrored. They are so many metaphors reflecting and implying something which, though thus variously expressed, is ineffable, though thus rendered multiform, remains inscrutable. Symbols hold the mind to truth but are not themselves the truth, hence it is delusory to borrow them. Each civilization, every age, must bring forth its own.

We shall therefore have to follow the difficult way of our own experiences, produce our own reactions, and assimilate our sufferings and realizations. Only then will the truth that we bring to manifestation be as much our own flesh and

From *The Philosophies of India,* by Heinrich Zimmer. Bollinger Series XXVI (Copyright © 1951 by Bollinger Foundation). Reprinted by permission of Princeton University Press.

blood as is the child its mother's; and the mother, in love with the Father, will then justly delight in her offspring as His duplication. The ineffable seed must be conceived, gestated, and brought forth from our own substance, fed by our blood, if it is to be the true child through which its mother is reborn: and the Father, the divine Transcendent Principle, will then also be reborn—delivered, that is to say, from the state of nonmanifestation, nonaction, apparent nonexistence. We cannot borrow God. We must effect His new incarnation from within ourselves. Divinity must descend, somehow, into the matter of our own existence and participate in this peculiar life-process.

According to the mythologies of India, this is a miracle that will undoubtedly come to pass. For in the ancient Hindu tales one reads that whenever the creator and sustainer of the world, Vishnu, is implored to appear in a new incarnation, the beseeching forces leave him no peace until he condescends. Nevertheless, the moment he comes down, taking flesh in a blessed womb, to be again made manifest in the world which itself is a reflex of his own ineffable being, self-willed demonic forces set themselves against him; for there are those who hate and despise the god and have no room for him in their systems of expansive egoism and domineering rule. These do everything within their power to hamper his career. Their violence, however, is not as destructive as it seems; it is no more than a necessary force in the historic process. Resistance is a standard part in the recurrent cosmic comedy that is enacted whenever a spark of supernal truth, drawn down by the misery of creatures and the imminence of chaos, is made manifest on the phenomenal plane.

"It is the same with our spirit," states Paul Valéry, "as with our flesh: both hide in mystery what they feel to be most important. They conceal it from themselves. They single it out and protect it by this profundity in which they ensconce it. Everything that really counts is well veiled; testimony and documents only render it the more obscure; deeds and works are designed expressly to misrepresent it."

The chief aim of Indian thought is to unveil and integrate into consciousness what has been thus resisted and hidden by the forces of life—not to explore and describe the visible world. The supreme and characteristic achievement of the Brāhman mind (and this has been decisive, not only for the course of Indian philosophy, but also for the history of Indian civilization) was its discovery of the Self (ātman) as an independent, imperishable entity, underlying the conscious personality and bodily frame. Everything that we normally know and express about ourselves belongs to the sphere of change, the sphere of time and space, but this Self (ātman) is forever changeless, beyond time, beyond space and the veiling net of causality, beyond measure, beyond the dominion of the eye. The effort of Indian philosophy has been, for millenniums, to know this adamantine Self and make the knowledge effective in human life. And this enduring concern is what has been responsible for supreme morning calm that pervades the terrible histories of the Oriental world—histories no less tremendous, no less horrifying, than our own. Through the vicissitudes of physical change a spiritual footing is maintained in the peaceful-blissful ground of Atman; eternal, timeless, and imperishable Being.

Indian, like Occidental, philosophy imparts information concerning the measurable structure and powers of the psyche, analyzes man's intellectual faculties and the operations of his mind, evaluates various theories of human understanding, establishes the methods and laws of logic, classifies the senses, and studies the processes by which experiences are apprehended and assimilated, interpreted and comprehended. Hindu philosophers, like those of the West, pronounce on ethical values and moral standards. They study also the visible traits of phenomenal existence, criticizing the data of external experience and drawing deductions with respect to the supporting principles. India, that is to say, has had, and still has, its own disciplines of psychology, ethics, physics, and metaphysical theory. But the primary concern—in striking contrast to the interests of the modern philosophers of the West—has always been, not information, but transformation: a radical changing of man's nature and, therewith, a renovation of his understanding both of the outer world and of his own existence; a transformation as complete as possible, such as will amount when successful to a total conversion or rebirth.

In this respect Indian philosophy sides with religion to a far greater extent than does the critical, secularized thinking of the modern West. It is on the side of such ancient philosophers as Pythagoras, Empedocles, Plato, the Stoics, Epicurus and his followers, Plotinus, and the Neoplatonic thinkers. We recognize the point of view again in St. Augustine, the medieval mystics such as Meister Eckhart, and such later mystics as Jakob Böhme of Silesia. Among the Romantic philosophers it reappears in Schopenhauer.

The attitudes toward each other of the Hindu teacher and the pupil bowing at his feet are determined by the exigencies of this supreme task of transformation. Their problem is to effect a kind of alchemical transmutation of the soul. Through the means, not of a merely intellectual understanding, but of a change of heart (a transformation that shall touch the core of his existence), the pupil is to pass out of bondage, beyond the limits of human imperfection and ignorance, and transcend the earthly plane of being.

There is an amusing popular fable which illustrates this pedagogical idea. It is recorded among the teachings of the celebrated Hindu saint of the nineteenth century, Sri Ramakrishna. Anecdotes of this childlike kind occur continually in the discourses of the Oriental sages; they circulate in the common lore of the folk and are known to everyone from infancy. They carry the lessons of India's timeless wisdom to the homes and hearts of the people, coming down through the millenniums as everybody's property. Indeed India is one of the great homelands of the popular fable; during the Middle Ages many of her tales were carried into Europe. The vividness and simple aptness of the images drive home the points of the teaching; they are like pegs to which can be attached no end of abstract reasoning. The best fable is but one of the many Oriental devices to make lessons catch hold and remain in the mind.

The present example is of a tiger cub that had been brought up among goats, but through the enlightening guidance of a spiritual teacher was made to realize its own unsuspected nature. Its mother had died in giving it birth. Big with young, she had been prowling for many days without discovering prey, when she came upon this herd of ranging wild goats. The tigress was ravenous at the time, and this fact may account for the violence of her spring; but in any case, the strain of the leap brought on the birth throes, and from sheer exhaustion she expired. Then the goats, who had scattered, returned to the grazing ground and found the little tiger whimpering at its mother's side. They adopted the feeble creature out of maternal compassion, suckled it together with their own offspring, and watched over it fondly. The cub grew and their care was rewarded; for the little fellow learned the language of the goats, adapted his voice to their gentle way of bleating, and displayed as much devotion as any kid of the flock. At first he experienced some difficulty when he tried to nibble thin blades of grass with his pointed teeth, but somehow he managed. The vegetarian diet kept him very slim and imparted to his temperament a remarkable meekness.

One night, when this young tiger among the goats had reached the age of reason, the herd was attacked again, this time by a fierce old male tiger, and again they scattered; but the cub remained where he stood, devoid of fear. He was of course surprised. Discovering himself face to face with the terrible jungle being, he gazed at the apparition in amazement. The first moment passed; then he began to fell self-conscious. Uttering a forlorn bleat, he plucked a thin leaf of grass and chewed it, while the other stared.

Suddenly the mighty intruder demanded: "What are you doing here among these goats? What are you chewing there?" The funny little creature bleated. The old one became really terrifying. He roared, "Why do you make this silly sound?" and before the other could respond, seized him roughly by the scruff and shook him, as though to knock him back to his senses. The jungle tiger then carried the frightened cub to a nearby pond, where he set him down, compelling him to look into the mirror surface, which was illuminated by the moon. "Now look at those two faces. Are they not alike? You have the pot-face of a tiger; it is like mine. Why do you fancy yourself to be a goat? Why do you bleat? Why do you nibble grass?"

The little one was unable to reply, but continued to stare, comparing the two reflections. Then it became uneasy, shifted its weight from paw to paw, and emitted another troubled, quavering cry. The fierce old beast seized it again and carried it off to his den, where he presented it with a bleeding piece of raw meat remaining from an earlier meal. The cub shuddered with disgust. The jungle tiger, ignoring the weak bleat of protest, gruffly ordered: "Take it! Eat it! Swallow it!" The cub resisted, but the frightening meat was forced between his teeth, and the tiger sternly supervised while he tried to chew and prepared to swallow. The toughness of the morsel was unfamiliar and was causing some difficulty, and he was just about to make his little noise again, when he began to get the taste of the blood. He was amazed; he reached with eagerness for the rest. He began to feel an unfamiliar gratification as the new food went down his gullet, and the meaty substance came into his stomach. A strange, glowing strength, starting from there, went out through his whole organism, and he commenced to feel elated, intoxicated. His lips smacked; he licked his jowls. He arose and opened his mouth with a mighty yawn, just as though he were waking from a night of sleep—a night that had held him long under its spell, for years and years. Stretching his form, he arched his back, extending and spreading his paws. The tail lashed the ground, and suddenly from his throat there burst the terrifying, triumphant roar of a tiger.

The grim teacher, meanwhile, had been watching closely and with increasing satisfaction. The transformation had actually taken place. When the roar was finished he demanded gruffly: "Now do you know what you really are?" and to complete the initiation of his young disciple into the secret lore of his own true nature, added: "Come, we shall go now for a hunt together in the jungle."

PAUL TILLICH

the three types of anxiety and the nature of man _____

I suggest that we distinguish three types of anxiety according to the three directions in which nonbeing threatens being. Nonbeing threatens man's ontic self-affirmation, relatively in terms of fate, absolutely in terms of death. It threatens man's spiritual self-affirmation, relatively in terms of emptiness, absolutely in terms of meaninglessness. It threatens man's moral self-affirmation, relatively in terms of guilt, absolutely in terms of condemnation. The awareness of this three-fold threat is anxiety appearing in three forms, that of fate and death (briefly, the anxiety of death), that of emptiness and loss of meaning (briefly, the anxiety of meaninglessness), that of guilt and condemnation (briefly, the anxiety of condemnation). In all three forms anxiety is existential in the sense that it belongs to existence as such and not to an abnormal state of mind as in neurotic (and psychotic) anxiety.

• • •

the anxiety of fate and death

The anxiety of death is the permanent horizon within which the anxiety of fate is at work. For the threat against man's ontic self-affirmation is not only the absolute threat of death but also the relative threat of fate. Certainly the anxiety of death overshadows all concrete anxieties and gives them their ultimate seriousness. They have, however, a certain independence and, ordinarily, a more

From *The Courage to Be,* by Paul Tillich. Yale University Press, New Haven, Conn., 1952.

immediate impact than the anxiety of death. The term "fate" for this whole group of anxieties stresses one element which is common to all of them: their contingent character, their unpredictability, the impossibility of showing their meaning and purpose. One can describe this in terms of the categorical structure of our experience. One can show the contingency of our temporal being, the fact that we exist in this and no other period of time, beginning in a contingent moment, ending in a contingent moment, filled with experiences which are contingent themselves with respect to quality and quantity. One can show the contingency of our spatial being (our finding ourselves in this and no other place, and the strangeness of this place in spite of its familiarity); the contingent character of ourselves and the place from which we look at our world; and the contingent character of the reality at which we look, that is, our world. Both could be different: this is their contingency and this produces the anxiety about our spatial existence. One can show the contingency of the causal interdependence of which one is a part, both with respect to the past and to the present, the vicissitudes coming from our world and the hidden forces in the depths of our own self. Contingent does not mean causally undetermined but it means that the determining causes of our existence have no ultimate necessity. They are given, and they cannot be logically derived. Contingently we are put into the whole web of causal relations. Contingently we are determined by them in every moment and thrown out by them in the last moment.

• • •

the anxiety of emptiness and meaninglessness

Nonbeing threatens man as a whole, and therefore threatens his spiritual as well as his ontic self-affirmation. Spiritual self-affirmation occurs in every moment in which man lives creatively in the various spheres of meaning. Creative, in this context, has the sense not of original creativity as performed by the genius but of living spontaneously, in action and reaction, with the contents of one's cultural life. In order to be spiritually creative one need not be what is called a creative artist or scientist or statesman, but one must be able to participate meaningfully in their original creations. Such a participation is creative insofar as it changes that in which one participates, even if in very small ways. The creative transformation of a language by the interdependence of the creative poet or writer and the many who are influenced by him directly or indirectly and react spontaneously to him is an outstanding example. Everyone who lives creatively in meanings affirms himself as a participant in these meanings. He affirms himself as participating in the spiritual life and as loving its contents. He loves them because they are his own fulfillment and because they are actualized through him. The scientist loves both the truth he discovers and himself insofar as he discovers it. He is held by the content of his discovery. This is what one can call "spiritual self-affirmation." And if he has not discovered but only participates in the discovery, it is equally spiritual self-affirmation. Such an experience presupposes that the spiritual life is taken seriously, that it is a matter of ultimate concern. And this again presupposes that in it and through it ultimate reality becomes manifest. A spiritual life in which this is not experienced is threatened by nonbeing in the two forms in which it attacks spiritual self-affirmation: emptiness and meaninglessness.

We use the term meaninglessness for the absolute threat of nonbeing to spiritual self-affirmation, and the term emptiness for the relative threat to it. They are no more identical than are the threat of death and fate. But in the background of emptiness lies meaninglessness as death lies in the background of the vicissitudes of fate.

The anxiety of meaninglessness is anxiety about the loss of an ultimate concern, of a meaning which gives meaning to all meanings. This anxiety is aroused by the loss of a spiritual center, of an answer, however symbolic and indirect, to the question of the meaning of existence.

The anxiety of emptiness is aroused by the threat of nonbeing to the special contents of the spiritual life. A belief breaks down through external events or inner processes: one is cut off from creative participation in a sphere of culture, one feels frustrated about something which one had passionately affirmed, one is driven from devotion to one object to devotion to another and again on to another, because the meaning of each of them vanishes and the creative eros is transformed into indifference or aversion. Everything is tried and nothing satisfies. The contents of the tradition, however excellent, however praised, however loved once, lose their power to give content today. And present culture is even less able to provide the content. Anxiously one turns away from all concrete contents and looks for an ultimate meaning, only to discover that it was precisely the loss of a spiritual center which took away the meaning from the special contents of the spiritual life. But a spiritual center cannot be produced intentionally, and the attempt to produce it only produces deeper anxiety. The anxiety of emptiness drives us to the abyss of meaninglessness.

. . .

the anxiety of guilt and condemnation

Nonbeing threatens from a third side: it threatens man's moral self-affirmation. Man's being, ontic as well as spiritual, is not only given to him but also demanded of him. He is responsible for it; literally, he is required to answer, if he is asked, what he has made of himself. He who asks him is his judge, namely he himself, who at the same time, stands against him. This situation produces the anxiety which, in relative terms, is the anxiety of guilt; in absolute terms, the anxiety of self-rejection or condemnation. Man is essentially "finite freedom"; freedom not in the sense of indeterminacy but in the sense of being able to determine himself through decisions in the center of his being. Man, as finite freedom, is free within the contingencies of his finitude. But within these limits he is asked to make of himself what he is supposed to become, to fulfill his destiny. In every act of moral self-affirmation man contributes to the fulfillment of his destiny, to the actualization of what he potentially is. It is the task of ethics to describe the nature of this fulfillment, in philosophical or theological terms. But however the norm is formulated, man has the power of acting against it, of contradicting his essential being, of losing his destiny. And under the conditions of man's estrangement from himself this is an actuality. Even in what he considers his best deed nonbeing is present and prevents it from being perfect. A profound ambiguity between good and evil permeates everything he does, because it permeates his personal being as such. Nonbeing is mixed with being in his moral self-affirmation as it is in his spiritual and ontic self-affirmation. The awareness of this ambiguity is the feeling of guilt. The judge who is oneself and who stands against oneself, he who "knows with" (conscience) everything we do and are gives a negative judgment, experienced by us as guilt. The anxiety of guilt shows the same complex characteristics as the anxiety about ontic and spiritual nonbeing. It is present in every moment of moral self-awareness and can drive us toward complete self-rejection, to the feeling of being condemned—not to an external punishment but to the despair of having lost our destiny.

To avoid this extreme situation man tries to transform the anxiety of guilt into moral action regardless of its imperfection and ambiguity. Courageously he takes nonbeing into his moral self-affirmation. This can happen in two ways, according to the duality of the tragic and the personal in man's situation, the first based on the contingencies of fate, the second on the responsibility of freedom. The first way can lead to a defiance of negative judgments and the moral demands on which they are based; the second way can lead to a moral rigor and the self-satisfaction derived from it. In both of them—usually called anomism and legalism—the anxiety of guilt lies in the background and breaks again and again into the open, producing the extreme situation of moral despair.

. . .

The three types of anxiety are interwoven in such a way that one of them gives the predominant color but all of them participate in the coloring of the state of anxiety. All of them and their underlying unity are existential, i.e., they are implied in the existence of man as man, his finitude, and his estrangement.

SHANKARACHARYA

the crest jewel of wisdom

The Atman is that by which the universe is pervaded, but which nothing pervades; which causes all things to shine, but which all things cannot make to shine. . . .

The nature of the one Reality must be known by one's own clear spiritual perception; it cannot be known through a pandit (learned man). Similarly the form of the moon can only be known through one's own eyes. How can it be known through others?

Who but the Atman is capable of removing the bonds of ignorance, passion and self-interested action? . . .

Liberation cannot be achieved except by the perception of the identity of the individual spirit with the universal Spirit. It can be achieved neither by Yoga (physical training), nor by Sankhya (speculative philosophy), nor by the practice of religious ceremonies, nor by mere learning. . . .

Disease is not cured by pronouncing the name of medicine, but by taking the medicine. Deliverance is not achieved by repeating the word "Brahman," but by directly experiencing Brahman. . . .

The Atman is the Witness of the individual mind and its operations. It is absolute knowledge. . . .

The wise man is one who understands that the essence of Brahman and of Atman is Pure Consciousness, and who realizes their absolute identity. The identity of Brahman and Atman is affirmed in hundreds of sacred texts. . . .

Caste, creed, family and lineage do not exist in Brahman. Brahman has neither name nor form, transcends merit and demerit, is beyond time, space and the objects of sense-experience. Such is Brahman, and "thou art That." Meditate upon this truth within your consciousness.

Supreme, beyond the power of speech to express, Brahman may yet be apprehended by the eye of pure illumination. Pure, absolute and eternal Reality—such is Brahman, and "thou art That." Meditate upon this truth within your consciousness. . . .

Though One, Brahman is the cause of many. There is no other cause. And yet Brahman is independent of the law of causation. Such is Brahman, and "thou art That." Meditate upon this truth within your consciousness. . . .

The truth of Brahman may be understood intellectually. But (even in those who so understand) the desire for personal separateness is deep-rooted and powerful, for it exists from beginningless time. It creates the notion, "I am the actor, I am he who experiences." This notion is the cause of bondage to conditional existence, birth and death. It can be removed only by the earnest effort to live constantly in union with Brahman. By the sages, the eradication of this notion and the craving for personal separateness is called Liberation.

It is ignorance that causes us to identify ourselves with the body, the ego, the senses, or anything that is not the Atman. He is a wise man who overcomes this ignorance by devotion to the Atman. . . .

When a man follows the way of the world, or the way of the flesh, or the way of tradition (i.e., when he believes in the religious rites and the letter of the scriptures, as though they were intrinsically sacred), knowledge of Reality cannot arise in him.

The wise say that this threefold way is like an iron chain, binding the feet of him who aspires to escape from the prison-house of this world. He who frees himself from the chain achieves Deliverance.

the bodhisattva vow

A Bodhisattva resolves: I take upon myself the burden of all suffering, I am resolved to do so, I will endure it. I do not turn or run away, do not tremble, am not terrified, nor afraid, do not turn back or despond.

And why? At all costs I must bear the burdens of all beings. In that I do not follow my own inclinations. I have made the vow to save all beings. All beings I must set free. The whole world of living beings I must rescue, from the terrors of birth, of old age, of sickness, of death and rebirth, of all kinds of moral offense, of all states of woe, of the whole cycle of birth-and-death, of the jungle of false views, of the loss of wholesome dharmas, of the concomitants of ignorance— from all these terrors I must rescue all beings. . . . I walk so that the kingdom of unsurpassed cognition is built up for all beings. My endeavors do not merely aim at my own deliverance. For with the help of the boat of the thought of all-knowledge, I must rescue all these beings from the stream of Samsara, which is so difficult to cross; I must pull them back from the great precipice, I must free them from all calamities, I must ferry them across the stream of Samsara. I myself must grapple with the whole mass of suffering of all beings. To the limit of my endurance I will experience in all the states of woe, found in any world system, all the abodes of suffering. And I must not cheat all beings out of my store of merit. I am resolved to abide in each single state of woe for numberless aeons; and so I will help all beings to freedom, in all the states of woe that may be found in any world system whatsoever.

And why? Because it is surely better that I alone should be in pain than that all these beings should fall into the states of woe. There I must give myself away as a pawn through which the whole world is redeemed from the terrors of the hells, of animal birth, of the world of Yama; and with this my own body I must experience, for the sake of all beings, the whole mass of all painful feelings. And on behalf of all beings, and in doing so I speak truthfully, am trustworthy, and do not go back on my word. I must not abandon all beings.

And why? There has arisen in me the will to win all-knowledge, with all beings for its object, that is to say, for the purpose of setting free the entire world of beings. And I have not set out for the supreme enlightenment from a desire

From *The Teachings of the Compassionate Buddha,* ed. Edwin A. Burtt. Copyright © 1955 by Edwin A. Burtt. Reprinted by arrangement with The New American Library, Inc., New York.

for delights, not because I hope to experience the delights of the five sense-qualities, or because I wish to indulge in the pleasures of the senses. And I do not pursue the course of a Bodhisattva in order to achieve the array of delights that can be found in the various worlds of sense-desire.

MARTIN BUBER

all real living is encounter _____

The world is twofold for man in accordance with his twofold attitude.

The attitude of man is twofold in accordance with the two basic words he can speak.

The basic words are not single words but word pairs.

One basic word is the word pair I-You.

The other basic word is the word pair I-It; but this basic word is not changed when He or She takes the place of It.

Thus the I of man is also twofold.

For the I of the basic word I-You is different from that in the basic word I-It.

Basic words do not state something that might exist outside them; by being spoken they establish a mode of existence.

Basic words are spoken with one's being.

When one says You, the I of the word pair I-You is said, too.

When one says It, the I of the word pair I-It is said, too.

The basic word I-You can only be spoken with one's whole being.

The basic word I-It can never be spoken with one's whole being.

There is no I as such but only the I of the basic word I-You and the I of the basic word I-It.

When a man says I, he means one or the other. The I he means is present when he says I. And when he says You or It, the I of one or the other basic word is also present.

Being I and saying I are the same. Saying I and saying one of the two basic words are the same.

Whoever speaks one of the basic words enters into the word and stands in it.

• • •

The You encounters me by grace—it cannot be found by seeking. But that I speak the basic word to it is a deed of my whole being, is my essential deed.

The You encounters me. But I enter into a direct relationship to it. Thus the relationship is election and electing, passive and active at once. An action of the whole being must approach passivity, for it does away with all partial actions and thus with any sense of action, which always depends on limited exertions.

The basic word I-You can be spoken only with one's whole being. The concentration and fusion into a whole being can never be accomplished by me, can never be accomplished without me. I require a You to become; becoming I, I say You.

All actual life is encounter.

$\bullet \quad \bullet \quad \bullet$

The You-sense of the man who in his relationships to all individual Yous experiences the disappointment of the change into It, aspires beyond all of them and yet not all the way toward his eternal You. Not the way one seeks something; in truth, there is no God-seeking because there is nothing where one could not find him. How foolish and hopeless must one be to leave one's way of life to seek God; even if one gained all the wisdom of solitude and all the power of concentration, one would miss him. It is rather as if a man went his way and merely wished that it might be *the* way; his aspiration finds expression in the strength of his wish. Every encounter is a way station that grants him a view of fulfillment; in each he thus fails to share, and yet also does share, in the one because he is ready. Ready, not seeking, he goes his way; this gives him the serenity toward all things and the touch that helps them. But once he has found, his heart does not turn away from them although he now encounters everything in the one. He blesses all the cells that have sheltered him as well as all those where he will still put up. For this finding is not an end of the way but only its eternal center.

It is a finding without seeking, a discovery of what is most original and the origin. The You-sense that cannot be satiated until it finds the infinite You sensed its presence from the beginning; this presence merely had to become wholly actual for it out of the actuality of the consecrated life of the world.

It is not as if God could be inferred from anything—say, from nature as its cause, or from history as its helmsman, or perhaps from the subject as the self that thinks itself through it. It is not as if something else were "given" and this were then deduced from it. This is what confronts us immediately and first and always, and legitimately it can only be addressed, not asserted.

a conversion

In my earlier years the "religious" was for me the exception. There were hours that were taken out of the course of things. From somewhere or other the firm crust of everyday was pierced. Then the reliable permanence of appearances broke down; the attack which took place burst its law asunder. "Religious experience" was the experience of an otherness which did not fit into the context of life. It could begin with something customary, with consideration of some familiar object, but which then became unexpectedly mysterious and uncanny, finally lighting a way into the lightning-pierced darkness of the mystery itself. But also, without any intermediate stage, time could be torn apart—first the firm world's structure then the still firmer self-assurance flew apart and you were delivered to fullness. The "religious" lifted you out. Over there now lay the accustomed existence with its affairs, but here illumination and ecstasy and rapture held, without time or sequence. Thus your own being encompassed a life here and a life beyond, and there was no bond but the actual moment of the transition.

The illegitimacy of such a division of the temporal life, which is streaming to death and eternity and which only in fulfilling its temporality can be fulfilled in face of these, was brought home to me by an everyday event, an event of judgment, judging with that sentence from closed lips and an unmoved glance such as the ongoing course of things loves to pronounce.

What happened was no more than that one forenoon, after a morning of "religious" enthusiasm, I had a visit from an unknown young man, without being there in spirit. I certainly did not fail to let the meeting be friendly, I did not treat him any more remissly than all his contemporaries who were in the habit of seeking me out about this time of day as an oracle that is ready to listen to reason. I conversed attentively and openly with him—only I omitted to guess the questions which he did not put. Later, not long after, I learned from one of his friends—he himself was no longer alive—the essential content of these questions; I learned that he had come to me not casually, but borne by destiny, not for a chat but for a decision. He had come to me, he had come in this hour. What do we expect when we are in despair and yet go to a man? Surely a presence by means of which we are told that nevertheless there is meaning.

Since then I have given up the "religious" which is nothing but the exception, extraction, exaltation, ecstasy; or it has given me up. I possess nothing but the everyday out of which I am never taken. The mystery is no longer disclosed, it has escaped or it has made its dwelling here where everything happens as it happens. I know no fullness but each mortal hour's fullness of claim and responsibility. Though far from being equal to it, yet I know that in the claim I am claimed and may respond in responsibility, and know who speaks and demands a response.

I do not know much more. If that is religion then it is just *everything,* simply all that is lived in its possibility of dialogue. Here is space also for religion's highest forms. As when you pray you do not thereby remove yourself from this life of yours but in your praying refer your thought to it, even though it may be in order to yield it; so too in the unprecedented and surprising, when you are called upon from above, required, chosen, empowered, sent, you with this your mortal bit of life are referred to, this moment is not extracted from it, it rests on what has been and beckons to the remainder which has still to be lived, you are not swallowed up in a fullness without obligation, you are willed for the life of communion.

HERMAN MELVILLE

the symphony _____

It was a clear steel-blue day. The firmaments of air and sea were hardly separable in that all-pervading azure; only, the pensive air was transparently pure and soft, with a woman's look, and the robust and man-like sea heaved with long, strong, lingering swells, as Samson's chest in his sleep.

Hither, and thither, on high, glided the snow-white wings of small, unspeckled birds; these were the gentle thoughts of the feminine air; but to and fro in the deeps, far down in the bottomless blue, rushed mighty leviathans, sword-fish, and sharks; and these were the strong, troubled, murderous thinkings of the masculine sea.

But though thus contrasting within, the contrast was only in shades and shadows without; those two seemed one; it was only the sex, as it were, that distinguished them.

Aloft, like a royal czar and king, the sun seemed giving this gentle air to this bold and rolling sea; even as bride to groom. And at the girdling line of the horizon, a soft and tremulous motion—most seen here at the equator—denoted the fond, throbbing trust, the loving alarms, with which the poor bride gave her bosom away.

Tied up and twisted; gnarled and knotted with wrinkles; haggardly firm and unyielding; his eyes glowing like coals, that still glow in the ashes of ruin; untottering Ahab stood forth in the clearness of the morn; lifting his splintered helmet of a brow to the fair girl's forehead of heaven.

Oh, immortal infancy, and innocency of the azure! Invisible winged creatures that frolic all round us! Sweet childhood of air and sky! how oblivious were ye

From *Moby Dick.*

of old Ahab's close-coiled woe! But so have I seen little Miriam and Martha, laughing-eyed elves, heedlessly gambol around their old sire; sporting with the circle of singed locks which grew on the marge of that burnt-out crater of his brain.

Slowly crossing the deck from the scuttle, Ahab leaned over the side, and watched how his shadow in the water sank and sank to his gaze, the more and the more that he strove to pierce the profundity. But the lovely aromas in that enchanted air did at last seem to dispel, for a moment, the cankerous thing in his soul. That glad, happy air, that winsome sky, did at last stroke and caress him; the step-mother world, so long cruel—forbidding—now threw affectionate arms round his stubborn neck, and did seem to joyously sob over him, as if over one, that however willful and erring, she could yet find it in her heart to save and to bless. From beneath his slouched hat Ahab dropped a tear into the sea; nor did all the Pacific contain such wealth as that one wee drop.

Starbuck saw the old man; saw him, how he heavily leaned over the side; and he seemed to hear in his own heart the measureless sobbing that stole out of the center of the serenity around. Careful not to touch him, or be noticed by him, he yet drew near to him, and stood there.

Ahab turned.

"Starbuck!"

"Sir."

"Oh, Starbuck! it is a mild, mild wind, and a mild looking sky. On such a day—very much such a sweetness as this—I struck my first whale—a boy-harpooneer of eighteen! Forty—forty—forty years ago!—ago! Forty years of continual whaling! forty years of privation, and peril, and storm-time! forty years on the pitiless sea! for forty years has Ahab forsaken the peaceful land, for forty years to make war on the horrors of the deep! Aye and yes, Starbuck, out of those forty years I have not spent three ashore. When I think of this life I have led; the desolation of solitude it has been; the masoned, walled-town of a Captain's exclusiveness, which admits but small entrance to any sympathy from the green country without—oh, weariness! heaviness! Guinea-coast slavery of solitary command!—when I think of all this; only half-suspected, not so keenly known to me before—and how for forty years I have fed upon dry salted fare—fit emblem of the dry nourishment of my soul!—when the poorest landsman has had fresh fruit to his daily hand, and broken the world's fresh bread, to my mouldy crusts—away, whole oceans away, from that young girl-wife I wedded past fifty, and sailed for Cape Horn the next day, leaving but one dent in my marriage pillow—wife? wife?—rather a widow with her husband alive! Aye, I widowed that poor girl when I married her, Starbuck; and then, the madness, the frenzy, the boiling blood and the smoking brow, with which, for a thousand low-erings old Ahab has furiously, foamingly chased his prey—more a demon than a man!—aye, aye! what a forty years' fool—fool—old fool, has old Ahab been! Why this strife of the chase? why weary, and palsy the arm at the oar, and the iron, and the lance? how the richer or better is Ahab now? Behold. Oh, Starbuck! is it not hard, that with this weary load I bear, one poor leg should have been snatched from under me? Here, brush this old hair aside; it blinds me, that I seem to weep. Locks so grey did never grow but from out some ashes! But do I look very old, so very, very old, Starbuck? I feel deadly faint, bowed, and humped, as though I were Adam, staggering beneath the piled centuries since Paradise. God! God! God!—crack my heart!—stave my brain!—mockery! mockery! bitter, biting mockery of grey hairs, have I lived enough joy to wear ye; and seem and feel thus intolerably old? Close! stand close to me, Starbuck; let me look into a human eye; it is better than to gaze into sea or sky; better than to gaze upon God. By the green land; by the bright hearth-stone! this is the magic glass, man; I see my wife and my child in thine eye. No, no; stay on board, on board!—lower not when I do; when branded Ahab gives chase to Moby Dick. That hazard shall not be thine. No, no! not with the far away home I see in that eye!"

"Oh, my Captain! my Captain! noble soul! grand old heart, after all! why should any one give chase to that hated fish! Away with me! let us fly these deadly waters! let us home! Wife and child, too, are Starbuck's—wife and child of his brotherly, sisterly, playfellow youth; even as thine, sir, are the wife and child of thy loving, longing, paternal old age! Away! let us away!—this instant let me alter the course! How cheerily, how hilariously, O my Captain, would we bowl on our way to see old Nantucket again! I think, sir, they have some such mild blue days, even as this, in Nantucket."

"They have, they have. I have seen them—some summer days in the morning. About this time—yes, it is his noon nap now—the boy vivaciously wakes; sits up in bed; and his mother tells him of me, of cannibal old me; how I am abroad upon the deep, but will yet come back to dance him again."

" 'Tis my Mary, my Mary herself! She promised that my boy, every morning, should be carried to the hill to catch the first glimpse of his father's sail! Yes, yes! no more! it is done! we head for Nantucket! Come, my Captain, study out the course, and let us away! See, see! the boy's face from the window! the boy's hand on the hill!"

But Ahab's glance was averted; like a blighted fruit tree he shook, and cast his last, cindered apple to the soil.

"What is it, what nameless, inscrutable, unearthly thing is it; what cozening, hidden lord and master, and cruel, remorseless emperor commands me; that against all natural lovings and longings, I so keep pushing, and crowding, and jamming myself on all the time; recklessly making me ready to do what in my own proper, natural heart, I durst not so much as dare? Is Ahab, Ahab? Is it I, God, or who, that lifts this arm? But if the great sun move not of himself; but is as an errand-boy in heaven; nor one single star can revolve, but by some invisible power; how then can this one small heart beat; this one small brain think thoughts; unless God does that beating, does that thinking, does that living, and not I. By heaven, man, we are turned round and round in this world, like yonder windlass, and Fate is the handspike. And all the time, lo! that smiling sky, and this unsounded sea! Look! see yon Albicore! who put it into him to chase and fang that flying-fish? Where do murderers go, man! Who's to doom, when the judge himself is dragged to the bar? But it is a mild, mild wind, and a mild looking sky; and the air smells now, as if it blew from a far-away meadow; they have been making hay somewhere under the slopes of the Andes, Starbuck, and the mowers are sleeping among the new-mown hay. Sleeping? Aye, toil we how we may, we all sleep at last on the field. Sleep? Aye, and rust amid greenness; as last year's scythes flung down, and left in the half-cut swaths—Starbuck!"

But blanched to a corpse's hue with despair, the mate had stolen away.

Ahab crossed the deck to gaze over on the other side; but started at two reflected, fixed eyes in the water there. Fedallah was motionlessly leaning over the same rail.

the good samaritan

One day a teacher of an adult Bible class got up and tested him with this question: "Doctor, what does one do to be saved?"

Jesus replied, "What does the Bible say? How do you interpret it?"

The teacher answered, "Love the Lord your God with all your heart and with all your soul and with all your physical strength and with all your mind; and love your neighbor as yourself."

"That is correct," answered Jesus. "Make a habit of this and you'll be saved."

But the Sunday school teacher, trying to save face, asked, "But . . . er . . . but . . . just who *is* my neighbor?"

Then Jesus laid into him and said, "A man was going from Atlanta to Albany and some gangsters held him up. When they had robbed him of his wallet and brand-new suit, they beat him up and drove off in his car, leaving him unconscious on the shoulder of the highway.

"Now it just so happened that a white preacher was going down that same highway. When he saw the fellow, he stepped on the gas and went scooting by.

"Shortly afterwards a white Gospel song leader came down the road, and when he saw what had happened, he too stepped on the gas.

"Then a black man traveling that way came upon the fellow, and what he saw moved him to tears. He stopped and bound up his wounds as best he could, drew some water from his water-jug to wipe away the blood and then laid him on the back seat. He drove on into Albany and took him to the hospital and said to the nurse, 'You all take good care of this white man I found on the highway. Here's

From *The Cotton Patch Version of Luke and Acts,* by Clarence Jordan, New York, Association Press, 1969.

the only two dollars I got, but you all keep account of what he owes, and if he can't pay it, I'll settle up with you when I make a pay-day.'

"Now if you had been the man held up by the gangsters, which of these three—the white preacher, the white song leader, or the black man—would you consider to have been your neighbor?"

The teacher of the adult Bible class said, "Why, of course, the nig—I mean, er . . . well, er . . . the one who treated me kindly."

Jesus said, "Well, then, *you* get going and start living like that!"

D. H. LAWRENCE

the proper study _____

If no man lives for ever, neither does any precept. And if even the weariest river winds somewhere safe to sea, so also does the weariest wisdom. And there it is lost. Also incorporated.

> Know then thyself, presume not God to scan;
> The proper study of mankind is man.

It was Alexander Pope who absolutely struck the note of our particular epoch: not Shakespeare or Luther or Milton. A man of first magnitude never fits his age perfectly.

> Know then thyself, presume not God to scan;
> The proper study of mankind is Man—*with a capital M.*

This stream of wisdom is very weary now: weary to death. It started such a gay little trickle, and is such a spent muddy ebb by now. It will take a big sea to swallow all its alluvia.

"Know then thyself." All right! I'll do my best. Honestly I'll do my best, sincerely to know myself. Since it is the great commandment to consciousness of our long era, let us be men, and try to obey it. Jesus gave the emotional commandment, "Love thy neighbor." But the Greeks set the even more absolute motto, in its way, a more deeply religious motto: "Know thyself."

Very well! Being man, and the son of man, I find it only honorable to obey. To do my best. To do my best to know myself. And particularly that part, or those parts of myself that have not yet been admitted into consciousness. Man is nothing, less than a tick stuck in a sheep's back, unless he adventures. Either into the unknown of the world, of his environment. Or into the unknown of himself.

From *Phoenix,* ed., Edward D. McDonald. *The Posthumous Papers of D. H. Lawrence,* Copyright 1936 by Frieda Lawrence, renewed © 1964 by The Estate of the late Frieda Lawrence Ravagli. Reprinted by permission of The Viking Press, Inc.

Allons! the road is before us. Know thyself! Which means, *really*, know thine own *unknown self*. It's no good knowing something you know already. The thing is to discover the tracts as yet unknown. And as the only unknown now lies deep in the passional soul, allons! the road is before us. We write a novel or two, we are called erotic or depraved or idiotic or boring. What does it matter, we go the road just the same. If you see the point of the great old commandment, *Know thyself,* then you see the point of all art.

But knowing oneself, like knowing anything else, is not a process that can continue to infinity, in the same direction. The fact that I myself *am* only myself makes me very specifically finite. True, I may argue that my Self is a mystery that impinges on the infinite. Admitted. But the moment my Self impinges on the infinite, it ceases to be just myself.

The same is true of all knowing. You start to find out the chemical composition of a drop of water, and before you know where you are, your river of knowledge is winding very unsatisfactorily into a very vague sea, called the ether. You start to study electricity, you track the wretch down till you get some mysterious and misbehaving atom of energy or unit of force that goes pop under your nose and leaves you with the dead body of a mere word.

You sail down your stream of knowledge, and you find yourself absolutely at sea. Which may be safety for the weary river, but is a sad look-out for you, who are a land animal.

Now all science starts gaily from the inland source of *I Don't Know.* Gaily it says: "I don't know, but I'm going to know." It's like a little river bubbling up cheerfully in the determination to dissolve the whole world in its waves. And science, like the little river, winds wonderingly out again into the final *I Don't Know* of the ocean.

All this is platitudinous as regards science. Science has learned an uncanny lot, *by the way*.

Apply the same to the Know Thyself motto. We have learned something by the way. But as far as I'm concerned, I see land receding, and the great ocean of the last *I Don't Know* enveloping me.

But the human consciousness is never allowed finally to say: "I Don't Know." It has got to know, even if it must metamorphose to do so.

Know then thyself, presume not God to scan.

Now as soon as you come across a Thou Shalt Not commandment, you may be absolutely sure that sometime or other, you'll have to break this commandment. You needn't make a practice of breaking it. But the day will come when you'll have to break it. When you'll have to take the name of the Lord Your God in vain, and have other gods, and worship idols, and steal, and kill, and commit adultery, and all the rest. A day will come. Because, as Oscar Wilde says, what's a temptation for, except to be succumbed to!

There comes a time to every man when he has to break one or other of the

Thou Shalt Not commandments. And then is the time to Know Yourself just a bit different from what you thought you were.

So that in the end, this Know Thyself commandment brings me up against the Presume-Not-God-to-Scan fence. Trespassers will be prosecuted. Know then thyself, presume not God to scan.

It's a dilemma. Because this business of knowing myself has led me slap up against the forbidden enclosure where, presumably, this God mystery is kept in corral. It isn't my fault. I followed the road. And it leads over the edge of a precipice on which stands up a sign-board: Danger! Don't go over the edge!

But I've *got* to go over the edge. The way lies that way.

Flop! Over we go, and into the endless sea. There drown.

No! Out of the drowning something else gurgles awake. And that's the best of the human consciousness. When you fall into the final sea of *I Don't Know,* then, if you can but gasp *Teach Me,* you turn into a fish, and twiddle your fins and twist your tail and grope in amazement, in a new element.

That's why they called Jesus: The Fish. Pisces. Because he fell, like the weariest river, into the great Ocean that is outside the shore, and there took on a new way of knowledge.

The Proper Study is Man, sure enough. But the proper study of man, like the proper study of anything else, will in the end leave you no option. You'll have to presume to study God. Even the most hard-boiled scientist, if he is a brave and honest man, is landed in this unscientific dilemma. Or rather, he is all at sea in it.

The river of human consciousness, like ancient Ocean, goes in a circle. It starts gaily, bubblingly, fiercely from an inland pool, where it surges up in obvious mystery and Godliness, the human consciousness. And here is the God of the Beginning, call him Jehovah or Ra or Ammon or Jupiter or what you like. One bubbles up in Greece, one in India, one in Jerusalem. From their various God-sources the streams of human consciousness rush variously down. Then begin to meander and to doubt. Then fall slow. Then start to silt up. Then pass into the great Ocean, which is the God of the End.

In the great ocean of the End, most men are lost. But Jesus turned into a fish, he had the other consciousness of the Ocean which is the divine End of us all. And then like a salmon he beat his way up stream again, to speak from the source.

And this is the greater history of man, as distinguished from the lesser history, in which figure Mr. Lloyd George and Monsieur Poincaré.

We are in the deep, muddy estuary of our era, and terrified of the emptiness of the sea beyond. Or we are at the end of the great road, that Jesus and Francis and Whitman walked. We are on the brink of a precipice, and terrified at the great void below.

No help for it. We are men, and for men there is no retreat. Over we go.

Over we must and shall go, so we may as well do it voluntarily, keeping our soul alive; and as we drown in our terrestrial nature, transmogrify into fishes. Pisces. That which knows the Oceanic Godliness of the End.

The proper study of mankind is man. Agreed entirely! But in the long run, it becomes again as it was before, man in his relation to the deity. The proper study of mankind is man in his relation to the deity.

And yet not as it was before. Not the specific deity of the inland source. The vast deity of the End. Oceanus whom you can only know by becoming a Fish. Let us become Fishes, and try.

They talk about the sixth sense. They talk as if it were an extension of the other senses. A mere *dimensional* sense. It's nothing of the sort. There is a sixth sense right enough. Jesus had it. The sense of the God that is the End and the Beginning. And the proper study of mankind is man in his relation to this Oceanic God.

We have come to the end, for the time being, of the study of man in his relation to man. Or man in his relation to himself. Or man in his relation to woman. There is nothing more of importance to be said, by us or for us, on this subject. Indeed, we have no more to say.

Of course, there is the literature of perversity. And there is the literature of little playboys and playgirls, not only of the western world. But the literature of perversity is a brief weed. And the playboy playgirl stuff, like the movies, though a very monstrous weed, won't live long.

As the weariest river winds by no means safely to sea, all the muddy little individuals begin to chirrup: "Let's play! Let's play at something! We're so god-like when we *play*."

But it won't do, my dears. The sea will swallow you up, and all your play and perversions and personalities.

You can't get any more literature out of man in his relation to man. Which, of course, should be writ large, to mean man in his relation to woman, to other men, and to the whole environment of men: or woman in her relation to man, or other women, or the whole environment of women. You can't get any more literature out of that. Because any new book must needs be a new stride. And the next stride lands you over the sandbar in the open ocean, where the first and greatest relation of every man and woman is to the Ocean itself, the great God of the End, who is the All-Father of all sources, as the sea is father of inland lakes and springs of water.

But get a glimpse of this new relation of men and women to the great God of the End, who is the Father, not the Son, of all our beginnings: and you get a glimpse of the new literature. Think of the true novel of St. Paul, for example. Not the sentimental looking-backward Christian novel, but the novel looking out to sea, to the great Source, and End, of all beginnings. Not the St. Paul with his human feelings repudiated, to give play to the new divine feelings. Not the St. Paul violent in reaction against worldliness and sensuality, and therefore a dogmatist with his sheaf of Shalt-Nots ready. But a St. Paul two thousand years older, having his own epoch behind him, and having again the great knowledge of the deity, the deity which Jesus knew, the vast Ocean God which is at the end of all our consciousness.

Because, after all, if chemistry winds wearily to sea in the ether, or some such universal, don't we also, not as chemists but as conscious men, also wind wearily to sea in a divine ether, which means nothing to us but space and words and emptiness? We wind wearily to sea in words and emptiness.

But man is a mutable animal. Turn into the Fish, the Pisces of man's final consciousness, and you'll start to swim again in the great life which is so frighteningly godly that you realize your previous presumption.

And then you realize the new relation of man. Men like fishes lifted on a great wave of the God of the End, swimming together, and apart, in a new medium. A new relation, in a new whole.

BANKEI-EITAKU

the zen
of birthlessness _____

How lucky you are these days! When I was young there wasn't a good master to be found. At least I couldn't uncover one. But the truth is I was rather simple when young, and made one blunder after another. And the fruitless efforts! I don't suppose I'll ever forget those days, if only because they were so painful. That's why I come here every day. I want to teach you how to avoid the blunders I made. How lucky you are these days!

I'm going to tell you about some of my mistakes, and I know you're clever enough—every one of you—to learn from what I say. If by chance one of you should be led astray by my example, the sin will be unpardonable. That must be avoided at all costs. Indeed it was only after great hesitation that I decided to tell you of my experiences. Remember then, you can learn from me without imitating.

My parents came here from the island of Shikoku, and it was right here (the province of Harima in Hyogo Prefecture) that I was born. My father was a lordless samurai and a Confucian scholar as well, but he died when I was a child and I was brought up by my mother. She was to tell me later that I was boss of all the children in the neighborhood (which led me to do a lot of mischief) and that roughly from my third year I began to loathe death, so much so in fact that when I cried all she had to do was mimic a corpse, or even say "death," and I'd stop crying and become good.

When yet a small boy I became interested in Confucianism, which in those days was very popular. One day while reading *Great Learning* (a classic of Chinese philosophy) I came upon the sentence, "The path of the Great Learning lies in clarifying illustrious virtue." This was completely beyond me, and I wondered about illustrious virtue for days on end, asking teacher after teacher, but to no avail. Finally one of them took me aside and said, "Go to a Zen priest. They know all about difficult things of this kind. All we do, day in, day out, is explain the meaning of the Chinese characters and, of course, lecture a bit. We know nothing about your 'illustrious virtue,' I'm afraid. Go ask a Zen priest, I tell you."

I'd have been happy to follow his advice, but there were no Zen priests around at the time. One of the chief motives for my wanting to know about illustrious virtue was that I felt duty bound to teach my mother the path of the Great Learning before she died. I kept going to hear all the Confucian and Buddhist lectures, and would return to her with the wisdom that had been imparted to me, but, alas, my questions remained unanswered.

One day I remembered a certain Zen master and went to him full of expectation. At once I asked him about illustrious virtue. He looked at me gravely and said that to understand I would have to sit in Zen meditation. Soon I would be able to grasp it. Well, I lost no time. Often I would go into the mountains and sit in Zen without taking a morsel for a week, or I would go to a rocky place and, choosing the sharpest rock, meditate for days on end, taking no food, until I toppled over. The results? Exhaustion, a shrunken stomach, and an increased desire to go on.

I returned to my village and entered a hermitage, where sleeping in an upright position and living arduously, I gave myself up to the old spiritual exercise of repeating the name of Amitabha. The results? More exhaustion, and huge painful sores on my bottom. It was impossible for me to sit in comfort, but in those days I was pretty tough. Nevertheless to ease the pain, I had to place layers of soft paper under me, which as they lost their effectiveness had constantly to be replaced. Sometimes I was forced to use cotton, so atrocious was the pain.

I knew I was overdoing it, of course, and finally I became seriously ill. Soon I was bringing up blood, lumps the size of a thumb end. One day I spat on the wall and watched fascinated as the lump of blood rolled down. I was in bad shape, I can tell you. On the advice of friends I engaged a servant to nurse me. Once for seven days running I could eat nothing but a gruel of thin rice. I felt my time was up and kept saying to myself, "No help for it. Soon I'll die without obtaining my old desire."

Suddenly, while at the very depths, it struck me like a thunderbolt that I had never been born, and that my birthlessness could settle any and every matter. This seemed to be my satori, the awakening I had been waiting for. I realized then that because I'd been ignorant of this simple truth, I'd suffered needlessly.

I began to feel better, and my appetite returned. I called my servant over and said, "I want a big bowl of rice. Right now." He looked puzzled, for he'd been expecting me to keel over; then he set about in a flurry to prepare the meal. In fact he made it so quickly, and in such a state, that the rice was only half-done and stiff. But I ate three bowls and, I can assure you, it didn't disagree with me. Daily my health improved, and soon I was able to accomplish the greatest desire of my life: I was able to get my mother to see the truth, the secret of birthlessness before she died.

SIMONE WEIL

the self

We possess nothing in the world—a mere chance can strip us of everything—except the power to say "I." That is what we have to give to God, in other words, to destroy. There is absolutely no other free act which it is given us to accomplish, only the destruction of the "I."

Offering: We cannot offer anything but the "I," and all we call an offering is merely a label attached to a compensatory assertion of the "I."

Nothing in the world can rob us of the power to say "I." Nothing except extreme affliction. Nothing is worse than extreme affliction which destroys the "I" from the outside, because after that we can no longer destroy it ourselves. What happens to those whose "I" has been destroyed from outside by affliction? It is not possible to imagine anything for them but annihilation according to the atheistic or materialistic conception.

Though they may have lost their "I," it does not mean that they have no more egoism. Quite the reverse. To be sure, this may occasionally happen when a doglike devotion is brought about, but at other times the being is reduced to naked, vegetative egoism. An egoism without an "I."

So long as we ourselves have begun the process of destroying the "I," we can prevent any affliction from causing harm. For the "I" is not destroyed by external pressures without a violent revolt. If for the love of God we refuse to give ourselves over to this revolt, the destruction does not take place from outside, but from within.

Redemptive suffering. If a human being who is in a state of perfection, and has through grace completely destroyed the "I" in himself, falls into that degree of affliction which corresponds for him to the destruction of the "I" from outside, we have there the cross in its fullness. Affliction can no longer destroy the "I" in him, for the "I" in him no longer exists, having completely disappeared and left the place to God. But affliction produces an effect which is equivalent, on the plane of perfection, to the exterior destruction of the "I." It produces the absence of God. "My God, why has thou forsaken me?"

What is this absence of God, produced by extreme affliction within the perfect soul? What is the value which is attached to it, and which is known as redemptive suffering?

Redemptive suffering is that by which evil really has fullness of being to the utmost extent of its capacity.

By redemptive suffering, God is present in extreme evil. For the absence of God is the mode of divine presence which corresponds to evil—absence which is felt. He who has not God within himself cannot feel his absence.

It is the purity, the perfection, the plenitude, the abyss of evil. Whereas hell is a false abyss. Hell is superficial. Hell is a nothingness which has the pretension and gives the illusion of being.

Purely external destruction of the "I" is quasi-infernal suffering. External destruction with which the soul associates itself through love is expiatory suffering. The bringing about of the absence of God in a soul completely emptied of self through love is redemptive suffering.

• • •

The sin in me says "I."

I am all. But this particular "I" is God. And it is not an "I."

Evil makes distinctions, prevents God from being equivalent to all.

It is because of my wretchedness that I am "I." It is on account of the wretchedness of the universe that, in a sense, God is I (that is to say, a person).

The Pharisees were people who relied on their own strength to be virtuous.

Humility consists in knowing that in what we call "I" there is no source of energy by which we can rise.

Everything, without exception, that is of value in me comes from somewhere other than myself, not as a gift, but as a loan which must be ceaselessly renewed. Everything, without exception, that is in me is absolutely valueless; and, among the gifts which have come to me from elsewhere, everything which I appropriate becomes valueless as soon as I do so.

Perfect joy excludes even the very feeling of joy, for in the soul filled by the object no corner is left for saying "I."

We cannot imagine such joys when they are absent, thus the incentive for seeking them is lacking.

the empty boat _____

He who rules men lives in confusion;
He who is ruled by men lives in sorrow.
Yao therefore desired
Neither to influence others
Nor to be influenced by them.
The way to get clear of confusion
And free of sorrow
Is to live with Tao
In the land of the great Void.

If a man is crossing a river
And an empty boat collides with his own skiff,
Even though he be a bad-tempered man
He will not become very angry.
But if he sees a man in the boat,
He will shout at him to steer clear.
If the shout is not heard, he will shout again,
And yet again, and begin cursing.
And all because there is somebody in the boat.
Yet if the boat were empty,
He would not be shouting, and not angry.

If you can empty your own boat
Crossing the river of the world,
No one will oppose you,
No one will seek to harm you.

The straight tree is the first to be cut down,
The spring of clear water is the first to be drained dry.
If you wish to improve your wisdom
And shame the ignorant,
To cultivate your character
And outshine others;
A light will shine around you
As if you had swallowed the sun and the moon:
You will not avoid calamity.

A wise man has said:
    "He who is content with himself
    Has done a worthless work.

Achievement is the beginning of failure.
Fame is the beginning of disgrace."

Who can free himself from achievement
And from fame, descend and be lost
Amid the masses of men?
He will flow like Tao, unseen,
He will go about like Life itself
With no name and no home.
Simple is he, without distinction.
To all appearances he is a fool.
His steps leave no trace. He has no power.
He achieves nothing, has no reputation.
Since he judges no one
No one judges him.
Such is the perfect man:
His boat is empty.

SIMONE WEIL

love

Love is a sign of our wretchedness. God can only love himself. We can only love
something else.

God's love for us is not the reason for which we should love him. God's love
for us is the reason for us to love ourselves. How could we love ourselves without
this motive?

It is impossible for man to love himself except in this roundabout way.

. . .

Supernatural love has no contact with force, but at the same time it does not
protect the soul against the coldness of steel. Only an earthly attachment, if it
has in it enough energy, can afford protection from the coldness of steel. Armor,
like the sword, is made of metal. Murder freezes the soul of the man who loves
only with pure love, whether he be the author or the victim, so likewise does
everything which, without going so far as actual death, constitutes violence. If
we want to have a love which will protect the soul from wounds, we must love
something other than God.

. . .

Among human beings, only the existence of those we love is fully recognized.
Belief in the existence of other human beings as such is love.

The mind is not forced to believe in the existence of anything (subjectivism, absolute idealism, solipsism, skepticism: cf. the Upanishads, the Taoists, and Plato, who, all of them, adopt this philosophical attitude by way of purification). That is why the only organ of contact with existence is acceptance, love. That is why beauty and reality are identical. That is why joy and the sense of reality are identical.

This need to be the creator of what we love is a need to imitate God. But the divinity toward which it tends is false unless we have recourse to the model seen from the other, the heavenly side. . . .

Pure love of creatures is not love in God, but love which has passed through God as through fire. Love which detaches itself completely from creatures to ascend to God, and comes down again associated with the creative love of God.

Thus the two opposites which rend human love are united: to love the beloved being just as he is, and to want to re-create him.

Imaginary love of creatures. We are attached by a cord to all the objects of attachment, and a cord can always be cut. We are also attached by a cord to the imaginary God, the God for whom love is also an attachment. But to the real God we are not attached, and that is why there is no cord which can be cut. He enters into us. He alone can enter into us. All other things remain outside, and our knowledge of them is confined to the tensions of varying degree and direction which affect the cord when there is a change of position on their part or on ours.

Love needs reality. What is more terrible than the discovery that through a bodily appearance we have been loving an imaginary being? It is much more terrible than death, for death does not prevent the beloved from having lived.

That is the punishment for having fed love on imagination.

• • •

To soil is to modify, it is to touch. The beautiful is that which we cannot wish to change. To assume power over is to soil. To possess is to soil.

To love purely is to consent to distance, it is to adore the distance between ourselves and that which we love.

The imagination is always united with a desire, that is to say a value. Only desire without an object is empty of imagination. There is the real presence of God in everything which imagination does not veil. The beautiful takes our desire captive and empties it of its object, giving it an object which is present and thus forbidding it to fly off toward the future.

Such is the price of chaste love. Every desire for enjoyment belongs to the future and the world of illusion, whereas if we desire only that a being should exist, he exists: what more is there to desire? The beloved being is then naked and real, not veiled by an imaginary future. The miser never looks at his treasure without imagining it n times larger. It is necessary to be dead in order to see things in their nakedness.

Thus in love there is chastity or the lack of chastity, according to whether the desire is or is not directed toward the future.

• • •

Do not allow yourself to be imprisoned by any affection. Keep your solitude. The day, if it ever comes, when you are given true affection there will be no opposition between interior solitude and friendship, quite the reverse. It is even by this infallible sign that you will recognize it. Other affections have to be severely disciplined.

THOMAS MERTON

an enemy of the state

On August 9, 1943, the Austrian peasant Franz Jägerstätter was beheaded by the German military authorities as an "enemy of the state" because he had repeatedly refused to take the military oath and serve in what he declared to be an "unjust war." His story has a very special importance at a time when the Catholic Church, in the Second Vatican Council, is confronting the moral problem of nuclear weaponry. This Austrian peasant was not only simultaneously a Catholic and a conscientious objector, but he was a fervent Catholic, so fervent that some who knew him believe him to have been a saint. His lucid and uncompromising refusal to fight for Germany in the Second World War was the direct outcome of his religious conversion. It was the political implementation of his desire to be a perfect Christian.

Franz Jägerstätter surrendered his life rather than take the lives of others in what he believed to be an "unjust war." He clung to this belief in the face of every possible objection not only on the part of the army and the state, but also from his fellow Catholics, the Catholic clergy and of course his own family. He had to meet practically every "Christian" argument that is advanced in favor of war. He was treated as a rebel, disobedient to lawful authority, a traitor to his country. He was accused of being selfish, self-willed, not considering his family, neglecting his duty to his children.

His Austrian Catholic friends understood that he was unwilling to fight for Hitler's Germany, but yet they argued that the war was justified because they hoped it would lead to the destruction of Bolshevism and therefore to the preservation of "European Christianity." He was therefore refusing to defend his faith. He was also told that he was not sufficiently informed to judge whether or not the war was just. That he had an obligation to submit to the "higher wisdom" of the state. The government and the Fuehrer know best. Thousands of

From *Faith and Violence*, Thomas Merton, University of Notre Dame Press, 1968.

Catholics, including many priests, were serving in the armies, and therefore he should not try to be "more Catholic than the Church."

He was even reminded that the bishops had not protested against this war, and in fact not only his pastor but even his bishop tried to persuade him to give up his resistance because it was "futile." One priest represented to him that he would have innumerable opportunities to practice Christian virtue and exercise an "apostolate of good example" in the armed forces. All these are very familiar arguments frequently met with in our present situation, and they are still assumed to be so conclusive that few Catholics dare to risk the disapproval they would incur by conscientious objection and dissent.

Jägerstätter's fellow villagers thought his refusal was evidence of fanaticism due to his religious conversion at the time of his marriage in 1936, followed by an "excess of Bible reading." His conscientious objection is still not fully understood in his native village, though on the local war memorial his name has been added to those of the villagers who were killed in action.

The peasant refused to give in to any of these arguments, and replied to them with all simplicity:

> I cannot and may not take an oath in favor of a government that is fighting an unjust war. . . . I cannot turn the responsibility for my actions over to the Führer. . . . Does anyone really think that this massive blood-letting can save European Christianity or bring it to a new flowering? . . . Is it not more Christian to offer oneself as a victim right away rather than first have to murder others who certainly have a right to live and want to live—just to prolong one's own life a little while?

When reminded that most Catholics had gone to war for Hitler without any such qualms of conscience, he replied that they obviously "had not received the grace" to see things as they were. When told that the bishops themselves expressed no such objections he repeated that "they had not received the grace" either.

Jägerstätter's refusal to fight for Hitler was not based on a personal repugnance to fighting in any form. As a matter of fact Jägerstätter was, by temperament, something of a fighter. In his wilder youthful days he had participated rather prominently in the inter-village gang wars. He had also undergone preliminary military training without protest, though his experience at that time had convinced him that army life presented a danger to morals.

Shortly after Hitler took over Austria in 1938, Jägerstätter had a dream in which he saw a splendid and shining express train coming round a mountain, and thousands of people running to get aboard. "No one could prevent them from getting on the train." While he was looking at this he heard a voice saying: "This train is going to hell." When he woke up he spontaneously associated the "train" with Nazism. His objection to military service was, then, the fruit of a particular religious interpretation of contemporary political events. His refusal to fight was not only a private matter of conscience: it also expressed a deep intuition concerning the historical predicament of the Catholic Church in the twentieth century. This intuition was articulated in several long and very impressive meditations or "commentaries" in which he says:

> The situation in which we Christians of Germany find ourselves today is much more bewildering than that faced by the Christians of the early centuries at the time of their bloodiest persecution. . . . We are not dealing with a small matter, but the great (apocalyptic) life and death struggle has already begun. Yet in the midst of it there are many who still go on living their lives as though nothing had changed. . . . That we Catholics must make ourselves tools of the worst and most dangerous anti-Christian power that has ever existed is something that I cannot and never will believe. . . . Many actually believe quite simply that things have to be the way they are. If this should happen to mean that they are obliged to commit injustice, then they believe that others are responsible. . . . I am convinced that it is still best that I speak the truth even though it costs me my life. For you will not find it written in any of the commandments of God or of the Church that a man is obliged under pain of sin to take an oath committing him to obey whatever might be commanded him by his secular ruler. We need no rifles or pistols for our battle, but instead spiritual weapons—and the foremost of these is prayer.

The witness of this Austrian peasant is in striking contrast to the career of another man who lived and worked for a time in the nearby city of Linz: Adolf Eichmann.

The American sociologist, Gordon Zahn, who is also a Catholic and a pacifist, has written an absorbing, objective, fully documented life of Jägerstätter, in which he studies with great care not only the motives and actions of the man himself, but the reactions and recollections of scores of people who knew him, from his family and neighbors to fellow prisoners and prison chaplains. One of the most striking things about the story is that repeated attempts were made to save the peasant-objector's life not only by his friends, by priests, by his attorney but even by his military judges (he was not in the hands of the SS).

Jägerstätter could have escaped execution if he had accepted noncombatant service in the medical corps, but he felt that even this would be a compromise, because his objection was not only to killing other men but to the act of saving his own life by an implicit admission that the Nazis were a legitimate regime carrying on a just war. A few minutes before his execution Jägerstätter still calmly refused to sign a document that would have saved him. The chaplain who was present, and who had tried like everyone else to persuade the prisoner to save himself, declared that Jägerstätter "lived as a saint and died as a hero."

It is important to observe that though the Catholic villagers of his native St. Radegund still tend to regard Jägerstätter as an extremist and a fanatic, or even as slightly touched in the head, the priests who knew him and others who have studied him have begun to admit the seriousness and supernatural impact of his heroic self-sacrifice. There are some who do not hesitate to compare his decision with that of Thomas More.

One of the prison chaplains who knew him said: "Not for an instant did I ever entertain the notion that Jägerstätter was 'fanatic' or even possibly mentally deranged. He did not give the slightest impression of being so." And a French cellmate said of him that he was "one of the heroes of our time, a fighter to the death for faith, peace and justice."

Finally, it is interesting to read the very reserved judgment of the bishop who, when consulted by Jägerstätter about this moral problem, urged him to renounce his "scruples" and let himself be inducted into the army.

I am aware of the "consistency" of his conclusions and respect them—especially in their intention. At that time I could see that the man thirsted after martyrdom and for the expiation of sin, and I told him that he was permitted to choose that path only if he knew he had been called to it through some special revelation originating from above and not in himself. He agreed with this. For this reason Jägerstätter represents a completely exceptional case, one more to be marveled at than copied.

The story of the Austrian peasant as told by Gordon Zahn is plainly that of a martyr, and of a Christian who followed a path of virtue with a dedication that cannot be fully accounted for by human motivation alone. In other words, it would seem that already in this biography one might find plausible evidence of what the Catholic Church regards as sanctity. But the Bishop of Linz, in hinting at the possibility of a special calling that might have made Jägerstätter an "exceptional case," does not mean even implicitly to approve the thesis that the man was a saint, still less a model to be imitated. In other words the bishop, while admitting the remote possibility of Catholic heroism in a conscientious objector, is not admitting that such heroism should be regarded as either normal or imitable.

The Second Vatican Council in its Constitution on the Church in the Modern World recognized, at least implicitly, the right of a Catholic to refuse on grounds of conscience to bear arms. It did not propose conscientious objection as a sweeping obligation. Nevertheless it clearly declared that no one could escape the obligation to *refuse obedience* to criminal orders issued by the state or the military command. The example of genocide was given. In view of the fact that total war tends more and more in fact to be genocidal, the Council's declaration obviously bears above all on war.

The Bishop of Linz, however, did not propose conscientious objection as a rational and Christian option. For him, the true heroes remain "those exemplary young Catholic men, seminarians, priests and heads of families who fought and died in heroic fulfillment of duty and in the firm conviction that they were fulfilling the will of God at their post. . . ."

It is still quite possible that even today after the Council and in an era of new war technology and new threats of global destruction, when the most urgent single problem facing modern man is the proliferation of atomic and nuclear weaponry, many Catholic bishops will continue to agree with this one. It is true, they admit that there is such a thing as an erroneous conscience which is to be followed provided it is "invincible." "All respect is due to the innocently erroneous conscience," says the Bishop of Linz, "it will have its reward from God."

Of whom is he speaking? Of the Catholic young men, the priests and the seminarians who died in Hitler's armies "in the firm conviction that they were fulfilling the will of God"? No. These, he says, were men (and the word is underlined) acting in the light of "a clear and correct conscience." Jägerstätter was "in error" but also "in good faith."

Certainly the bishop is entitled to his opinion: but the question of whose conscience was erroneous and whose was correct remains one that will ultimately be settled by God, not man. Meanwhile there is another question: the responsibility of those who help men to form their conscience—or fail to do so. And here, too, the possibility of firm convictions that are "innocently erroneous" gives food for some rather apocalyptic thought.

The real question raised by the Jägerstätter story is not merely that of the individual Catholic's right to conscientious objection (admitted in practice even by those who completely disagreed with Jägerstätter) but the question of the Church's own mission of protest and prophecy in the gravest spiritual crisis man has ever known.

JAMES NAYLOR

there is a spirit ───────────────────────────────────

There is a Spirit which I feel, that delights to do no Evil, nor to revenge any Wrong, but delights to endure all things, in hope to enjoy its own in the End: its hope is to outlive all Wrath and Contention, and to weary out all Exaltation and Cruelty, or whatever is of a Nature contrary to itself. It sees to the End of all Temptations: as it bears no Evil in itself, so it conceives none in Thoughts to any other: if it be betrayed it bears it; for its Ground and Spring is the Mercies and Forgiveness of God: its Crown is Meekness, its Life is Everlasting Love unfeigned, and takes its Kingdom with Entreaty, and not with Contention, and keeps it by Lowliness of Mind. In God alone it can rejoice, though none else regard it, or can own its Life. It's conceived in Sorrow, and brought forth without any to pity it; nor doth it murmur at Grief and Oppression. It never rejoiceth but through Sufferings; for with the World's Joy it is murdered. I found it alone, being forsaken; I have Fellowship therein, with them who lived in Dens, and desolate Places in the Earth, who through Death obtained this Resurrection and Eternal Holy Life.

the sunset of the century

1

The last sun of the century sets amidst the blood-red clouds of the West and the
    whirlwind of hatred.
The naked passion of self-love of Nations, in its drunken delirium of greed, is
    dancing to the clash of steel and the howling verses of vengeance.

2

The hungry self of the Nation shall burst in a violence of fury from its own
    shameless feeding.
For it has made the world its food.
And licking it, crunching it, and swallowing it in big morsels,
It swells and swells,
Till in the midst of its unholy feast descends the sudden shaft of heaven piercing
    its heart of grossness.

3

The crimson glow of light on the horizon is not the light of thy dawn of peace,
    my Motherland.
It is the glimmer of the funeral pyre burning to ashes the vast flesh—the self-love
    of the Nation—dead under its own excess.
Thy morning waits behind the patient dark of the East,
Meek and silent.

4

Keep watch, India.
Bring your offerings of worship for that sacred sunrise.
Let the first hymn of its welcome sound in your voice and sing
"Come, Peace, thou daughter of God's own great suffering.
Come with thy treasure of contentment, the sword of fortitude,
And meekness crowning thy forehead."

5

Be not ashamed, my brothers, to stand before the proud and the powerful
With your white robe of simpleness.
Let your crown be of humility, your freedom the freedom of the soul.
Build God's throne daily upon the ample bareness of your poverty
And know that what is huge is not great and pride is not everlasting.

From *Nationalism,* London, Macmillan, n.d. Permission of the Trustees of the Tagore Estate
and Macmillan London and Basingstoke.

RABÌNDRANĀTH TAGORE
where the mind
is without fear

Where the mind is without fear and the head is held high;
Where knowledge is free;
Where the world has not been broken up into fragments by narrow domestic
    walls;
Where words come out from the depth of truth;
Where tireless striving stretches its arms towards perfection;
Where the clear stream of reason has not lost its way into the dreary desert sand
    of dead habit;
Where the mind is led forward by thee into everwidening thought and action—
Into that heaven of freedom, my Father, let my country awake.

CHANDOGYA UPANISHAD
there is a light

Wherefrom do all these words come? They come from space. All beings arise from space, and into space they return: space is indeed their beginning, and space is their final end.   1. 9. 1

Prajapati, the Creator of all, rested in life-giving meditation over the worlds of his creation; and from them came the three *Vedas.* He rested in meditation and from those came the three sounds: Bhur, Bhuvas, Svar, earth, air, and sky. He rested in meditation and from the three sounds came the sound Om. Even as all leaves come from a stem, all words come from the sound Om. Om is the whole universe. Om is in truth the whole universe.   2. 23. 2

Great is the Gayatri, the most sacred verse of the Vedas; but how much greater is the Infinity of Brahman! A quarter of his being is this whole universe: the other three quarters are his heaven of Immortality.   3. 12. 5

There is a Light that shines beyond all things on earth, beyond us all, beyond the heavens, beyond the highest, the very highest heavens. This is the Light that shines in our heart.

All this universe is in truth Brahman. He is the beginning and end and life of all. As such, in silence, give unto him adoration.

Man in truth is made of faith. As his faith is in this life, so he becomes in the beyond: with faith and vision let him work.

There is a Spirit that is mind and life, light and truth and vast spaces. He contains all works and desires and all perfumes and all tastes. He enfolds the whole universe, and in silence is loving to all.

This is the Spirit that is in my heart, smaller than a grain of rice, or a grain of barley, or a grain of mustard-seed, or a grain of canary-seed, or the kernel of a grain of canary-seed. This is the Spirit that is in my heart, greater than the earth, greater than the sky, greater than heaven itself, greater than all these worlds.

He contains all works and desires and all perfumes and all tastes. He enfolds the whole universe and in silence is loving to all. This is the Spirit that is in my heart, this is Brahman.

CHANDOGYA UPANISHAD
thou art that _____

Svetaketu said: "Certainly my honored masters knew not this themselves. If they had known, why would they not have told me? Explain this to me, father."

"So be it, my child."

"Bring me a fruit from this banyan tree."

"Here it is, father."

"Break it."

"It is broken, Sir."

"What do you see in it?"

"Very small seeds, Sir."

"Break one of them, my son."

"It is broken, Sir."

"What do you see in it?"

"Nothing at all, Sir."

Then his father spoke to him: "My son, from the very essence in the seed which you cannot see comes in truth this vast banyan tree.

"Believe me, my son, an invisible and subtle essence is the Spirit of the whole universe. That is Reality. That is Atman. Thou Art That."

"Explain more to me, father," said Svetaketu.

"So be it, my son.

From *The Upanishads,* trans. Juan Mascaró, Penguin Books Ltd. Copyright © Juan Mascaró, 1965.

"Place this salt in water and come to me tomorrow morning."

Svetaketu did as he was commanded, and in the morning his father said to him: "Bring me the salt you put into the water last night."

Svetaketu looked into the water, but could not find it, for it had dissolved. His father then said: "Taste the water from this side. How is it?"

"It is salt."

"Taste it from the middle. How is it?"

"It is salt."

"Look for the salt again and come again to me."

The son did so, saying: "I cannot see the salt. I only see water."

His father then said: "In the same way, O my son, you cannot see the Spirit. But in truth he is here.

"An invisible and subtle essence is the Spirit of the whole universe. That is Reality. That is Truth. Thou Art That."

Is there anything higher than thought?

Meditation is in truth higher than thought. The earth seems to rest in silent meditation; and the waters and the mountains and the sky and the heavens seem all to be in meditation. Whenever a man attains greatness on this earth, he has his reward according to his meditation.

ST. PAUL

love _____

And now I will show you the best way of all.

I may speak in tongues of men or of angels, but if I am without love, I am a sounding gong or a clanging cymbal. I may have the gift of prophecy, and know every hidden truth; I may have faith strong enough to move mountains; but if I have no love, I am nothing. I may dole out all I possess, or even give my body to be burnt, but if I have no love, I am none the better.

Love is patient; love is kind and envies no one. Love is never boastful, nor conceited, nor rude; never selfish, not quick to take offense. Love keeps no score of wrongs; does not gloat over other men's sins, but delights in the truth. There is nothing love cannot face; there is no limit to its faith, its hope, and its endurance.

Love will never come to an end. Are there prophets? their work will be over. Are there tongues of ecstasy? they will cease. Is there knowledge? it will vanish away; for our knowledge and our prophecy alike are partial, and the partial van-

_____

From *The New English Bible.* © the Delegates of the Oxford University Press and the Syndics of the Cambridge University Press 1961, 1970. Reprinted by permission.

ishes when wholeness comes. When I was a child, my speech, my outlook, and my thoughts were all childish. When I grew up, I had finished with childish things. Now we see only puzzling reflections in a mirror, but then we shall see face to face. My knowledge now is partial; then it will be whole, like God's knowledge of me. In a word, there are three things that last for ever: faith, hope, and love; but the greatest of them all is love.

ST. PAUL

christ—god's secret

I want them to continue in good heart and in the unity of love, and to come to the full wealth of conviction which understanding brings, and grasp God's secret. That secret is Christ himself; in him lie hidden all God's treasures of wisdom and knowledge. I tell you this to save you from being talked into error by specious arguments. For though absent in body, I am with you in spirit, and rejoice to see your orderly array and the firm front which your faith in Christ presents.

Therefore, since Jesus was delivered to you as Christ and Lord, live your lives in union with him. Be rooted in him; be built in him; be consolidated in the faith you were taught; let your hearts overflow with thankfulness. Be on your guard; do not let your minds be captured by hollow and delusive speculations, based on traditions of man-made teaching and centered on the elemental spirits of the universe and not on Christ.

For it is in Christ that the complete being of the Godhead dwells embodied, and in him you have been brought to completion. Every power and authority in the universe is subject to him as Head.

ST. PAUL

life with christ

Were you not raised to life with Christ? Then aspire to the realm above, where Christ is, seated at the right hand of God, and let your thoughts dwell on that higher realm, not on this earthly life. I repeat, you died; and now your life lies hidden with Christ in God. When Christ, who is our life, is manifested, then you too will be manifested with him in glory.

Then put to death those parts of you which belong to the earth—fornication, indecency, lust, foul cravings, and the ruthless greed which is nothing less than idolatry. Because of these, God's dreadful judgment is impending; and in the life you once lived these are the ways you yourselves followed. But now you must yourselves lay aside all anger, passion, malice, cursing, filthy talk—have done with them! Stop lying to one another, now that you have discarded the old nature with its deeds and have put on the new nature, which is being constantly renewed in the image of its Creator and brought to know God. There is no question here of Greek and Jew, circumcised and uncircumcised, barbarian, Scythian, slave and freeman; but Christ is all, and is in all.

PART 2
the world
and transcendence

Transcendence is a metaphor that derives from the simple notion that some things are "above" other things. In this section we are concerned with the extension of this metaphor to its ultimate meaning. A remark of Einstein's will illustrate the point: "The most beautiful thing that we can experience is the mysterious. . . . To know that what is impenetrable to us really exists, manifesting itself as the highest wisdom and the most radiant beauty which our dull facilities can comprehend only in their most primitive form—this knowledge, this feeling, is at the center of true religiousness."

Such a notion of transcendence is opposed to the piety of what Wilfred Cantwell Smith calls the "cumulative tradition." It is also opposed to the "God Is Dead" tradition of Nietzsche, although in his case there is still the transcendent Superman—the humanity yet to emerge. Beckett's "Sucking Stones" is a better instance of man existing in complete nontranscendence.

Eiseley's story of his captured hawk is a beautiful example of another concept of transcendence, that of life infinitely transcending the notion of a machine. Pondering that story alone should give ample substance for thought.

The presence of transcendent experiences is a fact; the meaning of these experiences is something else. The major Western Semitic metaphor for transcendence is *Person* while for the East the metaphor is the *One*. Several selections illuminate these options. The passages from the Koran, for instance, illustrate the former: Allah is beyond all thought and experience possible to a man. Zimmer's "Parade of Ants" illustrates the latter. We have also included several short selections from the Chinese Taoist (the "t" is pronounced as a "d") tradition because of the simplicity and beauty of their expression, even in translation. The Western perspective shows itself again in Kierkegaard who contrasts the Eastern notion of the Knight of Infinite Resignation with Abraham who is the model for his Knight of Faith. Robert Capon's cookbook begins with an essay that shows the transcendent even in an onion.

There are those who prefer to think of the transcendent as part of the natural world. Some of these writers appear in later sections (for instance, Maslow's discussion in Part 5), but we have let Lord Russell speak for this point of view in his eloquent "A Free Man's Worship." More generally the religious mind sees the mysteriously transcendent as trustworthy and even gracious. The prodigal son parable from the Buddhist tradition beautifully illustrates this conviction.

that nature is a heraclitean fire
and of the comfort of the resurrection ⎯⎯⎯⎯⎯⎯⎯⎯⎯⎯⎯⎯⎯⎯

CLOUD-PUFFBALL, torn tufts, tossed pillows ǀ flaunt forth, then chevy on an air-
built thoroughfare: heaven-roysterers, in gay-gangs ǀ they throng; they glitter in marches.
Down roughcast, down dazzling whitewash, ǀ wherever an elm arches,
Shivelights and shadowtackle in long ǀ lashes lace, lance, and pair.
Delightfully the bright wind boisterous ǀ ropes, wrestles, beats earth bare
Of yestertempest's creases; ǀ in pool and rut peel parches
Squandering ooze to squeezed ǀ dough, crust, dust; stanches, starches
Squadroned masks and manmarks ǀ treadmire toil there
Footfretted in it. Million-fuelèd, ǀ nature's bonfire burns on.
But quench her bonniest, dearest ǀ to her, her clearest-selvèd spark
Man, how fast his firedint, ǀ his mark on mind, is gone!
Both are in an unfathomable, all is in an enormous dark
Drowned. O pity and indigǀnation! Manshape, that shone
Sheer off, disseveral, a star, ǀ death blots black out; nor mark
              Is any of him at all so stark
But vastness blurs and time ǀ beats level. Enough! the Resurrection,
A heart's-clarion! Away grief's gasping, ǀ joyless days, dejection.
              Across my foundering deck shone
A beacon, an eternal beam. ǀ Flesh fade, and mortal trash
Fall to the residuary worm; ǀ world's wildfire, leave but ash:
              In a flash, at a trumpet crash,
I am all at once what Christ is, ǀ since he was what I am, and
This Jack, joke, poor potsherd, ǀ patch, matchwood, immortal diamond,
              Is immortal diamond.

─────────
From *Poems of Gerard Manley Hopkins,* ed. W. H. Gardner, New York, Oxford, 1948.

the death of god ⎯⎯⎯⎯⎯⎯⎯⎯⎯⎯⎯⎯⎯⎯⎯⎯⎯⎯⎯⎯⎯⎯⎯⎯⎯⎯

The figs are falling from the trees; they are good and sweet; and, as they fall, their red skin bursts. I am a north wind to ripe figs.

     Thus, like figs, these teachings fall to you, my friends; now consume their

─────────
From *The Portable Nietzsche,* trans. Walter Kaufmann. Copyright 1954 by The Viking Press, Inc. Reprinted by permission of The Viking Press, Inc.

juice and their sweet meat. It is autumn about us, and pure sky and afternoon. Behold what fullness there is about us! And out of such overflow it is beautiful to look out upon distant seas; but now I have taught you to say: overman.

God is a conjecture; but I desire that your conjectures should not reach beyond your creative will. Could you create a god? Then do not speak to me of any gods. But you could well create the overman. Perhaps not you yourselves, my brothers. But into fathers and forefathers of the overman you could re-create yourselves: and let this be your best creation.

God is a conjecture; but I desire that your conjectures should be limited by what is thinkable. Could you think a god? But this is what the will to truth should mean to you: that everything be changed into what is thinkable for man, visible for man, feelable for man. You should think through your own senses to their consequences.

And what you have called world, that shall be created only by you: your reason, your image, your will, your love shall thus be realized. And verily, for your own bliss, you lovers of knowledge.

And how would you bear life without this hope, you lovers of knowledge? You could not have been born either into the incomprehensible or into the irrational.

But let me reveal my heart to you entirely, my friends: if there were gods, how could I endure not to be a god! Hence there are no gods. Though I drew this conclusion, now it draws me.

God is a conjecture; but who could drain all the agony of this conjecture without dying? Shall his faith be taken away from the creator, and from the eagle, his soaring to eagle heights?

God is a thought that makes crooked all that is straight, and makes turn whatever stands. How? Should time be gone, and all that is impermanent a mere lie? To think this is a dizzy whirl for human bones, and a vomit for the stomach; verily, I call it the turning sickness to conjecture thus. Evil I call it, and misanthropic—all this teaching of the One and the Plenum and the Unmoved and the Sated and the Permanent. All the permanent—that is only a parable. And the poets lie too much.

It is of time and becoming that the best parables should speak: let them be a praise and a justification of all impermanence.

Creation—that is the great redemption from suffering, and life's growing light. But that the creator may be, suffering is needed and much change. Indeed, there must be much bitter dying in your life, you creators. Thus are you advocates and justifiers of all impermanence. To be the child who is newly born, the creator must also want to be the mother who gives birth and the pangs of the birth-giver.

Verily, through a hundred souls I have already passed on my way, and through a hundred cradles and birth pangs. Many a farewell have I taken; I know the heart-rending last hours. But thus my creative will, my destiny, wills it. Or, to say it more honestly: this very destiny—my will wills.

Whatever in me has feeling, suffers and is in prison; but my will always comes to me as my liberator and joy-bringer. Willing liberates: that is the true teaching of will and liberty—thus Zarathustra teaches it. Willing no more and esteeming no more and creating no more—oh, that this great weariness might always remain far from me! In knowledge too I feel only my will's joy in begetting and becoming; and if there is innocence in my knowledge, it is because the will to beget is in it. Away from God and gods this will has lured me; what could one create if gods existed?

But my fervent will to create impels me ever again toward man; thus is the hammer impelled toward the stone. O men, in the stone there sleeps an image, the images of my images. Alas, that it must sleep in the hardest, the ugliest stone! Now my hammer rages cruelly against its prison. Pieces of rock rain from the stone: what is that to me? I want to perfect it; for a shadow came to me—the stillest and lightest of all things once came to me. The beauty of the overman came to me as a shadow. O my brothers, what are the gods to me now?

Thus spoke Zarathustra.

FRIEDRICH NIETZSCHE
beyond good and evil _____

There is an old illusion, which is called good and evil. So far the wheel of this illusion has revolved around soothsayers and stargazers, and therefore believed: "All is destiny: you ought to, for you must."

Then man again mistrusted all soothsayers and stargazers, and therefore believed: "All is freedom: you can, for you will." O my brothers, so far there have been only illusions about stars and the future, not knowledge; and therefore there have been only illusions so far, not knowledge, about good and evil.

"Thou shalt not rob! Thou shalt not kill!" Such words were once called holy; one bent the knee and head and took off one's shoes before them. But I ask you: where have there ever been better robbers and killers in this world than such holy words?

Is there not in all life itself robbing and killing? And that such words were called holy—was not truth itself killed thereby? Or was it the preaching of death that was called holy, which contradicted and contravened all life? O my brothers, break, break the old tablets!

This is my pity for all that is past: I see how all of it is abandoned—abandoned to the pleasure, the spirit, the madness of every generation, which comes along and reinterprets all that has been as a bridge to itself.

A great despot might come along, a shrewd monster who, according to his

From *The Portable Nietzsche,* trans. Walter Kaufmann. Copyright 1954 by The Viking Press, Inc. Reprinted by permission of The Viking Press, Inc.

pleasure and displeasure, might constrain and strain all that is past till it becomes a bridge to him, a harbinger and herald and cockcrow.

This, however, is the other danger and what prompts my further pity: whoever is of the rabble, thinks back as far as the grandfather; with the grandfather, however, time ends.

Thus all that is past is abandoned: for one day the rabble might become master and drown all time in shallow waters.

Therefore, my brothers, a new nobility is needed to be the adversary of all rabble and of all that is despotic and to write anew upon new tablets the word "noble."

For many who are noble are needed, and noble men of many kinds, that there may be a nobility. Or as I once said in a parable: "Precisely this is godlike that there are gods, but no God."

FRIEDRICH NIETZSCHE

god is dead

The background of our cheerfulness. The greatest recent event—that "God is dead," that the belief in the Christian God has ceased to be believable—is even now beginning to cast its first shadows over Europe. For the few, at least, whose eyes, whose suspicion in their eyes, is strong and sensitive enough for this spectacle, some sun seems to have set just now. . . . In the main, however, this may be said: the event itself is much too great, too distant, too far from the comprehension of the many even for the tidings of it to be thought of as having arrived yet, not to speak of the notion that many people might know what has really happened here, and what must collapse now that this belief has been undermined—all that was built upon it, leaned on it, grew into it; for example, our whole European morality. . . .

Even we born guessers of riddles who are, as it were, waiting on the mountains, put there between today and tomorrow and stretched in the contradiction between today and tomorrow, we firstlings and premature births of the coming century, to whom the shadows that must soon envelop Europe really should have appeared by now—why is it that even we look forward to it without any real compassion for this darkening, and above all without any worry and fear for ourselves? It is perhaps that we are still too deeply impressed by the first consequences of this event—and these first consequences, the consequences for us, are perhaps the reverse of what one might expect: not at all sad and dark, but rather like a new, scarcely describable kind of light, happiness, relief, exhilaration, encouragement, dawn? Indeed, we philosophers and "free spirits" feel as if a new dawn were shining on us when we receive the tidings that "the old god is dead"; our heart overflows with gratitude, amazement, anticipation, expectation. At last the horizon appears free again to us, even granted that it is not bright; at last our ships may venture out again, venture out to face any danger; all the daring of the lover of knowledge is permitted again; the sea, our sea, lies open again; perhaps there has never yet been such an "open sea."

SAMUEL BECKETT

sucking stones

I took advantage of being at the seaside to lay in a store of sucking-stones. They were pebbles but I call them stones. Yes, on this occasion I laid in a considerable store. I distributed them equally among my four pockets, and sucked them turn and turn about. This raised a problem which I first solved in the following way. I had say sixteen stones, four in each of my four pockets these being the two pockets of my trousers and the two pockets of my greatcoat. Taking a stone from the right pocket of my greatcoat, and putting it in my mouth, I replaced it in the right pocket of my greatcoat by a stone from the right pocket of my trousers, which I replaced by a stone from the left pocket of my trousers, which I replaced by a stone from the left pocket of my greatcoat, which I replaced by the stone which was in my mouth, as soon as I had finished sucking it. Thus there were still four stones in each of my four pockets, but not quite the same stones. And when the desire to suck took hold of me again, I drew again on the right pocket of my greatcoat, certain of not taking the same stone as the last time. And while I sucked it I rearranged the other stones in the way I have just described. And so on. But this solution did not satisfy me fully. For it did not escape me that, by an extraordinary hazard, the four stones circulating thus might always be the same four. In which case, far from sucking the sixteen stones turn and turn about, I was really only sucking four, always the same, turn and turn about. But I shuffled them well in my pockets, before I began to suck, and again, while I sucked, before transferring them, in the hope of obtaining a more general circulation of the stones from pocket to pocket. But this was only a makeshift that could not long content a man like me. So I began to look for something else. And the first thing I hit upon was that I might do better to transfer the stones four by four, instead of one by one, that is to say, during the sucking, to take the three stones remaining in the right pocket of my greatcoat and replace them by the four in the right pocket of my trousers, and these by the

four in the left pocket of my trousers, and these by the four in the left pocket of
my greatcoat, and finally these by the three from the right pocket of my greatcoat, plus the one, as soon as I had finished sucking it, which was in my mouth.
Yes, it seemed to me at first that by so doing I would arrive at a better result.
But on further reflection I had to change my mind and confess that the circulation of the stones four by four came to exactly the same thing as their circulation one by one. For if I was certain of finding each time, in the right pocket of
my greatcoat, four stones totally different from their immediate predecessors, the
possibility nevertheless remained of my always chancing on the same stone, within
each group of four, and consequently of my sucking, not the sixteen turn and turn
about as I wished, but in fact four only, always the same, turn and turn about. So I
had to seek elsewhere than in the mode of circulation. For no matter how I caused
the stones to circulate, I always ran the same risk. It was obvious that by increasing
the number of my pockets I was bound to increase my chances of enjoying my
stones in the way I planned, that is to say one after the other until their number
was exhausted. Had I had eight pockets, for example, instead of the four I did
have, then even the most diabolical hazard could not have prevented me from
sucking at least eight of my sixteen stones, turn and turn about. The truth is I
should have needed sixteen pockets in order to be quite easy in my mind. And
for a long time I could see no other conclusion than this, that short of having
sixteen pockets, each with its stone, I could never reach the goal I had set myself, short of an extraordinary hazard. And if at a pitch I could double the number of my pockets, were it only by dividing each pocket in two, with the help of
a few safety-pins let us say, to quadruple them seemed to be more than I could
manage. And I did not feel inclined to take all that trouble for a half-measure.
For I was beginning to lose all sense of measure, after all this wrestling and
wrangling, and to say, All or nothing. And if I was tempted for an instant to
establish a more equitable proportion between my stones and my pockets, by
reducing the former to the number of the latter, it was only for an instant. For it
would have been an admission of defeat. And sitting on the shore, before the
sea, the sixteen stones spread out before my eyes, I gazed at them in anger and
perplexity. For just as I had difficulty in sitting on a chair, or in an arm-chair,
because of my stiff leg you understand, so I had none in sitting on the ground,
because of my stiff leg, for it was about this time that my good leg, good in the
sense that it was not stiff, began to stiffen. I needed a prop under the ham you
understand, and even under the whole length of the leg, the prop of the earth.
And while I gazed thus at my stones, revolving interminable martingales all
equally defective, and crushing handfuls of sand, so that the sand ran through
my fingers and fell back on the strand, yes, while thus I lulled my mind and part
of my body, one day suddenly it dawned on the former, dimly, that I might
perhaps achieve my purpose without increasing the number of my pockets, or
reducing the number of my stones, but simply by sacrificing the principle of
trim. The meaning of this illumination, which suddenly began to sing within me,
like a verse of Isaiah, or of Jeremiah, I did not penetrate at once, and notably

the word trim, which I had never met with, in this sense, long remained obscure. Finally I seemed to grasp that this word trim could not here mean anything else, anything better, than the distribution of the sixteen stones in four groups of four, one group in each pocket, and that it was my refusal to consider any distribution other than this that had vitiated my calculations until then and rendered the problem literally insoluble. And it was on the basis of this interpretation, whether right or wrong, that I finally reached a solution, inelegant assuredly, but sound, sound. Now I am willing to believe, indeed I firmly believe, that other solutions to this problem might have been found, and indeed may still be found, no less sound, but much more elegant, than the one I shall now describe, if I can. And I believe too that had I been a little more insistent, a little more resistant, I could have found them myself. But I was tired, but I was tired, and I contented myself ingloriously with the first solution that was a solution, to this problem. But not to go over the heartbreaking stages through which I passed before I came to it, here it is, in all its hideousness. All (all!) that was necessary was to put for example, to begin with, six stones in the right pocket of my greatcoat, or supply-pocket, five in the right pocket of my trousers, and five in the left pocket of my trousers, that makes the lot, twice five ten plus six sixteen, and none, for none remained, in the left pocket of my greatcoat, which for the time being remained empty, empty of stones that is, for its usual contents remained, as well as occasional objects. For where do you think I hid my vegetable knife, my silver, my horn and the other things that I have not yet named, perhaps shall never name. Good. Now I can begin to suck. Watch me closely. I take a stone from the right pocket of my greatcoat, suck it, stop sucking it, put it in the left pocket of my greatcoat, the one empty (of stones). I take a second stone from the right pocket of my greatcoat, suck it, put it in the left pocket of my greatcoat. And so on until the right pocket of my greatcoat is empty (apart from its usual and casual contents) and the six stones I have just sucked, one after the other, are all in the left pocket of my greatcoat. Pausing then, and concentrating, so as not to make a balls of it, I transfer to the right pocket of my greatcoat, in which there are no stones left, the five stones in the right pocket of my trousers, which I replace by the five stones in the left pocket of my trousers, which I replace by the six stones in the left pocket of my greatcoat. At this stage then the left pocket of my greatcoat is again empty of stones, while the right pocket of my greatcoat is again supplied, and in the right way, that is to say with other stones than those I have just sucked. These other stones I then begin to suck, one after the other, and to transfer as I go along to the left pocket of my greatcoat, being absolutely certain, as far as one can be in an affair of this kind, that I am not sucking the same stones as a moment before, but others. And when the right pocket of my greatcoat is again empty (of stones), and the five I have just sucked are all without exception in the left pocket of my greatcoat, then I proceed to the same redistribution as a moment before, or a similar redistribution, that is to say I transfer to the right pocket of my greatcoat, now again available, the five stones in the right pocket of my trousers, which I replace by the six stones in the left pocket of my trousers, which I replace by the five stones in the left pocket of my greatcoat. And there I am ready to begin again. Do I have to go on? No, for it is clear that after the next series, of sucks and transfers, I shall be back where I started, that is to say with the first six stones back in the supply-pocket, the next five in the right pocket of my stinking old trousers and finally the last five in left pocket of same, and my sixteen stones will have been sucked once at least in impeccable succession, not one sucked twice, not one left unsucked. It is true that the next time I could scarcely hope to suck my stones in the same order as the first time and that the first, seventh and twelfth for example of the first cycle might very well be the sixth, eleventh and sixteenth respectively of the second, if the worst came to the worst. But that was a drawback I could not avoid. And if in the cycles taken together utter confusion was bound to reign, at least within each cycle taken separately I could be easy in my mind, at least as easy as one can be, in a proceeding of this kind. For in order for each cycle to be identical, as to the succession of stones in my mouth, and God knows I had set my heart on it, the only means were numbered stones or sixteen pockets. And rather than make twelve more pockets or number my stones, I preferred to make the best of the comparative peace of mind I enjoyed within each cycle taken separately. For it was not enough to number the stones, but I would have had to remember, every time I put a stone in my mouth, the number I needed and look for it in my pocket. Which would have put me off stone for ever, in a very short time. For I would never have been sure of not making a mistake, unless of course I had kept a kind of register, in which to tick off the stones one by one, as I sucked them. And of this I believed myself incapable. No, the only perfect solution would have been the sixteen pockets, symmetrically disposed, each one with its stone. Then I would have needed neither to number nor to think, but merely, as I sucked a given stone, to move on the fifteen others, each to the next pocket, a delicate business admittedly, but within my power, and to call always on the same pocket when I felt like a suck. This would have freed me from all anxiety, not only within each cycle taken separately, but also for the sum of all cycles, though they went on forever. But however imperfect my own solution was, I was pleased at having found it all alone, yes, quite pleased. And if it was perhaps less sound than I had thought in the first flush of discovery, its inelegance never diminished. And it was above all inelegant in this, to my mind, that the uneven distribution was painful to me, bodily. It is true that a kind of equilibrium was reached, at a given moment, in the early stages of each cycle, namely after the third suck and before the fourth, but it did not last long, and the rest of the time I felt the weight of the stones dragging me now to one side, now to the other. So it was something more than a principle I abandoned, when I abandoned the equal distribution, it was a bodily need. But to suck the stones in the way I have described, not haphazard, but with method, was also I think a bodily need. Here then were two incompatible bodily needs, at loggerheads. Such things happen. But deep down I didn't give a tinker's curse about being off my balance, dragged to the right hand and the left, backwards and forwards. And deep down it was all the same to me whether I sucked a different stone each time or always the same stone, until the end of time. For they all tasted exactly the same. And if I had collected sixteen, it was not in order to ballast myself in such and such a way, or to suck them turn about, but simply to have a little store, so as never to be without. But deep down I didn't give a fiddler's curse about being without, when they were all gone they would be all gone, I wouldn't be any the worse off, or hardly any. And the solution to which I rallied in the end was to throw away all the stones but one, which I kept now in one pocket, now in another, and which of course I soon lost, or threw away, or gave away, or swallowed.

WILFRED CANTWELL SMITH

the cumulative tradition ──────────────────────────

The man of religious faith lives in this world. He is subject to its pressures, limited within its imperfections, particularized within one or another of its always varying contexts of time and place, and he is observable. At the same time and because of his faith or through it, he is or claims to be in touch with another world transcending this. The duality of this position some would say is the greatness and some the very meaning of human life; the heart of its distinctive quality, its tragedy and its glory. Others would dismiss the claim as false, though not uninteresting. However that may be, the duality raises problems not only for the man of faith himself, for the formulator of faith whether theologian or artist, and for the philosopher. It raises problems also, we have seen, for the student of religious history. My suggestion is that these latter issues might be treated differently from what has been customary and more effectively, in such a way as to enable the more ultimate questions to be appreciated in truer perspective, and not prejudged.

We speak of the life of religious man seeming to be somehow in two worlds, the mundane realm of limiting and observable and changing actuality and a realm transcending this. What is the nature of that transcendent sphere, and what the nature of its relation to this mundane one, are questions on which, to put it mildly, there is no general agreement.

Whether the transcendence is the human imagination at work or the fantasy of subconscious neuroses, or the meaningless patter of language gone awry, or the ideological superstructure of a particular economic situation; or whether it is a real world, or more real than this immediate one, or this immediate one perceived more truly; and whether, if it is real, it is personal, Jesus-like, rational, formless, moral, punitive, unknowable—all these are questions on which intelligent men have taken varying stands. It would seem evident that if the study of man's religious history is to make progress at all as a cogent scholarly pursuit, it must do so without waiting for, or presupposing, agreement on these matters. In fact the divergence of answers is one part of the very matter that one is trying to understand. Room for this multiplicity must therefore be provided in the conceptual framework with which one approaches the task.

The nature of the mundane world, on the other hand, is becoming increasingly known, in a fashion that admits less and less of divergence. This is true also of the mundane aspect of man's own living. Men may differ as to the content of faith or as to its validity, but there is in principle little room for differing as to its overt manifestations across the centuries in their resplendent or grotesque variety. The unobservable part of man's history, especially his religious history, may and indeed must be acknowledged an open question so far as scholarship is concerned. Meanwhile the observable part, including that of his religious history, is because of that very scholarship accessible to open scrutiny.

From this ambivalent quality of religious life, our difficulty ineluctably stems. What is needed, then, is a device to give the ambivalence full play. Such a device is in fact fairly readily at hand. It may seem disarmingly simple, and at first blush just a trifle evasive, although this in fact is part of its virtue. For as scholars we cannot but also as scholars we need not and must not begin by "solving" the problem of the relation between transcendence and the world. It is both possible and rewarding to postpone it. Our academic and intellectual skills are not capable of letting us climb over a mountain whose summit is in the skies. While staying on the ground we may, if the road that I discern does not deceive me, quietly outflank it, and so get on with our task.

This is because, whatever the relation between our two realms may be metaphysically or theologically, so far as the historian is concerned the link is quite clear. It is man.

The history of what has been called religion in general and of each religion, is the history of man's participation in an evolving context of observable actualities, and in a something, not directly observable by historical scholarship.

Any historiography, we suggest, distorts what it is reporting if it omits either of these two aspects; and yet is doomed to flounder if it attempts to combine them. My suggestion is the basically rather simple one that we separate them in intellectual analysis, retaining both.

Phrased more historically: the study of man's religious life has in the past been inadequate insofar as its concept of religion has neglected either the mundane or the transcendent element in what it has studied, and has been confused in so far as its concept has attempted to embrace both. I ask whether these studies may not proceed more satisfactorily in future if, putting aside the concept "religion" or "the religions" to describe the two, we elect to work rather with two separate concepts.

I propose to call these "cumulative tradition," on the one hand, and "faith," on the other. The link between the two is the living person.

By "faith" I mean personal faith. For the moment let it stand for an inner religious experience or involvement of a particular person; the impingement on him of the transcendent, putative or real. By "cumulative tradition" I mean the entire mass of overt objective data that constitute the historical deposit, as it were, of the past religious life of the community in question: temples, scriptures, theological systems, dance patterns, legal and other social institutions, conventions, moral codes, myths, and so on; anything that can be and is transmitted from one person, one generation, to another, and that an historian can observe.

It is my suggestion that by the use of these two notions it is possible to conceptualize and to describe anything that has ever happened in the religious life of mankind, whether within one's own religious community (which is an important point) or in others' (which is also an important point). Also, so far as I can see, it is possible for these concepts to be used equally by skeptic or believer, by Muslim or Buddhist, Episcopalian or Quaker, Freudian or Marxist or Sufi.

These are rather sweeping claims. They would seem pretentious, did one not remember that I do not pretend to have solved vast problems that have outwitted better men; I am suggesting rather a method that will humbly yet deliberately allow man's long wrestling with those problems to be investigated without prior solution.

To illustrate the thesis, let us look at what has been called Hinduism.

Among the Hindus, the cumulative tradition does not begin at any particular time or place. When we first become aware of it, it was already diverse. For illustrative purposes, let us arbitrarily begin by considering the person, whoever he was, who composed what is now the well-known Creation Hymn in Book X of the Ṛg Veda. That one particular person composed it in its present form is not an assumption requisite to my argument: presumably some person did once compose a significant contribution to this poem.

Now that person, about whom we know almost nothing but can conjecture a little, was born into a specific historical context which included the cumulative Hindu religious tradition up to that point, or at least that branch of it that existed within the range of his awareness. The tradition was different for him from what it was further south, and was different also from what it later became. The basic point in this latter difference that I would here stress is that in particular it did not include in his day what it has included since, namely this particular poem. It did include, almost certainly, many of the other hymns now collected into the Ṛg Veda, and this is a fact obviously important for understanding the historico-religious event of his composing the new poem. It would be fascinating to know how much of the indigenous (pre-Aryan) cumulative tradition it included. Did he know any language other than Sanskrit, or ever talk with anyone who did?—and so on; there are many questions.

These questions need not be answered, or answerable; all that I am concerned to show is that he received, external to himself, in the form of rites and practices, norms, ideas, group pressures, family influences, vocabulary, social institutions, and what not, a religious tradition; and that he changed that tradition by adding to it. He added to it something that emerged from the interaction within his personality between that external tradition and some personal quality of his own that we may cheerfully leave undetermined. Orthodox Hindus may believe that he "heard"; Christians may believe that either the Logos or the devil was at work; literary critics may apply the same explanations that they use for poetic creation wherever they find it. However one may choose to interpret how it took place, the fact is, and on this surely all may agree, that inside that man's person something unobservable happened of which the outward consequence was a new hymn. And this product of his faith was therefore added to the cumulative tradition, which has therefore never been quite the same since.

That man's faith could not have been what it was had it not been for the particular form of the cumulative tradition to that point. Yet it was not simply the product of that previous tradition; if this poet had perchance died of malaria as a child, probably few would wish to argue that that hymn in just that form would have got written anyway. Therefore the subsequent form of the Hindu cumulative tradition, including this hymn, is not simply the continuation or extrapolation of its earlier history, not including it. Rather, its later history is the prolongation and enrichment of its earlier existence as modified by the intervention of the faith and activity of this man.

Multiply this kind of incident a thousand million times, I suggest, and one has the development of the Hindu religious tradition. It is a part of this world; it is the product of human activity; it is diverse, it is fluid, it grows, it changes, it accumulates. It crystallizes in material form the faith of previous generations, and it sets the context for the faith of each new generation as these come along. But it neither includes nor fully determines that later faith. It conditions it, certainly. Yet each man's faith is his own, is partly free, and results from an interaction within the personality between that confronting tradition along with all other mundane circumstances, external and inner, and the transcendent. A man's faith is what his tradition means to him. Yet it is, further, what the universe means to him, in the light of that tradition.

By choosing the author of this hymn, one may perhaps feel that I have invidiously selected genius. Certainly some persons are more important for the cumulative tradition than are others; and it is almost excusable to oversimplify the immense array of Hindu religiousness by thinking of its history in terms simply of those persons and movements that have conspicuously modified and ramified and enriched (or debased?) it in its developing course. Almost, but not quite. The tradition was what it was until it was changed by the creative activity of those who wrote the Upanishads and the Bhagavad Gita, who built the temples and introduced the dances, who formulated the rules and elaborated the practices, who fought it out with the Buddhist sectarians and took up the challenge of Islam, who developed and spread the Bhakti movement, who innovated with the West and against it, who reformed and revitalized and rethought. Almost, but not quite. The great creative leaders have been great and have been creative, and have led. They have led the cumulative tradition to new accumulations; the enormously multi-faceted panorama of Hindu life would not be what it is today without them. Yet the obscure, the average, Hindu is not to be neglected in the story. In the total, his role has been no less crucial. And indeed, finally his role has been in principle no different.

A Sankara or a Ramanuja, on the one hand stimulated and conditioned by an inherited cumulative tradition, and on the other inspired by his own understanding of its meaning and his own vision of a transcendent truth, conceived something new and bequeathed to the subsequent ongoing tradition an objective, public formulation of that private vision. Yet in the same way, though of course on a drastically smaller scale, some remote village mother receives that little segment of the cumulative tradition that obtains just then in her small corner of India, interiorizes it to make what she can or will of its meaning, translating the outer forms into a personal faith, petty or profound; and then in turn she hands it on to her son, modified in an outward sense perhaps only minutely or negligibly, yet personalized. If it meant nothing to her inside, the historian may be sure that the next generation would handle even its externals differently. No less important, in the religious history of man, than the creative faith of innovating leaders is the preservative faith of receptive followers.

It is because the materials of a cumulative tradition serve each generation as the ground of a transcendent faith that they persist. The objective data of a tradition exist in this world and are observable by an historian; but they continue to exist and to be observable because for the men and women who use them they serve as windows through which they see a world beyond.

Anyone familiar with the piety of the common Hindu will appreciate the observation that whatever role exceptional persons may play in setting up particular matters in the tradition, once those matters are launched they are entrusted to the entire community, and their subsequent history is in the hands of the whole.

Furthermore, although changes that are creative advances are perhaps largely the result of the work of outstanding individuals (though even this is disputable), there is another type of change, historically hardly less important, which perhaps more usually is brought about by the action of quite ordinary folk, often acting together in numbers. This is the change of neglect, decline, and retrogression. Elements in a cumulative tradition may be dropped as well as added; customs disappear, observances are not observed, temples fall into ruin. Lofty insights are degraded, warm spontaneities are gradually institutionalized, novelties become traditions. The community not only preserves the insights of its leaders, it can also misinterpret or lose them.

It should be clear that my analysis differs crucially from that of positivists or naturalists or any who would "reduce" "religion" to anything less than its devotees see. The cumulative tradition of which we are speaking lies wholly within this mundane world and is fully open to historical observation. Yet this is very different from saying that the whole history and nature of a religion lies within this sphere, so that a religion may be equated with its mundane observable career. From the position here proposed, one may insist that the mundane traditions persist only insofar as they are refreshed, each generation anew, by the faith of each of the participants; and that his faith, being personal, is not confined to what lies within history. The cumulative tradition is wholly historical; but history is not a closed system, since as agent within it stands man, his spirit in some degree open to the transcendent.

MOHAMMED

the idea of god _____

Do not hearts feel tranquil
whenever God is mentioned?   13:28, *Thunder*

SINCERITY (or UNITY)

(Chapter 112)

In the name of God, the Merciful, the Mercygiving!
    SAY: "God is Unique!
    God, the Source (for everything)!
    He has not fathered anything
    nor is He fathered,
    and there is nothing
    comparable to Him!"   112:1–4 (complete)

O My servants who have believed, My earth is broad, so Me should you worship! Every soul will taste death; then to Us shall you return.

29:56–57, *The Spider*

How many animals do not carry their own provision! God provides for them and for you. He is Alert, Aware.   29:60, *The Spider*

Your Lord creates and chooses anything He wishes; they have no choice. Praise be to God and Exalted is He over anything they may associate with Him. Your Lord knows whatever their breasts conceal and what they display; He is God, there is no god except Him. Praise is His from the first and in the Hereafter. Ruling belongs to Him, and to Him will you return.   28:68–70, *Tales*

From *Selections from the Noble Reading, An Anthology of Passages from the Qur'an,* trans. Thomas Ballantine Irving, Cedar Rapids, Iowa, Unity Publishing Company, 1968.

GOD'S SEAT

God! There is no god except Him,
the Living, the Eternal!
Slumber does not overtake Him, nor does sleep.
He has everything in heaven and everything on earth.
Who is there to intercede with Him
except with His permission?
He knows what lies before them and what's behind them,
while they do not embrace any of His knowledge
except whatever He may wish.
Vast is His seat as heaven and earth;
preserving them both does not weary Him.
He is the Sublime, the Almighty!   2:255, *The Cow*

GOD THE SOVEREIGN

SAY: "O God, Holder of control!
You give control to anyone You wish
and snatch control away from anyone You wish.
You strengthen anyone You wish
and humble anyone You wish.
Good lies within Your hand;
You are so Capable of everything!
    You wrap night up in daytime,
and wrap daytime up in night."
You draw the living from the dead,
and draw the dead from the living.
You provide for anyone You wish
without any reckoning.   3:26–27, *Imran's Family*

GOD'S FACE

The East and West are God's.
Wherever you may turn,
there is God's countenance;
God is so Ample, Aware!   2:115, *The Cow*

GOD THE LIGHT

God is the Light of heaven and earth!
His light may be compared to a niche
in which there is a lamp;
the lamp is in a glass; the glass
is just as if it were a glittering star
kindled from a blessed olive tree,

neither Eastern nor Western,
whose oil will almost glow though fire
has never touched it. Light upon light,
God guides anyone He wishes to His Light.
God makes up parables for mankind;
God is so Aware of everything!
　　There are houses God has permitted to be raised
where His name is mentioned; in them
He is glorified morning and evening
by men whom neither business nor selling
distract from remembering God,
keeping up prayer, and giving alms.
They fear a day when one's heart and eyesight
will feel upset, till God rewards them
for the finest things they may have done,
and gives them even more out of His bounty.
God provides for anyone He wishes
without any reckoning!
　　Those who disbelieve have deeds
like a mirage on a desert:
the thirsty man will reckon it is water
till when he comes up to it,
he finds it to be nothing.
Yet he finds God stands by him
and he must pay Him his account;
God is so Swift in reckoning!
　　Or like darkness on the boundless sea:
one wave covers up another wave,
over which there hangs a cloud;
darkness, one above the other!
When he holds his hand out,
he can scarcely see it. Yet anyone
whom God has not granted Light to
will have no Light!

Have you not seen how everyone in heaven and earth glorifies God, even to
the birds lined up? Each knows its prayer and glorification. God is Aware of
everything they do. God holds dominion over heaven and earth; towards God
lies one's goal!

Have you not seen how God drives along a cloud, then piles it up, next sets it
in a heap? You see a downpour coming from inside it. He sends down masses
from the sky with hail in them, and pelts anyone He wishes with it, and diverts it
from anyone He wishes. A flash from His lightning almost takes away one's
sight. God alternates night and daytime; in that lies a lesson for those possessing
sight.

God has created every animal out of water; some of them walk on their belly, while others walk on two legs, and still others walk on four. God creates anything He wishes; God is Capable of everything.   24:35–45, *Light*

SAY: "Have you seen what god besides God would bring you radiance, if God laid perpetual night over you until Resurrection day? Will you not listen?"

SAY: "Have you seen what god besides God would bring you night wherein you might repose, if God laid perpetual daylight over you until Resurrection day? Will you not observe?

"Out of His own mercy has He granted you night and daytime so you may repose in it and seek some of His bounty, and so you may be thankful."

                                                        28:71–73, *Tales*

GOD THE ONE

He is the one Who has furnished you with hearing, eyesight and vital organs; yet seldom do you thank [Him]. He is the one Who has spread you out over the earth, and to Him will you be summoned. He is the one Who gives life and brings death; He controls the change between night and daytime. Will you not reason?

Rather they say the same thing as the first men said; they say: "When we have died and become dust and bones, will we be raised up again? This was promised us and our forefathers long ago. These are only legends of primitive people!"

SAY: "Who owns the earth and everyone on it, if you have known?" They will say: "It is God's." SAY: "Will you not remember?"

SAY: "Who is Lord of the seven heavens and Lord of the mighty throne?" They will say: "They are God's." SAY: "Will you not heed?"

SAY: "In whose hand lies control over everything? He protects yet remains unprotected, if you only knew?" They will say: "In God's." SAY: "You must be bewitched." Rather We gave them truth while they deny it.

God has not adopted any son, nor is there any god alongside Him, otherwise every god would carry off whatever it has created, and some of them would get the upper hand over others. Glory be to God over what they describe! Knower of the Unseen and the Visible: Exalted is He over what they associate with Him!

                                                        23:78–92, *Believers*

GOD'S POWER

Have you not watched
how your Lord lengthens shadows?
If He so wished,
He would make them stand still.
    Then We placed the sun
as an indicator for them;
next We gradually pulled them towards us.

He is the one Who placed night
as a garment for you,
and sleep for repose.
He makes daytime for rising.
 He is the one Who has loosed the winds
as heralds announcing His mercy.
 We send down pure water from the sky,
so We may bring life to a dead land,
and let everything We have created
such as livestock and men aplenty drink.
 We have arranged it among them
so they may be reminded,
yet most men refuse anything
except denial.   25:45–50, *The Criterion*

GOD'S ATTRIBUTES

Or have they adopted sponsors instead of God? He is the [only] Sponsor; He
revives the dead. He is so Capable of everything!

No matter what you may have differed over in any way, its judgment is up to
God. Such is God, my Lord; on Him have I relied and to Him do I turn. Originator of heaven and earth, He has granted you spouses from among yourselves
and pairs of livestock by means of which He multiplies you.

There is nothing like Him! He is the Alert, Observant. He holds the controls
for heaven and earth; He extends sustenance to anyone He wishes, and withholds
it. He is so Aware of everything! He has instituted the [same] religion for you
that He recommended for Noah, and which We have inspired you with and recommended for Abraham, Moses and Jesus: "Keep up religion and do not stir up
any divisions in it."   42:9–13, *Consultation*

GORDON D. KAUFMAN

**the transcendent
as personal** _____

When a personal limiter is the analogical basis for understanding the ultimate
Limit, a doctrine of God results. The ultimate Limit is then conceived in quasi-
personal terms to be understood most decisively with notions drawn originally

From "Transcendence Without Mythology" in *God the Problem*. *Harvard Theological Review*. Copyright by the President and Fellows of Harvard College. The conception of God
suggested here, together with the corresponding conception of revelation, is worked out in

from the language used to deal with interpersonal experience. It is clear that this conception is the one operative in the biblical tradition where God is spoken of as lord, father, judge, king, and so on, and he is said to love and hate, to make covenants with his people, to perform "mighty acts," to be characterized by mercy, forgiveness, faithfulness, patience, wisdom, and the like—all terms drawn from the linguistic region of interpersonal discourse. Moreover, the biblical God is understood not to be accessible to man's every beck and call; he is not some structure or reality immanent in human experience and thus directly available to man. On the contrary, he resides in lofty transcendence, whence he acts in complete freedom to change the course of history or to reveal himself to his people through his prophets. Now it is clear that this image of inaccessible transcendence and freedom made known and effective through explicit acts of communication and power—through words and deeds—is built up analogically from the model of the hiddenness and transcendence and freedom of the finite self, who also can (in some significant measure) hide himself from his fellows and remain inaccessible, except as he chooses to manifest himself through acts and words. Though other terminology and images are also found in the biblical materials, there can be no doubt that personalistic language and conceptions most decisively shape the biblical view of the ultimate Limit.

I contended earlier in this paper, however, that the biblical and Christian traditions appear determined in large part by a metaphysical-cosmological dualism characteristic of mythology and no longer meaningful to many moderns. Moreover, it has often been held that precisely the anthropomorphic image of God as personal is an especially crude example of the mythological thinking of primitive man and therefore to be regarded as only symbolic or picture language, of significance in worship or prayer but not adequate for precise theological or philosophical work. We must now ask, therefore, how far a personalistic conception of God is essentially bound up with an inadequate mythology, how far it may be an independent and justifiable interpretation of the ultimate Limit.

It should be evident that to conceive the ultimate Limit personalistically is formally neither more nor less mythological than to conceive it on analogy with any of the other types of finite limiter. Each has its own peculiar appropriateness to certain dimensions of the self's experience of limitation, and each has difficulty in interpreting the other dimensions. With respect to the experience of limitation itself, then, no reason for preferring any of the four to the others can be given. Moreover, inasmuch as it is necessary to grasp the ultimate Limit in terms of *some* model if it is to be adequately conceived at all, the attempt to

---

much fuller detail in Chapter IV, "Two Models of Transcendence," Chapter V, "God as Symbol," and Chapter VII, "Revelation and Cultural History." The excerpt is taken from Chapter III, "Transcendence Without Mythology." We have included this excerpt because it is one of the clearest defenses of the notion of the Transcendent as Personal. The reader should be challenged by this view since our cultural preferences are overwhelmingly for impersonal models. This preference is buttressed by our interests in both scientific and Asian models.

grasp it personalistically should not be rejected as mythological (in the dubious sense of claiming unwarranted knowledge of that *beyond* the Limit) in any way not also applicable to every other attempt to apprehend and understand our finitude.

In a manner not characteristic of the other finite limiters, however, the personalistic image lends itself to a reopening of the question not only of the Limit, but of what is beyond it. For (as we noted above) it interprets man's relationship to that which ultimately limits him as being like his relationship to the finite selves with which he is in interaction. Such selves over against me always transcend in their subjectivity and freedom what is directly accessible to me in my experience (that is, their bodies) even though they "come to him" and communicate with him in and through this physical dimension of their being that is open to his view. What one directly experiences of the other are, strictly speaking, the external physical sights and sounds he makes, not the deciding, acting, purposing center of the self—though I have no doubt these externalities are not *merely* physical phenomena but are the outward and visible expression of inner thought, purpose, intention. Thus I do not speak merely of "sights and sounds" but of the "sights and sounds which *he* makes" in *his* attempt to act or to communicate.

In our interaction with other persons we presuppose a reality (the active center of the self) *beyond* that which we immediately perceive, a reality encountered by us and known to us not simply in physiologically-based perception (though that is of course also involved) but in and through the language that we jointly speak. It is in the act of communication that we discover that the other is more than merely physical being, is a conscious self; it is in the experience of speaking and hearing that we come to know the *personal* hidden behind and in the merely physical. This is the most powerful experience we have of *transcendence of the given* on the finite level, the awareness of genuine activity and reality *beyond* and *behind* what is directly open to our view.

When this type of complex interrelationship is used to interpret the ultimate Limit, it is clear that an active reality (or "self") beyond the Limit—beyond what is directly experienceable as such—will be implied. A self in its active center is never directly open to view, but is known only as he reveals himself in communication and communion. Likewise, on this model God cannot be identified with what is accessible to or within our experience, not even with the ultimate Limit of our experience; rather this Limit must be grasped as the *medium* through which God encounters us (as noises and gestures are media for finite selves), God himself being conceived as the dynamic acting reality beyond the Limit. In this way a certain reference to reality beyond the Limit of our experience is intrinsic to the personalistic image, and therefore such reference need not depend upon nor involve a reversion to mythology. It must be emphasized, however, that reference of this sort to transcendent reality is justifiable only when the ultimate Limit is understood in terms of a personal limiter; for only in the interaction with other selves do we encounter an active reality which comes to us from

beyond what is accessible in experience. Organic, physical, and normative limiters can all be interpreted exhaustively in terms of what is given in and to experience (though it is not essential to do so), and it is mythology, therefore, if
one speaks of a transcendent extra-experiential reality on the basis of one of
those models; a personal limiter alone necessarily and intrinsically involves genuine transcendence.

Correlative with this reference to a locus of reality beyond the Limit there
must be a conception of revelation. We know the transcendent reality of other
selves only as they act toward and communicate with us, as they reveal to us
their reality and character and purposes in word and deed. So also, only if we are
prepared to acknowledge some genuine encounter with God through his own
actions directed toward us, is it appropriate to speak of the ultimate Limit in
personalistic terms, that is, with "God-language." By definition we could know
nothing of any personal being beyond the Limit of our experience if that being
did not in some way manifest himself to us through our experience or its Limit.
Once again, the organic, physical, and normative analogies for understanding the
ultimate Limit require no doctrine of revelation, nor is any appropriate to them.
This is the mode of knowledge characteristic of interpersonal communion, and it
is when such encounters are taken as the model for understanding the Limit of
all experience that the category of revelation is required. Thus, to speak of God
acting or God revealing himself is not necessarily to make a mythological statement presupposing an unjustified and unjustifiable metaphysical-cosmological
dualism; such forms of conceptualization and speech are necessary if and whenever a personal limiter is taken as the model for grasping the ultimate Limit.

HEINRICH ZIMMER

the parade of ants ⎯⎯⎯⎯⎯⎯⎯⎯⎯⎯⎯⎯⎯⎯⎯⎯⎯⎯⎯⎯⎯⎯⎯⎯⎯⎯

Indra slew the dragon, a giant titan that had been couching on the mountains in
the limbless shape of a cloud serpent, holding the waters of heaven captive in its
belly. The god flung his thunderbolt into the midst of the ungainly coils; the
monster shattered like a stack of withered rushes. The waters burst free and
streamed in ribbons across the land, to circulate once more through the body of
the world.

This flood is the flood of life and belongs to all. It is the sap of field and
forest, the blood coursing in the veins. The monster had appropriated the common benefit, massing his ambitious, selfish hulk between heaven and earth, but

now was slain. The juices again were pouring. The titans were retreating to the underworlds; the gods were returning to the summit of the central mountain of the earth, there to reign from on high.

During the period of the supremacy of the dragon, the majestic mansions of the lofty city of the gods had cracked and crumbled. The first act of Indra was to rebuild them. All the divinities of the heavens were acclaiming him their savior. Greatly elated in his triumph and in the knowledge of his strength, he summoned Vishvakarman, the god of arts and crafts, and commanded him to erect such a palace as should befit the unequaled splendor of the king of the gods.

The miraculous genius, Vishvakarman, succeeded in constructing in a single year a shining residence, marvelous with palaces and gardens, lakes and towers. But as the work progressed, the demands of Indra became even more exacting and his unfolding visions vaster. He required additional terraces and pavilions, more ponds, groves, and pleasure grounds. Whenever Indra arrived to appraise the work, he developed vision beyond vision of marvels remaining to be contrived. Presently the divine craftsman, brought to despair, decided to seek succor from above. He would turn to the demiurgic creator, Brahma, the pristine embodiment of the Universal Spirit, who abides far above the troubled Olympian sphere of ambition, strife, and glory.

When Vishvakarman secretly resorted to the higher throne and presented his case, Brahma comforted the petitioner. "You will soon be relieved of your burden," he said. "Go home in peace." Then, while Vishvakarman was hurrying down again to the city of Indra, Brahma himself ascended to a still higher sphere. He came before Vishnu, the Supreme Being, of whom he himself, the Creator, was but an agent. In beatific silence Vishnu gave ear, and by a mere nod of the head let it be known that the request of Vishvakarman would be fulfilled.

Early next morning a brahmin boy, carrying the staff of a pilgrim, made his appearance at the gate of Indra, bidding the porter announce his visit to the king. The gate-man hurried to the master, and the master hastened to the entrance to welcome in person the auspicious guest. The boy was slender, some ten years old, radiant with the luster of wisdom. Indra discovered him amidst a cluster of enraptured, staring children. The boy greeted the host with a gentle glance of his dark and brilliant eyes. The king bowed to the holy child and the boy cheerfully gave his blessing. The two retired to the hall of Indra, where the god ceremoniously proffered welcome to his guest with oblations of honey, milk, and fruits, then said: "O Venerable Boy, tell me of the purpose of your coming."

The beautiful child replied with a voice that was as deep and soft as the slow thundering of auspicious rain clouds. "O King of Gods, I have heard of the mighty palace you are building, and have come to refer to you the questions in my mind. How many years will it require to complete this rich and extensive residence? What further feats of engineering will Vishvakarman be expected to accomplish? O Highest of the Gods,"—the boy's luminous features moved with a gentle, scarcely perceptible smile—"no Indra before you has ever succeeded in completing such a palace as yours is to be."

Full of the wine of triumph, the king of the gods was entertained by this mere boy's pretension to a knowledge of Indras earlier than himself. With a fatherly smile he put the question: "Tell me, Child! Are they then so very many, the Indras and Vishvakarmans whom you have seen—or at least, whom you have heard of?"

The wonderful guest calmly nodded. "Yes, indeed, many have I seen." The voice was as warm and sweet as milk fresh from the cow, but the words sent a slow chill through Indra's veins. "My dear child," the boy continued, "I knew your father, Kashyapa, the Old Tortoise Man, lord and progenitor of all the creatures of the earth. And I knew your grandfather, Marichi, Beam of Celestial Light, who was the son of Brahma. Marichi was begotten of the god Brahma's pure spirit; his only wealth and glory were his sanctity and devotion. Also, I know Brahma, brought forth by Vishnu from the lotus calix growing from Vishnu's navel. And Vishnu himself—the Supreme Being, supporting Brahma in his creative endeavor—him too I know.

"O King of Gods, I have known the dreadful dissolution of the universe. I have seen all perish, again and again, at the end of every cycle. At the terrible time, every single atom dissolves into the primal, pure waters of eternity, whence originally all arose. Everything then goes back into the fathomless, wild infinity of the ocean, which is covered with utter darkness and is empty of every sign of animate being. Ah, who will count the universes that have passed away, of the creations that have risen afresh, again and again, from the formless abyss of the vast waters? Who will number the passing ages of the world, as they follow each other endlessly? And who will search through the wide infinities of space to count the universes side by side, each containing its Brahma, its Vishnu, and its Shiva? Who will count the Indras in them all—those Indras side by side, who reign at once in all the innumerable worlds; those others who passed away before them; or even the Indras who succeed each other in any given line, ascending to godly kingship, one by one, and, one by one, passing away? King of Gods, there are among your servants certain who maintain that it may be possible to number the grains of sand on earth and the drops of rain that fall from the sky, but no one will ever number all those Indras. This is what the Knowers know.

"The life and kingship of an Indra endure seventy-one eons, and when twenty-eight Indras have expired, one Day and Night of Brahma has elapsed. But the existence of one Brahma, measured in such Brahma Days and Nights, is only one hundred and eight years. Brahma follows Brahma; one sinks, the next arises; the endless series cannot be told. There is no end to the number of those Brahmas—to say nothing of Indras.

"But the universes side by side at any given moment, each harboring a Brahma and an Indra: who will estimate the number of these? Beyond the farthest vision, crowding outer space, the universes come and go, an innumerable host. Like delicate boats they float on the fathomless, pure waters that form the body of Vishnu. Out of every hair-pore of that body a universe bubbles and breaks. Will you presume to count them? Will you number the gods in all those worlds—the worlds present and the worlds past?"

A procession of ants had made its appearance in the hall during the discourse of the boy. In military array, in a column four yards wide, the tribe paraded across the floor. The boy noted them, paused, and stared, then suddenly laughed with an astonishing peal, but immediately subsided into a profoundly indrawn and thoughtful silence.

"Why do you laugh?" stammered Indra. "Who are you, mysterious being, under this deceiving guise of a boy?" The proud king's throat and lips had gone dry, and his voice continually broke. "Who are you, Ocean of Virtues, enshrouded in deluding mist?"

The magnificent boy resumed: "I laughed because of the ants. The reason is not to be told. Do not ask me to disclose it. The seed of woe and the fruit of wisdom are enclosed within this secret. It is the secret that smites with an ax the tree of worldly vanity, hews away its roots, and scatters its crown. This secret is a lamp to those groping in ignorance. This secret lies buried in the wisdom of the ages, and is rarely revealed even to saints. This secret is the living air of those ascetics who renounce and transcend mortal existence; but worldlings, deluded by desire and pride, it destroys."

The boy smiled and sank into silence. Indra regarded him, unable to move. "O Son of a Brahmin," the king pleaded presently, with a new and visible humility, "I do not know who you are. You would seem to be Wisdom Incarnate. Reveal to me this secret of the ages, this light that dispels the dark."

Thus requested to teach, the boy opened to the god the hidden wisdom. "I saw the ants, O Indra, filing in long parade. Each was once an Indra. Like you, each by virtue of pious deeds once ascended the rank of a king of gods. But now, through many rebirths, each has become again an ant. This army is an army of former Indras.

"Piety and high deeds elevate the inhabitants of the world to the glorious realm of the celestial mansions, or to the higher domains of Brahma and Shiva and to the highest sphere of Vishnu; but wicked acts sink them into the worlds beneath, into pits of pain and sorrow, involving reincarnation among birds and vermin, or out of the wombs of pigs and animals of the wild, or among trees, or among insects. It is by deeds that one merits happiness or anguish, and becomes a master or a serf. It is by deeds that one attains to the rank of a king or a brahmin, or of some god, or of an Indra or a Brahma. And through deeds again, one contracts disease, acquires beauty and deformity, or is reborn in the condition of a monster.

"This is the whole substance of the secret. This wisdom is the ferry to beatitude across the ocean of hell.

"Life in the cycle of the countless rebirths is like a vision in a dream. The gods on high, the mute trees and the stones, are alike apparitions in this phantasy. But Death administers the law of time. Ordained by time, Death is the master of all. Perishable as bubbles are the good and the evil of the beings of the dream. In unending cycles the good and evil alternate. Hence, the wise are attached to neither, neither the evil nor the good. The wise are not attached to anything at all."

The boy concluded the appalling lesson and quietly regarded his host. The king of gods, for all his celestial splendor, had been reduced in his own regard to insignificance. Meanwhile, another amazing apparition had entered the hall.

The newcomer had the appearance of a kind of hermit. His head was piled with matted hair; he wore a black deerskin around his loins; on his forehead was painted a white mark; his head was shaded by a paltry parasol of grass; and a quaint, circular cluster of hair grew on his chest: it was intact at the circumference, but from the center many of the hairs, it seemed, had disappeared. This saintly figure strode directly to Indra and the boy, squatted between them on the floor, and there remained, motionless as a rock. The kingly Indra, somewhat recovering his hostly role, bowed and paid obeisance, offering sour milk with honey and other refreshments; then he inquired, falteringly but reverently, after the welfare of the stern guest, and bade him welcome. Whereupon the boy addressed the holy man, asking the very questions Indra himself would have proposed.

"Whence do you come, O Holy Man? What is your name and what brings you to this place? Where is your present home, and what is the meaning of this grass parasol? What is the portent of that circular hair-tuft on your chest: why is it dense at the circumference but at the center almost bare? Be kind enough, O Holy Man, to answer, in brief, these questions. I am anxious to understand."

Patiently the old saint smiled, and slowly began his reply. "I am a brahmin. Hairy is my name. And I have come here to behold Indra. Since I know that I am short-lived, I have decided to possess no home, to build no house, and neither to marry nor to seek a livelihood. I exist by begging alms. To shield myself from sun and rain I carry over my head this parasol of grass.

"As to the circle of hair on my chest, it is a source of grief to the children of the world. Nevertheless, it teaches wisdom. With the fall of an Indra, one hair drops. That is why, in the center all the hairs have gone. When the other half of the period allotted to the present Brahma will have expired, I myself shall die. O Brahmin Boy, it follows that I am somewhat short of days; what, therefore, is the use of a wife and a son, or of a house?

"Each flicker of the eyelids of the great Vishnu registers the passing of a Brahma. Everything below that sphere of Brahma is as insubstantial as a cloud taking shape and again dissolving. That is why I devote myself exclusively to meditating on the incomparable lotus-feet of highest Vishnu. Faith in Vishnu is more than the bliss of redemption; for every joy, even the heavenly, is as fragile as a dream, and only interferes with the one-pointedness of our faith in Him Supreme.

"Shiva, the peace-bestowing, the highest spiritual guide, taught me this wonderful wisdom. I do not crave to experience the various blissful forms of redemption: to share the highest god's supernal mansions and enjoy his eternal presence, or to be like him in body and apparel, or to become a part of his august substance, or even to be absorbed wholly in his ineffable essence."

Abruptly, the holy man ceased and immediately vanished. It had been the god Shiva himself; he had now returned to his supramundane abode. Simultaneously, the brahmin boy, who had been Vishnu, disappeared as well. The king was alone, baffled and amazed.

The king, Indra, pondered; and the events seemed to him to have been a dream. But he no longer felt any desire to magnify his heavenly splendor or to go on with the construction of his palace. He summoned Vishvakarman. Graciously greeting the craftsman with honeyed words, he heaped on him jewels and precious gifts, then with a sumptuous celebration sent him home.

The king, Indra, now desired redemption. He had acquired wisdom, and wished only to be free. He entrusted the pomp and burden of his office to his son, and prepared to retire to the hermit life of the wilderness. Whereupon his beautiful and passionate queen, Shachi, was overcome with grief.

Weeping, in sorrow and utter despair, Shachi resorted to Indra's ingenious house-priest and spiritual advisor, the Lord of Magic Wisdom, Brihaspati. Bowing at his feet, she implored him to divert her husband's mind from its stern resolve. The resourceful counselor of the gods, who by his spells and devices had helped the heavenly powers wrest the government of the universe from the hands of their titan rivals, listened thoughtfully to the complaint of the voluptuous, disconsolate goddess, and knowingly nodded assent. With a wizard's smile, he took her hand and conducted her to the presence of her spouse. In the role, then, of spiritual teacher, he discoursed sagely on the virtues of the spiritual life, but on the virtues also, of the secular. He gave to each its due. Very skillfully he developed his theme. The royal pupil was persuaded to relent in his extreme resolve. The queen was restored to radiant joy.

This Lord of Magic Wisdom, Brihaspati, once had composed a treatise on government, in order to teach Indra how to rule the world. He now issued a second work, a treatise on the polity and stratagems of married love. Demonstrating the sweet art of wooing ever anew, and of enchaining the beloved with enduring bonds, this priceless book established on sound foundations the married life of the reunited pair.

Thus concludes the marvelous story of how the king of gods was humiliated in his boundless pride, cured of an excessive ambition, and through wisdom, both spiritual and secular, brought to a knowledge of his proper role in the wheeling play of unending life.

HAROLD K. SCHILLING

post-modern science and man's sense
of depth and mystery _____

I

Something is happening to man that is so momentous as to constitute a new
creation (religiously speaking) or a major evolutionary emergence (scientifically
speaking). It is that man is experiencing a tremendous expansion of his consciousness—his ability to perceive, respond to, and understand reality. The aspect
of this to which I should like to call attention especially at this time is man's
recovery and intensification of his sense of depth and mystery in nature—and the
significance of this for Christian faith.

We now perceive that reality has depths, dimensions, and qualities quite unknown earlier. This is the case even in physical material, where it was to be expected least, since its "fundamental building blocks" were regarded as structure-
less and impenetrable. As I see it, this development in man is due in large part to
what I shall call *post-modern science,* that of the twentieth century, as distinguished from its predecessor, *modern science,* that of the few preceding centuries.

History is repeating itself. The Copernican revolution was characterized by
what Butterfield called "fundamental changes in outlook," "remarkable turns in
the current intellectual fashion," a "subtle . . . alteration in men's feeling for
things" and "for matter itself," and awareness of a "new texture of experience."[1] It is precisely this sort of thing that is happening again—now.

II

It seems there was a time when many men had faith in God that took into account their experience of nature. Luther, for instance, "felt the presence of God
very vividly" . . . "in the various phenomena of nature," and sensed that "all
creation is the most beautiful book or Bible," . . . "in which God has described
and portrayed himself."[2] Luther could say this while saying also that "although
He is everywhere, in all creatures, and although I could find Him in a stone, in
fire, in water, or even a rope (for He surely is there), still he does not want me to
look for Him apart from the Word." However these avowals may be interpreted,
it is clear that Luther had "an open delight in reality," and a "sense of genuine
primal wonder and awe," which enriched his faith, because they enabled him to
sense God's living presence in nature—the God mediated to him through the
Word.

Unfortunately, however, for many of Luther's later followers, as for many
theologians and others today, these sensitivities and insights with regard to nature seemed to disappear almost completely. While they profess to sense his presence in history, they fail to sense and they even deny it in nature. For still

From *McCormick Quarterly* 21, May 1968.

others, and they are legion, the denial of his activity in nature leads inevitably—
and logically—to the denial of it anywhere—and consequently to the loss of a
sense of depth and mystery, and of faith in God.

John Dillenberger speaks of this erosion, with special reference to evolutionary thought, as follows:

> The Darwinian impact was the final threat to all the vertical and depth dimen-
> sion within man and the cosmos. It marked the culmination of a period in
> which no adequate symbols were left for expressing and thinking about the
> classical Christian heritage. . . . The late nineteenth and early twentieth cen-
> turies may have been one of those rare periods in history in which theology
> was virtually impossible, when the crisis of language and imagination ex-
> cluded the essential depth of both God and man.[3]

Some scholars feel that Dillenberger's analysis is exaggerated. However that
may be, it seems undeniable that science did make it extremely difficult for
many men, scientists and nonscientists alike, to experience, conceptualize, or
intuit depth, and therefore to find meaning in such terms as "the vertical dimension" of life, or the "mystery" of the cosmos.

Thus well along in the twentieth century many religious thinkers espouse the
view of science expressed by Michael Foster:

> Modern science is knowledge which eliminates mystery. In contrast to Greek
> science it does not end in wonder but in the expulsion of wonder.
> Modern scientific knowledge does not contain degrees of depth or pro-
> fundity.
> Revealed truth by contrast offers depth after depth to the understanding
> without being exhausted.[4]

While I deny that science was ever actually like that, I admit that during the
modern period it came to seem so for many people, with obviously deleterious
effects upon those sensitivities and perceptivities without which there can be no
religious faith—and for that matter no adequate science either. The reason for
this lies, I suggest, in the character and content of the world view that was built
upon science in the modern period.

III

How is it possible for a world view to have such abrasive effects upon primal
human sensibilities? Because there is a close connection between a man's views
about the world and his capacity for perceiving it; between what he sees and can
then know, as well as between what he knows and can then see. Thus a world
view is not only a portrait of what he "sees," but a prehending probe that enables him to see. Perception is then an active two-way, incoming and outgoing,
feedback sort of process. In this way a world view may be either constricting or
expanding in its effects upon human perception and consciousness. While that of
the nineteenth century, as I see it, was in this sense constricting, that of today is
expanding in its influence.

For one thing, "genuine primal wonder and awe," and "open delight in reality" are probably more keen and meaningful today among scientists than ever before. If this seems surprising, it is probably because it has been fashionable recently to assert that the preoccupations of scientists have shifted away from the concrete immediacies of direct observation to the remote abstractions of theory, and thus away from nature itself. I regard this as a misconception. Theory in science is always anchored to data, and refers to actual phenomena. Insofar as science may have shifted its gaze from the "immediacies" of nature, it is in fact simply probing below the surface of things, penetrating farther into its interior, and thus entering into closer and more intimate relationship with nature. Thus Robert S. Millikan, recent Nobel laureate in chemistry, has said:

> The scientist must develop enormous tolerance in seeking for ideas which may please nature, and enormous patience, self-restraint, and humility when his ideas over and over again are rejected by nature before he arrives at one to please her. When the scientist does finally find such an idea, there is something very intimate in his feeling of communion with nature.[5]

Moreover, many scientists are finding that their studies do not "eliminate mystery" or "end in the expulsion of wonder," and that they do reveal "degrees of depth and profundity." And out of their explorations of nature, there is emerging a vision of the cosmos that, far from being constricting, is liberating the human mind *from* many of the inhibiting presuppositions and conceptions to which it fell prey in the modern period, and freeing it *for* more imaginative and daring thinking—and is expanding man's sensitivities and consciousness.

IV

The construction of overall world views is, of course, the business of philosophy, not science. Since, however, in recent times science has contributed much of the basic stuff that has gone into such views, it has become common practice to speak of "a scientific world view," even though it is derived from science only indirectly. In this sense, then, I shall speak of a modern and of a post-modern world view, and contrast them. Before doing this in detail, let us consider their general characteristics with the help of the accompanying two symbolic figures.

The first is merely a circle. The second is a ring of radially directed arrows, pointing outward and inward, that also clearly mark off a circular area, yet one without a definite boundary. The former regarded the world as closed, essentially completed and unchanging, basically simple and shallow, and fundamentally unmysterious—a deterministically conceived cosmic machine. The latter regards it more and more as open, uncompleted and changing, basically complex, with great depth and qualitative variety, and truly mysterious—a living, vibrant, growing organism forever pregnant with possibilities for novel emergences and developments in the future. The arrows are intended to symbolize the dynamism of the world, emphasizing action, event, and change more than substance and eternality. Their alternation in direction suggests a perpetual state of tension and dialectic opposition: advance and retreat, depths and heights, simplicity and complexity, outwardness and inwardness, evolution and involution, ex-plosion and im-plosion. Because it is impossible to consider all of these in detail in one lecture, we shall confine ourselves to only five of them—and briefly: depth, qual-itative variety, complexity, unboundedness (openness), and mystery. Before we do this, however, a few more general remarks may be in order.

While these differences in outlook are pronounced, they do not represent a sharp historical discontinuity. Twentieth-century science did, of course, come out of earlier centuries, where its roots are rather deep. Late in the nineteenth there was in the air a feeling that something strange was impending. And yet at the turn of the century many physical scientists felt that all significant problems posed by nature had been solved, and that all the fundamental knowledge of the physical world was in hand.

Moreover, it was thought that nature was deterministic in the sense that there could not in principle be any radically new developments or genuine surprises. This was the closed world conception. Then the lid blew off. Surprises, in the form of utterly unanticipated phenomena, such as X-rays and radioactivity, did put in their appearance, and refused to fit into the prevailing neat scheme of things. The closed world view was demolished, and the open one began to re-place it.

It would, of course, be a mistake to suppose that the older view was inher-ently stultifying. Far from it; it opened up vast vistas of the universe for human investigation, and brought forth novel ways of inquiry, and produced huge bodies of remarkable knowledge and understanding. It was imaginative and dar-ing. And yet, as often happens with even the greatest of human creations, this one in time lost much of its luster and its forward thrust, began to solidify, and thus became in many ways a roadblock to further advance. What had been glori-ously liberating and open became to a large extent inhibiting and closed.

Let us not, however, forget this important fact, that science has developed self-corrective, feedback attitudes and mechanisms that prove most effective in times of intellectual crisis. When triggered by unforeseen discoveries, they bring about modification, or at times even outright revolution that sweeps away much of the old and replaces it by the new—thus providing the foundation for new world views. This is precisely what happened in the early decades of this century in the sciences.

V

One of the epoch-making findings of post-modern science is that physical reality has a vast interior, with great depths and seemingly infinite variety of qualita-tively different structures. L. L. Foldy, physicist at the Case Institute of Tech-nology, speaks of this as follows, while discussing the prospects for exploring the inside of nucleons:

> ... with the examination of the structure of the proton and neutron one is investigating a new hierarchical level in the material organization of the physi-

cal universe, related to, but underlying, the now substantially explored level of atomic and nuclear structure. . . .[6]

Elsewhere in the article he speaks of

> . . . hierarchy or organized structures, each level of the hierarchy being characterized by a degree of internal logical structure of its own, in part independent of the hierarchies being above or below. . . .

There are three key concepts here: level, structure characteristic of a level, and partial independence of neighboring hierarchical structures.

Such a statement could not have been made fifty years ago. What is most astonishing about it is not only the idea of stacked hierarchies of matter, but that physical reality has another basic dimension: depth. For these levels must not be thought of as being "up" or "down" in the usual sense, but in the vast interior of even the smallest of particles. Thus an object, like a stone or bacterium or atom, has not only the dimensions of length, breadth, and thickness, but also that of interior depth.[7]

There is, of course, nothing new in the idea that if we would truly understand nature, we must look behind its facade, and penetrate *into* it. Until recently, however, science was unable to push very far inside, certainly not far enough to give us a keen sense of vast depth.

Now it can and does. Consider, for instance, how many levels we now recognize in the interior of, say, a cat. First, there is the level of the animal itself, then of its organs, then of its tissues making up the organs; thereafter in succession, each one inside the preceding ones, the levels of the cells, chromosomes, genes, molecules, atoms, atomic nuclei, protons and neutrons. In the modern era no one would have dreamt that the exploration of the interior of matter would disclose so many levels characterized by such radically different structures. And yet, as Foldy was saying, right now physics is investigating still another level, at which it is expecting to identify still another species of particle, which has already been given the fascinating name of *quark*. What a picture, wheels within wheels within wheels, so to speak!

But the picture is not yet complete. For one thing, one can also go outward, i.e., to the levels of the planets, then the planetary systems, the stellar systems (galaxies), the galactic systems (supergalaxy or supergalaxies). Then there are other kinds of interiors and depths, for instance, the immense depths of the human personality and psyche—in the realm of so-called depth-psychology. Thus the feeling for depth has come not only to physics and chemistry, but to astronomy, biology, psychology, anthropology, and sociology. Almost nothing was known about such depths in the nineteenth century.

What enabled post-modern science to reveal so much more? First, radically new instrumental techniques and correspondingly revolutionary thinking. Thus the "descent" to the micro-world became possible only when science developed methods of observing, measuring, and theoretically conceiving ever smaller micro-objects. Atoms have diameters measured in billionths of inches, and atomic nuclei millionths of billionths. Second, to get through to these ever smaller entities requires ever more powerful "probes" that can crack successive surrounding "shells" to disclose what is inside them. Actually these probes are high energy projectiles fired by atom-smashers we have all heard about, that are rated in millions and billions of so-called electron volts. Genuine understanding of depth in physical reality could not come until science was able by such means actually to descend to great depths and then to describe the structures actually found there. Of course, in other realms of reality, e.g., those of life, mind, and psyche, still other kinds of probes had to be devised. What has come out of all this in our time is genuinely new scientific experience and insight—those of interior depth in nature.

Recall now Foldy's assertion that there is "a hierarchy of organized structures, each level . . . characterized by a degree of internal logical structure of its own, in part independent of others." In other words, there are in a sense not only different forms, but different "kinds" of matter. Indeed matter is so different in kind in its great depths (in the micro-world) that it requires radically different concepts, laws, and theories for its description. To illustrate, one finds there entities called "particles" that are not particles at all in the usual sense, for much of the time they behave like waves. We know nothing in ordinary experience that acts like both particles and waves. Other entities encountered there, e.g., mesons, are somewhat like particles, somewhat like waves, and somewhat like forces. It was because of the strangeness of these peculiar kinds of matter-entities that new kinds of ideas and imagery had to be devised.

Furthermore in the micro-world there occur exceedingly strange happenings, such as transient existence, fusion, fission, transmutation, annihilation, and "creation." To understand these one must radically revise ideas derived from experience in the micro-world. For instance, matter does *not* persist from eternity to eternity. Object and subject are *not* completely separable. Observation does *not* leave unchanged what is to be observed. Indeterminacy and probability must to a significant extent replace determinacy and certainty in our thinking. Substance loses its primacy to relationship and event, among the basic categories of physical reality.

Awareness of depth brings with it then also awareness of great qualitative variety. To understand reality in depth means also to have conceptions and insights beyond those entailed by experience in the shallows of existence. When people come to feel at home with the idea of depth and with the strange notions this requires, their relationship to reality has changed, their consciousness has expanded, and they themselves have been transformed.

VI

From what we have seen thus far it follows that we can no longer regard the world as basically simple in the old sense, that not far below the surface of things there exists a ground level of simple order, by which all the bewildering physical complexities of the world can be resolved. Contrary to the expectations of the modern era, the deeper matter has been probed, the more complex—not more simple—it has revealed itself to be. While by no means all scientists are saying this explicitly, many are. For instance, C. P. Snow in the Introduction to a book entitled *Matter,* by physicist Ralph Lapp, says the following:

> Not too long ago one took it for granted that the final scientific picture of the world would be beautiful, orderly, and simple. . . . We have had a number of surprises. The beauty is there, but not of the expected kind. The order is there, but not of the sort to damp down our questions. The simplicity has disappeared.[8]

In the body of the text Lapp remarks, after recounting some remarkable recent research:

> Yet, for all that we have learned about matter . . . the more scientists probe, the greater complexities they encounter.

The supposed simplicity of a relatively few ultimate species of basic and completely predictable building-blocks has given way to an unexpected kind of "system" or hierarchy of many complex structures, each one hiding other complexities at successively deeper levels within it. It seems then that we shall have to become accustomed to the idea that physical reality is fundamentally complex in that sense—even though it must also be regarded as simple in another sense we cannot discuss now.

This raises another question: how many levels are there all told? Is there a "bottom" level—or for that matter, a "top" level—beyond which there are no others? Of course, *we do not know.* Science has no way of answering such a limiting question. Yet scientists do have opinions on the subject; witness the following creedal affirmation by H. Pais in an article "The Particles Jungle":

> Finding new forms of matter is exciting . . . also disquieting. Things are not as simple as they seemed. . . . It is a basic creed of physics . . . that Nature's ultimate design is simple. If something does not look simple it usually means that we have not reached the bottom of it. No one can *prove* that Nature must forever be simple, but this drive to simplicity has been an unfailing guide for 300 years. . . . We must continue to follow its lead.[9]

Contrast this with the view of Snow and Lapp noted earlier; and also with that of Gerald Holton, Harvard physicist, as follows:

> . . . in particle physics today one no longer believes that there are one or two or three very simple laws at the bottom of all this turmoil of spontaneous disintegration and creation of particles.
>
> On the contrary, a more correct view is that at the bottom of our simple laws there is a vast sea, a flux of chaotic disorder in which these particles continually change and rearrange, a whole zoo of "virtual" particles that for small intervals of time disobey all the classical laws. A nineteenth-century physicist would find this view intolerable. It may be that here is a warning to us that when things get very interesting, one has to give up these naive har-

monies and simplicities and must, as it were, face complexity on its own terms.[10]

David Bohm, also a distinguished physicist, approaches the question from still another angle. He suggests that

> ... nature may have in it an infinity of different kinds of things . . ., and un-limited variety of . . . properties, qualities, entities, systems, levels, etc.
> ... it is evidently quite possible that as we penetrate further still, we will find that the character of the organization of things into levels will change so fundamentally that even the pattern of levels itself will eventually fade out. . . .[11]

No, we cannot be sure. There can be no doubt, however, that thus far scientific experience shows that with increasing depth complexity increases. There is no evidence whatsoever of its decreasing toward a ground level. Also there is consid-erable support for the kind of thinking expressed by Holton and Bohm that makes meaningless any idea of such a level in the ordinary sense. It is far from unlikely therefore that with regard to its depths nature is unlimited, and there-fore unbounded and open. It seems then that the sense of depth includes also a sense of the unboundedness of physical reality—in its dimension of depth.

VII

When the implications of the post-modern vision first dawn upon one, he is apt to feel that "the bottom has dropped out of things." He finds himself facing a vast open abyss instead of a solid foundation. Complexity, disorder, uncertainty, and probability seem to play disconcertingly dominant roles in it. Virtually everything once regarded as absolute and immutable verities of nature seems to have been swept away. Later, however, this experience may turn out after all to be liberating, and even energizing. There comes a quickening of hope, a restora-tion of confidence in rationality, though it now has hitherto unsuspected dimen-sions and meanings. The new way of seeing and sensing things, and the new openness to reality then lead one to ask strangely haunting questions, questions not strictly scientific, yet not unscientific, and far from insignificant.

I saw this happen to a student not long ago. We had been talking about post-modern science and its impact upon our culture and upon individual conscious-ness. Said he: "Where then do we stand? Is there any ground to stand on? Before what do we stand? What are we encountering here?" The answer I suggested was, "We stand before Mystery—genuine awesome mystery." He seemed to know immediately what I meant. Indeed I had the feeling that he was aware of more than I was.

The feeling grows on me that contemporary science is slowly but insistently leading us toward a conception of nature that cannot be elaborated adequately in the last analysis without the trans-scientific category of mystery. The question is, however, whether a scientist or anybody else can today make any sense out of such talk.

In the modern era scientists spoke of mystery only rarely. Now they do it much more often. For example, notice once more Mr. Lapp's statement. When I quoted it earlier, I omitted the clause I now restore and emphasize: "Yet, for all we have learned about matter, *some of its fundamental mysteries persist*. The more scientists probe, the greater complexity they encounter." Nature, he feels, displays not only fundamental complexity, but also "fundamental mysteries." And somewhat later he asserts that ". . . the more is known, the more the mystery deepens."

The way he puts it is most interesting, and certainly unusual, for ordinarily one supposes that as knowledge grows mysteries vanish. "The more is *known*, the more the mystery deepens." He does not say just what he means by mystery. It is quite clear, however, from this and other contexts that he is not talking about the pseudo-mysteries of not-yet-solved-problems. Consciously or subconsciously he and many other scientists are aware, I think, that the term mystery should be reserved for something much more profound, having to do with the incomprehensible, unfathomable, inexhaustible, ineffable, enigmatic, awesome, infinite, numinous. I believe that many of them sense too that it pertains not only to the unknown, but even more to the known. They would find deep meaning in theologian Pelikan's distinction between two complementary aspects of mystery: mystery as the quantity of the unknown, and mystery as the glory quality of the known.

Consider the following assertions by scientists as all alluding, I believe, to the fundamentally mysterious character of nature and its realities—and not to mere temporary problems. Weiskopf: "Our knowledge is an island in the infinite ocean of the unknown." This is about the quantity of the unknown. Again Weiskopf: "Every great scientific discovery creates new problems when it solves old ones. When we know more, we have more questions to ask." This tells us something about the quality of the known. Shapley: "As science adds to what is *known* about nature, it does not thereby subtract from the total of what is *not known*." Clearly this is about both. Boulding: "As our knowledge grows so does our ignorance." What is evident here is a keen sense of the infinity, unfathomability, and inexhaustibility of physical reality—in all its dimensions and in both its unknown and known aspects. This is consistent with the contemporary feeling among scientists today that, contrary to the frustrated feelings prevailing so widely near the close of the modern era, science will never come to the end of its search. Henry Margenau symbolizes this feeling—and conviction—by the title of his book, *Open Vistas*.

Consider also Philip Frank's comment that "reality in its fullness can only be experienced, never presented." Most contemporary scientists would probably agree with philosopher Frederick Ferré that "an element of mystery must always veil the relation between conceptual synthesis—however intelligible—and reality." Along a similar line, Margenau: "I would be tempted to say that the ratio of what we know scientifically to what we do not understand in scientific terms has been, is and will always be zero." Surely what is being said here is that nature is to a significant degree ineffable. Reality is always more than can be said or known conceptually.

The sense of depth brings with it also a genuine sense of mystery. The two are, I think, inseparable. Post-modern science is contributing much to the recovery and intensification of that sense.

Finally I suggest that many men are so constituted that only if they come to sense and respond to mystery experienced in nature—where they work and live— are they able to sense and respond to ultimate, transcendent mystery in and beyond nature. Surely Tillich was correct in saying that while science itself cannot unveil and disclose ultimate, divine mystery, it does disclose genuine mystery within nature, which points beyond itself to transcendent mystery: "Reality, every bit of reality, is inexhaustible and points to mystery . . . that transcends the endless series of scientific questions and answers."

Perhaps then you can appreciate how I feel, and what I mean, when I say, without elaborating it further, that the expansion of human consciousness in our time is of tremendous significance for Christian faith—for at least some people, such as myself and many others like me in the science community.

> O *depth* of wealth, wisdom, and knowledge in God! How *unsearchable* his judgments, how *untraceable* his ways! . . . Source, Guide and Goal of all that is—to him be *glory* for ever! Amen." (NEB)

NOTES AND REFERENCES

1. Herbert Butterfield, *The Origins of Modern Science,* London: G. Bell & Sons, pp. 104 f.
2. G. Bornkamm, *Luther's World of Thought,* St. Louis: Concordia Publishing House, 1965, Ch.: "The Picture of Nature."
3. J. Dillenberger, *Protestant Thought and Natural Science,* Garden City, N.Y.: Doubleday, 1960.
4. Michael A. Foster, *Mystery and Philosophy,* London: SCM Press, 1957.
5. Quoted by Platt, *Science,* Nov. 1966, p. 746.
6. L. L. Foldy, "The Structure of Nucleons," *Physics Today,* Sept. 1965. Nucleons are the "particles" (protons and neutrons) that constitute the atomic nucleus.
7. The term "interior depth" is not standard in science, though the idea of it is.
8. Published by Time Incorporated, New York, 1963; pp. 7, 9.
9. *The Rockefeller University Review,* Feb. 1966.
10. *Christianity and Crisis,* May 30, 1966.
11. *Causality and Chance,* New York: Harper Torchbook, 1961, pp. 133, 139.

**the source
of the universe** _____

The lovers of Brahman ask:

What is the source of this universe? What is Brahman? From where do we come? By what power do we live? Where do we find rest? Who rules over our joys and sorrows, O seers of Brahman?

Shall we think of time, or of the own nature of things, or of a law of necessity, or of chance, or of the elements, or of the power of creation of woman or man? Not a union of these, for above them is a soul who thinks. But our soul is under the power of pleasure and pain!

By the Yoga of meditation and contemplation the wise saw the power of God, hidden in his own creation. It is he who rules over all the sources of this universe, from time to the soul of man.

And they saw the Wheel of his power made of one circle, three layers, sixteen parts, fifty spokes, twenty counterspokes, six groups of eight, three paths, one rope of innumerable strands, and the great illusion. . . .

. . .

They also saw the river of life impetuously rushing with the five streams of sense-feelings which come from five sources, the five elements. Its waves are moved by five breathing winds, and its origin is a fivefold fountain of consciousness. This river has five whirlpools, and the violent waves of five sorrows. It has five stages of pain and five dangerous windings and turnings.

In this vast Wheel of creation wherein all things live and die, wanders round the human soul like a swan in restless flying, and she thinks that God is afar. But when the love of God comes down upon her, then she finds her own immortal life.

Exalted in songs has been Brahman. In him are God and the world and the soul, and he is the imperishable supporter of all. When the seers of Brahman see him in all creation, they find peace in Brahman and are free from all sorrows.

God upholds the oneness of this universe: the seen and the unseen, the transient and the eternal. The soul of man is bound by pleasure and pain; but when she sees God she is free from all fetters.

There is the soul of man with wisdom and unwisdom, power and powerlessness; there is nature, Prakriti, which is creation for the sake of the soul; and there is God, infinite, omnipresent, who watches the work of creation. When a man knows the three he knows Brahman.

Matter in time passes away, but God is for ever in Eternity, and he rules both matter and soul. By meditation on him, by contemplation of him, and by communion with him, there comes in the end the destruction of earthly delusion.

_____

From *The Upanishads,* trans. Juan Mascaró, Penguin Books, Ltd. Copyright © Juan Mascaró, 1965.

When a man knows God, he is free: his sorrows have an end, and birth and death are no more. When in inner union he is beyond the world of the body, then the third world, the world of the Spirit, is found, where the power of the All is, and man has all: for he is one with the ONE.

Know that Brahman is for ever in thee, and nothing higher is there to be known. When one sees God and the world and the soul, one sees the Three: one sees Brahman.

Even as fire is not seen in wood and yet by power it comes to light **as** fire, so Brahman in the universe and in the soul is revealed by the power of OM.

The soul is the wood below that can burn and be fire, and OM is the whirling friction-rod above. Prayer is the power that makes OM turn round and then the mystery of God comes to light.

God is found in the soul when sought with truth and self-sacrifice, as fire is found in wood, water in hidden springs, cream in milk, and oil in the oil-fruit.

There is a Spirit who is hidden in all things, as cream is hidden in milk, and who is the source of self-knowledge and self-sacrifice. This is Brahman, the Spirit Supreme. This is Brahman, the Spirit Supreme.

LOREN EISELEY

the bird and the machine _____

I suppose their little bones have years ago been lost among the stones and winds of those high glacial pastures. I suppose their feathers blew eventually into the piles of tumbleweed beneath the straggling cattle fences and rotted there in the mountain snows, along with dead steers and all the other things that drift to an end in the corners of the wire. I do not quite know why I should be thinking of birds over the *New York Times* at breakfast, particularly the birds of my youth half a continent away. It is a funny thing what the brain will do with memories and how it will treasure them and finally bring them into odd juxtapositions with other things, as though it wanted to make a design, or get some meaning out of them, whether you want it or not, or even see it.

It used to seem marvelous to me, but I read now that there are machines that can do these things in a small way, machines that can crawl about like animals, and that it may not be long now until they do more things—maybe even make themselves—I saw that piece in the *Times* just now. And then they will, maybe— well, who knows—but you read about it more and more with no one making any protest, and already they can add better than we and reach up and hear things through the dark and finger the guns over the night sky.

This is the new world that I read about at breakfast. This is the world that

From *The Immense Journey,* New York, Random House, 1957.

confronts me in my biological books and journals, until there are times when I sit quietly in my chair and try to hear the little purr of the cogs in my head and the tubes flaring and dying as the messages go through them and the circuits snap shut or open. This is the great age, make no mistake about it; the robot has been born somewhat appropriately along with the atom bomb, and the brain they say now is just another type of more complicated feedback system. The engineers have its basic principles worked out; it's mechanical, you know; nothing to get superstitious about; and man can always improve on nature once he gets the idea. Well, he's got it all right and that's why, I guess, that I sit here in my chair, with the article crunched in my hand, remembering those two birds and that blue mountain sunlight. There is another magazine article on my desk that reads "Machines Are Getting Smarter Every Day." I don't deny it, but I'll still stick with the birds. It's life I believe in, not machines.

. . .

I sat once on a high ridge that fell away before me into a waste of sand dunes. I sat through hours of a long afternoon. Finally, as I glanced beside my boot an indistinct configuration caught my eye. It was a coiled rattlesnake, a big one. How long he had sat with me I do not know. I had not frightened him. We were both locked in the sleep-walking tempo of the earlier world, baking in the same high air and sunshine. Perhaps he had been there when I came. He slept on as I left, his coils, so ill-discerned by me, dissolving once more among the stones and gravel from which I had barely made him out.

. . .

Not many months thereafter I joined some colleagues heading higher into a remote windy tableland where huge bones were reputed to protrude like boulders from the turf. I had drowsed with reptiles and moved with the century-long pulse of trees; now, lethargically, I was climbing back up some invisible ladder of quickening hours. There had been talk of birds in connection with my duties. Birds are intense, fast-living creatures—reptiles, I suppose one might say, that have escaped out of the heavy sleep of time, transformed fairy creatures dancing over sunlit meadows. It is a youthful fancy, no doubt, but because of something that happened up there among the escarpments of that range, it remains with me a life-long impression. I can never bear to see a bird imprisoned.

We came into that valley through the trailing mists of a spring night. It was a place that looked as though it might never have known the foot of man, but our scouts had been ahead of us and we knew all about the abandoned cabin of stone that lay far up on one hillside. It had been built in the land rush of the last century and then lost to the cattlemen again as the marginal soils failed to take to the plow.

There were spots like this all over that country. Lost graves marked by unlettered stones and old corroding rim-fire cartridge cases lying where somebody had made a stand among the boulders that rimmed the valley. They are all that remain of the range wars; the men are under the stones now. I could see our cavalcade winding in and out through the mist below us: torches, the reflection of the truck lights on our collecting tins, and the far-off bumping of a loose dinosaur thigh bone in the bottom of a trailer. I stood on a rock a moment looking down and thinking what it cost in money and equipment to capture the past.

We had, in addition, instructions to lay hands on the present. The word had come through to get them alive—birds, reptiles, anything. A zoo somewhere abroad needed restocking. It was one of those reciprocal matters in which science involves itself. Maybe our museum needed a stray ostrich egg and this was the payoff. Anyhow, my job was to help capture some birds and that was why I was there before the trucks.

The cabin had not been occupied for years. We intended to clean it out and live in it, but there were holes in the roof and the birds had come in and were roosting in the rafters. You could depend on it in a place like this where everything blew away, and even a bird needed some place out of the weather and away from coyotes. A cabin going back to nature in a wild place draws them till they come in, listening at the eaves, I imagine, pecking softly among the shingles till they find a hole and then suddenly the place is theirs and man is forgotten.

Sometimes of late years I find myself thinking the most beautiful sight in the world might be the birds taking over New York after the last man has run away to the hills. I will never live to see it, of course, but I know just how it will sound because I've lived up high and I know the sort of watch birds keep on us. I've listened to sparrows tapping tentatively on the outside of air conditioners when they thought no one was listening, and I know how other birds test the vibrations that come up to them through the television aerials.

"Is he gone?" they ask, and the vibrations come up from below, "Not yet, not yet."

Well, to come back, I got the door open softly and I had the spotlight all ready to turn on and blind whatever birds there were so they couldn't see to get out through the roof. I had a short piece of ladder to put against the far wall where there was a shelf on which I expected to make the biggest haul. I had all the information I needed just like any skilled assassin. I pushed the door open, the hinges squeaking only a little. A bird or two stirred—I could hear them—but nothing flew and there was a faint starlight through the holes in the roof.

I padded across the floor, got the ladder up and the light ready, and slithered up the ladder till my head and arms were over the shelf. Everything was dark as pitch except for the starlight at the little place back of the shelf near the eaves. With the light to blind them, they'd never make it. I had them. I reached my arm carefully over in order to be ready to seize whatever was there and I put the flash on the edge of the shelf where it would stand by itself when I turned it on. That way I'd be able to use both hands.

Everything worked perfectly except for one detail—I didn't know what kind of birds were there. I never thought about it at all, and it wouldn't have mattered if I had. My orders were to get something interesting. I snapped on the flash and sure enough there was a great beating and feathers flying, but instead of my having them, they, or rather he, had me. He had my hand, that is, and for a small hawk not much bigger than my fist he was doing all right. I heard him give one short metallic cry when the light went on and my hand descended on the bird beside him; after that he was busy with his claws and his beak was sunk in my thumb. In the struggle I knocked the lamp over on the shelf, and his mate got her sight back and whisked neatly through the hole in the roof and off among the stars outside. It all happened in fifteen seconds and you might think I would have fallen down the ladder, but no, I had a professional assassin's reputation to keep up, and the bird, of course, made the mistake of thinking the hand was the enemy and not the eyes behind it. He chewed my thumb up pretty effectively and lacerated my hand with his claws, but in the end I got him, having two hands to work with.

He was a sparrow hawk and a fine young male in the prime of life. I was sorry not to catch the pair of them, but as I dripped blood and folded his wings carefully, holding him by the back so that he couldn't strike again, I had to admit the two of them might have been more than I could have handled under the circumstances. The little fellow had saved his mate by diverting me, and that was that. He was born to it, and made no outcry now, resting in my hand hopelessly, but peering toward me in the shadows behind the lamp with a fierce, almost indifferent glance. He neither gave nor expected mercy and something out of the high air passed from him to me, stirring a faint embarrassment.

I quit looking into that eye and managed to get my huge carcass with its fist full of prey back down the ladder. I put the bird in a box too small to allow him to injure himself by struggle and walked out to welcome the arriving trucks. It had been a long day, and camp still to make in the darkness. In the morning that bird would be just another episode. He would go back with the bones in the truck to a small cage in a city where he would spend the rest of his life. And a good thing, too. I sucked my aching thumb and spat out some blood. An assassin has to get used to these things. I had a professional reputation to keep up.

In the morning, with the change that comes on suddenly in that high country, the mist that had hovered below us in the valley was gone. The sky was a deep blue, and one could see for miles over the high outcroppings of stone. I was up early and brought the box in which the little hawk was imprisoned out onto the grass where I was building a cage. A wind as cool as a mountain spring ran over the grass and stirred my hair. It was a fine day to be alive. I looked up and all around and at the hole in the cabin roof out of which the other little hawk had fled. There was no sign of her anywhere that I could see.

"Probably in the next county by now," I thought cynically, but before beginning work I decided I'd have a look at my last night's capture.

Secretively, I looked again all around the camp and up and down and opened the box. I got him right out in my hand with his wings folded properly and I was careful not to startle him. He lay limp in my grasp and I could feel his heart pound under the feathers but he only looked beyond me and up.

I saw him look that last look away beyond me into a sky so full of light that I could not follow his gaze. The little breeze flowed over me again, and nearby a mountain aspen shook all its tiny leaves. I suppose I must have had an idea then of what I was going to do, but I never let it come up into consciousness. I just reached over and laid the hawk on the grass.

He lay there a long minute without hope, unmoving, his eyes still fixed on that blue vault above him. It must have been that he was already so far away in heart that he never felt the release from my hand. He never even stood. He just lay with his breast against the grass.

In the next second after that long minute he was gone. Like a flicker of light, he had vanished with my eyes full on him, but without actually seeing even a premonitory wing beat. He was gone straight into that towering emptiness of light and crystal that my eyes could scarcely bear to penetrate. For another long moment there was silence. I could not see him. The light was too intense. Then from far up somewhere a cry came ringing down.

I was young then and had seen little of the world, but when I heard that cry my heart turned over. It was not the cry of the hawk I had captured; for, by shifting my position against the sun, I was now seeing further up. Straight out of the sun's eye, where she must have been soaring restlessly above us for untold hours, hurried his mate. And from far up, ringing from peak to peak of the summits over us, came a cry of such unutterable and ecstatic joy that it sounds down across the years and tingles among the cups on my quiet breakfast table.

I saw them both now. He was rising fast to meet her. They met in a great soaring gyre that turned to a whirling circle and a dance of wings. Once more, just once, their two voices, joined in a harsh wild medley of question and response, struck and echoed against the pinnacles of the valley. Then they were gone forever somewhere into those upper regions beyond the eyes of men.

I am older now, and sleep less, and have seen most of what there is to see and am not very much impressed any more, I suppose, by anything. "What Next in the Attributes of Machines?" my morning headline runs. "It Might Be the Power to Reproduce Themselves."

I lay the paper down and across my mind a phrase floats insinuatingly: "It does not seem that there is anything in the construction, constituents, or behavior of the human being which it is essentially impossible for science to duplicate and synthesize. On the other hand. . . ."

All over the city the cogs in the hard, bright mechanisms have begun to turn. Figures move through computers, names are spelled out, a thoughtful machine selects the fingerprints of a wanted criminal from an array of thousands. In the laboratory an electronic mouse runs swiftly through a maze toward the cheese it can neither taste nor enjoy. On the second run it does better than a living mouse.

"On the other hand. . . ." Ah, my mind takes up, on the other hand the machine does not bleed, ache, hang for hours in the empty sky in a torment of hope to learn the fate of another machine, nor does it cry out with joy nor dance in the air with the fierce passion of a bird. Far off, over a distance greater than space, that remote cry from the heart of heaven makes a faint buzzing among my breakfast dishes and passes on and away.

LAOTZU

the tao ————————————————————————————————

Before creation a presence existed,
Self-contained, complete,
Formless, voiceless, mateless,
Changeless,
Which yet pervaded itself
With unending motherhood.
Though there can be no name for it,
I have called it "the way of life."
Perhaps I should have called it "the fullness of life,"
Since fullness implies widening into space,
Implies still further widening,
Implies widening until the circle is whole.
In this sense
The way of life is fulfilled,
Heaven is fulfilled,
Earth fulfilled
And a fit man also is fulfilled:
These are the four amplitudes of the universe
And a fit man is one of them:
Man rounding the way of earth,
Earth rounding the way of heaven,
Heaven rounding the way of life
Till the circle is full.

———————

the way life flows

What we look for beyond seeing
And call the unseen,
Listen for beyond hearing
And call the unheard,
Grasp for beyond reaching
And call the withheld,
Merge beyond understanding
In a oneness
Which does not merely rise and give light,
Does not merely set and leave darkness,
But forever sends forth a succession of living things as mysterious
As the unbegotten existence to which they return.
That is why men have called them empty phenomena,
Meaningless images,
In a mirage
With no face to meet,
No back to follow.
Yet one who is anciently aware of existence
Is master of every moment,
Feels no break since time beyond time
In the way life flows.

where is tao?

Master Tung Kwo asked Chuang:
"Show me where the Tao is found."
Chuang Tzu replied:
"There is nowhere it is not to be found."
The former insisted:
"Show me at least some definite place

Where Tao is found."
"It is in the ant," said Chuang.
"Is it in some lesser being?"
"It is in the weeds."
"Can you go further down the scale of things?"
"It is in this piece of tile."
"Further?"
"It is in this turd."
At this Tung Kwo had nothing more to say.
But Chuang continued: "None of your questions
Are to the point. They are like the questions
Of inspectors in the market,
Testing the weight of pigs
By prodding them in their thinnest parts.
Why look for Tao by going 'down the scale of being'
As if that which we call 'least'
Had less of Tao?
Tao is Great in all things,
Complete in all, Universal in all,
Whole in all. These three aspects
Are distinct, but the Reality is One.
Therefore come with me
To the palace of Nowhere
Where all the many things are One:
There at last we might speak
Of what has no limitation and no end.
Come with me to the land of Non-Doing:
What shall we there say—that Tao
Is simplicity, stillness,
Indifference, purity,
Harmony and ease? All these names leave me indifferent
For their distinctions have disappeared.
My will is aimless there.
If it is nowhere, how should I be aware of it?
If it goes and returns, I know not
Where it has been resting. If it wanders
Here then there, I know not where it will end.
The mind remains undetermined in the great Void.
Here the highest knowledge
Is unbounded. That which gives things
Their thusness cannot be delimited by things.
So when we speak of 'limits,' we remain confined
To limited things.
The limit of the unlimited is called 'fullness.'

The limitlessness of the limited is called 'emptiness.'
Tao is the source of both. But it is itself
Neither fullness nor emptiness.
Tao produces both renewal and decay,
But is neither renewal nor decay.
It causes being and non-being
But is neither being nor non-being.
Tao assembles and it destroys,
But it is neither the Totality nor the Void."

CHUANG TZU

tao _____

Cocks crow
Dogs bark
This all men know.
Even the wisest
Cannot tell
Whence these voices come
Or explain
Why dogs bark and cocks crow
When they do.
Beyond the smallest of the small
There is no measure.
Beyond the greatest of the great
There is also no measure.

Where there is no measure
There is no "thing."
In this void
You speak of "cause"
Or of "chance"?
You speak of "things"
Where there is "no-things."
To name a name
Is to delimit a "thing."

When I look beyond the beginning

I find no measure.
When I look beyond the end
I find also no measure.
Where there is no measure
There is no beginning of any "thing."
You speak of "cause" or "chance"?
You speak of the beginning of some "thing."

Does Tao exist?
Is it then a "thing that exists"?
Can it "non-exist"?
Is there then "thing that exists"
That "cannot not exist"?
To name Tao
Is to name no-thing.
Tao is not the name
Of "an existent."
"Cause" and "chance"
Have no bearing on Tao.
Tao is a name
That indicates
Without defining.

Tao is beyond words
And beyond things.
It is not expressed
Either in word or in silence.
Where there is no longer word or silence
Tao is apprehended.

ERIK H. ERIKSON

homo religiosus

At the time of the Ahmedabad strike, Gandhi was forty-eight years old: middle-aged Mahatma, indeed. That the very next year he emerged as the father of his country only lends greater importance to the fact that the middle span of life is under the dominance of the universal human need and strength which I have come to subsume under the term generativity. I have said that in this stage a man and a woman must have defined for themselves what and whom they have come to care for, what they care to do well, and how they plan to take care of what they have started and created. But it is clear that the great leader creates for himself and for many others new choices and new cares. These he derives from a mighty drivenness, an intense and yet flexible energy, a shocking originality, and a capacity to impose on his time what most concerns him—which he does so convincingly that his time believes this concern to have emanated "naturally" from ripe necessities. And historians must agree, for they are able only to study the confluences in what has come to pass and to be recorded—unless, of course, they come to the conclusion (and not a few have done so) that India, if not much better, would certainly not be much worse off if the man had never lived. And, indeed, compared with the charismatic men of his time, Gandhi and his "inner voice" may seem more moodily personal, more mystically religious, and more formless in ideology than any of them. There is nothing more consistent in the views of Gandhi's critics than the accusation of inconsistency: at one time he is accused of sounding like a socialist, and at another a dreamy conservative; or, again, a pacifist and a frantic militarist; a nationalist and a "communalist"; an anarchist and a devotee of tradition; a Western activist and an Eastern mysticist; a total religionist and yet so liberal that he could say he saw God even in the atheist's atheism. Did this polymorphous man have a firm center?

If, for the sake of this game, I should give his unique presence a name that would suit my views, I would call him a religious actualist. In my clinical ruminations I have found it necessary to split what we mean by "real" into that which can be known because it is demonstrably correct (factual reality) and that which feels effectively true in action (actuality). Gandhi absorbed from Indian culture a conception of truth (sat) which he attempted to make actual in all compartments of human life and along all the stages which make up its course. I will in the next section make the most of the claim that the Mahatma (in spite of his enmity toward all erotism) was a mighty good bodily specimen—as is attested in motion pictures which show him to be so much more agile and of one piece than most men seem to be.

At the same time, he was as actual an Indian as can be imagined, aware that the great majority of his country's massive population was held together only by an ancient culture which, even if disintegrating, was all there for India to rely on in the face of irreversible modernization. As an Indian, he had been born a Bania, and it was as a Bania and a Gujarati that he entered on the fateful path toward an all-India Mahatmaship. But while he learned to utilize craftily what was his first professional identity, namely, that of a barrister English style, and while he then became a powerful politician Indian style, he also strove to grasp the "business" of religious men, namely, to keep his eyes trained upon the all-embracing circumstance that each of us exists with a unique consciousness and a responsibility of his own which makes him at the same time zero and everything, a center of absolute silence, and the vortex of apocalyptic participation. A man who looks through the historical parade of cultures and civilizations, styles and isms which provide most of us with a glorious and yet miserably fragile sense of immortal identity, defined status, and collective grandeur faces the central truth of our nothingness—and, *mirabile dictu,* gains power from it.

Gandhi's actualism, then, first of all consisted in his knowledge of, and his ability to gain strength from, the fact that nothing is more powerful in the world than conscious nothingness if it is paired with the gift of giving and accepting actuality. It is not for me to say what this power is; yet obviously it demands the keenest minds and a most experienced heart, for otherwise it would be crushed between megalomania and self-destruction. As for the rest of mankind, I have an inkling that our response to such a man rests on the need of all men to find a few who plausibly take upon themselves—and seem to give meaning to—what others must deny at all times but cannot really forget for a moment. Freud, in one of his "economic" moods, might well have said that, psychologically speaking, such men save others not so much from their sins (this Freud would not have claimed to know), but from the fantastic effort not to see the most obvious of all facts: that life is bounded by not-life.

Indian culture has (as have all others) made out of this special mission of saintly men a universal and often utterly corrupt institution, and Gandhi was well aware of the fact that the Mahatmaship could type him to the point of in-actuality. He considered it all the more incumbent upon himself to make his spiritual power work in political realities—for which he brought along both a specific giftedness and, as we saw, favorable identifications. I think the man was right who said that Gandhi, when he listened to his inner voice, heard the clamor of the people. It may be just this alliance of inner voice and voice of mankind which must make such a man at times insensitive to those closest to him by fa-milial bond.

Swaraj in the sense of home-rule and self-rule was Gandhi's "way": if the power of actuality—as we now may add—is the mutual maximization of greater and higher unity among men, then each must begin to become actual by combin-ing what is given in his individual development and in his historical time. Gandhi, I think, would make his own those pronouncements of Luther which I once sin-gled out as the essence of religious actualism: Quotidianus Christi adventus—Christ comes today; via dei est qua nos ambulare facit—God's way is what makes us move; semper oportit nasci, novari, generari—we must always be reborn, re-newed, regenerated; proficere est nihil aliud nisi semper incipere—to do enough means nothing else than always to begin again. Thus, out of the acceptance of nothingness emerges what can be the most central and inclusive, timeless and actual, conscious and active position in the human universe. We have seen that Gandhi was never too proud to find universal meaning in petty circumstances, for he knew that one must build on the values of one's childhood as long as they are revalidated by experience, until one perceives a wider truth which may make them relative or obsolete. Thus Gandhi could be and remain a Jain—a religion which, of course, provides ritual choices in a multiplicity of images and values—and yet could also absorb some of the essence of other, all other, religions. By the same token, he could live in symbiosis with the technology of his time and yet comprehend and exploit the fact that some such symbolic and pragmatic item as the spinning wheel could dramatically activate in hundreds of thousands of localities what was at the time not at all ready for industrialization.

Here, as in many other aspects of his life, the appearance of inconsistency is only a function of the critics' confusion in regard to elusive ends and self-fulfilling means. For it is in the daily means the dharma, practicality, and ethics coincide, wherefore the devotee of the hum of the charkha is not necessarily further removed from actuality than is he who feels vitalized by the clang of industrial activity. If each worker continues with full attention to the mood and the style of his activity, and as long as this activity lifts him above otherwise fallow or regressive potentials, he adheres to the Gandhian dictum that means are "ends-in-the-making" or "ends in proccu." A "true" man, then, will not remain fixated on either means or ends for their own sake. He will not permit himself or others to use foul means with the illusory justification that their continuance "for a little while longer" will end in a utopian future when the truth will at last become the universal means—whereupon the world will forever after be free for democracy, or free for communism, or free for the stateless society, or whatever. What is true now will, if not attended to, never be true again: and what is untrue now will never, by any trick, become true later. Therefore I would interpret, and interpret with humility, the truth-force of the religious actualist thus: to be ready to die for what is true now means to grasp the only chance to have lived fully.

The religious actualist, however, inevitably becomes a religious innovator, for his very passion and power will make him want to make actual for others what actualizes him. This means to create or recreate institutions, and it can mean the attempt to institutionalize nothingness. The Hindu concept of the life cycle, as we saw, allots a time for the learning of eternal concerns in youth, and for the experience of near-nothingness at the end of life, while it reserves for the middle of life a time dedicated to the "maintenance of the world," that is, a time for the most intense actualization of erotic, procreative, and communal bonds: in this period of life, adult man must forget death for the sake of the newborn individual and the coming generations. But the middle-aged do need all the more the occasional man who can afford to remember, and they will travel regularly and far to partake of his elusive power. We have seen how deeply Gandhi at times minded having to become a householder, for without his becoming committed to a normal course of life by marriage, he might well have been a monastic saint instead of what he became: politician and reformer with an honorary sainthood. For the true saints are those who transfer the state of householdership to the house of God, becoming father and mother, brother and sister, son and daughter, to all creation, rather than to their own issue. But they do this in established "orders," and they create or partake in rituals which will envelop and give peace to those who must live in transitory reality.

SIGMUND FREUD
religion as an illusion _____

Religious ideas which profess to be dogmas, are not the residue of experience or the final result of reflection; they are illusions, fulfillments of the oldest, strongest and most insistent wishes of mankind; the secret of their strength is the strength of these wishes. We know already that the terrifying effect of infantile helplessness aroused the need for protection—protection through love—which the father relieved, and that the discovery that this helplessness would continue through the whole of life made it necessary to cling to the existence of a father—but this time a more powerful one. Thus the benevolent rule of divine providence allays our anxiety in face of life's dangers, the establishment of a moral order ensures the fulfillment of the demands of justice, which within human culture have so often remained unfulfilled, and the prolongation of earthly existence by a future life provides in addition the local and temporal setting for these wish-fulfillments. Answers to the questions that tempt human curiosity, such as the origin of the universe and the relation between the body and the soul, are developed in accordance with the underlying assumptions of this system; it betokens a tremendous relief for the individual psyche if it is released from the conflicts of childhood arising out of the father complex, which are never wholly overcome, and if these conflicts are afforded a universally accepted solution.

When I say that they are illusions, I must define the meaning of the word. An illusion is not the same as an error, it is indeed not necessarily an error. Aristotle's belief, to which ignorant people still cling, that vermin are evolved out of dung was an error; so was the belief of a former generation of doctors that tabes dorsalis was the result of sexual excess. It would be improper to call these errors illusions. On the other hand, it was an illusion on the part of Columbus that he had discovered a new sea-route to India. The part played by his wish in this error is very clear. One may describe as an illusion the statement of certain nationalists that the Indo-Germanic race is the only one capable of culture, or the belief, which only psychoanalysis destroyed, that the child is a being without sexuality. It is characteristic of the illusion that it is derived from men's wishes; in this respect it approaches the psychiatric delusion, but it is to be distinguished from this, quite apart from the more complicated structure of the latter. In the delusion we emphasize as essential the conflict with reality; the illusion need not be necessarily false, that is to say, unrealizable or incompatible with reality. For instance, a poor girl may have an illusion that a prince will come and fetch her home. It is possible; some such cases have occurred. That the Messiah will come and found a golden age is much less probable; according to one's personal attitude one will classify this belief as an illusion or as analogous to a delusion. Examples of illusions that have come true are not easy to discover, but the illusion of the alchemists that all metals can be turned into gold may prove to be one. The desire to have lots of gold, as much gold as possible, has been considerably damped by our modern insight into the nature of wealth, yet chemistry no longer considers a transmutation of metals into gold as impossible. Thus we call a belief an illusion when wish-fulfillment is a prominent factor in its motivation, while disregarding its relations to reality, just as the illusion itself does.

If after this survey we turn again to religious doctrines, we may reiterate that they are all illusions, they do not admit of proof, and no one can be compelled to consider them as true or to believe in them. Some of them are so improbable, so very incompatible with everything we have laboriously discovered about the reality of the world, that we may compare them—taking adequately into account the psychological differences—to delusions. Of the reality value of most of them we cannot judge; just as they cannot be proved, neither can they be refuted. We still know too little to approach them critically. The riddles of the universe only reveal themselves slowly to our inquiry, to many questions science can as yet give no answer; but scientific work is our only way to the knowledge of external reality. Again, it is merely illusion to expect anything from intuition or trance; they can give us nothing but particulars, which are difficult to interpret, about our own mental life, never information about the questions that are so lightly answered by the doctrines of religion. It would be wanton to let one's own arbitrary action fill the gap, and according to one's personal estimate declare this or that part of the religious system to be more or less acceptable. These questions are too momentous for that; too sacred, one might say.

At this point it may be objected: well, then, if even the crabbed skeptics admit that the statements of religion cannot be confuted by reason, why should I not believe in them, since they have so much on their side—tradition, the concurrence of mankind, and all the consolation they yield? Yes, why not? Just as no one can be forced into belief, so no one can be forced into unbelief. But do not deceive yourself into thinking that with such arguments you are following the path of correct reasoning. If ever there was a case of facile argument, this is one. Ignorance is ignorance; no right to believe anything is derived from it. No reasonable man will behave so frivolously in other matters or rest content with such feeble grounds for his opinions or for the attitude he adopts; it is only in the highest and holiest things that he allows this. In reality these are only attempts to delude oneself or other people into the belief that one still holds fast to religion, when one has long cut oneself loose from it. Where questions of religion are concerned people are guilty of every possible kind of insincerity and intellectual misdemeanor. Philosophers stretch the meaning of words until they retain scarcely anything of their original sense; by calling "God" some vague abstraction which they have created for themselves, they pose as deists, as believers, before the world; they may even pride themselves on having attained a higher and purer idea of God, although their God is nothing but an insubstantial shadow and no longer the mighty personality of religious doctrine. Critics persist in calling "deeply religious" a person who confesses to a sense of man's insignificance and impotence in face of the universe, although it is not this feeling that constitutes the essence of religious emotion, but rather the next step, the reaction to it, which seeks a remedy against this feeling. He who goes no further, he who humbly acquiesces in the insignificant part man plays in the universe, is, on the contrary, irreligious in the truest sense of the word.

It does not lie within the scope of this inquiry to estimate the value of religious doctrines as truth. It suffices that we have recognized them, psychologically considered, as illusions. But we need not conceal the fact that this discovery strongly influences our attitude to what must appear to many the most important of questions. We know approximately at what periods and by what sort of men religious doctrines were formed. If we now learned from what motives this happened, our attitude to the problem of religion will suffer an appreciable change. We say to ourselves: it would indeed be very nice if there were a God, who was both creator of the world and a benevolent providence, if there were a moral world order and a future life, but at the same time it is very odd that this is all just as we should wish it ourselves. And it would be still odder if our poor, ignorant, enslaved ancestors had succeeded in solving all these difficult riddles of the universe.

PAUL TILLICH

what faith is _____

1. faith as ultimate concern

Faith is the state of being ultimately concerned: the dynamics of faith are the dynamics of man's ultimate concern. Man, like every living being, is concerned about many things, above all about those which condition his very existence, such as food and shelter. But man, in contrast to other living beings, has spiritual concerns—cognitive, aesthetic, social, political. Some of them are urgent, often extremely urgent, and each of them as well as the vital concerns can claim ultimacy for a human life or the life of a social group. If it claims ultimacy it demands the total surrender of him who accepts this claim, and it promises total fulfillment even if all other claims have to be subjected to it or rejected in its name. If a national group makes the life and growth of the nation its ultimate concern, it demands that all other concerns, economic well-being, health and life, family, aesthetic and cognitive truth, justice and humanity, be sacrificed. The extreme nationalisms of our century are laboratories for the study of what

Abridged from pp. 1–13 in *Dynamics of Faith* by Paul Tillich. Copyright © 1957 by Paul Tillich.

ultimate concern means in all aspects of human existence, including the smallest concern of one's daily life. Everything is centered in the only god, the nation—a god who certainly proves to be a demon, but who shows clearly the unconditional character of an ultimate concern.

But it is not only the unconditional demand made by that which is one's ultimate concern, it is also the promise of ultimate fulfillment which is accepted in the act of faith. The content of this promise is not necessarily defined. It can be expressed in indefinite symbols or in concrete symbols which cannot be taken literally, like the "greatness" of one's nation in which one participates even if one has died for it, or the conquest of mankind by the "saving race," etc. In each of these cases it is "ultimate fulfillment" that is promised, and it is exclusion from such fulfillment which is threatened if the unconditional demand is not obeyed.

An example—and more than an example—is the faith manifest in the religion of the Old Testament. It also has the character of ultimate concern in demand, threat and promise. The content of this concern is not the nation—although Jewish nationalism has sometimes tried to distort it into that—but the content is the God of justice, who, because he represents justice for everybody and every nation, is called the universal God, the God of the universe. He is the ultimate concern of every pious Jew, and therefore in his name the great commandment is given: "You shall love the Lord your God with all your heart, and with all your soul, and with all your might" (Deut. 6:5). This is what ultimate concern means and from these words the term "ultimate concern" is derived. They state unambiguously the character of genuine faith, the demand of total surrender to the subject of ultimate concern. The Old Testament is full of commands which make the nature of this surrender concrete, and it is full of promises and threats in relation to it. Here also are the promises of symbolic indefiniteness, although they center around fulfillment of the national and individual life, and the threat is the exclusion from such fulfillment through national extinction and individual catastrophe. Faith, for the men of the Old Testament, is the state of being ultimately and unconditionally concerned about Jahweh and about what he represents in demand, threat and promise.

Another example—almost a counter-example, yet nevertheless equally revealing—is the ultimate concern with "success" and with social standing and economic power. It is the god of many people in the highly competitive Western culture and it does what every ultimate concern must do: it demands unconditional surrender to its laws even if the price is the sacrifice of genuine human relations, personal conviction, and creative *eros*. Its threat is social and economic defeat, and its promise—indefinite as all such promises—the fulfillment of one's being. It is the breakdown of this kind of faith which characterizes and makes religiously important most contemporary literature. Not false calculations but a misplaced faith is revealed in novels like *Point of No Return*. When fulfilled, the promise of this faith proves to be empty.

Faith is the state of being ultimately concerned. The content matters infinitely for the life of the believer, but it does not matter for the formal definition of faith. And this is the first step we have to make in order to understand the dynamics of faith.

2. faith as a centered act

Faith as ultimate concern is an act of the total personality. It happens in the center of the personal life and includes all its elements. Faith is the most centered act of the human mind. It is not a movement of a special section or a special function of man's total being. They all are united in the act of faith. But faith is not the sum total of their impacts. It transcends every special impact as well as the totality of them and it has itself a decisive impact on each of them.

Since faith is an act of the personality as a whole, it participates in the dynamics of personal life. These dynamics have been described in many ways, especially in the recent developments of analytic psychology. Thinking in polarities, their tensions and their possible conflicts, is a common characteristic of most of them. This makes the psychology of personality highly dynamic and requires a dynamic theory of faith as the most personal of all personal acts. The first and decisive polarity in analytic psychology is that between the so-called unconscious and the conscious. Faith as an act of total personality is not imaginable without the participation of the unconscious elements in the personality structure. They are always present and decide largely about the content of faith. But, on the other hand, faith is a conscious act and the unconscious elements participate in the creation of faith only if they are taken into the personal center which transcends each of them. If this does not happen, if unconscious forces determine the mental status without a centered act, faith does not occur, and compulsions take its place. For faith is a matter of freedom. Freedom is nothing more than the possibility of centered personal acts. The frequent discussion in which faith and freedom are contrasted could be helped by the insight that faith is a free, namely, centered act of the personality. In this respect freedom and faith are identical.

. . .

This leads to the question of how faith as a personal, centered act is related to the rational structure of man's personality which is manifest in his meaningful language, in his ability to know the true and to do the good, in his sense of beauty and justice. All this, and not only his possibility to analyze, to calculate and to argue, makes him a rational being. But in spite of this larger concept of reason we must deny that man's essential nature is identical with the rational character of his mind. Man is able to decide for or against reason, he is able to create beyond reason or to destroy below reason. This power is the power of his self, the center of self-relatedness in which all elements of his being are united. Faith is not an act of any of his rational functions, as it is not an act of the unconscious, but it is an act in which both the rational and the nonrational elements of his being are transcended.

Faith as the embracing and centered act of the personality is "ecstatic." It transcends both the drives of the nonrational unconscious and the structures of the rational conscious. It transcends them, but it does not destroy them. The ecstatic character of faith does not exclude its rational character although it is not identical with it, and it includes nonrational strivings without being identical with them. In the ecstasy of faith there is an awareness of truth and of ethical value; there are also past loves and hates, conflicts and reunions, individual and collective influences. "Ecstasy" means "standing outside of oneself"—without ceasing to be oneself—with all the elements which are united in the personal center.

A further polarity in these elements, relevant for the understanding of faith, is the tension between the cognitive function of man's personal life, on the one hand, and emotion and will, on the other hand.

• • •

In every act of faith there is cognitive affirmation, not as the result of an independent process of inquiry but as an inseparable element in a total act of acceptance and surrender. This also excludes the idea that faith is the result of an independent act of "will to believe." There is certainly affirmation by the will of what concerns one ultimately, but faith is not a creation of the will. In the ecstasy of faith the will to accept and to surrender is an element, but not the cause. And this is true also of feeling. Faith is not an emotional outburst: this is not the meaning of ecstasy. Certainly, emotion is in it, as in every act of man's spiritual life. But emotion does not produce faith. Faith has a cognitive content and is an act of the will. It is the unity of every element in the centered self. Of course, the unity of all elements in the act of faith does not prevent one or the other element from dominating in a special form of faith. It dominates the character of faith but it does not create the act of faith.

This also answers the question of a possible psychology of faith. Everything that happens in man's personal being can become an object of psychology. And it is rather important for both the philosopher of religion and the practical minister to know how the act of faith is embedded in the totality of psychological processes. But in contrast to this justified and desirable form of a psychology of faith there is another one which tries to derive faith from something that is not faith but is most frequently fear. The presupposition of this method is that fear or something else from which faith is derived is more original and basic than faith. But this presupposition cannot be proved. On the contrary, one can prove that in the scientific method which leads to such consequences faith is already effective. Faith precedes all attempts to derive it from something else, because these attempts are themselves based on faith.

3. the source of faith

We have described the act of faith and its relation to the dynamics of personality. Faith is a total and centered act of the personal self, the act of unconditional, infinite and ultimate concern. The question now arises: what is the source of this all-embracing and all-transcending concern? The word "concern" points to two sides of a relationship, the relation between the one who is concerned and his concern. In both respects we have to imagine man's situation in itself and in his world. The reality of man's ultimate concern reveals something about his being, namely, that he is able to transcend the flux of relative and transitory experiences of his ordinary life. Man's experiences, feelings, thoughts are conditioned and finite. They not only come and go, but their content is of finite and conditional concern—unless they are elevated to unconditional validity. But this presupposes the general possibility of doing so; it presupposes the element of infinity in man. Man is able to understand in an immediate personal and central act the meaning of the ultimate, the unconditional, the absolute, the infinite. This alone makes faith a human potentiality.

Human potentialities are powers that drive toward actualization. Man is driven toward faith by his awareness of the infinite to which he belongs, but which he does not own like a possession. This is in abstract terms what concretely appears as the "restlessness of the heart" within the flux of life.

The unconditional concern which is faith is the concern about the unconditional. The infinite passion, as faith has been described, is the passion for the infinite. Or, to use our first term, the ultimate concern is concern about what is experienced as ultimate. In this way we have turned from the subjective meaning of faith as a centered act of the personality to its objective meaning, to what is meant in the act of faith. It would not help at this point of our analysis to call that which is meant in the act of faith "God" or "a god." For at this step we ask: What in the idea of God constitutes divinity? The answer is: It is the element of the unconditional and of ultimacy. This carries the quality of divinity. If this is seen, one can understand why almost every thing "in heaven and on earth" has received ultimacy in the history of human religion. But we also can understand that a critical principle was and is at work in man's religious consciousness, namely, that which is really ultimate over against what claims to be ultimate but is only preliminary, transitory, finite.

The term "ultimate concern" unites the subjective and the objective side of the act of faith—the *fides qua creditur* (the faith through which one believes) and the *fides quae creditur* (the faith which is believed). The first is the classical term for the centered act of the personality, the ultimate concern. The second is the classical term for that toward which this act is directed, the ultimate itself, expressed in symbols of the divine. This distinction is very important, but not ultimately so, for the one side cannot be without the other. There is no faith without a content toward which it is directed. There is always something meant in the act of faith. And there is no way of having the content of faith except in the act of faith. All speaking about divine matters which is not done in the state of ultimate concern is meaningless. Because that which is meant in the act of faith cannot be approached in any other way than through an act of faith.

In terms like ultimate, unconditional, infinite, absolute, the difference between subjectivity and objectivity is overcome. The ultimate of the act of faith and the ultimate that is meant in the act of faith are one and the same. This is symbolically expressed by the mystics when they say that their knowledge of God is the knowledge God has of himself; and it is expressed by Paul when he says (I Cor. 13) that he will know as he is known, namely, by God. God never can be object without being at the same time subject. Even a successful prayer is, according to Paul (Rom. 8), not possible without God as Spirit praying within us. The same experience expressed in abstract language is the disappearance of the ordinary subject-object scheme in the experience of the ultimate, the unconditional. In the act of faith that which is the source of this act is present beyond the cleavage of subject and object. It is present as both and beyond both.

This character of faith gives an additional criterion for distinguishing true and false ultimacy. The finite which claims infinity without having it (as, e.g., a nation or success) is not able to transcend the subject-object scheme. It remains an object which the believer looks at as a subject. He can approach it with ordinary knowledge and subject it to ordinary handling. There are, of course, many degrees in the endless realm of false ultimacies. The nation is nearer to true ultimacy than is success. Nationalistic ecstasy can produce a state in which the subject is almost swallowed by the object. But after a period the subject emerges again, disappointed radically and totally, and by looking at the nation in a skeptical and calculating way does injustice even to its justified claims. The more idolatrous a faith the less it is able to overcome the cleavage between subject and object. For that is the difference between true and idolatrous faith. In true faith the ultimate concern is a concern about the truly ultimate; while in idolatrous faith preliminary, finite realities are elevated to the rank of ultimacy. The inescapable consequence of idolatrous faith is "existential disappointment," a disappointment which penetrates into the very existence of man! This is the dynamics of idolatrous faith: that it is faith, and as such, the centered act of a personality; that the centering point is something which is more or less on the periphery; and that, therefore, the act of faith leads to a loss of the center and to a disruption of the personality. The ecstatic character of even an idolatrous faith can hide this consequence only for a certain time. But finally it breaks into the open.

4. faith and the dynamics of the holy
He who enters the sphere of faith enters the sanctuary of life. Where there is faith there is an awareness of holiness. This seems to contradict what has just been said about idolatrous faith. But it does not contradict our analysis of idolatry. It only contradicts the popular way in which the word "holy" is used. What concerns one ultimately becomes holy. The awareness of the holy is awareness of the presence of the divine, namely of the content of our ultimate concern. This awareness is expressed in a grand way in the Old Testament from the visions of the patriarchs and Moses to the shaking experiences of the great prophets and psalmists. It is a presence which remains mysterious in spite of its appearance, and it exercises both an attractive and a repulsive function on those who encounter it. In his classical book, *The Idea of the Holy*, Rudolph Otto has described these two functions as the fascinating and the shaking character of the

holy. (In Otto's terminology: *mysterium fascinans et tremendum.*) They can be found in all religions because they are the way in which man always encounters the representations of his ultimate concern. The reason for these two effects of the holy is obvious if we see the relation of the experience of the holy to the experience of ultimate concern. The human heart seeks the infinite because that is where the finite wants to rest. In the infinite it sees its own fulfillment. This is the reason for the ecstatic attraction and fascination of everything in which ultimacy is manifest. On the other hand, if ultimacy is manifest and exercises its fascinating attraction, one realizes at the same time the infinite distance of the finite from the infinite and, consequently, the negative judgment over any finite attempts to reach the infinite. The feeling of being consumed in the presence of the divine is a profound expression of man's relation to the holy. It is implied in every genuine act of faith, in every state of ultimate concern.

the prodigal son and the seeking father

It is like a youth who, on attaining manhood, leaves his father and runs away. For long he dwells in some other country, ten, twenty, or fifty years. The older he grows, the more needy he becomes. Roaming about in all directions to seek clothing and food, he gradually wanders along till he unexpectedly approaches his native country. From the first the father searched for his son, but in vain, and meanwhile has settled in a certain city. His home becomes very rich; his goods and treasures are incalculable; gold, silver, lapis lazuli, corals, amber, crystal, and other gems so increase that his treasures overflow; many others and slaves has he, retainers and attendants, and countless elephants, horses, carriages, animals to ride, and kine and sheep. His revenues and investments spread to other countries, and his traders and customers are many in the extreme.

At this time, the poor son, wandering through village after village, and passing through countries and cities, at last reached the city where his father has settled. Always has the father been thinking of his son, yet, though he has been parted from him over fifty years, he has never spoken of the matter to any one, only pondering over it within himself and cherishing regret in his heart, as he reflects: "Old and worn, I own much wealth; gold, silver, and jewels, granaries and treasuries overflowing; but I have no son. Some day my end will come and my wealth be scattered and lost, for there is no one to whom I can leave it." Thus does he often think of his son, and earnestly repeats this reflection: "If I could only get back my son and commit my wealth to him, how contented and happy should I be, with never a further anxiety!''

World-honored One! Meanwhile the poor son, hired for wages here and there, unexpectedly arrives at his father's house. Standing by the gate, he sees from afar his father seated on a jeweled footstool, revered and surrounded by brahmanas, kshatriyas, and citizens, and with strings of pearls, worth thousands and myriads, adorning his body; attendants and young slaves with white chowries wait upon him right and left; he is covered by a rich canopy from which hang streamers of flowers; perfume is sprinkled on the earth, all kinds of famous flowers are scattered around, and precious things are placed in rows for his acceptance or rejection. Such is his glory, and the honor of his dignity. The poor son, seeing his father possessed of such great power, is seized with fear, regretting that he has come to this place, and secretly reflects thus: "This must be a king, or some one of royal rank; it is no place for me to obtain anything for the hire of my labor. I had better go to some poor hamlet, where there is a place for letting out my labor, and food and clothing are easier to get. If I tarry here long, I may suffer oppression and forced service."

Having reflected thus, he hastens away. Meanwhile, the rich elder on his lion-seat has recognized his son at first sight, and with great joy in his heart has also reflected: "Now I have some one to whom my treasures of wealth are to be made over. Always have I been thinking of this my son, with no means of seeing him; but suddenly he himself has come and my longing is satisfied. Though worn with years, I yearn for him as of old."

Instantly he dispatches his attendants to pursue him quickly and fetch him back. Thereupon the messengers hasten forth to seize him. The poor son, surprised and scared, loudly cries his complaint: "I have committed no offense against you; why should I be arrested?" The messengers all the more hasten to lay hold of him and compel him to go back. Thereupon, the poor son, thinking within himself that though he is innocent yet he will be imprisoned, and that now he will surely die, is all the more terrified; he faints away and falls prostrate on the ground. The father, seeing this from afar, sends word to the messengers: "I have no need for this man. Do not bring him by force. Sprinkle cold water on his face to restore him to consciousness and do not speak to him any further." Wherefore? The father, knowing that his son's disposition is inferior, knowing that his own lordly position has caused distress to his son, yet convinced that he is his son, tactfully does not say to others: "This is my son."

A messenger says to the son: "I now set you free; go wherever you will." The poor son is delighted, thus obtaining the unexpected. He rises from the ground and goes to a poor hamlet in search of food and clothing. Then the elder, desiring to attract his son, sets up a device. Secretly he sends two men, doleful and shabby in appearance, saying—"You go and visit that place and gently say to the poor man—'There is a place for you to work here: you will be given double wages.' If the poor man agrees, bring him back and give him work. If he asks what work you wish him to do, then you may say to him—'We will hire you for scavenging, and we both also will work along with you.' " Then the two messengers go in search of the poor son and, having found him, place before him the above proposal. Thereupon the poor son, having received his wages beforehand, joins with them in removing a dirt-heap.

His father, beholding the son, is struck with compassion for, and wonder at, him. Another day he sees at a distance, through a window, his son's figure, gaunt, lean, and doleful, filthy and unclean with dirt and dust; thereupon he takes off his strings of jewels, his soft attire, and ornaments, and puts on a coarse, torn, and dirty garment, smears his body with dust, takes a dust-hod in his right hand, and with an appearance fear-inspiring says to the laborers: "Get on with your work, don't be lazy." By such a device he gets near to his son, to whom he afterwards says: "Aye, my man, you stay and work here, do not go again elsewhere; I will increase your wages; give whatever you need, bowls, utensils, rice, wheat-flour, salt, vinegar, and so on; have no hesitation; besides, there is an old and worn-out servant whom you shall be given if you need him. Be at ease in your mind; I am, as it were, your father; do not be worried again. Wherefore? I am old and advanced in years, but you are young and vigorous; all the time you have been working, you have never been deceitful, lazy, angry or grumbling; I have never seen you, like the other laborers, with such vices as these. From this time forth you shall be as my own begotten son."

Thereupon the elder gives him a new name and calls him a son. The poor son, though he rejoices at this happening, still thinks of himself as a humble hireling. For this reason, during twenty years he continues to be employed in scavenging. After this period, there grows mutual confidence between them, and he goes in and out and is at his ease, though his abode is still the original place.

World-honored One! Then the elder becomes ill and, knowing that he will die before long, says to the poor son: "Now I possess abundance of gold, silver, and precious things, and my granaries and treasuries are full to overflowing. The quantities of these things, and the amounts which should be received and given, I want you to understand in detail. Such is my mind, and you must agree to this my wish. Wherefore? Because, now, I and you are of the same mind. Be increasingly careful so that there be no waste."

The poor son accepts his instruction and commands, and becomes acquainted with all the goods, gold, silver, and precious things, as well as all the granaries and treasuries, but has no idea of expecting to inherit so much as a meal, while his abode is still the original place and he is yet unable to abandon his sense of inferiority.

After a short time has again passed, the father, knowing that his son's ideas have gradually been enlarged, his aspirations developed, and that he despises his previous state of mind, on seeing that his own end is approaching, commands his son to come, and gathers together his relatives, and the kings, ministers, kshatriyas, and citizens. When they are all assembled, he thereupon addresses them saying: "Now, gentlemen, this is my son, begotten by me. It is over fifty years since, from a certain city, he left me and ran away to endure loneliness and misery. His former name was so-and-so and my name was so-and-so. At that time in that city I sought him sorrowfully. Suddenly in this place I met and regained him. This is really my son and I am really his father. Now all the wealth which I possess entirely belongs to my son, and all my previous disbursements and receipts are known by this son."

World-honored One! When the poor son heard these words of his father, great was his joy at such unexpected news, and thus he thought: "Without any mind for, or effort on my part, these treasures now come of themselves to me."

THOMAS MERTON

hagia sophia

There is in all visible things an invisible fecundity, a dimmed light, a meek namelessness, a hidden wholeness. This mysterious Unity and Integrity is Wisdom, the Mother of all, *Natura naturans.* There is in all things an inexhaustible sweetness and purity, a silence that is a fount of action and joy. It rises up in wordless gentleness and flows out to me from the unseen roots of all created being, welcoming me tenderly, saluting me with indescribable humility. This is at once my own being, my own nature, and the Gift of my Creator's Thought and Art within me, speaking as Hagia Sophia, speaking as my sister, Wisdom.

ST. JOHN OF THE CROSS

possessing everything and nothing

In order to arrive at having pleasure in everything,
Desire to have pleasure in nothing.
In order to arrive at possessing everything,
Desire to possess nothing.
In order to arrive at being everything,
Desire to be nothing.
In order to arrive at knowing everything,
Desire to know nothing.
In order to arrive at that wherein thou hast no pleasure,

Thou must go by a way wherein thou hast no pleasure.
　　In order to arrive at that which thou knowest not,
Thou must go by a way that thou knowest not.
　　In order to arrive at that which thou possessest not,
Thou must go by a way that thou possessest not.
　　In order to arrive at that which thou art not,
Thou must go through that which thou art not.

　　When thy mind dwells upon anything,
Thou art ceasing to cast thyself upon the All.
　　For, in order to pass from the all to the All,
Thou hast to deny thyself wholly in all.
　　And, when thou comest to possess it wholly,
Thou must possess it without desiring anything.
　　For, if thou wilt have anything in having all,
Thou hast not thy treasure purely in God.

SÖREN KIERKEGAARD

the knight of infinite resignation and the knight of faith ──────────

We read in those holy books: "And God tempted Abraham, and said unto him, Abraham, Abraham, where art thou? And he said, Here am I." Thou to whom my speech is addressed, was such the case with thee? When afar off thou didst see the heavy dispensation of providence approaching thee, didst thou not say to the mountains, Fall on me, and to the hills, Cover me? Or if thou wast stronger, did not thy foot move slowly along the way, longing as it were for the old path? When a call was issued to thee, didst thou answer, or didst thou not answer perhaps in a low voice, whisperingly? Not so Abraham: joyfully, buoyantly, confidently, with a loud voice, he answered, "Here am I." We read further: "And Abraham rose early in the morning"—as though it were to a festival, so he hastened, and early in the morning he had come to the place spoken of, to Mount Moriah. He said nothing to Sarah, nothing to Eleazar. Indeed who could understand him? Had not the temptation by its very nature exacted of him an oath of silence? He cleft the wood, he bound Isaac, he lit the pyre, he drew the knife. My hearer, there was many a father who believed that with his son he lost everything that was dearest to him in the world, that he was deprived of every hope for the future, but yet there was none that was the child of promise in the sense that Isaac was for Abraham. There was many a father who lost his child; but

From Sören Kierkegaard, *Fear and Trembling and The Sickness Unto Death*, trans. with an Introduction and Notes by Walter Lowrie (copyright 1941, 1954 by Princeton University Press; Princeton Paperback, 1968). Reprinted by permission of Princeton University Press.

then it was God, it was the unalterable, the unsearchable will of the Almighty, it was His hand took the child. Not so with Abraham. For him was reserved a harder trial, and Isaac's fate was laid along with the knife in Abraham's hand. And there he stood, the old man, with his only hope! But he did not doubt, he did not look anxiously to the right or to the left, he did not challenge heaven with his prayers. He knew that it was God the Almighty who was trying him, he knew that it was the hardest sacrifice that could be required of him; but he knew also that no sacrifice was too hard when God required it—and he drew the knife.

But what did Abraham do? He arrived neither too soon nor too late. He mounted the ass, he rode slowly along the way. All that time he believed—he believed that God would not require Isaac of him, whereas he was willing nevertheless to sacrifice him if it was required. He believed by virtue of the absurd; for there could be no question of human calculation, and it was indeed the absurd that God who required it of him should the next instant recall the requirement. He climbed the mountain, even at the instant when the knife glittered he believed . . . that God would not require Isaac. He was indeed astonished at the outcome, but by a double-movement he had reached his first position, and therefore he received Isaac more gladly than the first time. Let us go further. We let Isaac be really sacrificed. Abraham believed. He did not believe that some day he would be blessed in the beyond, but that he would be happy here in the world. God could give him a new Isaac, could recall to life him who had been sacrificed. He believed by virtue of the absurd; for all human reckoning had long since ceased to function. That sorrow can derange a man's mind, that we see, and it is sad enough. That there is such a thing as strength of will which is able to haul up so exceedingly close to the wind that it saves a man's reason, even though he remains a little queer, that too one sees. I have no intention of disparaging this; but to be able to lose one's reason, and therefore the whole of finiteness of which reason is the broker, and then by virtue of the absurd to gain precisely the same finiteness—that appalls my soul, but I do not for this cause say that it is something lowly, since on the contrary it is the only prodigy.

Upon this pinnacle stands Abraham. The last stage he loses sight of is the infinite resignation. He really goes further, and reaches faith.

· · ·

The knights of the infinite resignation are easily recognized: their gait is gliding and assured. Those on the other hand who carry the jewel of faith are likely to be delusive, because their outward appearance bears a striking resemblance to that which both the infinite resignation and faith profoundly despise . . . to Philistinism.

I candidly admit that in my practice I have not found any reliable example of the knight of faith, though I would not therefore deny that every second man may be such an example. I have been trying, however, for several years to get on the track of this, and all in vain. People commonly travel around the world to see rivers and mountains, new stars, birds of rare plumage, queerly deformed fishes, ridiculous breeds of men—they abandon themselves to the bestial stupor which gapes at existence, and they think they have seen something. This does not interest me. But if I knew where there was such a knight of faith, I would make a pilgrimage to him on foot, for this prodigy interests me absolutely. I would not let go of him for an instant, every moment I would watch to see how he managed to make the movements, I would regard myself as secured for life, and would divide my time between looking at him and practicing the exercises myself, and thus would spend all my time admiring him. As was said, I have not found any such person, but I can well think him. Here he is. Acquaintance made, I am introduced to him. The moment I set eyes on him I instantly push him from me, I myself leap backwards, I clasp my hands and say half aloud, "Good Lord, is this the man? Is it really he? Why, he looks like a tax-collector!" However, it is the man after all. I draw closer to him, watching his least movements to see whether there might not be visible a little heterogeneous fractional telegraphic message from the infinite, a glance, a look, a gesture, a note of sadness, a smile, which betrayed the infinite in its heterogeneity with the finite. No! I examine his figure from tip to toe to see if there might not be a cranny through which the infinite was peeping. No! He is solid through and through. His tread? It is vigorous, belonging entirely to finiteness; no smartly dressed townsman who walks out to Fresberg on a Sunday afternoon treads the ground more firmly, he belongs entirely to the world, no Philistine more so. One can discover nothing of that aloof and superior nature whereby one recognizes the knight of the infinite. He takes delight in everything, and whenever one sees him taking part in a particular pleasure, he does it with the persistence which is the mark of the earthly man whose soul is absorbed in such things. He tends to his work. So when one looks at him one might suppose that he was a clerk who had lost his soul in an intricate system of bookkeeping, so precise is he. He takes a holiday on Sunday. He goes to church. No heavenly glance or any other token of the incommensurable betrays him; if one did not know him, it would be impossible to distinguish him from the rest of the congregation, for his healthy and vigorous hymn-singing proves at the most that he has a good chest. In the afternoon he walks to the forest. He takes delight in everything he sees, in the human swarm, in the new omnibuses, in the water of the Sound; when one meets him on the Beach Road one might suppose he was a shopkeeper taking his fling, that's just the way he disports himself, for he is not a poet, and I have sought in vain to detect in him the poetic incommensurability. Toward evening he walks home, his gait is as indefatigable as that of the postman. On his way he reflects that his wife has surely a special little warm dish prepared for him, e.g., a calf's head roasted, garnished with vegetables. If he were to meet a man like-minded, he could continue as far as East Gate to discourse with him about that dish, with a passion befitting a hotel chef. As it happens, he hasn't four pence to his name, and yet he fully and firmly believes that his wife has that dainty dish for him. If she had it, it would then be an invidious sight for superior people and an inspiring one for the plain man, to see him eat; for his appetite is greater than Esau's. His wife hasn't it—strangely enough, it is quite the same to him.

. . .

In the evening he smokes his pipe; to look at him one would swear that it was the grocer over the way vegetating in the twilight. He lives as carefree as a ne'er-do-well, and yet he buys up the acceptable time at the dearest price, for he does not do the least thing except by virtue of the absurd. And yet, and yet—actually I could become furious over it, for envy if for no other reason—this man has made and every instant is making the movements of infinity. With infinite resignation he has drained the cup of life's profound sadness, he knows the bliss of the infinite, he senses the pain of renouncing everything, the dearest things he possesses in the world, and yet finiteness tastes to him just as good as to one who never knew anything higher, for his continuance in the finite did not bear a trace of the cowed and fearful spirit produced by the process of training; and yet he has this sense of security in enjoying it, as though the finite life were the surest thing of all. And yet, and yet the whole earthly form he exhibits is a new creation by virtue of the absurd. He resigned everything infinitely, and then he grasped everything again by virtue of the absurd. He constantly makes the movements of infinity, but he does this with such correctness and assurance that he constantly gets the finite out of it, and there is not a second when one has a notion of anything else. It is supposed to be the most difficult task for a dancer to leap into a definite posture in such a way that there is not a second when he is grasping after the posture, but by the leap itself he stands fixed in that posture. Perhaps no dancer can do it—that is what this knight does. Most people live dejectedly in worldly sorrow and joy; they are the ones who sit along the wall and do not join in the dance. The knights of infinity are dancers and possess elevation. They make the movements upward, and fall down again; and this too is no mean pastime, nor ungraceful to behold. But whenever they fall down they are not able at once to assume the posture, they vacillate an instant, and this vacillation shows that after all they are strangers in the world. This is more or less strikingly evident in proportion to the art they possess, but even the most artistic knights cannot altogether conceal this vacillation. One need not look at them when they are up in the air, but only the instant they touch or have touched the ground—then one recognizes them. But to be able to fall down in such a way that the same second it looks as if one were standing and walking, to transform the leap of life into a walk, absolutely to express the sublime in the pedestrian—that only the knight of faith can do—and this is the one and only prodigy.

. . .

In the infinite resignation there is peace and rest; every man who wills it, who has not abased himself by scorning himself (which is still more dreadful than being proud), can train himself to make this movement which in its pain reconciles one with existence. Infinite resignation is that shirt we read about in the old fable. The thread is spun under tears, the cloth bleached with tears, the shirt sewn with tears; but then too it is a better protection than iron and steel. The imperfection in the fable is that a third party can manufacture this shirt. The secret in life is that everyone must sew it for himself, and the astonishing thing is that a man can sew it fully as well as a woman. In the infinite resignation there is peace and rest and comfort in sorrow—that is, if the movement is made normally. It would not be difficult for me, however, to write a whole book, were I to examine the various misunderstandings, the preposterous attitudes, the deceptive movements, which I have encountered in my brief practice. People believe very little in spirit, and yet making this movement depends upon spirit, it depends upon whether this is or is not a one-sided result of a *dira necessitas,* and if this is present, the more dubious it always is whether the movement is normal. If one means by this that the cold, unfruitful necessity must necessarily be present, one thereby affirms that no one can experience death before he actually dies, and that appears to me a crass materialism. However, in our time people concern themselves rather little about making pure movements. In case one who was about to learn to dance were to say, "For centuries now one generation after another has been learning positions, it is high time I drew some advantage out of this and began straightway with the French dances"—then people would laugh at him; but in the world of spirit they find this exceedingly plausible. What is education? I should suppose that education was the curriculum one had to run through in order to catch up with oneself, and he who will not pass through this curriculum is helped very little by the fact that he was born in the most enlightened age.

The infinite resignation is the last stage prior to faith, so that one who has not made this movement has not faith; for only in the infinite resignation do I become clear to myself with respect to my eternal validity, and only then can there be any question of grasping existence by virtue of faith.

Now we will let the knight of faith appear in the rôle just described. He makes exactly the same movements as the other knight, infinitely renounces claim to the love which is the content of his life, he is reconciled in pain; but then occurs the prodigy, he makes still another movement more wonderful than all, for he says, "I believe nevertheless that I shall get her, in virtue, that is, of the absurd, in virtue of the fact that with God all things are possible."

.   .   .

The movements are frequently confounded, for it is said that one needs faith to renounce the claim to everything, yea, a stranger thing than this may be heard, when a man laments the loss of his faith, and when one looks at the scale to see where he is, one sees, strangely enough, that he has only reached the point where he should make the infinite movement of resignation. In resignation I make renunciation of everything, this movement I make by myself, and if I do not make it, it is because I am cowardly and effeminate and without enthusiasm and do not feel the significance of the lofty dignity which is assigned to every man, that of being his own censor, which is a far prouder title than that of Censor General to the whole Roman Republic. This movement I make by myself, and what I gain is myself in my eternal consciousness, in blissful agreement with my love for the Eternal Being. By faith I make renunciation of nothing, on the contrary, by faith I acquire everything, precisely in the sense in which it is said that he who has faith like a grain of mustard can remove mountains. A purely human courage is required to renounce the whole of the temporal to gain the eternal; but this I gain, and to all eternity I cannot renounce it—that is a self-contradiction. But a paradoxical and humble courage is required to grasp the whole of the temporal by virtue of the absurd, and this is the courage of faith. By faith Abraham did not renounce his claim upon Isaac, but by faith he got Isaac.

ALBERT CAMUS

on becoming a man _____

As November drew to a close, the mornings turned much colder. Heavy downpours had scoured the streets and washed the sky clean of clouds. In the mornings a weak sunlight bathed the town in a cold, sparkling sheen. The air warmed up, however, as night approached. It was such a night that Tarrou chose for telling something of himself to Dr. Rieux.

• • •

"A pleasant spot," said Rieux as he lowered himself into a chair. "You'd think that plague had never found its way up here."

Tarrou was gazing seawards, his back to the doctor.

"Yes," he replied after a moment's silence, "it's good to be here."

Then, settling into the chair beside Rieux, he fixed his eyes on his face. Three times the glow spread up the sky and died **away**. A faint clatter of crockery rose from a room opening on the street below. A door banged somewhere in the house.

"Rieux," Tarrou said in a quite ordinary tone, "do you realize that you've never tried to find out anything about me—the man I am? Can I regard you as a friend?"

"Yes, of course, we're friends; only so far we haven't had much time to show it."

"Good. That gives me confidence. Suppose we now take an hour off—for friendship?"

Rieux smiled by way of answer.

"Well, here goes!"

"I've had to dwell on my start in life, since for me it really was the start of everything. I'll get on more quickly now. I came to grips with poverty when I

From *The Plague*, trans. Stuart Gilbert, New York, Modern Library, 1948.

was eighteen, after an easy life till then. I tried all sorts of jobs, and I didn't do too badly. But my real interest in life was the death penalty; I wanted to square accounts with that poor blind owl in the dock. So I became an agitator, as they say. I didn't want to be pestiferous, that's all. To my mind the social order around me was based on the death sentence, and by fighting the established order I'd be fighting against murder. That was my view, others had told me so, and I still think that this belief of mine was substantially true. I joined forces with a group of people I then liked, and indeed have never ceased to like. I spent many years in close cooperation with them, and there's not a country in Europe in whose struggles I haven't played a part. But that's another story.

"Needless to say, I knew that we, too, on occasion, passed sentences of death. But I was told that these few deaths were inevitable for the building up of a new world in which murder would cease to be. That also was true up to a point—and maybe I'm not capable of standing fast where that order of truths is concerned. Whatever the explanation, I hesitated. But then I remembered that miserable owl in the dock and it enabled me to keep on. Until the day when I was present at an execution—it was in Hungary—and exactly the same dazed horror that I'd experienced as a youngster made everything reel before my eyes.

"Have you ever seen a man shot by a firing-squad? No, of course not; the spectators are hand-picked and it's like a private party, you need an invitation. The result is that you've gleaned your ideas about it from books and pictures. A post, a blindfolded man, some soldiers in the offing. But the real thing isn't a bit like that. Do you know that the firing-squad stands only a yard and a half from the condemned man? Do you know that if the victim took two steps forward his chest would touch the rifles? Do you know that, at this short range, the soldiers concentrate their fire on the region of the heart and their big bullets make a hole into which you could thrust your fist? No, you didn't know all that; those are things that are never spoken of. For the plague-stricken their peace of mind is more important than a human life. Decent folks must be allowed to sleep easy o' nights, mustn't they? Really it would be shockingly bad taste to linger on such details, that's common knowledge. But personally I've never been able to sleep well since then. The bad taste remained in my mouth and I've kept lingering on the details, brooding over them.

"And thus I came to understand that I, anyhow, had had plague through all those long years in which, paradoxically enough, I'd believed with all my soul that I was fighting it. I learned that I had had an indirect hand in the deaths of thousands of people; that I'd even brought about their deaths by approving of acts and principles which could only end that way. Others did not seem embarrassed by such thoughts, or anyhow never voiced them of their own accord. But I was different; what I'd come to know stuck in my gorge. I was with them and yet I was alone. When I spoke of these matters they told me not to be so squeamish; I should remember what great issues were at stake. And they advanced arguments, often quite impressive ones, to make me swallow what none the less I couldn't bring myself to stomach. I replied that the most eminent of the plague-stricken, the men who wear red robes, also have excellent arguments to justify what they do, and once I admitted the arguments of necessity and *force majeure* put forward by the less eminent, I couldn't reject those of the eminent. To which they retorted that the surest way of playing the game of the red robes was to leave to them the monopoly of the death penalty. My reply to this was that if you gave in once, there was no reason for not continuing to give in. It seems to me that history has borne me out; today there's a sort of competition who will kill the most. They're all mad over murder and they couldn't stop killing men even if they wanted to.

"In any case, my concern was not with arguments. It was with the poor owl; with that foul procedure whereby dirty mouths stinking of plague told a fettered man that he was going to die, and scientifically arranged things so that he should die, after nights and nights of mental torture while he waited to be murdered in cold blood. My concern was with that hole in a man's chest. And I told myself that meanwhile, so far anyhow as I was concerned, nothing in the world would induce me to accept any argument that justified such butcheries. Yes, I chose to be blindly obstinate, pending the day when I could see my way more clearly.

"I'm still of the same mind. For many years I've been ashamed, mortally ashamed, of having been, even with the best intentions, even at many removes, a murderer in my turn. As time went on I merely learned that even those who were better than the rest could not keep themselves nowadays from killing or letting others kill, because such is the logic by which they live; and that we can't stir a finger in this world without the risk of bringing death to somebody. Yes, I've been ashamed ever since; I have realized that we all have plague, and I have lost my peace. And today I am still trying to find it; still trying to understand all those others and not to be the mortal enemy of anyone. I only know that one must do what one can to cease being plague-stricken, and that's the only way in which we can hope for some peace or, failing that, a decent death. This, and only this, can bring relief to men and, if not save them, at least do them the least harm possible and even, sometimes, a little good. So that is why I resolved to have no truck with anything which, directly or indirectly, for good reasons or for bad, brings death to anyone or justifies others' putting him to death.

"That, too, is why this epidemic has taught me nothing new, except that I must fight it at your side. I know positively—yes, Rieux, I can say I know the world inside out, as you may see—that each of us has the plague within him; no one, no one on earth is free from it. And I know, too, that we must keep endless watch on ourselves lest in a careless moment we breathe in somebody's face and fasten the infection on him. What's natural is the microbe. All the rest—health, integrity, purity (if you like)—is a product of the human will, of a vigilance that must never falter. The good man, the man who infects hardly anyone, is the man who has the fewest lapses of attention. And it needs tremendous will-power, a never ending tension of the mind, to avoid such lapses. Yes, Rieux, it's a wearying business, being plague-stricken. But it's still more wearying to refuse to be it. That's why everybody in the world today looks so tired; everyone is more or less sick of plague. But that is also why some of us, those who want to get the plague out of their systems, feel such desperate weariness, a weariness from which nothing remains to set us free except death.

"Pending that release, I know I have no place in the world of today; once I'd definitely refused to kill, I doomed myself to an exile that can never end. I leave it to others to make history. I know, too, that I'm not qualified to pass judgment on those others. There's something lacking in my mental make-up, and its lack prevents me from being a rational murderer. So it's a deficiency, not a superiority. But as things are, I'm willing to be as I am; I've learned modesty. All I maintain is that on this earth there are pestilences and there are victims, and it's up to us, so far as possible, not to join forces with the pestilences. That may sound simple to the point of childishness; I can't judge if it's simple, but I know it's true. You see, I'd heard such quantities of arguments, which very nearly turned my head, and turned other people's heads enough to make them approve of murder; and I'd come to realize that all our troubles spring from our failure to use plain, clean-cut language. So I resolved always to speak—and to act—quite clearly, as this was the only way of setting myself on the right track. That's why I say there are pestilences and there are victims; no more than that. If, by making that statement, I, too, become a carrier of the plague-germ, at least I don't do it willfully. I try, in short, to be an innocent murderer. You see, I've no great ambitions.

"I grant we should add a third category: that of the true healers. But it's a fact one doesn't come across many of them, and anyhow it must be a hard vocation. That's why I decided to take, in every predicament, the victims' side, so as to reduce the damage done. Among them I can at least try to discover how one attains to the third category; in other words, to peace."

Tarrou was swinging his leg, tapping the terrace lightly with his heel, as he concluded. After a short silence the doctor raised himself a little in his chair and asked if Tarrou had an idea of the path to follow for attaining peace.

"Yes," he replied. "The path of sympathy."

Two ambulances were clanging in the distance. The dispersed shouts they had been hearing off and on drew together on the outskirts of the town, near the stony hill, and presently there was a sound like a gunshot. Then silence fell again. Rieux counted two flashes of the revolving light. The breeze freshened and a gust coming from the sea filled the air for a moment with the smell of brine. And at the same time they clearly heard the low sound of waves lapping the foot of the cliffs.

"It comes to this," Tarrou said almost casually; "what interests me is learning how to become a saint."

"But you don't believe in God."

"Exactly! Can one be a saint without God?—that's the problem, in fact the only problem, I'm up against today."

A sudden blaze sprang up above the place the shouts had come from and, stemming the wind-stream, a rumor of many voices came to their ears. The blaze died down almost at once, leaving behind it only a dull red glow. Then in a break of the wind they distinctly heard some strident yells and the discharge of a gun, followed by the roar of an angry crowd. Tarrou stood up and listened, but nothing more could be heard.

"Another skirmish at the gates, I suppose."

"Well, it's over now," Rieux said.

Tarrou said in a low voice that it was never over, and there would be more victims, because that was in the order of things.

"Perhaps," the doctor answered. "But, you know, I feel more fellowship with the defeated than with saints. Heroism and sanctity don't really appeal to me, I imagine. What interests me is being a man."

"Yes, we're both after the same thing, but I'm less ambitious."

Rieux supposed Tarrou was jesting and turned to him with a smile. But, faintly lit by the dim radiance falling from the sky, the face he saw was sad and earnest. There was another gust of wind and Rieux felt it warm on his skin. Tarrou gave himself a little shade.

"Do you know," he said, "what we now should do for friendship's sake?"

"Anything you like, Tarrou."

"Go for a swim. It's one of these harmless pleasures that even a saint-to-be can indulge in, don't you agree?" Rieux smiled again, and Tarrou continued: "With our passes, we can get out on the pier. Really, it's too damn silly living only in and for the plague. Of course, a man should fight for the victims, but if he ceases caring for anything outside that, what's the use of his fighting?"

"Right," Rieux said. "Let's go."

. . .

Once they were on the pier they saw the sea spread out before them, a gently heaving expanse of deep-piled velvet, supple and sleek as a creature of the wild. They sat down on a boulder facing the open. Slowly the waters rose and sank, and with their tranquil breathing sudden oily glints formed and flickered over the surface in a haze of broken lights. Before them the darkness stretched out into infinity. Rieux could feel under his hand the gnarled, weather-worn visage of the rocks, and a strange happiness possessed him. Turning to Tarrou, he caught a glimpse on his friend's face of the same happiness, a happiness that forgot nothing, not even murder.

ROBERT FARRAR CAPON

the supper of the lamb _____

the first session

Let me concede a point to the reader. You no doubt feel that, whatever else may be forthcoming in this book, I owe you at least an attempt to make good on the obviously pretentious and apparently ordinary recipe with which I began. You are right; I intend to address myself to it immediately. I must ask, however, that you permit me to do it at my own rate. These things take time.

For the moment, therefore, set aside the leg of lamb. If you are a hardy soul, and do not mind getting cold fingers cutting up meat, return it to the refrigerator; alternatively, if comfort is a consideration with you, let it warm up a bit on the kitchen counter. In any case, we do not need it yet. I must teach you first how to deal with onions.

Select three or four medium-size onions—I have in mind the common, or yellow, onion normally available in the supermarket. The first movement (IA) of my recipe is simply a stew; small white onions, while more delicate as a vegetable in their own right, are a nuisance to cut up for inclusion in something else. The labor of peeling is enlarged beyond reason, and the attempt to slice up the small slippery balls you are left with can be painful.

Next take one of the onions (preferably the best-looking), a paring knife, and a cutting board and sit down at the kitchen table. Do not attempt to stand at a counter through these opening measures. In fact, to do it justice, you should arrange to have sixty minutes or so free for this part of the exercise. Admittedly, spending an hour in the society of an onion may be something you have never done before. You feel, perhaps, a certain resistance to the project. Please don't. As I shall show later, a number of highly profitable members of the race have undertaken it before you. Onions are excellent company.

Once you are seated, the first order of business is to address yourself to the onion at hand. (You must firmly resist the temptation to feel silly. If necessary, close the doors so no one will see you; but do not give up out of embarrassment.) You will note, to begin with, that the onion is a *thing*, a being, just as you are. Savor that for a moment. The two of you sit here in mutual confrontation. Together with knife, board, table, and chair, you are the constituents of a *place* in the highest sense of the word. This is a *Session*, a meeting, a society of things.

You have, you see, already discovered something: The uniqueness, the *placiness,* of places derives not from abstractions like *location,* but from confrontations like man-onion. Erring theologians have strayed to their graves without learning what you have come upon. They have insisted, for example, that heaven is no place because it could not be defined in terms of spatial coordinates. They have written off man's eternal habitation as a "state of mind." But look what your onion has done for you: It has given you back the possibility of heaven as a place without encumbering you with the irrelevancy of location.

This meeting between the two of you could be moved to a thousand different latitudes and longitudes and still remain the *session* it started out to be. Indeed, by the motions of the earth, the solar system, the galaxy, and the universe (if that can be defined), every place—every meeting of matter—becomes a kind of cosmic floating crap game: Location is accidental to its deepest meaning. What really matters is not where we are, but who—what real beings—are with us. In that sense, heaven, where we see God face to face through the risen flesh of Jesus, may well be the placiest of all places, as it is the most *gloriously* material of all meetings. Here, perhaps, we do indeed see only through a glass darkly; we mistake one of the earthly husks of place for the heart of its mattering.

But back to the onion itself. As nearly as possible now, try to look at it as if you have never seen an onion before. Try, in other words, to meet it on its own terms, not to dictate yours to it. You are convinced, of course, that you know what an onion is. You think perhaps that it is a brownish yellow vegetable, basically spherical in shape, composed of fundamentally similar layers. All such prejudices should be abandoned. It is what it is, and your work here is to find it out.

For a start, therefore, notice that your onion has two ends: a lower, now marked only by the blackish gray spot from which the root filaments descended into the earth; and an upper, which terminates (unless your onions are over the hill, or have begun to sprout because you store them under a leaky sink trap) in a withered peak of onion paper. Note once again what you have discovered: an onion is not a sphere in repose. It is a linear thing, a bloom of vectors thrusting upward from base to tip. Stand your onion, therefore, root end down upon the board and see it as the paradigm of life that it is—as one member of the vast living, gravity-defying troop that, across the face of the earth, moves light- and airward as long as the world lasts.

Only now have you the perspective needed to enter the onion itself. Begin with the outermost layer of paper, or onion skin. Be careful. In the ordinary processes of cooking, the outer skin of a sound onion is removed by peeling away the immediately underlying layers of flesh with it. It is a legitimate short cut; the working cook cannot afford the time it takes to loosen only the paper. Here, however, it is not time that matters, but the onion. Work gently then, lifting the skin with the point of your knife so as not to cut or puncture the flesh beneath. It is harder than you may have thought. Old onion skins give up easily, but new ones can be stubborn.

Look now at the fall of stripped and flakèd skin before you. It is dry. It is, all things considered, one of the driest things in the world. Not dusty dry like potatoes, but smoothly and thinly dry, suggesting not accidental desiccation, not the withering due to age or external circumstance, but a fresh and essential dryness.

Dryness as an achievement, not as a failure. Elegant dryness. Deliberate dryness. More than that, onion paper is, like the onion itself, directional, vectored, ribbed. (It will, oddly, split as easily across its striations as with them: Its grain has been reduced by dryness to a merely visual quality.) Best of all, though, it is of two colors: the outside, a brownish yellow of no particular brightness; but the inside a soft, burnished, coppery gold, ribbed—especially near the upper end— with an exquisiteness only hinted at on the outside. Accordingly, when you have removed all the paper, turn the fragments inside-up on the board. They are elegant company.

For with their understated display of wealth, they bring you to one of the oldest and most secret things of the world: the sight of what no one but you has ever seen. This quiet gold, and the subtly flattened sheen of greenish yellow white onion that now stands exposed, are virgin land. Like the incredible fit of twin almonds in a shell, they present themselves to you as the animals to Adam: as nameless till seen by man, to be met, known and christened into the city of being. They come as deputies of all the hiddennesses of the world, of all the silent competencies endlessly at work deep down in things. And they come to *you*— to you as their priest and voice, for oblation by your heart's astonishment at their great glory.

Only now are you ready for the first cut. Holding the onion vertically, slice it cleanly in half right down the center line, and look at what you have done. You have opened the floodgates of being. First, as to the innards. The mental diagram of sphere within sphere is abolished immediately. *Structurally,* the onion is not a ball, but a nested set of fingers within fingers, each thrust up from the base through the center of the one before it. The outer digits are indeed swollen to roundness by the pressure of the inner, but their sphericity is incidental to the linear motion of flame inthrusting flame.

Next, the colors. The cross-section of each several flame follows a rule: On its inner edge it is white, on its outer, pigmented; the color varying from the palest greenish yellow in the middle flames, to more recognizably onion shades as you proceed outward. The centermost flames of all are frankly and startlingly green; it is they which will finally thrust upward into light. Thus the spectrum of the onion: green through white to green again, and ending all in the brown skin you have peeled away. Life inside death. The forces of being storming the walls of the void. Freshness in the face of the burning, oxidizing world which maderizes all life at last to the color of cut apples and old sherry.

Next, pressure. Look at the cut surface: moisture. The incredible, utter wetness of onions, of course, you cannot know yet: This is only the first hinted pressing of juice. But the sea within all life has tipped its hand. You have cut open no inanimate thing, but a living tumescent being—a whole that is, as all life is, smaller, simpler than its parts; which holds, as all life does, the pieces of its being in compression. To prove it, try to fit the two halves of the onion back together. It cannot be done. The faces which began as two plane surfaces drawn by a straight blade are now mutually convex, and rock against each other. Put them together on one side and the opposite shows a gap of more than two minutes on a clock face.

Again, pressure. But now pressure toward you. The smell of onion, released by the flowing of its juices. Hardly a discovery, of course—even the boor knows his onions to that degree. But pause still. Reflect how little smell there is to a whole onion—how well the noble reek was contained till now by the encompassing dryness. Reflect, too, how it is the humors and sauces of being that give the world flavor, how all life came from the sea, and how, without water, nothing can hold a soul. Reflect finally what a soul the onion must have, if it boasts such juices. Your eyes will not yet have begun to water, nor the membranes of your nose to recoil. The onion has only, if you will, *whispered* to you. Yet you have not mistaken a syllable of its voice, not strained after a single word. How will you stop your senses when it raises this stage whisper to a shout?

Now, however, the two halves of the onion lie, cut face up, before you. With the point of your paring knife, carefully remove the base, or bottom (or heart) much as you would do to free the leaves of an artichoke or of a head of lettuce. Take away only as much as will make it possible to lift out, one by one, the several layers. Then gently pry them out in order, working from the center to the outside. Arrange them in a line as you do, with matching parts from the separate halves laid next to each other, making them ascend thus by twos from the smallest green fingers, through white flames, up to the outer shells which sit like paired Russian church spires.

Then look. The myth of sphericity is finally dead. The onion, as now displayed, is plainly all vectors, rissers and thrusts. *Tongues of fire.* But the pentecost they mark is that of nature, not grace: the Spirit's first brooding on the face of the waters. Lift one of the flames; feel its lightness and rigidity, its crispness and strength. Make proof of its membranes. The inner: thin, translucent, easily removed; the outer, however, thinner, almost transparent—and so tightly bonded to the flesh that it protests audibly against separation. (You will probably have to break the flesh to free even a small piece.) The membranes, when in place, give the onion its fire, its sheen, soft within and brighter without. But when they are removed, the flesh is revealed in a new light. Given a minute to dry, it acquires a pale crystalline flatness like nothing on earth. Eggshell is the only word for it; but by comparison to the stripped flesh of an onion, an eggshell is only as delicate as poured concrete.

Set aside your broken flame now and pick up a fresh one. Clear a little space on the board. Lay it down on its cut face and slice it lengthwise into several strips. (You will want to tap it lightly with the edge of the knife first. There is a hollow crisp sound to be gotten that way—something between a *tock* and a *tunk*. It is the sound of health and youth, the audible response of cellularity when it is properly addressed. Neither solid nor soft, it is the voice of life itself.)

Next take one of the slivers and press it. Here you will need firmness. If you have strong nails, use the back of the one on your middle finger; if not, steamroller the slice with a round pencil. Press and roll it until it yields all the water it will. You have reached the deepest revelation of all.

First, and obviously, the onion is now part of you. It will be for days. For the next two mornings at least, when you wash your hands and face, your meeting with it will be reconvened in more than memory. It has spoken a word with power, and even the echo is not in vain.

But, second, the onion itself is all but gone. The flesh, so crisp and solid, turns out to have been an aqueous house of cards. If you have done your pressing well, the little scraps of membrane and cell wall are nearly nonexistent. The whole infolded next of flames was a blaze of water, a burning bush grown from the soil of the primeval oceans. All life is from the sea.

And God said, Let the waters bring forth abundantly. . . . And God saw that it was good. This juice, this liquor, this rough-and-ready cordial, runs freely now on board and hands and knife. Salt, sweet, and yet so much itself as to speak for no other, it enters the city of being. What you have seen, to be sure, is only the smallest part of its singularity, the merest hint of the stunning act of being that it is, but it is enough perhaps to enable you to proceed, if not with safety, then with caution.

For somehow, beneath this gorgeous paradigm of unnecessary being, lies the Act by which it exists. You have just now reduced it to its parts, shivered it into echoes, and pressed it to a memory, but you have also caught the hint that a thing is more than the sum of all the insubstantialities that comprise it. Hopefully, you will never again argue that the solidities of the world are mere matters of accident, creatures of air and darkness, temporary and meaningless shapes out of nothing. Perhaps now you have seen at least dimly that the uniquenesses of creation are the result of continuous creative support, of effective regard by no mean lover. He *likes* onions, therefore they are. The fit, the colors, the smell, the tensions, the tastes, the textures, the lines, the shapes are a response, not to some forgotten decree that there may as well be onions as turnips, but to His present delight—His intimate and immediate joy in all you have seen, and in the thousand other wonders you do not even suspect. With Peter, the onion says, Lord, it is good for us to *be* here. Yes, says God. *Tov. Very* good.

Fair enough then. All life is from the sea. It takes water to hold a soul. Living beings are full of juices.

But watch out.

I once gave a dinner party at which I conned my wife (then hardly more than a bride) into garnishing a main dish (I think it was a mixed grill) with fried parsley. *Persil frit* is one of the traps that is laid to teach humility to men beset by culinary presumption. I had spent the better part of a morning off devising a way of making attractive bunches of parsley for frying, and I had finally come up with what I still consider (apart from the disaster that followed) the perfect presentation of persil frit. I took bread sticks and, with a coping saw, carefully cut them into three-quarter-inch lengths. Then, ever so gently, I bored out the centers with a small twist drill. This provided me with a number of neckerchief slides, as it were, into each of which I thrust a sufficient number of parsley sprigs to make a snug fit. Since my wife had bought excellent parsley, they made magnificent little sheaves of green.

Unfortunately, however, I neglected to tell my wife that, in spite of all this artsy-crafty ingenuity, I had never prepared, cooked, eaten, or even seen fried parsley before. What she trustingly accepted from me as a manageable fact was nothing but a conceit. We sow, on bright, clear days, the seeds of our own destruction.

For a young thing she had done more than well. Hors d'oeuvres, soup, and fish had come off beautifully—but at an expense of spirit to which I was blind. The working cook of a major meal operates under pressure, and the ivory tower gourmet should never forget it. The mixed grill was in the broiler, the french fryer was heating on the stove, and my wife, tense but still game, picked up my little parsley masterpieces and dropped them into the fat.

What followed was the nearest thing we have ever had to a kitchen fire, and one of the nearest to a marital disaster. Parsley: freshness: water. All life is from the sea. Water: heat: steam. When the bouquets hit the fat, the whole business blew up. Steam: sound: fury. And grease all over the kitchen. Fury: wife: tears. All waters return to the sea.

I spent the fish course in the kitchen mending my fences, trying to bluff my way out. To this day, I remember nothing about the rest of the meal. Except one thing. The parsley was glorious. It fries in ten seconds or so and turns the most stunning green you can imagine. It was parsley transfigured, and I shall never forget it. It is just as well. My wife has never cooked it again.

Between the onion and the parsley, therefore, I shall give the summation of my case for paying attention. Man's real work is to look at the things of the world and to love them for what they are. That is, after all, what God does, and man was not made in God's image for nothing. The fruits of his attention can be seen in all the arts, crafts, and sciences. It can cost him time and effort, but it pays handsomely. If an hour can be spent on one onion, think how much regarding it took on the part of that old Russian who looked at onions and church spires long enough to come up with St. Basil's Cathedral. Or how much curious and loving attention was expended by the first man who looked hard enough at the insides of trees, the entrails of cats, the hind ends of horses and the juice of pine trees to realize he could turn them all into the first fiddle. No doubt his wife urged him to get up and do something useful. I am sure that he was a stalwart enough lover of things to pay no attention at all to her nagging; but how wonderful it would have been if he had known what we know now about his dawdling. He could have silenced her with the greatest riposte of all time: Don't bother me; I am creating the possibility of the Bach unaccompanied sonatas.

But if man's attention is repaid so handsomely, his inattention costs him dearly. Everytime he diagrams something instead of looking at it, everytime he regards not what a thing *is* but what it can be made to *mean* to him—everytime he substitutes a conceit for a fact—he gets grease all over the kitchen of the world.

Reality slips away from him; and he is left with nothing but the oldest monstrosity in the world: an idol. Things must be met for themselves. To take them only for their meaning is to convert them into gods—to make them too important, and therefore to make *them* unimportant altogether. Idolatry has two faults. It is not only a slur on the true God; it is also an insult to true things.

They made a calf in Horeb; thus they turned their Glory into the similitude of a calf that eateth hay. Bad enough, you say. Ah, but it was worse than that. Whatever good may have resided in the Golden Calf—whatever loveliness of gold or beauty of line—went begging the minute the Israelites got the idea that *it* was their savior out of the bondage of Egypt. In making the statue a matter of the greatest *point,* they missed the point of its *matter* altogether.

Berate me not therefore for carrying on about slicing onions in a world under the sentence of nuclear overkill. The heaviest weight on the shoulders of the earth is still the age-old idolatry by which man has cheated himself of both Creator and creation. And this age is no exception. If you prefer to address yourself to graver matters, well and good: Idolatry needs all the enemies it can get. But if I choose to break enemies in the kitchen, I cannot be faulted. We are both good men, in a day when good men are hard to find. Let us join hands and get on with our iconoclasm.

There is a Russian story about an old woman whose vices were so numerous that no one could name even one of her virtues. She was slothful, spiteful, envious, deceitful, greedy, foul-mouthed, and proud. She lived by herself and in herself; she loved no one and no thing. One day a beggar came to her door. She upbraided him, abused him, and sent him away. As he left, however, she unaccountably threw an onion after him. He picked it up and ran away. In time the women died and was dragged down to her due reward in hell. But just as she was about to slip over the edge of the bottomless pit, she looked up. Above her, descending from the infinite distances of heaven, was a great archangel, and in his hand was an onion. "Grasp this," he said. "If you hold it, it will lift you up to heaven."

One real thing is closer to God than all the diagrams in the world.

BERTRAND RUSSELL

a free man's worship _____

To Dr. Faustus in his study Mephistopheles told the history of the Creation, saying:

"The endless praises of the choirs of angels had begun to grow wearisome;

From *Mysticism and Logic,* New York, Barnes and Noble, 1918. Reprinted also with permission of George Allen & Unwin Ltd.

for, after all, did he not deserve their praise? Had he not given them endless joy? Would it not be more amusing to obtain undeserved praise, to be worshipped by beings whom he tortured? He smiled inwardly, and resolved that the great drama should be performed.

"For countless ages the hot nebula whirled aimlessly through space. At length it began to take shape, the central mass threw off planets, the planets cooled, boiling seas and burning mountains heaved and tossed, from black masses of cloud hot sheets of rain deluged the barely solid crust. And now the first germ of life grew in the depths of the ocean, and developed rapidly in the fructifying warmth into vast forest trees, huge ferns springing from the damp mould, sea monsters breeding, fighting, devouring, and passing away. And from the monsters, as the play unfolded itself, Man was born, with the power of thought, the knowledge of good and evil, and the cruel thirst for worship. And Man saw that all is passing in this mad, monstrous world, that all is struggling to snatch, at any cost, a few brief moments of life before Death's inexorable decree. And Man said: 'There is a hidden purpose, could we but fathom it, and the purpose is good; for we must reverence something, and in the visible world there is nothing worthy of reverence.' And Man stood aside from the struggle, resolving that God intended harmony to come out of chaos by human efforts. And when he followed the instincts which God had transmitted to him from his ancestry of beasts of prey, he called it Sin, and asked God to forgive him. But he doubted whether he could be justly forgiven, until he invented a divine Plan by which God's wrath was to have been appeased. And seeing the present was bad, he made it yet worse, that thereby the future might be better. And he gave God thanks for the strength that enabled him to forgo even the joys that were possible. And God smiled; and when he saw that Man had become perfect in renunciation and worship, he sent another sun through the sky, which crashed into Man's sun; and all returned again to nebula.

" 'Yes,' he murmured, 'it was a good play; I will have it performed again.' "

Such, in outline, but even more purposeless, more void of meaning, is the world which Science presents for our belief. Amid such a world, if anywhere, our ideals henceforward must find a home. That Man is the product of causes which had no prevision of the end they were achieving; that his origin, his growth, his hopes and fears, his loves and his beliefs, are but the outcome of accidental collocations of atoms; that no fire, no heroism, no intensity of thought and feeling, can preserve an individual life beyond the grave; that all the labors of the ages, all the devotion, all the inspiration, all the noonday brightness of human genius, are doomed to extinction in the vast death of the solar system, and that the whole temple of Man's achievement must inevitably be buried beneath the debris of a universe in ruins—all these things, if not quite beyond dispute, are yet so nearly certain, that no philosophy which rejects them can hope to stand. Only within the scaffolding of these truths, only on the firm foundation of unyielding despair, can the soul's habitation henceforth be safely built.

How, in such an alien and inhuman world, can so powerless a creature as Man preserve his aspirations untarnished? A strange mystery it is that Nature, omnipotent but blind, in the revolutions of her secular hurryings through the abysses of space, has brought forth at last a child, subject still to her power, but gifted with sight, with knowledge of good and evil, with the capacity of judging all the works of his unthinking Mother. In spite of Death, the mark and seal of the parental control, Man is yet free, during his brief years, to examine, to criticize, to know, and in imagination to create. To him alone, in the world with which he is acquainted, this freedom belongs; and in this lies his superiority to the resistless forces that control his outward life.

. . .

When, without the bitterness of impotent rebellion, we have learnt both to resign ourselves to the outward rule of Fate and to recognize that the nonhuman world is unworthy of our worship, it becomes possible at last so to transform and refashion the unconscious universe, so to transmute it in the crucible of imagination, that a new image of shining gold replaces the old idol of clay. In all the multiform facts of the world—in the visual shapes of trees and mountains and clouds, in the events of the life of man, even in the very omnipotence of Death—the insight of creative idealism can find the reflection of a beauty which its own thoughts first made. In this way mind asserts its subtle mastery over the thoughtless forces of Nature. The more evil the material with which it deals, the more thwarting to untrained desire, the greater is its achievement in inducing the reluctant rock to yield up its hidden treasures, the prouder its victory in compelling the opposing forces to swell the pageant of its triumph.

. . .

Victory, in this struggle with the powers of darkness, is the true baptism into the glorious company of heroes, the true initiation into the overmastering beauty of human existence. From that awful encounter of the soul with the outer world, enunciation, wisdom, and charity are born; and with their birth a new life begins. To take into the inmost shrine of the soul the irresistible forces whose puppets we seem to be—Death and change, the irrevocableness of the past, and the powerlessness of man before the blind hurry of the universe from vanity to vanity—to feel these things and know them is to conquer them.

This is the reason why the Past has such magical power. The beauty of its motionless and silent pictures is like the enchanted purity of late autumn, when the leaves, though one breath would make them fall, still glow against the sky in golden glory. The Past does not change or strive; like Duncan, after life's fitful fever it sleeps well; what was eager and grasping, what was petty and transitory, has faded away, the things that were beautiful and eternal shine out of it like stars in the night. Its beauty, to a soul not worthy of it, is unendurable; but to a soul which has conquered Fate it is the key of religion.

The life of Man, viewed outwardly, is but a small thing in comparison with the forces of Nature. The slave is doomed to worship Time and Fate and Death, because they are greater than anything he finds in himself, and because all his thoughts are of things which they devour. But, great as they are, to think of them greatly, to feel their passionless splendour, is greater still. And such thought makes us free men; we no longer bow before the inevitable in Oriental subjection, but we absorb it, and make it a part of ourselves. To abandon the struggle for private happiness, to expel all eagerness of temporary desire, to burn with passion for eternal things—this is emancipation, and this is the free man's worship. And this liberation is effected by a contemplation of Fate; for Fate itself is subdued by the mind which leaves nothing to be purged by the purifying fire of Time.

United with his fellow-men by the strongest of all ties, the tie of a common doom, the free man finds that a new vision is with him always, shedding over every daily task the light of love. The life of Man is a long march through the night, surrounded by invisible foes, tortured by weariness and pain, towards a goal that few can hope to reach, and where none may tarry long. One by one, as they march, our comrades vanish from our sight, seized by the silent orders of omnipotent Death. Very brief is the time in which we can help them, in which their happiness or misery is decided. Be it ours to shed sunshine on their path, to lighten their sorrows by the balm of sympathy, to give them the pure joy of a never-tiring affection, to strengthen failing courage, to instill faith in hours of despair. Let us not weigh in grudging scales their merits and demerits, but let us think only of their need—of the sorrows, the difficulties, perhaps the blindnesses, that make the misery of their lives; let us remember that they are fellow-sufferers in the same darkness, actors in the same tragedy with ourselves. And so, when their day is over, when their good and their evil have become eternal by the immortality of the past, be it ours to feel that, where they suffered, where they failed, no deed of ours was the cause; but wherever a spark of the divine fire kindled in their hearts, we were ready with encouragement, with sympathy, with brave words in which high courage glowed.

Brief and powerless is Man's life; on him and all his race the slow, sure doom falls pitiless and dark. Blind to good and evil, reckless of destruction, omnipotent matter rolls on its relentless way; for Man, condemned to-day to lose his dearest, to-morrow himself to pass through the gate of darkness, it remains only to cherish, yet the blow falls, the lofty thoughts that ennoble his little day; disdaining the coward terrors of the slave of Fate, to worship at the shrine that his own hands have built; undismayed by the empire of chance, to preserve a mind free from the wanton tyranny that rules his outward life; proudly defiant of the irresistible forces that tolerate, for a moment, his knowledge and his condemnation, to sustain alone, a weary but unyielding Atlas, the world that his own ideals have fashioned despite the trampling march of unconscious power.

JAMES JOYCE

i love flowers _____

I love flowers Id love to have the whole place swimming in roses God of heaven
theres nothing like nature the wild mountains then the sea and the waves rushing
then the beautiful country with fields of oats and wheat and all kinds of things
and all the fine cattle going about that would do your heart good to see rivers
and lakes and flowers all sorts of shapes and smells and colors springing up even
out of the ditches primroses and violets nature it is as for them saying theres no
God I wouldnt give a snap of my two fingers for all their learning why dont they
go and create something I often asked him atheists or whatever they call themselves go and wash the cobbles off themselves first then they go howling for the
priest and they dying and why why because theyre afraid of hell on account of
their bad conscience ah yes I know them well who was the first person in the
universe before there was anybody that made it all who ah that they dont know
neither do I so there you are they might as well try to stop the sun from rising
tomorrow the sun shines for you he said the day we were lying among the
rhododendrons on Howth head in the grey tweed suit and his straw hat the day I
got him to propose to me yes first I gave him the bit of seedcake out of my
mouth and it was leapyear like now yes 16 years ago my God after that long kiss
I near lost my breath yes he said I was a flower of the mountain yes so we are
flowers all a womans body yes that was one true thing he said in his life and the
sun shines for you today yes that was why I liked him because I saw he understood or felt what a woman is and I knew I could always get round him and I
gave him all the pleasure I could leading him on till he asked me to say yes and I
wouldnt answer first only looked out over the sea and the sky I was thinking of
so many things he didnt know of Mulvey and Mr Stanhope and Hester and father
and old captain Groves and the sailors playing all birds fly and I say stoop and
washing up dishes they called it on the pier and the sentry in front of the gover-
nors house with the thing round his white helmet poor devil half roasted and the
Spanish girls laughing in their shawls and their tall combs and the auctions in the
morning the Greeks and the jews and the Arabs and the devil knows who else
from all the ends of Europe and Duke street and the fowl market all clucking
outside Larby Sharons and the poor donkeys slipping half asleep and the vague
fellows in the cloaks asleep in the shade on the steps and the big wheels of the
carts of the bulls and the old castle thousands of years old yes and those handsome Moors all in white and turbans like kings asking you to sit down in their
little bit of a shop and Ronda with the old windows of the posadas glancing eyes
a lattice hid for her lover to kiss the iron and the wineshops half open at night
and the castanets and the night we missed the boat at Algeciras the watchman
going about serene with his lamp and O that awful deepdown torrent O and the

From *Ulysses,* New York, Modern Library, 1946.

sea the sea crimson sometimes like fire and the glorious sunsets and the figtrees in the Alameda gardens yes and all the queer little streets and pink and blue and yellow houses and the rosegardens and the jessamine and geraniums and cactuses and Gibraltar as a girl where I was a Flower of the mountain yes when I put the rose in my hair like the Andalusian girls used or shall I wear a red yes and how he kissed me under the Moorish wall and I thought well as well him as another and then I asked him with my eyes to ask again yes and then he asked me would I yes to say yes my mountain flower and first I put my arms around him yes and drew him down to me so he could feel my breasts all perfume yes and his heart was going like mad and yes I said yes I will Yes

HENRY DAVID THOREAU

the ponds

Sometimes, having had a surfeit of human society and gossip, and worn out all my village friends, I rambled still farther westward than I habitually dwell, into yet more unfrequented parts of the town, "to fresh woods and pastures new," or, while the sun was setting, made my supper of huckleberries and blueberries on Fair-Haven Hill, and laid up a store for several days. The fruits do not yield their true flavor to the purchaser of them, nor to him who raises them for the market. There is but one way to obtain it, yet few take that way. If you would know the flavor of huckleberries, ask the cow-boy or the partridge. It is a vulgar error to suppose that you have tasted huckleberries who never plucked them. A huckleberry never reaches Boston; they have not been known there since they grew on her three hills. The ambrosial and essential part of the fruit is lost with the bloom which is rubbed off in the market-cart, and they become mere provender. As long as Eternal Justice reigns, not one innocent huckleberry can be transported thither from the country's hills.

Occasionally, after my hoeing was done for the day, I joined some impatient companion who had been fishing on the pond since morning, as silent and motionless as a duck or a floating leaf, and, after practicing various kinds of philosophy, had concluded commonly, by the time I arrived, that he belonged to the ancient sect of Coenobites. There was one older man, an excellent fisher and skilled in all kinds of woodcraft, who was pleased to look upon my house as a building erected for the convenience of fishermen; and I was equally pleased when he sat in my doorway to arrange his lines. Once in a while we sat together on the pond, he at one end of the boat and I at the other; but not many words passed between us, for he had grown deaf in his later years, but he occasionally hummed a psalm, which harmonized well enough with my philosophy. Our intercourse was thus altogether one of unbroken harmony, far more pleasing to remember than if it had been carried on by speech. When, as was commonly the case, I had none to commune with, I used to raise the echoes by striking with a paddle on the side of my boat, filling the surrounding woods with circling and dilating sound, stirring them up as the keeper of a menagerie his wild beasts, until I elicited a growl from every wooded vale and hillside.

In warm evenings I frequently sat in the boat playing the flute, and saw the perch, which I seemed to have charmed, hovering around me, and the moon traveling over the ribbed bottom, which was strewed with the wrecks of the forest. Formerly I had come to this pond adventurously, from time to time, in dark summer nights, with a companion, and making a fire close to the water's edge, which we thought attracted the fishes, we caught pouts with a bunch of worms strung on a thread, and when we had done, far in the night, threw the burning brands high into the air like sky-rockets, which, coming down into the pond, were quenched with a loud hissing, and we were suddenly groping in total darkness. Through this, whistling a tune, we took our way to the haunts of men again. But now I had made my home by the shore.

Sometimes, after staying in a village parlor till the family had all retired, I have returned to the woods, and, partly with a view to the next day's dinner, spent the hours of midnight fishing from a boat by moonlight, serenaded by owls and foxes, and hearing, from time to time, the creaking note of some unknown bird close at hand. These experiences were very memorable and valuable to me,—anchored in forty feet of water, and twenty or thirty rods from the shore, surrounded sometimes by thousands of small perch and shiners, dimpling the surface with their tails in the moonlight, and communicating by a long flaxen line with mysterious nocturnal fishes which had their dwelling forty feet below, or sometimes dragging sixty feet of line about the pond as I drifted in the gentle night breeze, now and then feeling a slight vibration along it, indicative of some life prowling about its extremity, of dull uncertain blundering purpose there, and slow to make up its mind. At length you slowly raise, pulling hand over hand, some horned pout squeaking and squirming to the upper air. It was very queer, especially in dark nights, when your thoughts had wandered to vast and cosmogonal themes in other spheres, to feel this faint jerk, which came to interrupt your dreams and link you to Nature again. It seemed as if I might next cast my line upward into the air, as well as downward into this element which was scarcely more dense. Thus I caught two fishes, as it were, with one hook.

PART 3
the future

The future is a form of transcendence for modern man who must bear the full thrust of the uncertain perils of a future that may be the end of man himself. For us the future can no longer be a repetition of patterns of past events. Eliade makes this clear in his essay on the "Terror of History." Alvin Toffler's expression "future shock" is a happy coinage for the present state of mind, for we move at an accelerated rate into a time which contains the grim possibility of universal disaster through population explosion, nuclear or biological weaponry, environmental pollution, or genetic deterioration. No doubt other elements will soon appear to threaten man in a similar way.

These melancholy visions of the future, illustrated by MacLeish's poem, suggest that we live in what the New Testament called the "last days." The word for this is "eschatology." ("Eschaton" is the Greek word for "end.") Our thought becomes more and more eschatological, which is another way of saying that we cannot think about the future without assuming a somewhat religious coloring. Religious thought arises when man is at his extremity, beyond his power to understand and control.

Teilhard de Chardin is optimistic about the possibilities. "The Spirit of the

Earth" suggests that we are now entering a new phase, a new evolutionary level of world consciousness. This he projects on the basis of a larger evolutionary hypothesis. That a Roman Catholic writer should be quoted in this matter illustrates the changing aspect of our times. Spengler's piece on the "Second Religiousness" is, on the other hand, pessimistic. He sees the renewed religiousness as a symptom of social decay, the winter of Western culture that has presently engulfed the world. On these issues the reader will have to make up his own mind and take his own stand.

the second coming _____

Turning and turning in the widening gyre
The falcon cannot hear the falconer;
Things fall apart; the centre cannot hold;
Mere anarchy is loosed upon the world,
The blood-dimmed tide is loosed, and everywhere
The ceremony of innocence is drowned;
The best lack all conviction, while the worst
Are full of passionate intensity.

Surely some revelation is at hand;
Surely the Second Coming is at hand.
The Second Coming! Hardly are those words out
When a vast image out of *Spiritus Mundi*
Troubles my sight: somewhere in sands of the desert
A shape with lion body and the head of a man,
A gaze blank and pitiless as the sun,
Is moving its slow thighs, while all about it
Reel shadows of the indignant desert birds.
The darkness drops again; but now I know
That twenty centuries of stony sleep
Were vexed to nightmare by a rocking cradle,
And what rough beast, its hour come round at last,
Slouches towards Bethlehem to be born?

the 800th lifetime _____

In the three short decades between now and the twenty-first century, millions of ordinary, psychologically normal people will face an abrupt collision with the future. Citizens of the world's richest and most technologically advanced nations, many of them will find it increasingly painful to keep up with the in-

From *Future Shock,* New York, Random House, 1971.

cessant demand for change that characterizes our time. For them, the future will have arrived too soon.

. . .

Western society for the past 300 years has been caught up in a fire storm of change. This storm, far from abating, now appears to be gathering force. Change sweeps through the highly industrialized countries with waves of ever accelerating speed and unprecedented impact. It spawns in its wake all sorts of curious social flora—from psychedelic churches and "free universities" to science cities in the Arctic and wife-swap clubs in California.

It breeds odd personalities, too: children who at twelve are no longer childlike; adults who at fifty are children of twelve. There are rich men who playact poverty, computer programmers who turn on with LSD. There are anarchists who, beneath their dirty denim shirts, are outrageous conformists, and conformists who, beneath their button-down collars, are outrageous anarchists. There are married priests and atheist ministers and Jewish Zen Buddhists. We have pop . . . and op . . . and *art cinétique* . . . There are Playboy Clubs and homosexual movie theaters . . . amphetamines and tranquilizers . . . anger, affluence, and oblivion. Much oblivion.

Is there some way to explain so strange a scene without recourse to the jargon of psychoanalysis or the murky clichés of existentialism? A strange new society is apparently erupting in our midst. Is there a way to understand it, to shape its development? How can we come to terms with it?

Much that now strikes us as incomprehensible would be far less so if we took a fresh look at the racing rate of change that makes reality seem, sometimes, like a kaleidoscope run wild. For the acceleration of change does not merely buffet industries or nations. It is a concrete force that reaches deep into our personal lives, compels us to act out new roles, and confronts us with the danger of a new and powerfully upsetting psychological disease. This new disease can be called "future shock," and a knowledge of its sources and symptoms helps explain many things that otherwise defy rational analysis.

the unprepared visitor

The parallel term "culture shock" has already begun to creep into the popular vocabulary. Culture shock is the effect that immersion in a strange culture has on the unprepared visitor. Peace Corps volunteers suffer from it in Borneo or Brazil. Marco Polo probably suffered from it in Cathay. Culture shock is what happens when a traveler suddenly finds himself in a place where yes may mean no, where a "fixed price" is negotiable, where to be kept waiting in an outer office is no cause for insult, where laughter may signify anger. It is what happens when the familiar psychological cues that help an individual to function in society are suddenly withdrawn and replaced by new ones that are strange or incomprehensible.

The culture shock phenomenon accounts for much of the bewilderment, frustration, and disorientation that plagues Americans in their dealings with other societies. It causes a breakdown in communication, a misreading of reality, an inability to cope. Yet culture shock is relatively mild in comparison with the much more serious malady, future shock. Future shock is the dizzying disorientation brought on by the premature arrival of the future. It may well be the most important disease of tomorrow.

Future shock will not be found in *Index Medicus* or in any listing of psychological abnormalities. Yet, unless intelligent steps are taken to combat it, millions of human beings will find themselves increasingly disoriented, progressively incompetent to deal rationally with their environments. The malaise, mass neurosis, irrationality, and free-floating violence already apparent in contemporary life are merely a foretaste of what may lie ahead unless we come to understand and treat this disease.

Future shock is a time phenomenon, a product of the greatly accelerated rate of change in society. It arises from the superimposition of a new culture on an old one. It is culture shock in one's own society. But its impact is far worse. For most Peace Corps men, in fact most travelers, have the comforting knowledge that the culture they left behind will be there to return to. The victim of future shock does not.

Take an individual out of his own culture and set him down suddenly in an environment sharply different from his own, with a different set of cues to react to—different conceptions of time, space, work, love, religion, sex, and everything else—then cut him off from any hope of retreat to a more familiar social landscape, and the dislocation he suffers is doubly severe. Moreover, if this new culture is itself in constant turmoil, and if—worse yet—its values are incessantly changing, the sense of disorientation will be still further intensified. Given few clues as to what kind of behavior is rational under the radically new circumstances, the victim may well become a hazard to himself and others.

Now imagine not merely an individual but an entire society, an entire generation—including its weakest, least intelligent, and most irrational members—suddenly transported into this new world. The result is mass disorientation, future shock on a grand scale.

This is the prospect that man now faces. Change is avalanching upon our heads and most people are grotesquely unprepared to cope with it.

break with the past

Is all this exaggerated? I think not. It has become a cliché to say that what we are now living through is a "second industrial revolution." This phrase is supposed to impress us with the speed and profundity of the change around us. But in addition to being platitudinous, it is misleading. For what is occurring now is, in all likelihood, bigger, deeper, and more important than the industrial revolution. Indeed, a growing body of reputable opinion asserts that the present movement represents nothing less than the second great divide in human history, comparable in magnitude only with that first great break in historic continuity, the shift from barbarism to civilization.

This idea crops up with increasing frequency in the writings of scientists and technologists. Sir George Thomson, the British physicist and Nobel prizewinner, suggests in *The Foreseeable Future* that the nearest historic parallel with today is not the industrial revolution but rather the "invention of agriculture in the neolithic age." John Diebold, the American automation expert, warns that "the effects of the technological revolution we are now living through will be deeper than any social change we have experienced before." Sir Leon Bagrit, the British computer manufacturer, insists that automation by itself represents "the greatest change in the whole history of mankind."

Nor are the men of science and technology alone in these views. Sir Herbert Read, the philosopher of art, tells us that we are living through "a revolution so fundamental that we must search many past centuries for a parallel. Possibly the only comparable change is the one that took place between the Old and the New Stone Age. . . ." And Kurt W. Marek, who under the name C. W. Ceram is best known as the author of *Gods, Graves and Scholars,* observes that "we, in the twentieth century, are concluding an era of mankind five thousand years in length. . . . We are not, as Spengler supposed, in the situation of Rome at the beginning of the Christian West, but in that of the year 3000 B.C. We open our eyes like prehistoric man, we see a world totally new."

One of the most striking statements of this theme has come from Kenneth Boulding, an eminent economist and imaginative social thinker. In justifying his view that the present moment represents a crucial turning point in human history, Boulding observes that "as far as many statistical series related to activities of mankind are concerned, the date that divides human history into two equal parts is well within living memory." In effect, our century represents The Great Median Strip running down the center of human history. Thus he asserts, "The world of today . . . is as different from the world in which I was born as that world was from Julius Caesar's. I was born in the middle of human history, to date, roughly. Almost as much has happened since I was born as happened before."

This startling statement can be illustrated in a number of ways. It has been observed, for example, that if the last 50,000 years of man's existence were divided into lifetimes of approximately sixty-two years each, there have been about 800 such lifetimes. Of these 800, fully 650 were spent in caves.

Only during the last seventy lifetimes has it been possible to communicate effectively from one lifetime to another—as writing made it possible to do. Only during the last six lifetimes did masses of men ever see a printed word. Only during the last four has it been possible to measure time with any precision. Only in the last two has anyone anywhere used an electric motor. And the overwhelming majority of all the material goods we use in daily life today have been developed within the present, the 800th, lifetime.

This 800th lifetime marks a sharp break with all past human experience because during this lifetime man's relationship to resources has reversed itself. This is most evident in the field of economic development. Within a single lifetime, agriculture, the original basis of civilization, has lost its dominance in nation after nation. Today in a dozen major countries agriculture employs fewer than 15 percent of the economically active population. In the United States, whose farms feed 200,000,000 Americans plus the equivalent of another 160,000,000 people around the world, this figure is already below 6 percent and it is still shrinking rapidly.

Moreover, if agriculture is the first stage of economic development and industrialism the second, we can now see that still another stage—the third—has suddenly been reached. In about 1956 the United States became the first major power in which more than 50 percent of the nonfarm labor force ceased to wear the blue collar of factory or manual labor. Blue collar workers were outnumbered by those in the so-called white-collar occupations—in retail trade, administration, communications, research, education, and other service categories. Within the same lifetime a society for the first time in human history not only threw off the yoke of agriculture, but managed within a few brief decades to throw off the yoke of manual labor as well. The world's first service economy had been born.

Since then, one after another of the technologically advanced countries have moved in the same direction. Today, in those nations in which agriculture is down to the 15 percent level or below, white collars already outnumber blue in Sweden, Britain, Belgium, Canada, and the Netherlands. Ten thousand years for agriculture. A century or two for industrialism. And now, opening before us—super-industrialism.

Jean Fourastié, the French planner and social philosopher, has declared that "nothing will be less industrial than the civilization born of the industrial revolution." The significance of this staggering fact has yet to be digested. Perhaps U Thant, Secretary General of the United Nations, came closest to summarizing the meaning of the shift to super-industrialism when he declared that "the central stupendous truth about developed economics today is that they can have—in anything but the shortest run—the kind and scale of resources they decide to have. . . . It is no longer resources that limit decisions. It is the decision that makes the resources. This is the fundamental revolutionary change—perhaps the most revolutionary man has ever known." This monumental reversal has taken place in the 800th lifetime.

This lifetime is also different from all others because of the astonishing expansion of the scale and scope of change. Clearly, there have been other lifetimes in which epochal upheavals occurred. Wars, plagues, earthquakes, and famine rocked many an earlier social order. But these shocks and upheavals were contained within the borders of one or a group of adjacent societies. It took generations, even centuries, for their impact to spread beyond these borders.

In our lifetime the boundaries have burst. Today the network of social ties is so tightly woven that the consequences of contemporary events radiate instantaneously around the world. A war in Vietnam alters basic political alignments in Peking, Moscow, and Washington, touches off protests in Stockholm, affects financial transactions in Zurich, triggers secret diplomatic moves in Algiers.

Indeed, not only do *contemporary* events radiate instantaneously—now we can be said to be feeling the impact of all *past* events in a new way. For the past is doubling back on us. We are caught in what might be called a "time skip."

An event that affected only a handful of people at the time of its occurrence in the past can have large-scale consequences today. The Peloponnesian War, for example, was little more than a skirmish by modern standards. While Athens, Sparta and several nearby city-states battled, the population of the rest of the globe remained largely unaware of and undisturbed by the war. The Zapotec Indians living in Mexico at the time were wholly untouched by it. The ancient Japanese felt none of its impact.

Yet the Peloponnesian War deeply altered the future course of Greek history. By changing the movement of men, the geographical distribution of genes, values, and ideas, it affected later events in Rome, and, through Rome, all Europe. Today's Europeans are to some small degree different people because that conflict occurred.

In turn, in the tightly wired world of today, these Europeans influence Mexicans and Japanese alike. Whatever trace of impact the Peloponnesian War left on the genetic structure, the ideas, and the values of today's Europeans is now exported by them to all parts of the world. Thus today's Mexicans and Japanese feel the distant, twice-removed impact of that war even though their ancestors, alive during its occurrence, did not. In this way, the events of the past, skipping as it were over generations and centuries, rise up to haunt and change us today.

When we think not merely of the Peloponnesian War but of the building of the Great Wall of China, the Black Plague, the battle of the Bantu against the Hamites—indeed, of all the events of the past—the cumulative implications of the time-skip principle take on weight. Whatever happened to some men in the past affects virtually all men today. This was not always true. In short, all history is catching up with us, and this very difference, paradoxically, underscores our break with the past. Thus the scope of change is fundamentally altered. Across space and through time, change has a power and reach in this, the 800th lifetime, that it never did before.

But the final, qualitative difference between this and all previous lifetimes is the one most easily overlooked. For we have not merely extended the scope and scale of change, we have radically altered its pace. We have in our time released a totally new social force—a stream of change so accelerated that it influences our sense of time, revolutionizes the tempo of daily life, and affects the very way we "feel" the world around us. We no longer "feel" life as men did in the past. And this is the ultimate difference, the distinction that separates the truly contemporary man from all others. For this acceleration lies behind the impermanence—the transience—that penetrates and tinctures our consciousness, radically affecting the way we relate to other people, to things, to the entire universe of ideas, art and values.

To understand what is happening to us as we move into the age of super-industrialism, we must analyze the processes of acceleration and confront the concept of transience. If acceleration is a new social force, transience is its psychological counterpart, and without an understanding of the role it plays in contemporary human behavior, all our theories of personality, all our psychology, must remain pre-modern. Psychology without the concept of transience cannot take account of precisely those phenomena that are peculiarly contemporary.

By changing our relationship to the resources that surround us, by violently expanding the scope of change, and, most crucially, by accelerating its pace, we have broken irretrievably with the past. We have cut ourselves off from the old ways of thinking, of feeling, of adapting. We have set the stage for a completely new society and we are now racing toward it. This is the crux of the 800th lifetime. And it is this that calls into question man's capacity for adaptation—how will he fare in this new society? Can he adapt to its imperatives? And if not, can he alter these imperatives?

ROBERT N. BELLAH

beyond belief ———————————————————————

the autobiography of a modern sociologist

David Riesman has reversed Gilbert Murray's phrase to speak of "the nerve of failure" so perhaps one can transpose another phrase common today and speak of "the faith of loss." "The nerve of failure" and "the faith of loss" point to a situation in which the idols are broken and the gods are dead, but the darkness of negation turns out to be full of rich possibility. Out of the nothingness which has swallowed up all tradition there comes nihilism but also the possibility of a new ecstatic consciousness. The yes and the no, joyfulness and despair, are terribly close together. No one can say whether in this generation we shall have global suicide or New Being.

· · ·

The first Bellah to arrive on this continent came in the late seventeenth century to Charleston, South Carolina. He was of Scottish descent, Presbyterian, and had come from Northern Ireland. In successive generations my ancestors—preachers, farmers, tradesmen—moved west, county by county, state by state. My father was born in Texas and grew up in Oklahoma. My mother's family was

Abridged and adapted "Introduction" to *Beyond Belief: Essays on Religion in a Post-Traditional World* by Robert N. Bellah. Copyright © 1970 by Robert N. Bellah.

of English and Scottish descent, and also Presbyterian. She was born in Arkansas where her father was a planter and she met my father at the University of Oklahoma. My father became the editor and publisher of a small-town newspaper in southwest Oklahoma, where I was born in 1927, but he died before I was three and I grew up with my mother in Los Angeles.

I was raised among the fragments of a once coherent, southern Protestant culture. My mother's memories of sober Sundays devoted to churchgoing, reading the Bible and *Pilgrim's Progress,* and visiting the cemetery were communicated to me and indeed I seldom missed attending the Presbyterian Sunday School. There the atmosphere was conservative without being fundamentalist. I remember being shocked and a bit outraged when I first heard a public school teacher discuss the theory of evolution in the third grade, for up till then I had only known the Bible story of creation.

When I first read Max Weber's *Protestant Ethic and the Spirit of Capitalism* at Harvard College it spoke to me of an atmosphere I knew well. I remembered an old gentleman speaking to my Sunday School class about "the calling." He told a lugubrious story about a young boy who had a calling from God to be an undertaker, which, the old man said, may not seem pleasant but like all honest callings is necessary and pleasing to God. Although the relatives that I knew were not at all intellectual, my mother communicated to me a love of books and writing which had been characteristic of her mother and my father. I grew up with an unself-conscious American patriotism, in which no basic questions about American society ever arose, and with a trace of southern sentimentalism about the Confederacy and prejudice against Republicans.

But I grew up not in the Bible belt but in Los Angeles in a heterogeneous neighborhood. I was exposed from an early age to people different from my family. Since my father had died when I was small I had no compelling figure with whom to identify, whose views could mold my own. My mother early looked to me for opinions. Thus I had both the necessity and the possibility of forging my own identity and worldview in adolescence out of the fragments of the past and the diversity of the present. In the heterogeneous environment of the Los Angeles public schools the people who were most interesting to me often turned out to be Jews. Among them I found that the culture for which I had learned a formal respect at home was a living reality, especially in the realms of music and literature.

And it was in high school that I met a girl whose refusal to accept sham, whose love of life and whose quest for perfection helped me define my own direction—a girl I later married.

In the atmosphere of the Second World War when I was coming to consciousness I became progressively more liberal, both religiously and politically. With an intensity which has become much more familiar recently I began to test the ideals I had been taught against the realities of life in America and came to doubt the entire structure of religious and political beliefs that I had earlier taken for granted. In my last year in high school I began to read Marxist literature loaned to me by one or two friends.

Harvard was in many ways a liberation for me. Instead of the isolation I felt in high school I felt supported in the intellectual and cultural as well as political ideas I was beginning to develop. The atmosphere was far less radical than it was in the thirties or would be again in the sixties, but there were sizable groups and remarkably intelligent individuals who shared my views. In many ways my Marxism was but a transposition of my Protestantism: idealistic, moral, puritanical. Instead of a mythical apocalypse I looked forward to what I thought was a real one. There would indeed be a new heaven and a new earth at the end of history when man's exploitation of man had finally been overcome. For the moment my religious and political concerns were fused in a single apocalyptic vision. Christianity I no longer took seriously. Marxism fulfilled my needs for personal identity and group belonging. It provided a great escape from the constrictions of provincial American culture—it gave a sweeping view of world history which allowed me to relate critically to my past and present. But even then I had half-conscious doubts that I could at such an early age have found a completely satisfactory worldview that had answers to all questions. My search for alternative visions went on in other realms as well. While Russia never interested me, even repelled me though I tried not to think about it, I was drawn to primitive and exotic cultures. I majored in social anthropology and, long before the hippies, was attracted to the American Indians and other primitive peoples. I was intrigued with what I thought was the wholeness and integrity of those cultures in contrast to the fragmentation I saw around me. I wrote my undergraduate honors thesis on Apache kinship systems. In my last year in college I took a course on East Asian civilization which was the beginning of an abiding interest. The aesthetic intensity of Japanese culture appealed to my parched Protestant soul and even in the midst of my Marxism I began reading about Zen Buddhism. Also as an undergraduate I was first exposed to psychoanalysis and the multiple levels of the inner life which it has revealed. Under the cover of an apparently satisfactory total worldview, multiple apprehensions of reality were growing.

The months after the disaster of the Henry Wallace campaign in 1948 were not easy ones for those in the dwindling American left. In the face of a growing persecution which was being carried out with great publicity by certain congressional and state legislative committees, and of the far more extensive purge which was quietly going on in many institutions of American society, the Marxist left turned upon itself, as the Navaho used to do in time of drought, and began to discover witches in its own midst. It was an ugly picture from any point of view and one that produced great human suffering. I never became a compulsive anti-Communist, a man trapped in a love-hate embrace with that which he has consciously rejected, but for me finally this idol too was broken.

The years of graduate school that followed were a time of spiritual vacuum. I was wrapped up in the time-consuming task of learning Japanese and Chinese and meeting the many requirements of a joint degree in sociology and Far Eastern languages. But it was also in these years that I began a tentative reappropriation of what I had earlier rejected. Talcott Parsons, and through him Max Weber and Emile Durkheim, opened up to me a view of human society and of historical development which was as sweeping as that of Marxism but in its openness and lack of dogmatism more appealing. The last years of Stalin's rule made the somber face of Soviet despotism ever clearer and I began to doubt the likelihood of any earthly utopia. For all its failures I came to believe that American society needed to be reformed rather than abandoned. In other words politically I became a liberal, but it was the chastened liberalism of a man with few illusions.

The religious need, the need for wholeness, which has been strong in me from adolescence, was partly filled in these years through my encounter with the theology of Paul Tillich. Here was the Protestantism of my childhood transmuted through the deepest encounter with the twentieth century. The recognition of despair in Tillich's Christian existentialism corresponded to my mood. His book *The Courage to Be* with its magnificent closing lines made a deep impression on me:

> The courage to take the anxiety of meaninglessness upon oneself is the boundary line up to which the courage to be can go. Beyond it is mere non-being. Within it all forms of courage are re-established in the power of the God above the God of theism. *The courage to be is rooted in the God who appears when God has disappeared in the anxiety of doubt.*[1]

Toward the end of my graduate years the reappropriations I had been making, reappropriations not on the basis of simple affirmations but of doubt and disillusion, were tested by a new series of events. It was perhaps inevitable that I should not escape the McCarthyism which was so pervasive in American universities in those days. First my fellowship was threatened unless I would speak with "complete candor" which meant informing on all those I had ever known politically. There were those who came to my defense and my fellowship was saved for one more year. Then the offer of an instructorship after I had completed my doctoral work was hedged with vaguer but similar conditions. I turned down this proposal and accepted a research fellowship at the Islamic Institute at McGill University, starting in the fall of 1955.

The next two years were in some ways rather grim. I understand how the young men who have gone to Canada rather than Vietnam must feel. I did not know if I could ever come back to the United States or if I would be able to get an academic job even in Canada after my fellowship had ended. I don't want to exaggerate the difficulties. The Islamic Institute was a wonderful place and the work I did there opened up many new opportunities for me later. But for a while it was a kind of personal low ebb. Those were also the years of the Khrushchev revelations of the terror of Stalin's regime and not long after of the drowning in blood of the Hungarian people's uprising. Exiled from my own country there was no other in which I could place hope.

It was in this situation that the new attitude toward Christianity which I had been developing with the help of Paul Tillich came to a kind of fruition. It was then that I understood existentially the Christian doctrine of sin. I saw that the worst is only a hair's breadth away from the best in any man and any society. I saw that unbroken commitment to any individual or any group is bound to be demonic. Nothing human can bear such a weight. The totalism of Communism and the totalism of the "Free World" are equally destructive. And I learned to see the darkness within, that we are all assassins in our hearts. If I am not a murderer it is because of the grace I have received through the love and support of others, not through the lack of murderous impulses within me. The only difference between me and the man on death row is that he somehow received less grace. Feeling all this I could no longer hate, or rather justify hatred. Since I participate in the guilt of every man there is no man I can reject or declare unforgivable. This is what the New Testament taught me in those months contradicting culture Christianity and Marxism, both of which make idolatrous commitments to particular structures and persons and foster a consequent self-righteousness. It was then that I saw that identification with the body of Christ meant identification with all men without exception.

In 1957 I accepted an appointment without conditions and returned to Harvard. The dark clouds of McCarthyism had almost blown away. During most of the decade that followed . . . there was room for cautious optimism, not only about America but also about most of the rest of the world. America seemed to be facing up to the scandal of racism and a period of "liberalization" seemed to have set in in Eastern Europe. Nothing in my experience justified any kind of elation but there did seem to be a basis for what I might call a pessimistic optimism which characterizes my writings of those years. My essay on religious evolution, which states the main presuppositions underlying my book, *Tokugawa Religion,* and the earlier essays in this collection, is not a paean to progress for I point out that at every stage the increase in freedom is also an increase in the freedom to choose destruction. But all the same there is a judicious confidence in the Reformation as a model for ideological transformation in the modern world. . . . Modern Western society, especially American society, in spite of all its problems, is *relatively* less problematic than the developing societies with their enormous difficulties in economic growth and political stability. Though my position is far more cautious than that of other American social scientists who have been concerned with the problem of "modernization" it partakes to some extent of the same ethos.

Perhaps my paper on "Civil Religion in America" written late in this period (1966) epitomizes this earlier attitude at the same time that it contains seeds of a new orientation. It is a strong endorsement of core American values, at least in their most self-critical form, but it also, especially in response to the deepening involvement in the Vietnam War, expresses a fundamental doubt about the future.

Later essays reflect a changed situation and a changed reaction on my part.

Behind them lies my dismay at the failure of our society to move quickly and efficiently to correct racial injustice, distress at the growing turbulence, much of it meaningless and self-destructive, in the academic community and above all horror at the profoundly immoral and unjustified war in Vietnam. These experiences have led me increasingly in the last few years to feel that the problems of American society, not of the developing societies, are the really most serious ones today. But my thinking has also been influenced by the emergence of a counter-culture in America, a culture of imagination and not of calculation. Even with all its pathological fringes the liberation of the expressive life which we have seen in the hippie movement and more broadly in popular culture in recent years seems to me of great significance. This too seems to be saying that we can take nothing for granted in our culture. There are entirely new possibilities which we must open up.

The move from Harvard to Berkeley in 1967 was an outward expression of an inward change. Harvard is in many ways the finest institution of Protestant culture in this country, confident and self-assured in its own value-commitments in a way most American universities are not. I have seen it at its best and I have seen it at less than its best but in any case after twenty years of close association with it it is an integral part of my life. As against the magisterial certainty of Harvard Berkeley stands in sharpest antithesis: not the calm order of Protestant tradition but the wide-open chaos of the post-Protestant, post-modern era. For all of its inner problems, for all of its tensions with an increasingly unsympathetic environment, Berkeley evinces the intensity, the immediacy, the openness and the precariousness of an emergent social order. For one trying to grapple with and define what that order is it is a good place to be.

As against the pessimistic optimism of earlier papers the later ones evince a kind of optimistic pessimism. Perhaps Yeats expresses the mood:

All things fall and are built again,
And those that build them again are gay.[2]

In this situation the playful radicalism of Norman O. Brown seems to me healing while the solemn radicalism of Herbert Marcuse seems destructive. I have learned much from the youthful outpouring of recent years but I am no more inclined to idolize this group than any other. They have brought new styles of freedom, new modes of access to the unconscious, but these styles and modes have been remarkably fragile and have easily disintegrated into cultural nihilism or political fanaticism. Behind the mask of the struggle for liberation one often sees the hard face of the authoritarian who will strangle the young rebels of the next generation.

These last papers do not signal a retreat from political responsibility. They do imply, more strongly than ever, the rejection of any kind of political totalism. But they suggest that in the present situation a politics of the imagination, a politics of religion, may be the only sane politics. There is no hope in any of the competing absolutisms. If the forces at war are locked in their own deathlike scenarios perhaps the only responsible politics is to unmask the pretensions of all the contending parties and give witness to the enormous possibilities in human experience, in a word, to waken the actors out of their trance. To this end a human science can perhaps join with a human religion to help create a human politics.

The relation between the personal search for meaning and wholeness which I have sketched above and the work which follows is a close one. Some of the intellectual influences on me have been mentioned above and others can be discovered from the inspection of footnotes in the various chapters. But the work is not the product just of intellectual influences but of the experience of a particular person at a particular place in history. I have discussed my reaction to successive phases of the history of my society but those phases have not dictated my reaction. Others have reacted very differently. One's life and work are an effort to find a form which will reconcile inner needs and outer pressures. The form itself is unique and personal even though both the inner needs and the outer pressures are transpersonal. In my life there has been a long preoccupation with fragmentation and wholeness and it is this which has made religion such an abiding concern.

In the beginning of my life there was a culture and a family which was incomplete, though, in the sense that I yet had no alternatives, total. In attempting to find a form which would be more complete and more satisfying in late adolescence I adopted the totalistic religio-political system of Marxism. Though this ideology played a valuable integrative role at an important transition stage it proved ultimately to be as much of a straitjacket as an uncritical acceptance of established religious and political values had been. After the rejection of Marxism there was no way back even if I had wanted one. A return to the bosom of American society in the middle fifties could only be made by the suicidal sacrifice of my own integrity. For me the search for wholeness from then on had to be made without totalism. A critical stance toward every society, ideology and religion was thenceforth essential. This did not mean that there was no longer any basis for values nor even that various aspects of tradition could not be appropriated. The loss of faith could become the faith of loss. The self-critical, self-revising, nontotalistic aspects of the tradition could be reclaimed. With respect to Christianity this meant Christ crucified, the assertion of faith in spite of the brokenness of every human structure. With respect to America this meant a society dedicated to its own transcendence, to the realization of human values. In neither case was there a total commitment to the existing church or state but rather to that within them which is always questioning their existing reality. Nor did the reassertion in broken form of a commitment to the Christian and American traditions exclude a deep involvement with other traditions and cultures. Wholeness was not to be obtained through exclusion but through a multi-layered inclusion.

In much of my work up until about 1965 there is to be seen an effort to discern a new system which would be an alternative to Marxism but rival it in sweep and comprehensiveness. To some extent this was a modern apology for liberal society and an attempt to show its relevance to the developing areas. I am by no means ready to repudiate this stage of my work, though I am increasingly aware of its limitations. I still believe that some equivalent of Protestant individualism and voluntaristic social organization is a necessary phase for any person or group who would fully participate in the potential freedom of the modern world.

More recently my attention has turned to the problems of post-Protestant man, man who is not only post-traditional—for Protestantism and some of its functional equivalents, among which I would place humanistic Marxism, are already post-traditional—but also in a sense post-modern.

This post-modern phase cannot be seen as simply a continuous projection of the major trends of present relatively modernized societies. Theorists of modernization have been tempted to assume that once a certain degree of individualism, civic culture and industrial development were achieved the future of a society was essentially nonproblematic. It is hard in 1970 to make that assumption. In fact we do not know where the most advanced societies are going. The more we understand the recent past the better, but the future is a new project full of contingency. The best guides in a time like this may not be the systematic theorists, the public opinion pollers or the scanners of indices and indicators, but poets and ecstatic aphorists like Norman O. Brown. If modernization has brought far greater knowledge, wealth and power than men have ever had before, then, potentially at least, we are freer than men have ever been and our future is more open to make it what we will. But the same resources which can bring us freedom can also be used for oppression and control. Men are not oppressed by armies and unfair economic systems alone. They are also oppressed by dead ideologies which can be locked into personalities and societies and program them on a course of fatal disaster, often in the name of "realism" and "necessity." Under these conditions we have need more than ever for the dreamers of dreams and the seers of visions. Freedom of the imagination, the ability to live in many realities at once, may be our strongest weapons in the struggle for human liberation.

The theme of loss, I now realize, is even more pervasive in this story than I had thought when I touched upon it in the beginning of this introduction. It is a story of loss: the lost father, the lost religion, the lost ideology, the lost country. And yet it is not, finally, a story of existential despair. Even Tillich who was so important in expressing my feelings at certain moments was not in his somberest moods wholly convincing. For the deepest truth I have discovered is that if one accepts the loss, if one gives up clinging to what is irretrievably gone, then the nothing which is left is not barren but enormously fruitful. Everything that one has lost comes flooding back again out of the darkness, and one's relation to it is new—free and unclinging. But the richness of the nothing contains far more, it is the all-possible, it is the spring of freedom. In that sense the faith of loss is closer to joy than to despair.

NOTES AND REFERENCES
1. Paul Tillich, *The Courage to Be*, New Haven, Conn.: Yale University Press, 1952, p. 190.
2. From "Lapis Lazuli," in William Butler Yeats, *The Variorum Edition of the Poems*, New York: Macmillan, 1968, p. 566.

TEILHARD DE CHARDIN

the spirit of the earth

a. mankind

Mankind: the idea of mankind was the first image in terms of which, at the very moment that he awoke to the idea of progress, modern man had to try to reconcile the hopes of an unlimited future with which he could no longer dispense, with the perspective of the inevitability of his own individual death. "Mankind" was at first a vague entity, felt rather than thought out, in which an obscure feeling of perpetual growth was allied to a need for universal fraternity. Mankind was the object of a faith that was often naive but whose magic, being stronger than all vicissitudes and criticisms, goes on working with persuasive force upon the present-day masses and on the "intelligentsia" alike. Whether one takes part in the cult or makes fun of it, even today no one can escape being haunted or even dominated by the idea of mankind.

In the eyes of the "prophets" of the eighteenth century, the world appeared really as no more than a jumble of confused and loose relationships; and the divination of a believer was required to feel the beating heart of that sort of embryo. Now, less than two hundred years later, here we are committed (though hardly conscious of the fact) to the reality, at any rate the material reality, of what our fathers expected. In the course of a few generations all sorts of economic and cultural links have been forged around us and they are multiplying in geometric progression. Nowadays, over and above the bread which to simple Neolithic man symbolized food, each man demands his daily ration of iron, copper and cotton, of electricity, oil and radium, of discoveries, of the cinema and of international news. It is no longer a simple field, however big, but the whole earth which is required to nourish each one of us. If words have any meaning, is this not like some great body which is being born—with its limbs, its nervous system, its perceptive organs, its memory—the body in fact of that great Thing which had come to fulfill the ambitions aroused in the reflective being by the newly acquired consciousness that he was at-one with and responsible to an evolutionary All?

Abridged from pp. 147–160, 245–253 in *The Phenomenon of Man* by Pierre Teilhard de Chardin, trans. by Bernard Wall. Copyright 1955 by Editions du Seuil. Copyright © 1959 in the English translation by Wm. Collins Sons & Co. Ltd., London, and Harper & Row, Publishers, New York.

Indeed, following logically upon our effort to coordinate and organize the lines of the world, it is to an outlook recalling the initial intuition of the first philanthropists that our minds constantly return, with the elimination of individualist and racial heresies. No evolutionary future awaits man except in association with all other men. The dreamers of yesterday glimpsed that. And in a sense we see the same thing. But what we are better able to perceive, because we stand on their shoulders, are its cosmic roots, its particular physical substance, and finally the specific nature of this mankind of which they could only have a presentiment—and for us not to see this we have to shut our eyes.

Cosmic roots. For the earliest humanitarians, man, in uniting with his fellows, was following a natural precept whose origins people hardly bothered to analyze and hence to measure their gravity. In those days, was not nature treated as a personage or as a poetic metaphor? What she required of us at a particular time she might have just thought up yesterday and perhaps would no longer want tomorrow. For us, more aware of the dimensions and structural demands of the world, the forces which converge upon us from without or arise from within and drive us ever closer together are losing any semblance of arbitrariness and any danger of instability.

Mankind was a fragile and even fictitious construction so long as it could only have a limited, plural and disjointed cosmos as setting; but it becomes consistent and at the same time probable as soon as it is brought within the compass of a biological space-time and appears as a continuation of the very lines of the universe amongst other realities as vast as itself.

Physical stuff. For many of our contemporaries, mankind still remains something unreal, unless materialized in an absurd way. For some it is only an abstract entity or even a mere conventional expression; for others it becomes a closely knit organic group in which the social element can be transcribed literally in terms of anatomy and physiology. It appears either as a general idea, a legal entity, or else as a gigantic animal. In both views we find the same inability, by default or by excess, to think the whole correctly. Does not the only way out of this dead-end lie in introducing boldly into our intellectual framework yet another category to serve for the super-individual?

. . .

To the eye that has become adjusted to the perspectives of evolution, the directed groups of phyla, layers, branches, etc., become perforce as clear, as physically real, as any isolated object. And in this class of particular size mankind naturally takes its place. But, for it to become representable to us, it is enough that by a mental re-orientation we should reach the point of seeing it directly, exactly as it is, without attempting to put it into terms of anything simpler which we know already.

Specific nature. Here, lastly, we pick up the problem again at the point at which the realization of the confluence of human thoughts had already led us. Being a collective reality, and therefore *sui generis,* mankind can only be understood to the extent that, leaving behind its body of tangible constructions, we try to determine the particular type of conscious synthesis emerging from its laborious and industrious concentration. It is in the last resort only definable as a mind.

Now from this point of view and in the present condition of things, there are two ways, through two stages, in which we can picture the form mankind will assume tomorrow—either (and this is simpler) as a common power and act of knowing and doing, or (and this goes much deeper) as an organic super-aggregation of souls. In short: knowledge or unanimity.

b. knowledge

Taken in the full modern sense of the word, knowledge is the twin sister of mankind. Born together, the two ideas (or two dreams) grew up together to attain an almost religious valuation in the course of the last century. Subsequently they fell together into the same disrepute. But that does not prevent them, when mutually supporting one another as they do, from continuing to represent (in fact more than ever) the ideal forces upon which our imagination falls back whenever it seeks to materialize in terrestrial form its reasons for believing and hoping.

The future of knowledge . . . As a first approximation it is outlined on our horizon as the establishment of an overall and completely coherent perspective of the universe. There was a time when the only part ascribed to knowledge lay in lighting up for our speculative pleasure the objects made ready and given around us. Nowadays, thanks to a philosophy which has given a meaning and a consecration to our thirst to think all things, we can glimpse that unconsciousness is a sort of ontological inferiority or evil, since the world can only fulfill itself in so far as it expresses itself in a systematic and reflective perception. Even (above all, in fact) in mathematics, is not "discovery" the bringing into existence of something new? From this point of view, intellectual discovery and synthesis are no longer merely speculation but creation. From this point onwards, some physical consummation of things is bound up with the explicit perception we make of them. And from this point onwards they are (at least partially) right who situate the crown of evolution in a supreme act of collective vision obtained by a panhuman effort of investigation and construction.

Knowledge for its own sake. But also, and perhaps still more, *knowledge for power.*

Since its birth, knowledge has made its greatest advances when stimulated by some particular problem of life needing a solution; and its most sublime theories would always have drifted, rootless, on the flood of human thought if they had not been promptly incorporated into some way of mastering the world. Accordingly the march of humanity, as a prolongation of that of all other animate forms, develops indubitably in the direction of a conquest of matter put to the service of mind. *Increased power for increased action.* But, finally and above all, *increased action for increased being.*

Of old, the forerunners of our chemists strove to find the philosopher's stone. Our ambition has grown since then. It is no longer to find gold but life; and in view of all that has happened in the last fifty years, who would dare to say that this is a mere mirage? With our knowledge of hormones we appear to be on the eve of having a hand in the development of our bodies and even of our brains. With the discovery of genes it appears that we shall soon be able to control the mechanism of organic heredity. And with the synthesis of albuminoids imminent, we may well one day be capable of producing what the earth, left to itself, seems no longer able to produce: a new wave of organisms, an artificially provoked neo-life. Immense and prolonged as the universal groping has been since the beginning, many possible combinations have been able to slip through the fingers of chance and have had to await man's calculated measures in order to appear. Thought artificially perfects the thinking instrument itself; life rebounds forward under the collective effect of its reflection. The dream which human research obscurely fosters is fundamentally that of mastering, beyond all atomic or molecular affinities, the ultimate energy of which all other energies are merely servants; and thus, by grasping the very mainspring of evolution, seizing the tiller of the world.

I salute those who have the courage to admit that their hopes extend that far; they are at the pinnacle of mankind; and I would say to them that there is less difference than people think between research and adoration. But there is a point I would like them to note, one that will lead us gradually to a more complete form of conquest and adoration. However far knowledge pushes its discovery of the "essential fire" and however capable it becomes some day of remodeling and perfecting the human element, it will always find itself in the end facing the same problem—how to give to each and every element its final value by grouping them in the unity of an organized whole.

c. unanimity

We have used the term mega-synthesis. When based on a better understanding of the collective, it seems to me that the word should be understood without attenuation or metaphors when applied to the sum of all human beings. The universe is necessarily homogeneous in its nature and dimensions. Would it still be so if the loops of its spiral lost one jot or tittle of their degree of reality or consistence in ascending ever higher? The still unnamed Thing which the gradual combination of individuals, peoples and races will bring into existence, must needs be *supra-physical,* not *infra-physical,* if it is to be coherent with the rest. Deeper than the common act in which it expresses itself, more important than the common power of action from which it emerges by a sort of self-birth, lies reality itself, constituted by the living reunion of reflective particles.

And what does that amount to if not (and it is quite credible) that the stuff of the universe, by becoming thinking, has not yet completed its evolutionary cycle, and that we are therefore moving forward towards some new critical point that lies ahead. In spite of its organic links, whose existence has everywhere become apparent to us, the biosphere has so far been no more than a network of divergent lines, free at their extremities. By effect of reflection and the recoils it involves, the loose ends have been tied up, and the noosphere tends to constitute a single closed system in which each element sees, feels, desires and suffers for itself the same things as all the others at the same time.

We are faced with a harmonized collectivity of consciousnesses equivalent to a sort of super-consciousness. The idea is that of the earth not only becoming covered by myriads of grains of thought, but becoming enclosed in a single thinking envelope so as to form, functionally, no more than a single vast grain of thought on the sidereal scale, the plurality of individual reflections grouping themselves together and reinforcing one another in the act of a single unanimous reflection.

This is the general form in which, by analogy and in symmetry with the past, we are led scientifically to envisage the future of mankind, without whom no terrestrial issue is open to the terrestrial demands of our action.

To the common sense of the "man-in-the-street" and even to a certain philosophy of the world to which nothing is possible save what has always been, perspectives such as these will seem highly improbable. But to a mind become familiar with the fantastic dimensions of the universe they will, on the contrary, seem quite natural, because they are directly proportionate with astronomical immensities.

In the direction of thought, could the universe terminate with anything less than the measureless—any more than it could in the direction of time and space?

One thing at any rate is sure—from the moment we adopt a thoroughly realistic view of the noosphere and of the hyper-organic nature of social bonds, the present situation of the world becomes clearer; for we find a very simple meaning for the profound troubles which disturb the layer of mankind at this moment.

The two-fold crisis whose onset began in earnest as early as the Neolithic age and which rose to a climax in the modern world, derives in the first place from a *mass-formation* (we might call it a "planetization") of mankind. Peoples and civilizations reached such a degree either of physical communion or economic interdependence or frontier contact that they could no longer develop save by interpenetration of one another. But it also arises out of the fact that, under the combined influence of machinery and the super-heating of thought, we are witnessing *a formidable upsurge of unused powers.* Modern man no longer knows what to do with the time and the potentialities he has unleashed. We groan under the burden of this wealth. We are haunted by the fear of "unemployment." Sometimes we are tempted to trample this super-abundance back into the matter from which it sprang without stopping to think how impossible and monstrous such an act against nature would be.

When we consider the increasing compression of elements at the heart of a

free energy which is also relentlessly increasing, how can we fail to see in this
two-fold phenomenon the two perennial symptoms of a leap forward of the
"radial"—that is to say of a new step in the genesis of mind?

In order to avoid disturbing our habits we seek in vain to settle international
disputes by adjustments of frontiers—or we treat as "leisure" (to be whiled
away) the activities at the disposal of mankind. As things are now going it will
not be long before we run full tilt into one another. Something will explode if
we persist in trying to squeeze into our old tumble-down huts the material and
spiritual forces that are henceforward on the scale of a world.

A new domain of psychical expansion—that is what we lack. And it is staring
us in the face if we would only raise our heads to look at it.

Peace through conquest, work in joy. These are waiting for us beyond the line
where empires are set up against other empires, in an interior totalization of the
world upon itself, in the unanimous construction of a *spirit of the earth.*

a new heaven
and a new earth _____

Then I saw a new heaven and a new earth; for the first heaven and the first earth
had passed away, and the sea was no more. And I saw the holy city, new Jerusalem, coming down out of heaven from God, prepared as a bride adorned for her
husband; and I heard a great voice from the throne saying, "Behold, the dwelling
of God is with men. He will dwell with them, and they shall be his people, and
God himself will be with them; he will wipe away every tear from their eyes, and
death shall be no more, neither shall there be mourning nor crying nor pain any
more, for the former things have passed away."

And he who sat upon the throne said, "Behold, I make all things new." Also
he said, "Write this, for these words are trustworthy and true." And he said to
me, "It is done! I am the Alpha and the Omega, the beginning and the end. To
the thirsty I will give water without price from the fountain of the water of life.
He who conquers shall have this heritage, and I will be his God and he shall be
my son. But as for the cowardly, the faithless, the polluted, as for murderers,
fornicators, sorcerers, idolaters, and all liars, their lot shall be in the lake that
burns with fire and brimstone, which is the second death."

And he who talked to me had a measuring rod of gold to measure the city
and its gates and walls. The city lies foursquare, its length the same as its breadth;
and he measured the city with his rod, twelve thousand stadia; its length and

From *The Revelation to John,* chap. 21. Revised Standard Version Bible copyright 1946,
1952 by the Division of Christian Education, National Council of Churches, used by permission. Also selections on pp. 281, 312, 313, 315, 316, 318, and 319.

breadth and height are equal. He also measured its wall, a hundred and forty-four cubits by a man's measure, that is, an angel's. The wall was built of jasper, while the city was pure gold, clear as glass. The foundations of the wall of the city were adorned with every jewel; the first was jasper, the second sapphire, the third agate, the fourth emerald, the fifth onyx, the sixth carnelian, the seventh chrysolite, the eighth beryl, the ninth topaz, the tenth chrysoprase, the eleventh jacinth, the twelfth amethyst. And the twelve gates were twelve pearls, each of the gates made of a single pearl, and the street of the city was pure gold, transparent as glass.

Then came one of the seven angels who had the seven bowls full of the seven last plagues, and spoke to me saying, "Come, I will show you the Bride, the wife of the Lamb." And in the Spirit he carried me away to a great, high mountain, and showed me the holy city Jerusalem coming down out of heaven from God, having the glory of God, its radiance like a most rare jewel, like a jasper, clear as crystal. It had a great, high wall, with twelve gates, and at the gates twelve angels, and on the gates the names of the twelve tribes of the sons of Israel were inscribed; on the east three gates, on the north three gates, on the south three gates, and on the west three gates. And the wall of the city had twelve foundations, and on them the twelve names of the twelve apostles of the Lamb.

And I saw no temple in the city, for its temple is the Lord God the Almighty and the Lamb. And the city has no need of sun or moon to shine upon it, for the glory of God is its light, and its lamp is the Lamb. By its light shall the nations walk; and the kings of the earth shall bring their glory into it, and its gates shall never be shut by day—and there shall be no night there; they shall bring into it the glory and the honor of the nations. But nothing unclean shall enter it, nor any one who practices abomination or falsehood, but only those who are written in the Lamb's book of life.

BORIS PASTERNAK

the garden of gethsemane _____

The turn in the road was illumined
By the indifferent glimmer of the remote stars.
The road led around the Mount of Olives;
Below, in its valley, the Brook Kedron ran.

Halfway, the small meadow dipped in a sharp break;
Beyond it began the great Milky Way,

Trans. Bernard Guilbert Guerney, from *Doctor Zhivago,* trans. Max Hayward and Manya Harari, New York, Pantheon, 1958.

While the silver-gray olives still strained forward
As if to stride onward upon empty air.

Furthest away was someone's garden plot.
He left His disciples outside the stone fence
Saying, "My soul is exceeding sorrowful, even unto death;
Tarry ye here, and watch with me."

He had rejected without resistance
Dominion over all things and the power to work miracles,
As though these had been His only on loan
And now was as all mortals are, even as we.

Night's distance seemed the very brink
Of annihilation, of nonexistence.
The universe's span was void of any life;
The garden only was a coign of being.

And peering into these black abysses—
Void, without end and without beginning—
His brow sweating blood, He pleaded with His Father
That this cup of death might pass from Him.

Having eased His mortal anguish through prayer,
He left the garden. Beyond its wall His disciples,
Overcome with sleep, sprawled on the ground
In the wayside feathergrass.

He awakened them: "God hath granted you to live
During my days on earth, and yet you lie there sprawling.
Behold, the hour is at hand, and the Son of Man
Shall betray Himself into the hands of sinners."

He had scarcely spoken when, coming from none knew where,
A throng of slaves sprang up, a host of vagrant men
With swords and torches, and at their head stood Judas
With the perfidious kiss writhing on his lips.

Peter drew sword and thrust the cutthroats back
And struck a man and smote off his ear.
Whereon he heard, "No metal can resolve dissension.
Put up thy sword again into his place.

Thinkest thou my Father would not send
Sky-darkening hosts of winged legions to my succor?
And without harming even a hair of mine
My enemies would scatter, leaving no trace behind.

But now the book of life has reached a page
Which is more precious than are all the holies.

That which was written now must be fulfilled.
Fulfillèd be it, then. Amen.

Seest thou, the passing of the ages is like a parable
And in its passing it may burst to flame.
In the name, then, of its awesome majesty
I shall, in voluntary torments, descend into my grave.

I shall descend into my grave. And on the third day rise again.
And, even as rafts float down a river,
So shall the centuries drift, trailing like a caravan,
Coming for judgment, out of the dark, to me."

ARCHIBALD MAC LEISH

epistle to be left in the earth _____

. . . It is colder now,
                        there are many stars,
                                    we are drifting
North by the Great Bear,
                        the leaves are falling,
The water is stone in the scooped rocks,
                                    to southward
Red sun grey air:
                the crows are
Slow on their crooked wings,
                                    the jays have left us:
Long since we passed the flares of Orion.
Each man believes in his heart he will die.
Many have written last thoughts and last letters.
None know if our deaths are now or forever:
None know if this wandering earth will be found.

We lie down and the snow covers our garments.
I pray you,
                you (if any open this writing)
Make in your mouths the words that were our names.
I will tell you all we have learned,
                                    I will tell you everything:

From *The Collected Poems of Archibald MacLeish,* Boston, Houghton Mifflin, 1962.

The earth is round,
>   There are springs under the orchards,
The loam cuts with a blunt knife,
>   beware of
Elms in thunder,
>   the lights in the sky are stars—
We think they do not see,
>   we think also
The trees do not know nor the leaves of the grasses hear us:
The birds too are ignorant.
>   Do not listen.
Do not stand at dark in the open windows.
We before you have heard this:
>   they are voices:
They are not words at all but the wind rising.
Also none among us has seen God.
(. . . We have thought often
The flaws of sun in the late and driving weather
Pointed to one tree but it was not so.)
As for the nights I warn you the nights are dangerous:
The wind changes at night and the dreams come.

It is very cold,
>   there are strange stars near Arcturus,
Voices are crying an unknown name in the sky.

MIRCEA ELIADE

the terror of history

The reappearance of cyclical theories in contemporary thought is pregnant with meaning. Incompetent as we are to pass judgment upon their validity, we shall confine ourselves to observing that the formulation, in modern terms, of an archaic myth betrays at least the desire to find a meaning and a transhistorical justification for historical events. Thus we find ourselves once again in the pre-Hegelian position, the validity of the "historicistic" solutions, from Hegel to Marx, being implicitly called into question. From Hegel on, every effort is direct-

From *The Myth of the Eternal Return* by Mircea Eliade, trans. Willard R. Trask, Bollinger Series XLVI (copyright © 1954 by Bollinger Foundation), reprinted by permission of Princeton University Press.

ed toward saving and conferring value on the historical event as such, the event in itself and for itself. In his study of the German Constitution, Hegel wrote that if we recognize that things are necessarily as they are, that is, that they are not arbitrary and not the result of chance, we shall at the same time recognize that they *must* be as they are. A century later, the concept of historical necessity will enjoy a more and more triumphant practical application: in fact, all the cruelties, aberrations, and tragedies of history have been, and still are, justified by the necessities of the "historical moment." Probably Hegel did not intend to go so far. But since he had resolved to reconcile himself with his own historical moment, he was obliged to see in every event the will of the Universal Spirit. This is why he considered "reading the morning papers a sort of realistic benediction of the morning." For him, only daily contact with events could orient man's conduct in his relations with the world and with God.

· · ·

The terror of history becomes more and more intolerable from the viewpoints afforded by the various historicistic philosophies. For in them, of course, every historical event finds its full and only meaning in its realization alone.

· · ·

For our purpose, only one question concerns us: How can the "terror of history" be tolerated from the viewpoint of historicism? Justification of a historical event by the simple fact that it is a historical event, in other words, by the simple fact that it "happened that way," will not go far toward freeing humanity from the terror that the event inspires. Be it understood that we are not here concerned with the problem of evil, which, from whatever angle it be viewed, remains a philosophical and religious problem; we are concerned with the problem of history as history, of the "evil" that is bound up not with man's condition but with his behavior toward others. We should wish to know, for example, how it would be possible to tolerate, and to justify, the sufferings and annihilation of so many peoples who suffer and are annihilated for the simple reason that their geographical situation sets them in the pathway of history; that they are neighbors of empires in a state of permanent expansion. How justify, for example, the fact that southeastern Europe had to suffer for centuries—and hence to renounce any impulse toward a higher historical existence, toward spiritual creation on the universal plane—for the sole reason that it happened to be on the road of the Asiatic invaders and later the neighbor of the Ottoman Empire? And in our day, when historical pressure no longer allows any escape, how can man tolerate the catastrophes and horrors of history—from collective deportations and massacres to atomic bombings—if beyond them he can glimpse no sign, no transhistorical meaning; if they are only the blind play of economic, social, or political forces, or, even worse, only the result of the "liberties" that a minority takes and exercises directly on the stage of universal history?

We know how, in the past, humanity has been able to endure the sufferings we have enumerated: they were regarded as a punishment inflicted by God, the syndrome of the decline of the "age," and so on. And it was possible to accept them precisely because they had a metahistorical meaning, because, for the greater part of mankind, still clinging to the traditional viewpoint, history did not have, and could not have, value in itself. Every hero repeated the archetypal gesture, every war rehearsed the struggle between good and evil, every fresh social injustice was identified with the sufferings of the Saviour (or, for example, in the pre-Christian world, with the passion of a divine messenger or vegetation god), each new massacre repeated the glorious end of the martyrs. It is not our part to decide whether such motives were puerile or not, or whether such a refusal of history always proved efficacious. In our opinion, only one fact counts: by virtue of this view, tens of millions of men were able, for century after century, to endure great historical pressures without despairing, without committing suicide or falling into that spiritual aridity that always brings with it a relativistic or nihilistic view of history.

· · ·

It is worth noting that the work of two of the most significant writers of our day—T. S. Eliot and James Joyce—is saturated with nostalgia for the myth of eternal repetition and, in the last analysis, for the abolition of time. There is also reason to foresee that, as the terror of history grows worse, as existence becomes more and more precarious because of history, the positions of historicism will increasingly lose in prestige. And, at a moment when history could do what neither the cosmos, nor man, nor chance have yet succeeded in doing—that is, wipe out the human race in its entirety—it may be that we are witnessing a desperate attempt to prohibit the "events of history" through a reintegration of human societies within the horizon (artificial, because decreed) of archetypes and their repetition. In other words, it is not inadmissible to think of an epoch, and an epoch not too far distant, when humanity, to ensure its survival, will find itself reduced to desisting from any further "making" of history in the sense in which it began to make it from the creation of the first empires, will confine itself to repeating prescribed archetypal gestures, and will strive to forget, as meaningless and dangerous, any spontaneous gesture which might entail "historical" consequences. It would even be interesting to compare the anhistorical solution of future societies with the paradisal or eschatological myths of the golden age of the beginning or the end of the world. But as we have it in mind to pursue these speculations elsewhere, let us now return to our problem: the position of historical man in relation to archaic man, and let us attempt to understand the objections brought against the latter on the basis of the historicistic view.

· · ·

In this total adherence, on the part of archaic man, to archetypes and repetition, modern man would be justified in seeing not only the primitives' amazement at their own first spontaneous and creative free gestures and their veneration, repeated *ad infinitum,* but also a feeling of guilt on the part of man hardly emerged from the paradise of animality (i.e., from nature), a feeling that urges him to reidentify with nature's eternal repetition the few primordial, creative, and spontaneous gestures that had signalized the appearance of freedom. Continuing his critique, modern man could even read in this fear, this hesitation or fatigue in the presence of any gesture without an archetype, nature's tendency toward equilibrium and rest; and he would read this tendency in the anticlimax that fatally follows upon any exuberant gesture of life and that some have gone so far as to recognize in the need felt by human reason to unify the real through knowledge. In the last analysis, modern man, who accepts history or claims to accept it, can reproach archaic man, imprisoned within the mythical horizon of archetypes and repetition, with his creative impotence, or, what amounts to the same thing, his inability to accept the risks entailed by every creative act. For the modern man can be creative only insofar as he is historical; in other words, all creation is forbidden him except that which has its source in his own freedom; and, consequently, everything is denied him except the freedom to make history by making himself.

To these criticisms raised by modern man, the man of the traditional civilizations could reply by a countercriticism that would at the same time be a defense of the type of archaic existence. It is becoming more and more doubtful, he might say, if modern man can make history. On the contrary, the more modern he becomes—that is, without defenses against the terror of history—the less chance he has of himself making history.

• • •

Whatever be the truth in respect to the freedom and the creative virtualities of historical man, it is certain that none of the historicistic philosophies is able to defend him from the terror of history. We could even imagine a final attempt: to save history and establish an ontology of history, events would be regarded as a series of "situations" by virtue of which the human spirit should attain knowledge of levels of reality otherwise inaccessible to it. This attempt to justify history is not without interest, and we anticipate returning to the subject elsewhere. But we are able to observe here and now that such a position affords a shelter from the terror of history only insofar as it postulates the existence at least of the Universal Spirit. What consolation should we find in knowing that the sufferings of millions of men have made possible the revelation of a limitary situation of the human condition if, beyond that limitary situation, there should be only nothingness? Again, there is no question here of judging the validity of a historicistic philosophy, but only of establishing to what extent such a philosophy can exorcise the terror of history. If, for historical tragedies to be excused, it suffices that they should be regarded as the means by which man has been enabled to know the limit of human resistance, such an excuse can in no way make man less haunted by the terror of history.

Basically, the horizon of archetypes and repetition cannot be transcended with impunity unless we accept a philosophy of freedom that does not exclude God. And indeed this proved to be true when the horizon of archetypes and repetition was transcended, for the first time, by Judaeo-Christianism, which introduced a new category into religious experience: the category of *faith*. It must not be forgotten that, if Abraham's faith can be defined as "for God everything is possible," the faith of Christianity implies that everything is also possible for man. "Have faith in God. For verily I say unto you, That whosoever shall say unto this mountain, Be thou removed, and be thou cast into the sea; and shall not doubt in his heart, but shall believe that those things which he saith shall come to pass; he shall have whatsoever he saith. Therefore I say unto you, What things soever ye desire, when ye pray, believe that ye receive them, and ye shall have them" (Mark 11:22–24). Faith, in this context, as in many others, means absolute emancipation from any kind of natural "law" and hence the highest freedom that man can imagine: freedom to intervene even in the ontological constitution of the universe. It is, consequently, a pre-eminently creative freedom. In other words, it constitutes a new formula for man's collaboration with the creation—the first, but also the only such formula accorded to him since the traditional horizon of archetypes and repetition was transcended. Only such a freedom (aside from its soteriological, hence, in the strict sense, its religious value) is able to defend modern man from the terror of history—a freedom, that is, which has its source and finds its guaranty and support in God. Every other modern freedom, whatever satisfactions it may procure to him who possesses it, is powerless to justify history; and this, for every man who is sincere with himself, is equivalent to the terror of history.

We may say, furthermore, that Christianity is the "religion" of modern man and historical man, of the man who simultaneously discovered personal freedom and continuous time (in place of cyclical time).

· · ·

Since the "invention" of faith, in the Judaeo-Christian sense of the word (= for God all is possible), the man who has left the horizon of archetypes and repetition can no longer defend himself against that terror except through the idea of God. In fact, it is only by presupposing the existence of God that he conquers, on the one hand, freedom (which grants him autonomy in a universe governed by laws or, in other words, the "inauguration" of a mode of being that is new and unique in the universe) and, on the other hand, the certainty that historical tragedies have a transhistorical meaning, even if that meaning is not always visible for humanity in its present condition. Any other situation of modern man leads, in the end, to despair. It is a despair provoked not by his own human existentiality, but by his presence in a historical universe in which almost the whole of mankind lives prey to a continual terror (even if not always conscious of it).

In this respect, Christianity incontestibly proves to be the religion of "fallen man": and this to the extent to which modern man is irremediably identified with history and progress, and to which history and progress are a fall, both implying the final abandonment of the paradise of archetypes and repetition.

the second religiousness ⎯⎯⎯⎯⎯⎯⎯⎯⎯⎯⎯⎯⎯⎯⎯⎯⎯⎯

We have in the European-American world of today the occultist and theophist
fraud, the American Christian Science, the untrue Buddhism of drawing-rooms,
the religious arts-and-crafts business (brisker in Germany than even in England)
that caters for groups and cults of Gothic or Late Classical or Taoist sentiment.
Everywhere it is just a toying with myths that no one really believes, a tasting of
cults that it is hoped might fill the inner void. The real belief is always the belief
in atoms and numbers, but it requires this highbrow hocus-pocus to make it
bearable in the long run. Materialism is shallow and honest, mock-religion shallow and dishonest. But the fact that the latter is possible at all foreshadows a
new and genuine spirit of seeking that declares itself, first quietly, but soon emphatically and openly, in the civilized waking-consciousness.

This next phase I call the *Second Religiousness*. It appears in all civilizations
as soon as they have fully formed themselves as such and are beginning to pass,
slowly and imperceptibly, into the nonhistorical state in which time-periods
cease to mean anything. (So far as the Western Civilization is concerned, therefore, we are still many generations short of that point.) The Second Religiousness is the necessary counterpart of Caesarism, which is the final *political* constitution of Late Civilizations; it becomes visible, therefore, in the Augustan Age of
the Classical and about the time of Shi-hwang-ti's time in China. In both phenomena the creative young strength of the Early Culture is lacking. But both
have their greatness nevertheless. That of the Second Religiousness consists in a
deep piety that fills the waking-consciousness—the piety that impressed Herodotus in the (Late) Egyptians and impresses West-Europeans in China, India, and
Islam—and that of Caesarism consists in its unchained might of colossal facts.
But neither in the creations of this piety nor in the form of the Roman Imperi-
um is there anything primary and spontaneous. Nothing is built up, no idea unfolds itself—it is only as if a mist cleared off the land and revealed the old forms,
uncertainly at first, but presently with increasing distinctness. The material of
the Second Religiousness is simply that of the first, genuine, young religiousness—only otherwise experienced and expressed. It starts with Rationalism's
fading out in helplessness, then the forms of the Springtime become visible, and
finally the whole world of the primitive religion, which had receded before the
grand forms of the early faith, returns to the foreground, powerful, in the guise
of the popular syncretism that is to be found in every Culture at this phase.

Every "Age of Enlightenment" proceeds from an unlimited optimism of the
reason—always associated with the type of megalopolitan—to an equally unquali-
fied skepticism. The sovereign waking-consciousness, cut off by walls and artifi-
cialities from living nature and the land about it and under it, cognizes nothing

⎯⎯⎯⎯⎯⎯
From *The Decline of the West,* New York, Knopf, 1937.

outside itself. It applies criticism to its imaginary world, which it has cleared of everyday sense-experience, and continues to do so till it has found the last and subtlest result, the form of the form—itself: namely, nothing. With this the possibilities of physics as a critical mode of world-understanding are exhausted, and the hunger for metaphysics presents itself afresh. But it is not the religious pastimes of educated and literature-soaked cliques, still less is it the intellect, that gives rise to the Second Religiousness. Its source is the naive belief that arises, unremarked but spontaneous, among the masses that there is some sort of mystic constitution of actuality (as to which formal proofs are presently regarded as barren and tiresome word-jugglery), and an equally naive heart-need reverently responding to the myth with a cult. The forms of neither can be foreseen, still less chosen—they appear of themselves, and as far as we are ourselves concerned, we are as yet far distant from them. But already the opinions of Comte and Spencer, the Materialism and the Monism and the Darwinism, which stirred the best minds of the nineteenth century to such passion, have become the world-view proper to country cousins.

The Classical philosophy had exhausted its ground by about 250 B.C. From that time on, "knowledge" was no longer a continually tested and augmented stock, but a belief therein, due basically to force of habit, but still able to convince, thanks to an old and well-tried methodology. In the time of Socrates there had been Rationalism as the religion of educated men, with, above it, the scholar-philosophy and, below it, the "superstition" of the masses. Now, philosophy developed towards an intellectual, and the popular syncretism towards a tangible, religiousness. The tendency was the same in both, and myth-belief and piety spread, not downwards, but upwards. Philosophy had much to receive and little to give. The Stoa had begun in the materialism of the Sophists and Cynics, and had explained the whole mythology on allegorical lines, but the prayer to Zeus at table—one of the most beautiful relics of the Classical Second Religiousness—dates from as early as Cleanthes (d. 232). In Sulla's time there was an upper-class Stoicism that was religious through and through, and a popular syncretism which combined Phrygian, Syrian, and Egyptian cults with numberless Classical mysteries that had become almost forgotten—corresponding exactly to the development of Buddha's enlightened wisdom into Hinayana for the learned and Mahayana for the masses, and to the relation between learned Confucianism and Taoism as the vessel of Chinese syncretism which it soon became.

Contemporary with the "Positivist" Meng-tse (372–289 B.C.) there suddenly began a powerful movement toward alchemy, astrology, and occultism. It has long been a favorite topic of dispute whether this was something new or a recrudescence of old Chinese myth-feeling—but a glance at Hellenism supplies the answer. This syncretism appears "simultaneously" in the Classical, in India and China, and in popular Islam. It starts always on rationalist doctrines—the Stoa, Laotse, Buddha—and carries these through with peasant and springtime and exotic motives of every conceivable sort. From about 200 B.C. the Classical Syncretism—which must not be confused with that of the later Magian Pseudo-

morphosis—raked in motives from Orphism, from Egypt, from Syria; from 67
B.C. the Chinese brought in Indian Buddhism in the popular Mahayana form,
and the potency of the holy writings as charms, and the Buddha figures as fet-
ishes, was thought to be all the greater for their alien origin. The original doctrine of Laotse disappeared very quickly. At the beginning of Han times (c. A.D.
200) the troops of the Sen had ceased to be "moral representations" and become kindly beings. The wind-, cloud-, thunder-, and rain-gods came back.
Crowds of cults which purported to drive out the evil spirits by the aid of the
gods acquired a footing. It was in that time that there arose—doubtless out of
some basic principle of pre-Confucian philosophy—the myth of Pan-ku, the
prime principle from which the series of mythical emperors descended. As we
know, the Logos-idea followed a similar line of development.

The theory and practice of the conduct of life that Buddha taught were the
outcome of world-weariness and intellectual disgusts, and were wholly unrelated
to religious questions. And yet at the very beginning of the Indian "Imperial"
period (250 B.C.) he himself had already become a seated god-figure; and the
Nirvana theories, comprehensible only to the learned, were giving place more
and more to solid and tangible doctrines of heaven, hell, salvation, which were
probably borrowed, as in other syncretisms, from an alien source—namely, Per-
sian Apocalyptic. Already in Asoka's time there were eighteen Buddhist sects.
The salvation doctrine of Mahayana found its first great herald in the port-
scholar Asvagosha (c. 50 B.C.) and its fulfillment proper in Nagarjuna (c. A.D.
150). But side by side with such teaching, the whole mass of proto-Indian mythology came back into circulation. The Vishnu and Shiva religions were already
in 300 B.C. in definite shape, and, moreover, in syncretic form, so that the
Krishna and the Rama legends were now transferred to Vishnu. We have the
same spectacle in the Egyptian New Empire, where Amen of Thebes formed the
center of a vast syncretism, and again in the Arabian world of the Abbassids,
where the folk-religion, with its images of Purgatory, Hell, Last Judgment, the
heavenly Kaaba, Logos-Mohammed, fairies, saints, and spooks drove pristine
Islam entirely into the background.

There are still in such times a few high intellects like Nero's tutor Seneca and
his antitype Psellus the philosopher, royal tutor and politician of Byzantium's
Caesarism-phase; like Marcus Aurelius the Stoic and Asoka the Buddhist, who
were themselves the Caesars; like the Pharaoh Amenhotep IV (Akhenaton),
whose deeply significant experiment was treated as heresy and brought to
naught by the powerful Amen priesthood—a risk that Asoka, too, had, no doubt,
to face from the Brahmins.

But Caesarism itself, in the Chinese as in the Roman Empire, gave birth to an
emperor cult, and thereby concentrated Syncretism. It is an absurd notion that
the veneration of the Chinese for the living emperor is a relic of ancient religion.
During the whole course of the Chinese Culture there were no emperors at all.
The rulers of the States were called Wang (that is, kings), and scarcely a century
before the final victory of the Chinese Augustus Meng-tse wrote—in the vein of

our nineteenth century—"The people is the most important element in the country; next come the useful gods of the soil and the crops, and least in importance comes the ruler." The mythology of the pristine emperors was without doubt put together by Confucius and his contemporaries, its constitutional and socioethical form was dictated by their rationalist aims, and from this myth the first Chinese Caesar borrowed both title and cult idea. The elevation of men to divinity is the full-cycle return to the springtime in which gods were converted into heroes—exactly like these very emperors and the figures of Homer—and it is a distinguishing trait of almost all religions of this second degree. Confucius himself was deified in A.D. 57, with an official cult, and Buddha had been so long before. Al Ghazali (c. 1050), who helped to bring about the "Second Religiousness" of the Islamic world, is now, in the popular belief, a divine being and is beloved as a saint and helper. In the philosophy schools of the Classical there was a cult of Plato, and of Epicurus, and Alexander's claim to descent from Heracles and Caesar's to descent from Venus lead directly to the cult of the *Divus,* in which immemorial Orphic imaginings and family religions crop up afresh, just as the cult of Hwang-ti contains traits of the most ancient mythology of China.

But with the coming of the emperor cults there begins at once, in each of the two, an attempt to bring the Second Religiousness into fixed organizations, which, however named—sects, orders, Churches—are always stiff reconstructions of what had been living forms of the Springtime, and bear the same relation to these as "caste" bears to "status."

There are signs of the tendency even in the Augustan reforms, with their artificial revival of long-dead city cults, such as the rites of the Fratres Arvales, but it is only with the Hellenistic mystery religions, or even with Mithraism, that community or Church organization proper begins, and its development is broken off in the ensuing downfall of the Classical. The corresponding feature in Egypt is the theocratic state set up by the priest-kings of Thebes in the eleventh century. The Chinese analogue is the Tao churches of the Han period and especially that founded by Chang-lu, which gave rise to the fearful insurrection of the Yellow Turbans (recalling the religious provincial rebellions of the Roman Empire), which devastated whole regions and brought about the fall of the Han dynasty. And the very counterpart of these ascetic Churches of Taoism, with their rigidity and wild mythology, is to be found in the late Byzantine monk states such as Studion and the autonomous group of monasteries on Athos, founded in 1100, which are as suggestive of Buddhism as anything could well be.

In the end Second Religiousness issues in the *fellah religions.* Here the opposition between cosmopolitan and provincial piety has vanished again, as completely as that between primitive and higher Culture. What this means the conception of the fellah people . . . tells us. Religion becomes entirely historyless; where formerly decades constituted an epoch, now whole centuries pass unimportantly, and the ups and downs of superficial changes only serve to show the unalterable finality of the inner state. It matters nothing that "Chufucianism" appeared in China (1200) as a variant of the Confucian state doctrine, when it appeared, and whether or not it succeeded. Equally, it signifies nothing that Indian Buddhism, long become a polytheistic religion of the people, went down before Neo-Brahmanism (whose great divine, Sankhara, lived about 800), nor is it of importance to know the date at which the latter passed over into the Hinduism of Brahma, Vishnu, and Shiva. There always are and always will be a handful of superlatively intellectual, thoughtful, and perfectly self-sufficing people, like the Brahmins in India, the Mandarins in China, and the Egyptian priests who amazed Herodotus. But the fellah religion itself is once more primitive through and through.

PART 4
new directions

We considered putting a question mark after this title, since we are not sure whether any of these tentative out-reachings are in a viable direction. Some of them no doubt represent fundamental elements in any possible future. The urge toward fresh immediate experience in religion, for instance, may not take the form of drug-induced ecstasies, but it almost certainly will not settle back content with second-hand reports. Similar things may be said of the longing for a more total educational experience as called for by Brown and Keen. With the breakdown of many aspects of societal life the search for new forms of community will certainly continue. We have included a couple of selections on communes.

Changes in the religious scene are so numerous that it is hard to be sure that we are representative, but Franck's account of the Roman Catholic renewal in Holland, "The Exploding Church," has wide implications beyond that denomination. It is hard to assess the so-called charismatic renewal, symbolized by such phenomena as speaking in tongues, that has appeared in both Catholic and Protestant circles. We have included one essay on this, "The Groovy Christians of Rye, N.Y." Franck's essay points to a more humanistic dimension in renewal while the "Groovy Christians" points in a somewhat different direction.

Certainly there is an upsurge in the ecstatic dimension, the urge toward more feeling and emotion in the place of institutional patterning and rational reflection. This is not new in the history of religion. We have for this reason included a selection from the biblical Song of Solomon and a poem of the greatest Christian mystic, St. John of the Cross.

Among other new things is an exciting dialogue between former enemies and rivals in religion. Selections from the Marxist-Christian and Buddhist-Christian dialogue serve to illustrate this trend.

The psychologists also have things to say about new directions. The short essay by B. F. Skinner is introduced to indicate the possibility that science may condemn man to a purely horizontal existence in which reference to religion will be unnecessary. Jung's essay, an introduction to the Chinese classic, the *I-Ching,* now popular among students, is useful because it contrasts some Western scientific modes of thought with the ancient Taoist perspective on the world. It also stands for the rise of magical forms of thought in our highly rational world. Less credible expressions of that thrust—astrology and palmistry, for instance—have not been represented. But there is no question that a more intuitive approach to existence is in the wind.

We have let a single but important movement, Transcendental Meditation, stand for the fact that many young people in the Western world are now experimenting with meditation in one way or another. A Zen example appears in Part 5. It was tempting to include some Western examples, but space precluded it despite the fact that the Western tradition of prayer and meditation may be less well known than Eastern variations on this theme.

a light exists in spring _____

A light exists in spring
    Not present on the year
At any other period.
    When March is scarcely here

A color stands abroad
    On solitary hills
That science cannot overtake,
    But human nature *feels*.

It waits upon the lawn;
    It shows the furthest tree
Upon the furthest slope we know;
    It almost speaks to me.

Then, as horizons step,
    Or noons report away,
Without the formula of sound,
    It passes, and we stay:

A quality of loss
    Affecting our content,
As trade had suddenly encroached
    Upon a sacrament.

From *Selected Poems and Letters of Emily Dickinson,* New York, Anchor Books, 1959.

the joyous cosmology _____

Eastern teachers work on the esoteric and aristocratic principle that the student must learn the hard way and find out almost everything for himself. Aside from occasional hints, the teacher merely accepts or rejects the student's attainments. But Western teachers work on the exoteric and democratic principle that everything possible must be done to inform and assist the student so as to make his mastery of the subject as easy as possible. Does the latter approach, as purists insist, merely vulgarize the discipline? The answer is that it depends upon the type of discipline. If everyone learns enough mathematics to master quadratic

From *The Joyous Cosmology,* New York, Vintage Books, 1962.

equations, the attainment will seem small in comparison with the much rarer comprehension of the theory of numbers. But the transformation of consciousness undertaken in Taoism and Zen is more like the correction of faulty perception or the curing of a disease. It is not an acquisitive process of learning more and more facts or greater and greater skills, but rather an unlearning of wrong habits and opinions. As Laotzu said, "The scholar gains every day, but the Taoist loses every day."

.   .   .

My own main interest in the study of comparative mysticism has been to cut through these tangles and to identify the essential psychological processes underlying those alterations of perception which enable us to see ourselves and the world in their basic unity. I have perhaps had some small measure of success in trying, Western fashion, to make this type of experience more accessible. I am therefore at once gratified and embarrassed by a development in Western science which could possibly put this unitive vision of the world, by almost shockingly easy means, within the reach of many who have thus far sought it in vain by traditional methods.

Is it possible, then, that Western science could provide a medicine which would at least give the human organism a start in releasing itself from its chronic self-contradiction? The medicine might indeed have to be supported by other procedures—psychotherapy, "spiritual" disciplines, and basic changes in one's pattern of life—but every diseased person seems to need some kind of initial lift to set him on the way to health. The question is by no means absurd if it is true that what afflicts us is a sickness not just of the mind but of the organism, of the very functioning of the nervous system and the brain. Is there, in short, a medicine which can give us temporarily the sensation of being integrated, of being fully one with ourselves and with nature as the biologist knows us, theoretically, to be? If so, the experience might offer clues to whatever else must be done to bring about full and continuous integration. It might be at least the tip of an Ariadne's thread to lead us out of the maze in which all of us are lost from our infancy.

.   .   .

Despite the widespread and undiscriminating prejudice against drugs as such, and despite the claims of certain religious disciplines to be the sole means to genuine mystical insight, I can find no essential difference between the experiences induced, under favorable conditions, by these chemicals and the states of "cosmic consciousness" recorded by R. M. Bucke, William James, Evelyn Underhill, Raynor Johnson, and other investigators of mysticism. "Favorable conditions" means a setting which is socially and physically congenial; ideally this would be some sort of retreat house (*not* a hospital or sanitarium) supervised by religiously oriented psychiatrists or psychologists. The atmosphere should be homelike rather than clinical, and it is of the utmost importance that the supervisor's attitude be supportive and sympathetic. Under insecure, bizarre, or unfriendly circumstances the experience can easily degenerate into a highly unpleasant paranoia. Two days should be set aside—one for the experience itself, which lasts for six or eight hours, and one for evaluation in the calm and relaxed frame of mind that normally follows.

. . .

In using lysergic acid or psilocybin, I usually start with some such theme as polarity, transformation (as of food into organism), competition for survival, the relation of the abstract to the concrete, or of Logos to Eros, and then allow my heightened perception to elucidate the theme in terms of certain works of art or music, of some such natural object as a fern, a flower, or a sea shell, of a religious or mythological archetype (it might be the Mass), and even of personal relationships with those who happen to be with me at the time. Or I may concentrate upon one of the senses and try, as it were, to turn it back upon itself so as to see the process of seeing, and from this move on to trying to know knowing, so approaching the problem of my own identity.

From these reflections there arise intuitive insights of astonishing clarity, and because there is little difficulty in remembering them after the effects of the drug have ceased (especially if they are recorded or written down at the time), the days or weeks following may be used for testing them by the normal standards of logical, aesthetic, philosophical, or scientific criticism. As might be expected, some prove to be valid and others not. It is the same with the sudden hunches that come to the artist or inventor in the ordinary way; they are not always as true or as applicable as they seem to be in the moment of illumination. The drugs appear to give an enormous impetus to the creative intuition, and thus to be of more value for constructive invention and research than for psychotherapy in the ordinary sense of "adjusting" the disturbed personality. Their best sphere of use is not the mental hospital but the studio and the laboratory, or the institute of advanced studies.

. . .

I have written this account as if the whole experience had happened on one day in a single place, but it is in fact a composite of several occasions. Except where I am describing visions before closed eyes, and this is always specified, none of these experiences are hallucinations.

. . .

To begin with, this world has a different kind of time. It is the time of biological rhythm, not of the clock and all that goes with the clock. There is no hurry. Our sense of time is notoriously subjective and thus dependent upon the quality of our attention, whether of interest or boredom, and upon the alignment of our behavior in terms of routines, goals, and deadlines. Here the present is self-sufficient, but it is not a static present. It is a dancing present—the unfolding of a pattern which has no specific destination in the future but is simply its own point. It leaves and arrives simultaneously, and the seed is as much the goal as the flower. There is therefore time to perceive every detail of the movement with infinitely greater richness of articulation. Normally we do not so much look at things as overlook them. The eye sees types and classes—flower, leaf, rock, bird, fire—mental pictures of things rather than things, rough outlines filled with flat color, always a little dusty and dim.

But here the depth of light and structure in a bursting bud go on forever. There is time to see them, time for the whole intricacy of veins and capillaries to develop in consciousness, time to see down and down into the shape of greenness, which is not green at all, but a whole spectrum generalizing itself as green—purple, gold, the sunlit turquoise of the ocean, the intense luminescence of the emerald. I cannot decide where shape ends and color begins. The bud has opened and the fresh leaves fan out and curve back with a gesture which is unmistakably communicative but does not say anything except, "Thus!" And somehow that is quite satisfactory, even startlingly clear. The meaning is transparent in the same way that the color and the texture are transparent, with light which does not seem to fall upon surfaces from above but to be right inside the structure and color. Which is of course where it is, for light is an inseparable trinity of sun, object, and eye, and the chemistry of the leaf is its color, its light.

But at the same time color and light are the gift of the eye to the leaf and the sun. Transparency is the property of the eyeball, projected outward as luminous space, interpreting quanta of energy in terms of the gelatinous fibers in the head. I begin to feel that the world is at once inside my head and outside it, and the two, inside and outside, begin to include or "cap" one another like an infinite series of concentric spheres. I am unusually aware that everything I am sensing is also my body—that light, color, shape, sound, and texture are terms and properties of the brain conferred upon the outside world. I am not looking *at* the world, not confronting it; I am knowing it by a continuous process of transforming it into myself, so that everything around me, the whole globe of space, no longer feels away from me but in the middle.

This is at first confusing. I am not quite sure of the direction from which sounds come. The visual space seems to reverberate with them as if it were a drum. The surrounding hills rumble with the sound of a truck, and the rumble and the color-shape of the hills become one and the same gesture. I use that word deliberately and shall use it again. The hills are moving into their stillness. They mean something because they are being transformed into my brain, and my brain is an organ of meaning. The forests of redwood trees upon them look like green fire, and the copper-gold of the sun-dried grass heaves immensely into the sky. Time is so slow as to be a kind of eternity, and the flavor of eternity transfers itself to the hills—burnished mountains which I seem to remember from an immeasurably distant past, at once so unfamiliar as to be exotic and yet as familiar as my own hand. Thus transformed into consciousness, into the electric, interior luminosity of the nerves, the world seems vaguely insubstantial—developed upon a color film, resounding upon the skin of a drum, pressing, not with weight, but with vibrations interpreted as weight. Solidity is a neurological invention, and, I wonder, can the nerves be solid to themselves? Where do we begin? Does the order of the brain create the order of the world, or the order of the world the brain? The two seem like egg and hen, or like back and front.

The physical world is vibration, quanta, but vibrations of what? To the eye, form and color; to the ear, sound; to the nose, scent; to the fingers, touch. But these are all different languages for the same thing, different qualities of sensitivity, different dimensions of consciousness. The question, "Of what are they differing forms?" seems to have no meaning. What is light to the eye is sound to the ear. I have the image of the senses being terms, forms, or dimensions not of one thing common to all, but of each other, locked in a circle of mutuality. Closely examined, shape becomes color, which becomes vibration, which becomes sound, which becomes smell, which becomes taste, and then touch, and then again shape. (One can see, for example, that the shape of a leaf *is* its color. There is no outline around the leaf; the outline is the limit where one colored surface becomes another.) I see all these sensory dimensions as a round dance, gesticulations of one pattern being transformed into gesticulations of another. And these gesticulations are flowing through a space that has still other dimensions, which I want to describe as tones of emotional color, of light or sound being joyous or fearful, gold elated or lead depressed. These, too, form a circle of reciprocity, a round spectrum so polarized that we can only describe each in terms of the others.

Sometimes the image of the physical world is not so much a dance of gestures as a woven texture. Light, sound, touch, taste, and smell become a continuous warp, with the feeling that the whole dimension of sensation is a single continuum or field. Crossing the warp is a woof representing the dimension of meaning—moral and aesthetic values, personal or individual uniqueness, logical significance, and expressive form—and the two dimensions interpenetrate so as to make distinguishable shapes seem like ripples in the water of sensation. The warp and the woof stream together, for the weaving is neither flat nor static but a many-directioned cross-flow of impulses filling the whole volume of space. I feel that the world is *on* something in somewhat the same way that a color photograph is on a film, underlying and connecting the patches of color, though the film here is a dense rain of energy. I see that what it is on is my brain—"that enchanted loom," as Sherrington called it. Brain and world, warp of sense and woof of meaning, seem to interpenetrate inseparably. They hold their boundaries or limits in common in such a way as to define one another and to be impossible without each other.

· · ·

The more prosaic, the more dreadfully ordinary anyone or anything seems to be, the more I am moved to marvel at the ingenuity with which divinity hides in order to seek itself, at the lengths to which this cosmic *joie de vivre* will go in elaborating its dance. I think of a corner gas station on a hot afternoon. Dust and exhaust fumes, the regular Standard guy all baseball and sports cars, the billboards halfheartedly gaudy, the flatness so reassuring—nothing around here but just us folks! I can see people just pretending not to see that they are avatars of Brahma, Vishnu, and Shiva, that the cells of their bodies aren't millions of gods, that the dust isn't a haze of jewels. How solemnly they would go through the act of not understanding me if I were to step up and say, "Well, who do you think you're kidding? Come off it, Shiva, you old rascal! It's a great act, but it doesn't fool me." But the conscious ego doesn't know that it is something which that divine organ, the body, is only pretending to be. When people go to a *guru,* a master of wisdom, seeking a way out of darkness, all he really does is to humor them in their pretense until they are outfaced into dropping it. He tells nothing, but the twinkle in his eye speaks to the unconscious—"You know. . . . *You* know!"

THEODORE ROSZAK

the counterfeit infinity:
the use and abuse of psychedelic experience ─────────────

a dusky light—a purple *flash*
crystalline splendor—light blue—
        Green lightnings.—
in that eternal and delirious misery—
        wrathfires—
                inward desolations—
an horror of great darkness
great things—on the ocean
        counterfeit infinity—

—COLERIDGE
(From *The Notebooks* for 1796.)

At the bohemian fringe of our disaffected youth culture, all roads lead to psychedelia. The fascination with hallucinogenic drugs emerges persistently as the common denominator of the many protean forms the counter culture has assumed in the post-World War II period. Correctly understood (which it all too seldom is), psychedelic experience participates significantly in the young's most radical rejection of the parental society. Yet it is their frantic search for the pharmacological panacea which tends to distract many of the young from all that is most valuable in their rebellion, and which threatens to destroy their most promising sensibilities.

If we accept the proposition that the counter culture is, essentially, an exploration of the politics of consciousness, then psychedelic experience falls into place as one, but only one, possible method of mounting that exploration. It becomes a limited chemical means to a greater psychic end, namely, the refor-

From *The Making of a Counter Culture* by Theodore Roszak. New copyright © 1968, 1969 by Theodore Roszak. Reprinted by permission of Doubleday & Company, Inc.

mulation of the personality, upon which social ideology and culture generally are ultimately based.

This was the spirit in which, at the turn of the century, both William James and Havelock Ellis undertook their study of hallucinogenic agents. The prospectus of these early experimenters—James using nitrous oxide and Ellis, the newly discovered peyote (on which James was able to achieve only bad stomach cramps)—was highly exuberant with respect to the cultural possibilities that might flow from an investigation of hallucinatory experience.

•   •   •

James was even more emphatic in hailing the philosophical importance of the nonintellective powers he had discovered not only directly through his experiments with narcotics, but more academically by way of his groundbreaking survey, *The Varieties of Religious Experience*. The enthusiasm on James' part is especially noteworthy since, as a founder of both pragmatism and behavioral psychology, he was much beholden to the standard forms of cerebration that belong to the scientific world view. Still, James was convinced that:

> . . . our normal waking consciousness, rational consciousness as we call it, is but one special type of consciousness, whilst all about it, parted from it by the filmiest of screens, there lie potential forms of consciousness entirely different. . . . No account of the universe in its totality can be final which leaves these other forms of consciousness quite disregarded. . . . they forbid a premature closing of our accounts with reality.[1]

When, some fifty years later, Aldous Huxley and Alan Watts undertook psychedelic experiments that were destined to have far greater social influence than those of Ellis and James, the investigations were still characterized by the same controlled samplings and urbane observations. Once again, the object was to gain a new, internal perspective on modes of consciousness and on religious traditions that the narrowly positivist science of the day had swept into an outsized pigeonhole labeled "mysticism"—meaning . . . "meaningless."

•   •   •

The hypothesis Ellis and James, Watts and Huxley were testing has always seemed to me wholly sensible, even from the most rigorously scientific viewpoint. If the province of science is the disciplined examination of human experience, then surely abnormal (or transnormal) states of consciousness must also constitute a field of scientific study. As James had contended, the mystics, by relating their insights to direct personal experience, would seem to qualify as rigorous empiricists. Why then should their experience and the knowledge that appears to flow from it be screened out by science as somehow illegitimate? Is it perhaps the case that the mystics, in accepting the fullness of human experience, have been more truly scientific than the conventional scientist, who insists that only what makes itself apparent to an arbitrarily limited range of consciousness deserves attention? Such a prejudice would seem all the more untenable once artificial chemical agents have been developed which provide discriminate access

to these transnormal forms of consciousness. Why should they not be used as a
kind of psychic depth charge with which to open up courses of perception that
have become severely log-jammed due to the entrenched cerebral habits of our
Western intelligence?

As an intellectual proposition, such experimentation may have been sound.
But the experiments were destined to become more than a form of exotic psychological research. Instead, they have been sucked into the undertow of a major
social movement—and in this context, their influence has been far from wholesome.

With hindsight, it is clear enough what went wrong. Both Huxley and Watts
drew the analogy between the drug experience and such exploratory devices as
the microscope. Accordingly, the hallucinogens were to function as a lens through
which the shadowy layers of consciousness could be studied. But a microscope
in the hands of a child or the laboratory janitor becomes a toy that produces
nothing but a kind of barbarous and superficial fascination. Perhaps the drug
experience bears significant fruit when rooted in the soil of a mature and cultivated mind. But the experience has, all of a sudden, been laid hold of by a generation of youngsters who are pathetically a-cultural and who often bring nothing to the experience but a vacuous yearning. They have, in adolescent rebellion,
thrown off the corrupted culture of their elders and, along with that soiled bath
water, the very body of the Western heritage—at best, in favor of exotic traditions they only marginally understand; at worst, in favor of an introspective
chaos in which the seventeen or eighteen years of their own unformed lives float
like atoms in a void.

I think one must be prepared to take a very strong line on the matter and
maintain that there are minds too small and too young for such psychic adventures—and that the failure to recognize this fact is the beginning of disaster.
There is nothing whatever in common between a man of Huxley's experience
and intellectual discipline sampling mescaline, and a fifteen-year-old tripper
whiffing airplane glue until his brain turns to oatmeal. In the one case, we have a
gifted mind moving sophisticatedly toward cultural synthesis; in the other, we
have a giddy child out to "blow his mind" and bemused to see all the pretty
balloons go up. But when all the balloons have gone up and gone pop, what is
there left behind but the yearning to see more pretty balloons? And so one
reaches again for the little magic tube . . . and again and again.

At the level of disaffiliated adolescence, the prospect held forth by psychedelic experience—that of consciousness expansion—is bound to prove abortive.
The psychedelics, dropped into amorphous and alienated personalities, have precisely the reverse effect: they diminish consciousness by way of fixation. The
whole of life comes to center despotically on one act, one mode of experience.
Whether or not marijuana, LSD, and amphetamine are addictive remains a moot
point—largely because of the ambiguity of the term "addiction." Are fingernails
addictive? We all know people who bite them constantly and compulsively. Is
chess addictive? There are players who will go without food or drink rather than

abandon the board. Where does the dependency of compulsive fascination leave off and addiction begin?

What *is* obvious, however, is that the psychedelics are a heavyweight obsession which too many of the young cannot get over or around. For them, psychic chemistry is no longer a means for exploring the perennial wisdom; it has become an end in itself, a source of boundless lore, study, and aesthetic elaboration. It is becoming the whole works. It is not that the young have all become hopheads; it is rather that, at the bohemian fringe, they are in the process of trying strenuously to inflate the psychedelics to the size of an entire culture. Ironically, the vice is typical of the worst sort of American commercialism. Start with a gimmick; end with a *Weltanschauung*. Madison Avenue's strategy of strategies: don't just sell them a new can opener; sell them a new way of life.

Here, then, is an example of how, at last, the dimensions of "expanded consciousness" measure up in the hippest versions of the underground press. (In this case, the October 1967 issue of the Southern California *Oracle*—but the point could be made with any number of other underground journals.) The art throughout is officially psychedelic: melting, soft-edged, bejeweled . . . not *good,* but official. The lead article is an interview with Timothy Leary, the subject exclusively under discussion being (what else?) LSD. The substance is slight and garbled, but the tone is pontifical and the piece strings together all the right slogans.

There follows a feature by a local "philosopher-ecologist" who has permitted the *Oracle* "to plug a tape recorder into his frontal lobe for a view of paradise as he perceives it." It begins: "When I turned on once in Yosemite with 250 micrograms of acid. . . ." Thereafter, we have another interview, this time with a rock star (again, "a tape recorded probe of his lobes"), and it is all about "How I Get High." Next, there is the first of a new series on "Ecstatic Living," which is described as "insights gleaned from a three-year creativity study conducted in Mexico under the sponsorship of Sandoz Company, makers of LSD-25"—which would seem to be in about the same category as research in international relations under the sponsorship of the CIA. The subtitle of the piece is: "Your Ecstatic Home—cheap ways of changing your home to reflect the changes in your consciousness."

· · ·

There is a word we have to describe such fastidious immersion in a single idea and all its most trivial ramifications, such precious efforts to make the marginal part stand for the whole of culture. The word is "decadent." And that, unhappily, is the direction in which a substantial segment of our youth culture is currently weakening.

If the psychedelic obsession were no more than a symptom of cultural impoverishment, things would be bad enough. But one must complete the grim picture by adding the sweaty, often vicious, and, in a few instances, even murderous relationships that inevitably grow up around an illegal trade. Money is still what it takes to survive in an urban environment, even if one is only eking out a subsistence. And narcotics, with their subsidiary merchandise, are what brings the money into communities like the East Village and the Haight-Ashbury.

. . .

To be sure, the authorities with their single-minded determination to treat the use of psychedelics as a police problem, and the mass media with their incorrigible penchant for simplifying and sensationalizing, are both to blame for turning the often innocent curiosity of the young into ugly and furtive channels. But the young bear a primary responsibility for letting themselves be trapped in the vicious ambience that the dominant society has created. One must insist that, on their own terms, they are old enough to know better than to let themselves be driven into the same bag with drug merchandisers, who are only the criminal caricature of the American business ethos, and who will scarcely be reformed by being given docile new populations to exploit.

It is no easy matter to establish responsibility for the psychedelic fascination of the young. The high-touting of narcotics has been going on since the days of the San Francisco Renaissance, and by now the number of those who have added to their lore and glamor is legion. Still, one figure—that of Timothy Leary—stands out as that of promoter, apologist, and high priest of psychedelia nonpareil. Surely if we look for the figures who have done the most to push psychedelic experience along the way toward becoming a total and autonomous culture, it is Leary who emerges as the Ultra of the campaign. Indeed, he would probably be insulted if we denied him the distinction.

It is remarkable, and more than a little suspicious, how Leary came to exert his brief but significant influence on the youth culture of the sixties. For while Leary had been a much-publicized pioneer in the field of psychedelic research since the early sixties, it was not until his academic career had been washed up (he was dismissed from Harvard in 1963) and he had twice run a-foul of the narcotics laws, that he blossomed forth—and then almost overnight—as a self-proclaimed cultic swami. This rather makes it difficult to avoid seeing more than a fortuitous connection between Leary's legal entanglements (one of which saddled him with the absurdly severe sentence of thirty years imprisonment and a $30,000 fine) and his subsequent claims to visionary prophecy. Such an interpretation of Leary's career may be too cynical, but the fact remains that the first, splashy "psychedelic celebration" of his League for Spiritual Discovery was held in September 1966, within six months of the time his lawyer had appealed that one of Leary's narcotics convictions be reversed as a violation of religious freedom.

. . .

By way of a mystic religiosity, Leary has succeeded in convincing vast numbers of the young that his "neurological politics" must function as an integral, if not a central, factor in their dissenting culture. "The LSD kick is a spiritual ecstasy. The LSD trip is a religious pilgrimage." Psychedelic experience is *the* way "to groove to the music of God's great song."

But the promise of nirvana is not all. Leary has begun of late to assimilate the psychedelics to a bizarre form of psychic Darwinism which admits the tripper to a "new race" still in the process of evolution. LSD, he claims, is "the sacrament that will put you in touch with the ancient two-million-year-old wisdom inside you"; it frees one "to go on to the next stage, which is the evolutionary timelessness, the ancient reincarnation thing that we always carry inside." After this fashion, the "politics of ecstasy" become the wave of the future, moving in mysterious ways to achieve the social revolution. When Leary is criticized, as he often is, for preaching a form of a-political quietism, his critics overlook the fact that his pitch to the young actually makes ambitious political claims.

• • •

When the claims of psychedelia take on such proportions, one is surely justified in digging in one's heels and registering heated protest. But the trouble is: dope is not simply an excrescence that can be surgically removed from our youth culture by indignant rejection. Leary and his followers have succeeded in endowing it with such a mystique that it now seems the very essence of that politics of the nervous system in which the young are so deeply involved. And this is ironic in the extreme, because one could make an excellent case that the revolution which Leary purports to be leading is the most lugubrious of illusions.

• • •

The young who take their psychedelic text from Huxley's *Doors of Perception* forget that in his *Brave New World* Huxley envisaged the unbearable being made bearable by a visionary chemical called "soma"—the purpose of which was to produce "sane men, obedient men, stable in their contentment."

Recently, when some young Englishmen, aided by a small number of radical psychiatrists, launched a group whose purpose it is to investigate the psychotropic drugs and "methods of altering consciousness in general," and to liberalize the narcotics laws in Great Britain, they appropriated the name SOMA for the organization: Society of Mental Awareness. I suspect they are tempting fate. For, on the face of it, it is difficult to see why the psychedelics cannot be assimilated to the requirements of the technocracy. Such an incorporation would seem to be an excellent example of Marcuse's "repressive desublimation."

• • •

"Better Things For Better Living Through Chemistry." So reads one of the prominent hippy buttons, quoting E. I. duPont. But the slogan isn't being used satirically. The wearers mean it the way duPont means it. The gadget-happy American has always been a figure of fun because of his facile assumption that there exists a technological solution to every human problem. It only took the great psychedelic crusade to perfect the absurdity by proclaiming that personal salvation and the social revolution can be packed in a capsule.

NOTES AND REFERENCES
1. William James, *The Varieties of Religious Experience,* New York: Modern Library, 1936, pp. 378–379.

NORMAN O. BROWN

apocalypse ——————————————————————————————

Columbia University
May 31, 1960

I didn't know whether I should appear before you—there is a time to show and a time to hide; there is a time to speak, and also a time to be silent. What time is it? It is fifteen years since H. G. Wells said Mind was at the End of its Tether— with a frightful queerness come into life: there is no way out or around or through, he said; it is the end. It is because I think mind is at the end of its teth- er that I would be silent. It is because I think there is a way out—a way down and out—the title of Mr. John Senior's new book on the occult tradition in literature—that I will speak.

Mind at the end of its tether: I can guess what some of you are thinking—*his* mind is at the end of its tether—and this could be; it scares me but it deters me not. The alternative to mind is certainly madness. Our greatest blessings, says Socrates in the *Phaedrus,* come to us by way of madness—provided, he adds, that the madness comes from the god. Our real choice is between holy and unholy madness: open your eyes and look around you—madness is in the saddle any- how. Freud is the measure of our unholy madness, as Nietzsche is the prophet of the holy madness, of Dionysus, the mad truth. Dionysus has returned to his na- tive Thebes; mind—at the end of its tether—is another Pentheus, up a tree. Re- sisting madness can be the maddest way of being mad.

And there is a way out—the blessed madness of the maenad and the bacchant: "Blessed is he who has the good fortune to know the mysteries of the gods, who sanctifies his life and initiates his soul, a bacchant on the the mountains, in holy purifications." It is possible to be mad and to be unblest; but it is not possible to get the blessing without the madness: it is not possible to get the illumina- tions without the derangement. Derangement is disorder: the Dionysian faith is that order as we have known it is crippling, and for cripples; that what is past is prologue; that we can throw away our crutches and discover the supernatural power of walking; that human history goes from man to superman.

No superman I: I come to you not as one who has supernatural powers, but as one who seeks for them, and who has some notions which way to go to find them.

Sometimes—most times—I think that the way down and out leads out of the university, out of the academy. But perhaps it is rather that we should recover the academy of earlier days—the Academy of Plato in Athens, the Academy of Ficino in Florence, Ficino who says, "The spirit of the god Dionysus was be- lieved by the ancient theologians and Platonists to be the ecstasy and abandon of disencumbered minds, when partly by innate love, partly at the instigation of the god, they transgress the natural limits of intelligence and are miraculously transformed into the beloved god himself: where, inebriated by a certain new draft of nectar and by an immeasurable joy, they rage, as it were, in a bacchic frenzy. In the drunkenness of this Dionysian wine, our Dionysius (the Areopagite) expresses his exultation. He pours forth enigmas, he sings in dithyrambs. To penetrate the profundity of his meanings, to imitate his quasi-Orphic manner of speech, we too require the divine fury."

At any rate the point is first of all to find again the mysteries. By which I do not mean simply the sense of wonder—that sense of wonder which is indeed the source of all true philosophy—by mystery I mean secret and occult; therefore unpublishable; therefore outside the university as we know it; but not outside Plato's Academy, or Ficino's.

Why are mysteries unpublishable? First because they cannot be put into words, at least not the kind of words which earned you your Phi Beta Kappa keys. Mysteries display themselves in words only if they can remain concealed; this is poetry, isn't it? We must return to the old doctrine of the Platonists and Neo-Platonists, that poetry is veiled truth; as Dionysus is the god who is both manifest and hidden; and as John Donne declared, with the Pillar of Fire goes the Pillar of Cloud. This is also the new doctrine of Ezra Pound, who says: "Prose is not education but the outer courts of the same. Beyond its doors are the mysteries. Eleusis. Things not to be spoken of save in secret. The mysteries self-defended, the mysteries that cannot be revealed. Fools can only profane them. The dull can neither penetrate the secretum nor divulge it to others." The mystic academies, whether Plato's or Ficino's, knew the limitations of words and drove us on beyond them, to go over, to go under, to the learned ignorance, in which God is better honored and loved by silence than by words, and better seen by closing the eyes to images than by opening them.

And second, mysteries are unpublishable because only some can see them, not all. Mysteries are intrinsically esoteric, and as such an offense to democracy: is not publicity a democratic principle? Publication makes it republican—a thing of the people. The pristine academies were esoteric and aristocratic, self-consciously separate from the profane vulgar. Democratic resentment denies that there can be anything that can't be seen by everybody; in the democratic academy truth is subject to public verification; truth is what any fool can see. This is what is meant by the so-called scientific method: so-called science is the attempt to substitute method for insight, mediocrity for genius, by getting a standard operating procedure. The great equalizers dispensed by the scientific method are the tools, those analytical tools. The miracle of genius is replaced by the standardized mechanism. But fools with tools are still fools, and don't let your Phi Beta Kappa key fool you. Tibetan prayer wheels are another way of arriving at the same result: the degeneration of mysticism into mechanism—so that any fool can do it. Perhaps the advantage is with Tibet: for there the mechanism is external while the mind is left vacant; and vacancy is not the worst condition of the mind. And the resultant prayers make no futile claim to originality or immortality; being nonexistent, they do not have to be catalogued or stored.

The sociologist Simmel sees showing and hiding, secrecy and publicity, as two poles, like Yin and Yang, between which societies oscillate in their historical development. I sometimes think I see that civilizations originate in the disclosure of some mystery, some secret; and expand with the progressive publication of their secret; and end in exhaustion when there is no longer any secret, when the mystery has been divulged, that is to say profaned. The whole story is illustrated in the difference between ideogram and alphabet. The alphabet is indeed a democratic triumph; and the enigmatic ideogram, as Ezra Pound has taught us, is a piece of mystery, a piece of poetry, not yet profaned. And so there comes a time—I believe we are in such a time—when civilization has to be renewed by the discovery of new mysteries, by the undemocratic but sovereign power of the imagination, by the undemocratic power which makes poets the unacknowledged legislators of mankind, the power which makes all things new.

The power which makes all things new is magic. What our time needs is mystery: what our time needs is magic. Who would not say that only a miracle can save us? In Tibet the degree-granting institution is, or used to be, the College of Magic Ritual. It offers courses in such fields as clairvoyance and telepathy; also (attention physics majors) internal heat: internal heat is a yoga bestowing supernatural control over body temperature. Let me succumb for a moment to the fascination of the mysterious East and tell you of the examination procedure for the course in internal heat. Candidates assemble naked, in midwinter, at night, on a frozen Himalayan lake. Beside each one is placed a pile of wet frozen undershirts; the assignment is to wear, until they are dry, as many as possible of these undershirts before dawn. Where the power is real, the test is real, and the grading system dumbfoundingly objective. I say no more. I say no more; Eastern Yoga does indeed demonstrate the existence of supernatural powers, but it does not have the particular power our Western society needs; or rather I think that each society has access only to its own proper powers; or rather each society will only get the kind of power it knows how to ask for.

The Western consciousness has always asked for freedom: the human mind was born free, or at any rate born to be free, but everywhere it is in chains; and now at the end of its tether. It will take a miracle to free the human mind: because the chains are magical in the first place. We are in bondage to authority outside ourselves: most obviously—here in a great university it must be said—in bondage to the authority of books. There is a Transcendentalist anticipation of what I want to say in Emerson's Phi Beta Kappa address on the American Scholar:

> The books of an older period will not fit this. Yet hence arises a grave mischief. The sacredness which attaches to the act of creation, the act of thought, is transferred to the record. Instantly the book becomes noxious: the guide is a tyrant. The sluggish and perverted mind of the multitude having once received this book, stands upon it, and makes an outcry if it is destroyed. Col-

leges are built on it. Meek young men grow up in libraries. Hence, instead of Man Thinking, we have the bookworm. I had better never see a book than to be warped by its attraction clean out of my own orbit, and make a satellite instead of a system. The one thing in the world, of value, is the active soul.

How far this university is from that ideal is the measure of the defeat of our American dream.

This bondage to books compels us not to see with our own eyes; compels us to see with the eyes of the dead, with dead eyes. Whitman, likewise in a Transcendentalist sermon, says, "You shall no longer take things at second or third hand, nor look through the eyes of the dead, nor feed on the specters in books." There is a hex on us, the specters in books, the authority of the past; and to exorcise these ghosts is the great work of magical self-liberation. Then the eyes of the spirit would become one with the eyes of the body, and god would be in us, not outside. God in us: *entheos:* enthusiasm; this is the essence of the holy madness. In the fire of the holy madness even books lose their gravity, and let themselves go up into the flame: "Properly," says Ezra Pound, "we should read for power. Man reading should be man intensely alive. The book should be a ball of light in one's hand."

I began with the name of Dionysus; let me be permitted to end with the name of Christ: for the power I seek is also Christian. Nietzsche indeed said the whole question was Dionysus versus Christ; but only the fool will take these as mutually exclusive opposites. There is a Dionysian Christianity, an apocalyptic Christianity, a Christianity of miracles and revelations. And there always have been some Christians for whom the age of miracle and revelation is not over; Christians who claim the spirit; enthusiasts. The power I look for is the power of enthusiasm; as condemned by John Locke; as possessed by George Fox, the Quaker; through whom the houses were shaken; who saw the channel of blood running down the streets of the city of Litchfield; to whom, as a matter of fact, was even given the magic internal heat—"The fire of the Lord was so in my feet, and all around me, that I did not matter to put on my shoes any more."

Read again the controversies of the seventeenth century and discover our choice: we are either in an age of miracles, says Hobbes, miracles which authenticate fresh revelations; or else we are in an age of reasoning from already received Scripture. Either miracle or Scripture. George Fox, who came up in spirit through the flaming sword into the paradise of God, so that all things were new, he being renewed to the state of Adam which he was in before he fell, sees that none can read Moses aright without Moses' spirit; none can read John's words aright, and with a true understanding of them, but in and with the same divine spirit by which John spake them, and by his burning shining light which is sent from God. Thus the authority of the past is swallowed up in new creation; the word is made flesh. We see with our own eyes and to see with our own eyes is second sight. To see with our own eyes is second sight.

Twofold Always. May God us keep
From single vision and Newton's sleep.

education for serendipity _____

I would like to propose that every educational institution, if it is to fulfill its central purpose of conserving and creating, should establish a department of "Wonder, Wisdom, and Serendipitous Knowledge" which would be charged with the prophetic task of discovering the unfashionable questions which are not being asked and the life options which are not being explored within the educational system. In the university such a department would study the university. It would look at its rhetoric, its ideology, and its performance. It might offer courses in antique virtues, strange potentialities, and odd patterns of personal and corporate life. Certainly it should make students aware of the options, lifestyles, and questions which are considered disrespectable, out of fashion, outgrown, simplistic, taboo, dangerous, or politically forbidden. It might even be well for the government to set up a new cabinet position devoted to raising embarrassing questions, considering neglected alternatives, and dramatizing different models of the fully human community.

• • •

I will sketch out some of the courses which might be offered in a department of Wonder, Wisdom, and Serendipitous Knowledge. . . . They represent an effort to focus curriculum upon the problems and questions which I have found to be central in the years since I ended my schooling and started my education. I would not want to argue that the cognitive, abstract, scientific, disciplines which currently dominate our schools should be thrown out and education focused wholly upon development of the individual. However the time seems ripe to recover the personalistic (as opposed to the mere humanistic) dimension of education. If we neglect to educate for identity and wholeness our abstract and technological knowledge will only form a shell around a painful vacuum. I should add that the listing of courses reflects more areas of need than exact educational techniques for satisfying these needs. It is more a catalogue of experiments which need doing than a syllabus of instructions.

silence, wonder, and the art of surrender

Aim. This course will explore the basic attitude which ancient philosophers insisted was the prerequisite for all wisdom—the attitude of wonder. It will aid students to develop an inner silence, to cultivate the ability to let things happen, to welcome, to listen, to allow, to be at ease in situations in which surrender rather than striving for control is appropriate.

Rationale. By the time a student reaches what we insist upon calling "higher" education (why not "deeper"?), his patterns of perception and style of life have

_____
From pp. 41–52 in *To a Dancing God* by Sam Keen. Copyright © 1970 by Sam Keen.

been rigidly shaped by the linguistic climate in which he has been immersed since birth. Learning to speak is the model and principle of all education, since language is the earliest tool used to cut up, structure, and control the chaos of reality. The language system of a culture therefore incarnates the values and beliefs into which the child must be initiated if he is to become a man. Currently we are so anxious to accomplish this initiation before rebellion may set in that a major educational preoccupation has become how early we can teach Johnny to read, how fast and economically we can get the accumulated data of culture programed into his head (read, computer.) Since Sputnik, childhood is in danger of becoming a national resource, a warehouse for stockpiling data necessary for furthering the aims of a cybernated society.

It is difficult to avoid the impression that Western culture has formed a conspiracy against silence. Words and noise are everywhere. Our education is dominantly verbal, conceptual, and dialectic. We read, or listen, or watch, in order to be entertained. The verbal diarrhea of disc jockeys pours from the omnipresent transistor into the waiting ears of millions. Chatter fills every corner into which silence might creep. Even what we call thinking is most often a highly refined form of inner conversation. Dialectic is dialogue with an invisible partner.

A psychoanalysis of chatter would suggest that our ca ververbalization is an effort to avoid something which is fearful—silence. But why should silence be threatening? Words are a way of structuring, manipulating, and controlling; thus, when they are absent the specter of loss of control arises. If we cannot name it we cannot control it. Naming gives us power. Hence silence is impotence, the surrender of control. Control is power, and power is safety. Being out of control is impotence and danger—so, at least, our fear warns us. Thus we avoid silence in order to preserve the illusion that we live in a world we control and to avoid confronting our fear of being out of control.

This obsession with controlling which characterizes technological culture blinds us to the necessity for alternative styles of perception and life. If we are unable to surrender control, to appreciate, to welcome, to wonder, to allow things and persons to speak with their own voice, to listen, we are condemned to perpetual aggression, to an unrelaxing Promethean effort to master the environment. No doubt there is a time for speaking, for dialectic, for control. But there is also a time for silence, for wonder, for surrender. It is this time we are in danger of forgetting in the contemporary world.

Content and Techniques. A course in the art of silence would, by definition, be difficult to teach. Would there be lectures, reading? How would we judge what learning had taken place? How would we grade improved skill in wondering? Where, indeed, would we find professors of silence, and how would we establish criteria for their promotion? (Perhaps those who published would be punished.) Although the difficulties are legion, it is helpful to remember that there are precedents for this experiment. Zen masters were professors of silence. By the use of koans they destroyed the naive faith of their pupils in the final adequacy of words and concepts to grasp reality, and by meditation they taught techniques by which the mind could be emptied of dialectic without losing awareness. The testimony of Zen is that once the art of interior silence is learned, control of the interior and exterior worlds may be maintained or surrendered at will. In the Western philosophical tradition there is also precedent for education in the art of silence. Platonism, Christian mysticism, and romanticism cultivated and valued the attitudes of wonder and silent appreciation.

A course in silence might, simply, begin with silence. Imposing a period of linguistic asceticism would sensitize students to the omnipresence of words and the threat of silence. It would foster the awareness that words and silence, ideas and feelings, concepts and sensations, controlling and surrendering, remain vital only so long as they are in continual relationship. Coming home to speaking after a sojourn in silent exile, a student might have gained sufficient reverence for language to become outraged at chatter, propaganda, and noise. Perhaps a new revolution might emerge which would insist upon the right to silence.

Many of the meditation techniques developed in the Zen tradition, which are currently being explored at Esalen and other centers devoted to the study of the "nonverbal humanities" (Aldous Huxley), would be useful to the student of silence. With practice it is possible to observe the stream of consciousness without interfering, to silence dialectic and become aware without self-consciousness, to experience greater immediacy and spontaneity than in "normal" consciousness. The "doors of perception" may be cleansed, silence may be recovered, the art of surrendering control may be learned.

It would also be necessary to explore our nonverbal ways of learning and communicating. We rely on speech because we are never systematically trained to communicate in any other way. Yet it is clear that much is said without words. Touch, taste, and smell are largely uneducated in our culture, although they are far more intimate organs of knowledge than hearing or seeing. Getting in touch, educating the more intimate senses might help to fill the vacuum within and between persons which now is cluttered with words. We might then, as they say in Maine, speak only when we could improve on silence.

introduction to carnality

Aim. The intent of this course is to help students experience a deeper integration between body, mind, and world, to develop a life-style richly infused with sensual and kinesthetic awareness, and to discover the sustaining certainties which arise from fully rooted and incarnate existence.

Rationale. Contemporary rhetoric gives all glory to flesh and matter. The combined impact of pragmatism, existentialism, scientific methodology, and the fruits of the technological revolution have convinced us that man's true home is in the kingdom of the body. The older idealistic view which saw man as a mind to which a body was accidentally attached, a spirit sadly encased in matter, is all but universally rejected in the twentieth century.

It is only in practice, never in theory, that idealistic and gnostic dualism remains a working presupposition of contemporary society. Our hymns of praise cannot drown out the hatred of the flesh which our actions reveal. Consider, for instance, our carelessness of the body in the educational process. Minds, not bodies, are taught in the classroom. At no point in the curriculum is an effort made to help students learn to read the language of the body, to acquire techniques of relaxation and control, to understand the relationship between body and personality structure, "character armor" (Reich) and defense mechanisms, motion and emotion. Our schools function as if the fact of incarnation was incidental to the task of education. Sometimes attention to the body sneaks in through courses in "personal hygiene," but these usually are a cross between internal plumbing, sex education, and edifying lessons on the value of cleanliness. What we call physical education most often consists of a series of competitive games (in season) which actually desensitize the body by focusing attention on the competitive goal of winning rather than increasing kinesthetic awareness.

The result of the hidden idealistic assumptions of our educational system is the perpetuation of a dualism, not unlike gnosticism, which separates mind from body, spirit from flesh, and appearance from feeling. The most painful symptom of this disease (a culturally condoned form of schizophrenia) is the twin phenomena of style and cosmetics. The body which displays clothing according to what is stylish is designed to be seen by others. Its dignity is in being seen, not in feeling. *Esse est percipi.* Likewise the face which is "made up" is a mask created by Helena Rubenstein which must be put on. It is a mirror face, not a flesh face, constructed with constant reference to how it will be viewed from without. To the degree that we design our bodies to be seen, we are divorced from the perspective of carnal feeling. Our education cannot be absolved of responsibility for perpetuating this style of bodily existence in which there is dominance of the visual body over the sensual body. If our bodies are hollow shells to be painted and decorated it is because we have never cared enough to educate the sensitive core; we have not undertaken to resurrect the body from deadness.

It may also be the case that the neglect of the body lies at the root of the political problem of the deterioration of the sense of public responsibility. The notion of public space is meaningful only in contrast to what is not public space, namely, private space. And the model of privacy is my relationship with my body. If I lack a sense of the density and inviolability of my own body I will have weak ego boundaries and an impaired ability to enter into social relationships. The extreme example of this simultaneous disintegration of private and public space is in the schizophrenic who lacks the feeling of being connected with his body. His body is weightless and transparent. It can be blown away by the wind or seen through by all eyes. It has no limits, boundaries, no privacy. Thus the schizophrenic child fears that his every thought and feeling can be read by the parent. There is no secret place, no fertile darkness in which tender things may take root and grow, hidden from prying eyes. Lacking a sense of potent incarnation, the schizophrenic also lacks the ability to be a member of a community. Privacy and community are related as the physical body is to the body politic. Without incarnation there is no incorporation. Embodiment is indivisible. The question is not (as the right wing insists) whether we will educate individuals to respect the integrity of private space, or (as the left wing insists) whether we will educate the community to re-create a sense of public space and responsibility. But whether we will do both, or neither. Carnal education is political and vice versa.

Content and Techniques. There is a wealth of theoretical material from physiology, psychology, and philosophy which might serve as a prelude to the study of incarnate existence. Knowledge of the basics of anatomy and physiology, not of the human body but of my body, would be a good starting point. Once a factual foundation has been provided, a physiosomatic study might draw heavily upon Freud's theory of repression and Wilhelm Reich's theory of character armor. Phenomenological analyses of the body, such as have been made by Marcel, Sartre, and Merleau-Ponty would also be valuable. It might also be useful to reflect upon the history and sociology of the body. McLuhan has pointed out that the balance between the senses changes to compensate for the dominant technology of a given age. It is also clear that different senses have provided the models for our understanding of what it means to know. Knowledge in Greek culture, as in idealistic philosophy, was likened to seeing. To know was to have a vision or a clear and distinct idea which corresponded to the reality known. In Hebrew culture, knowing was more often understood as a mode of touch and involvement. It is no accident that the biblical tradition speaks of knowing in the sexual sense in which a man "knows" a woman. There is, at any rate, sufficient "hard" conceptual, historical, psychological, and philosophical material demonstrating the way in which the body constitutes knowledge to render a course in carnality academically respectable (if that is a concern).

The difficulty lies not with the theoretical but with the visceral dimensions of this source. Education for carnality cannot evade the problem of sex . . . which is at once a moral, religious, and political problem. How are we to deal with our sexuality? It is most often assumed that if we are to retain civilization we must pay the price of repression. Norman Brown and Herbert Marcuse have raised questions about this ancient presupposition which demand consideration if the revolutionary promise of education is to be fulfilled. Our genital preoccupation represents one possible form of organizing energy and time, of structuring the concerns of the body. Both Brown and Marcuse suggest that sexual, personal, and political organization are all open to change. They are matters of choice. Thus, if education aims at creating or revealing the freedom necessary to change, it would necessarily need to sensitize students to the manner in which their energies are organized. Education which avoids the erogenous zones, the sensitive areas, neglects the power structure. It would seem self-evident that if education avoids the question of power and change, it more properly deserves the name "indoctrination," and has no place in a democratic society. A democratic form of political organization distributes power and therefore consistently demands a style of bodily existence in which erotic sensibility is homogenized into the total body rather than localized in representative genital organs. It may be that a democratic society can only survive in a sensitive milieu. It is significant that the most serious revolutionary threat America has confronted in the universities arises in a time of free sexuality. It is not against the repressive superego that forbids free genital sexuality that the rebellion is directed, but against the careless pollution, desecration, and insensitive killing of the loveless technological society. The new demands are not for sex but love, not for new tyrants but participatory democracy, not for a greater share of the wealth but a more caring society. It is difficult to avoid the conclusion that the fundamental question education must deal with in the coming years is the question of alternative ways of organizing the energy and power of the physical and the political body.

There are many techniques which could be used to increase awareness of the inseparability of body, psyche, and world. Fritz Perls, the father of Gestalt therapy, has suggested a series of exercises which might form an introduction to the art of reading the language of the body. He maintains that if we single out and pay attention to any of the fundamental conscious bodily functions, such as eating, eliminating, or making love, we can construct a model of the personality. How, for instance do you eat? How do you take the world into yourself? Do you choose food carefully for its aesthetic and nutritional value? Do you pay attention to taste and texture? Chew carefully? Read when eating? As you incorporate nourishment, so you will take in and digest the world which surrounds you. If you doubt this, give full attention to your style of eating for one week and try drawing parallels to the way in which you read, listen, think, understand, and relate to persons.

Many techniques for educating and resensitizing the body might also be borrowed from therapeutic and religious disciplines. Eastern religions have centuries of experience in educating the body which to date have not been taken seriously by Western educators. It is possible to separate the idealistic metaphysics and the presuppositions of Eastern spirituality from yoga practices and make use of its technology of body awareness and control. One example of how this might be done: the Zen technique of focusing attention upon breathing provides an immediate experimental basis for understanding and integrating the involuntary and the voluntary; it provides a bodily model of the tension between unconscious and conscious functions of the personality. The moment one *tries* to breathe spontaneously it becomes obvious that it is futile to try to make happen those things which can only be allowed to happen. Enlightenment (the state at which education aims) consists in being able to discern the appropriate moments for acceptance and action, wonder and work, relaxation and willfulness. It should be obvious that this ability is a prerequisite for happiness so long as man must both accept the limits of mortality and strive to extend his control.

Another ancient educational medium which might be revived is dance. In primitive cultures dance was a central way of exhibiting and celebrating values and beliefs. As Arthur Darby Nock, the Harvard historian of religions, was fond of saying, "Primitive religion is not believed. It is danced." Even Plato knew that dance and gymnastics were essential for political education; if the values of a culture are to be deeply rooted they must be celebrated with all the facilities— reason, emotion, and sensation. The body has wisdom to teach that the mind knows not of. It understands much of rhythm and timing which is easily forgotten when life is ruled too exclusively by ideas. Such fundamental themes as the relation between activity and passivity, strength and weakness, tension and relaxation, disease and grace are more easily learned from bodily movement than from conceptual analysis. As Zorba knew, there are times when only dance can say what must be said. There are certain emotions which are difficult to entertain without motion. We are moved by joy, or shaken by grief. It may be that the sparsity of joy in contemporary life is closely related to the loss of dance as a central vehicle for the education and articulation of values and beliefs. We do not share the same dances. Perhaps corporate bonds are strongly forged only when bodies join together in celebration. If so, re-education of the body is essential for creating a community. Is it really possible to be in touch without touching, to be moved without moving?

a cup of tea

Nan-in, a Japanese master during the Meiji era (1868–1912), received a university professor who came to inquire about Zen.

Nan-in served tea. He poured his visitor's cup full, and then kept on pouring.

The professor watched the overflow until he no longer could restrain himself. "It is overfull. No more will go in!"

"Like this cup," Nan-in said, "you are full of your own opinions and speculations. How can I show you Zen unless you first empty your cup?"

From *Zen Flesh, Zen Bones,* ed., Paul Reps, Rutland, Vt., Charles E. Tuttle Co. Reprinted by permission.

LEWIS YABLONSKY

strawberry fields forever _____

I was pretty much living by myself when I completely dropped out. I was a pro-
bation officer, which is a pretty dropped-out kind of a job to begin with. I
worked in a camp where you work three days and then have four days off. Well,
you can drop a lot further out on these four days than you can on a weekend, if
you're working a five-day-a-week job. I had started taking acid about eight
months before I quit work and it just occurred to me that it would be interesting
to see what would happen if I just did what I FELT like doing all the time. You
know, get up when I feel like it, wear what I feel like wearing, go to sleep, think,
say, do whatever the fuck I felt like. And you can't do that if you're working for
somebody else. So I did! I was thirty-three years old, and it was the first time in
my life that I ever did really feel free. I'd had vacations before, but always, even
in the vacations, you're thinking about what you're going to do after the vacation is over. I was on unemployment for about ten months once. I couldn't really enjoy that because I had a certain amount of guilt. You shouldn't be drawing
unemployment. (YOU SHOULD BE THIS, YOU SHOULD BE THAT.) But I
was able to accept the freedom, and I seem to be able to accept it more and
more all the time.

Around October, when I quit work, a bunch of us from various places started
getting tighter and tighter and closer and closer together. We had hit on the game
of pushing each other to be open about our feelings all the time. We found that
the more we were together in this kind of atmosphere, the more we opened up,
the more we enjoyed each other and life. At the time I was renting a house in
Malibu Canyon and it just started filling up with people. At night it was wall-to-
wall with people. It was in a pretty residential neighborhood and things were
getting hot. We were using a lot of acid, staying up all night with music and mo-
torcycles coming and going and so on. One of my partners heard about some
property out in Decker Canyon. We decided to move in there and at the same
time decided to let anybody else that wanted to come there, come. I kind of laid
down that there would be no structure. There would be complete acceptance of
everybody's trip, simply because I found the more I had been able to accept MY-
SELF and people around me, and they were able to accept me, the higher we
got. I wanted to see a whole community where this could happen.

The word just spread all over. Half our population came from the San Francisco area. The average number of people there was about thirty to thirty-five.
On the weekends it would go up to over a hundred. And I'd say probably anywhere from fifteen hundred to two thousand people passed through.

We got the name Strawberry Fields from the Beatles' song. Actually I gave the

From *The Hippie Trip* by Lewis Yablonsky, copyright © 1968 by Western Publishing Company, Inc., reprinted by permission of the publishers, The Bobbs-Merrill Company, Inc.

community two names: STRAWBERRY FIELDS and DESOLATION ROW. Everybody remembers Strawberry Fields, it's a lot pleasanter.

It was pitch black and horrible, and the depths of misery. Yet it was also the fairest, lightest, purest thing. Everybody, including myself, had some images and expectations as to what it would be. It *was* everybody's image and expectation, and the opposite. It was all things.

It was a beautiful place where people could go and take acid in a relatively paranoia-free atmosphere of trust about the community. It was a place of accelerated evolutionary change. A way of people seeing themselves and, as a result, seeing life. It was accelerated to a degree that, to my mind, I have never before experienced. Evolutionary change is a process which is a result of being open, being trusting, and not being defensive.

I feel that the reason an infant begins to close up, the reason that it needs to build ego defenses, is because it is threatened by the hypocrisy and lies of the civilization into which it was born. This is represented usually by its parents, later on by the school, and later on the police. The defense is against the fantasy that is laid on children that they are not perfect. That they are slightly imbecilic, that they are definitely inadequate until they become SOMETHING sometime in the future. They should grow up intelligent, mature, respectable, ambitious, and successful, with no underarm smells, or bad breath, or shitty diapers. This is, of course, a lie. But the lie is enforced by threatening vibrations communicated to the child.

At Strawberry we used drugs to break these threatening repressive fears. We believed that psychedelic drugs, given and received in an atmosphere of trust, enable man to know his God nature and his unity with life.

The only ritual about taking acid was that people at Strawberry were asked not to leave the property. If they wanted to freak out and take their clothes off, yell, scream, on the property they were safe.

I think that our community did the community-at-large a tremendous service by having a place where people could go, take acid, and could freak out without harming themselves or the community. REALITY is that more and more people are going to use acid. Whether we like it or not. Unethical, immoral, depraved, call it what you want, sick, whatever! REALITY is that more and more people are going to use it. Repressive laws, paranoia-producing laws are going to cause more flip-outs. Our place was as paranoia-free a place as has ever been where there is a lot of dope.

sexual freedom and children

A principal of our religion was that dynamic spiritual growth happens in an atmosphere of complete acceptance of infant and childhood sexuality. Which means, to get right down to it, that eight-year-old kids should play with each other sexually. And you let them do it because that's what they feel like doing. At one time we had thirteen kids at Strawberry Fields. They had complete sexual freedom.

Of course, some adult under these rules could try to lay his trip on a young kid. . . . I wouldn't dig fucking a prepubescent female. It may be somebody else's trip. I would hope that adults would be turned in enough not to impose this on the kid if the kid wasn't behind it. In an open community it's difficult to think of someone that would impose that kind of trip on a kid. That was the only negative "no no" raised about sex in our religion. Obviously if you're going to have free infant and childhood sexuality, it's implied that there is complete acceptance of adult sexuality.

A lot of people feel that sexual freedom is a very bad thing. This culture accepts that little kids want to play with their penis. It's all right for LITTLE kids to masturbate. But somehow after a certain age, say around three, sex isn't supposed to happen. This is a fantasy because it's an anthropological fact that we alone of the creatures on this earth, our species is capable of sexual enjoyment, play, and pleasure from the day it's born to the day it dies. That is the one place that evolution has brought us that is different from every other species of animal.

The first time I ever saw this idea in print was in a book by Philip Wylie called *They Both Were Naked*. The whole book is pretty absurd except for this one rap where Wylie delivers that whole scene about kids and sex. I saw that this is the way it IS, man, out at Strawberry Fields, because we had kids there. One time we had twelve kids; the oldest was thirteen.

I never saw people go through such rapid changes as those kids did where everybody's accepting them. Where, when an adult is trying to lay their game on them the kid can say, "Fuck off, man" and not be afraid to say it. No human being has reached enlightenment till they can say "fuck off" to their mother or dad.

We only had one casualty to the Establishment. One of our kids was taken from the community. The petition filed in behalf of the child by the Establishment stated that the child was in danger of leading a lewd and immoral life. But in our community the words "lewd" and "immoral" have been thrown out. [In the case cited, the five-year-old child was regularly smoking marijuana.]

I remember one time, I guess I was twelve or thirteen, I was living with my aunt and uncle. And my aunt was always rapping about how you had to be a certain way because you have to be thinking about what people say. I just said to her, "Who the fuck CARES what people say!" I guess that's when you start dropping out, when you see your identity doesn't have anything to do with what people say.

. . .

I have a very strong negative reaction to the movement being characterized as the Flower Children and the Love Children and love-ins and love trips, because all that is saying that hate is bad, which is a lie. It's a refuge in another fantasy. There never has been a man who didn't have hostile feelings. There never has been a man who hasn't had the feelings of grief. Hate is righteous, if you can accept it, and you express it. When it doesn't become violence. But if it's repressed because you "OUGHT" to repress it, and you HAVE to, and it's NOT NICE to express feelings unless they're acceptable to somebody else, then it builds up to where violence can eventually become the expression. But I know that some of the most far-out feelings of love I've had have been when I've been confronted in relationships with hurtful experiences, reacted to them, expressed my hate as vehemently as I could, and almost instantly I became suffused with far-out feelings of love and acceptance.

the demise of strawberry fields

I kind of took on more than I could handle with Strawberry Fields. I got pneumonia and hepatitis, which I think is my body telling me that a lot of things aren't quite in harmony. I think a community, unless it's going to have an awful lot of money behind it, is going to have to be restricted to productive people for a while. It would be righteous if there were a community that was so far-out that it could accommodate people who are still in a state of being slobs. You know, some people have been told what they HAVE to do for so long, man, that they get into a place where they're free and they just don't know what to do. They just sit around in their own filth. Which is where they're at, at that time. It would be righteous if there were people who could be on a trip to pick up after them and produce for them, and provide them with food and clothing and things like that, but there doesn't seem to be the money right now, or, more important, the people. Most communities are going to have to be pretty restrictive. There was a community up in Gorda, near Big Sur, which has just been closed down for the same reason. It just got too big and became like a refugee camp.

You have to have a leadership with a broader base than just one or two people to even begin with. You'd have to have a council. Then if somebody wants to live in the community, they could rap with the council. Presumably the council will be comprised of tuned-in people who can tune-in on the person that wants to come in. Maybe we'll take some grass or acid with the applicant and really get down to it. They won't have to have an application blank or references.

I had a image when Strawberry Fields started as to what it should be. I would like to see it be a more or less self-sustaining commune where there would be such a complete atmosphere of freedom and acceptance that creative people could really get right into the expression of their creativity. What happened was that it turned into kind of a retreat or a refugee camp. The people who were around were kind of tired of the cities, and run down physically, and kind of up-tight. They would come out there and stay and take acid and smoke grass and kind of get their heads straightened out a little bit and split.

We never got to the point where we could produce anything or be self-supporting. Success? I don't know. I was a success in terms of MY growth. I went through more far-out changes in the six months that that place existed than I have in any other period of my life. For me it was a success.

HERBERT A. OTTO

communes:
the alternative life-style _____

Angelina is a tall, striking blonde in her mid-forties, with a husky voice and a motherly, forthright air about her. She had been a successful interior decorator in a well-known college town in Oregon. Following her divorce, Angelina decided to rent some of the extra bedrooms in her house to students.

"I was shocked seeing people dirty and with unwashed hair—until I got to know them better and saw their soul reflected in their eyes. They wanted country life and animals. They wanted to be creative and to be themselves. At that time, I was attending a Unitarian church. I talked to the minister about starting a commune. He said it wouldn't work."

Angelina felt she needed new ideas and viewpoints, and she went to the Esalen Institute at Big Sur, California. She stayed three months. "I could see so much, feel so much, I thought I was really called."

Upon returning to her business, which she had left in competent hands, Angelina decided to sell out and was able to do so at a favorable price. "I made up my mind I wanted the family feeling. At this point, it was like Providence when I heard about the hundred and fifty acres. The price was so reasonable. I thought there was something wrong with the place. But when I saw it—with the half-dozen springs, three streams, and mixed timber—I knew this was the spot for a nature commune."

Angelina started the commune two-and-a-half years ago with a young couple she had met at Esalen. Today, there are thirty young people and eight children in the community. Twelve of this group are called "stable"; they have made a commitment to the commune. Median age within the commune is in the mid-twenties. Sixty-five percent of the group are young men. There are many high school and college dropouts, but also a number of successful former businessmen and professionals, several teachers, and two engineers.

This commune, with Angelina as its prime mover and guiding spirit, is just one of many such living arrangements that have mushroomed around the country. Over the past few years, the commune movement has grown at an unprecedented and explosive rate, and there is every indication that this is only the initial phase of a trend that is bound to have far-reaching implications for the function and structure of our contemporary society. Some traditional institutions are already beginning to feel the impact of this explosive growth.

The commune movement has passed far beyond its contemporary origins in hippie tribalism and can no longer be described as a movement for youth exclusively. There are a rapidly growing number of communes composed of persons in their mid-twenties to upper thirties. A source at the National Institute of Health

From "Communes: The Alternative Life-Style," *Saturday Review* (April 24, 1971). Copyright 1971 Saturday Review, Inc. Reprinted also with permission of the author.

has estimated that more than 3,000 urban communes are now in operation. This figure closely corresponds to a recent *New York Times* inquiry that uncovered 2,000 communes in thirty-four states.

Certain common viewpoints, almost a *Weltanschauung,* are shared by members of the contemporary commune movement. First, there is a deep respect and reverence for nature and the ecological system. There is a clear awareness that 70 percent of the population lives on 1 percent of the land and that this 1 percent is severely polluted, depressingly ugly, and psychologically overcrowded. Commune members generally believe that a very small but politically influential minority with no respect for the ecological system or the beauty of nature exploits all of the land for its own gain. Surpassing the credo of conservationist organizations, most commune members stress the rehabilitation of *all* lands and the conservation of *all* natural resources for the benefit of *all* the people.

Anti-Establishment sentiment is widespread, as is the conviction that a change in social and institutional structures is needed to halt man's dehumanization and to give him an opportunity to develop his potential. Considerable divergence of opinion exists on how social change is to be brought about, but there is general agreement that the commune movement contributes to change by bringing man closer to himself and to his fellow man through love and understanding.

Communes widely accept the idea that life is meant to be fundamentally joyous and that this is of the essence in doing, and enjoying, what you want to do— "doing your thing." Work in this context becomes a form of joyous self-expression and self-realization. Many commune members believe that existence can be an almost continuous source of joyous affirmation. They usually trace the absence of authentic joy in contemporary society to the confining nature of many of our social institutions, the stifling of spontaneity, and the preponderance of game-playing and of devitalized artificial ways of relating socially.

A strong inner search for the meaning of one's own life, an openness and willingness to communicate and encounter, coupled with a compelling desire for personal growth and development, are hallmarks of the movement. A strong anti-materialistic emphasis prevails; it decries a consumption-oriented society. In many communes, what does not fit into a room becomes commune property. A considerable number of communes aim for the type of self-sufficiency through which they can exist independently of "the system."

There is a strong trend toward ownership of land and houses by communes. Leasing arrangements have not proved satisfactory; in too many instances, landlords have canceled leases when community pressures were exerted. The nonurban communes I have visited are strongly aware of ecological factors, and, because of this, members usually had consulted with local health authorities concerning the construction and placement of sanitary facilities. Among the urban communes, toilet and bath facilities were in most cases short of the demand.

Marked preferences for vegetarianism and for organically grown food are noticeable in the commune movement. Many individual members also experiment with different health diets. Roughly 40 percent of the communes I visited were vegetarian; 20 percent served both vegetarian and nonvegetarian meals. The remainder served meat when available—usually two to six times a week. This third group, although not vegetarian by choice, liked their vegetarian meals and expressed very little craving for meat. Whenever possible, communes concentrate on growing and raising their own food. An estimated 60 percent of the urban communes are now purchasing some or most of their supplies from health-food stores or similar sources.

Not surprisingly, the commune has become the repository of repressed man's erotic fantasy. I was continuously told that visitors who come not to learn and understand but to peek and ogle invariably ask two questions: "Who sleeps with whom?" And, "Do you have group sex?" There appears to be much fantasizing by outsiders about the sex life in communes.

Although there is considerable sexual permissiveness, I found a high degree of pairing with a strong tendency toward interpersonal commitment in a continuing relationship. Nudism is casual and accepted, as is the development of a healthy sensuality, and natural childbirth, preferably within the commune, is encouraged. Group sex involving the whole commune occurs quite rarely, although there may be sexual experimentation involving two or more couples or combinations.

The research team of Larry and Joan Constantine has studied multilateral (group) marriage for the past three years. They have written and published more studies in this area than other behavioral scientists, but have found only one commune practicing group marriage. Most likely, there are others. About two dozen independent families are known to be engaged in multilateral marriage, taking as their model Bob Rimmer's novel *Proposition 31,* which presents a case for group marriage. Many others prefer to keep their arrangement totally secret for fear of reprisals. According to an article by the Constantines, entitled "Personal Growth in Multiple Marriages," failure rate is better than one out of two, because "group marriage is a marathon that does not end—it takes a real commitment to genuine, substantial, and unrelenting personal growth to really make it function and work."

Interest in spiritual development is a dominant theme in most communes. Study of and acquaintance with Eastern and Western mystics and religious philosophies is widespread. Religiosity and denominationalism were seldom encountered. On the other hand, I was struck by the deep commitment to spiritual search of so many members in all the communes I visited. Many members were trying different forms of meditation, and books on Eastern religions and mysticism were prominent on shelves.

I find that although there is some overlapping of functions and categories, a number of distinct types of communes can be recognized and are found in operation.

• The Agricultural Subsistence Commune: The main thrust is to farm or till the soil (mostly organic farming) so that the land will provide most, if not all, needs and make the commune independent and self-supporting. Many of these communes cultivate such specialized crops as organically grown grain, vegetables, and other produce, which are then sold to health-food stores, health-food wholesalers, or supermarkets.

• The Nature Commune: Emphasis is on supporting the ecological system and on the enjoyment of nature. Buildings and gardening or farming plots are designed to fit into the landscape to preserve its natural beauty. Everyone "does his own thing," and economic support for subsistence usually comes from such varied sources as sale of produce and handicrafts, wages from part-time work, welfare support, etc.

• The Craft Commune: One or several crafts, such as weaving, pottery making, or carpentry (including construction or work on buildings outside the commune), occupy the interest of members. They often spend considerable blocks of time enjoying the exercise of their craft with the income contributed to the commune. Many of the craft communes sell directly to the consumer as a result of local, regional, or sometimes national advertisements and publicity. Profit margins vary since the vast majority of such communes do not subscribe to the amassing of profits as the primary aim of their enterprise. Included in this category are the multimedia communes that specialize in light shows, video tape, and film-making.

• The Spiritual/Mystical Commune: The ongoing spiritual development of members is recognized to be of primary importance. There may be adherence to a religious system, such as Buddhism, Sufism, or Zen, and a teacher or guru may be involved. Studies of various texts and mystical works, use of rituals, a number of forms of meditation (such as transcendental or Zen meditation), and spontaneous spiritual celebrations play key roles in the life of the commune. Several of these communes also describe themselves as Christian and have a strong spiritual, but not denominational, emphasis.

• The Denominational Commune: There is a religious emphasis with membership restricted to those of a particular denomination. Examples are the Episcopalian Order of St. Michael, in Crown Point, Indiana, and the Catholic Worker Farm, in Tivoli, New York.

• The Church-sponsored Commune: Such a commune may be originated or sponsored by a church. There is usually a religious emphasis, but denominationalism is not stressed.

• The Political Commune: Members subscribe to or share a common ideology. They may identify themselves as anarchists, socialists, pacifists, etc. Emphasis is on the communal living experience with others sharing the same viewpoint. This is seen as fostering the individuals' political development. The commune is rarely engaged in direct social action in opposition to the Establishment.

• The Political Action Commune: Members are committed and practicing political activists (or activists-in-training) for the purpose of changing the social system. Classes are conducted, strategy formulated and carried out. The commune may be identified with a minority cause or be interested in organizing an industry, community, or ghetto neighborhood. It often identifies itself by the single word "revolutionary."

• The Service Commune: The main goal is social service. Emphasis is on organizing communities, helping people to plan and carry out community projects, offering professional or case-aide services, etc. Some of these communes include members from the helping professions. There are several such communes in the Philadelphia and New York ghettos; another example is the Federation of Communities, which services several locations in the Appalachians.

• The Art Commune: Artists from different fields or the same field come together to share in the stimulating climate of communal artistic creativity. As compared with the craft commune, members of the art commune are often painters, sculptors, or poets, who usually sell their art works independently rather than collectively. There are poetry and street theater communes in Berkeley and San Francisco.

• The Teaching Commune: Emphasis is on training and developing people who are able both to live and to teach others according to a particular system of techniques and methods. Communes whose purpose or mainstay is to conduct a school or schools also fall into this category.

• The Group Marriage Commune: Although members may be given the freedom to join in the group marriage or not, the practice of group marriage plays an important and often central role in the life of the commune. All adults are considered to be parents of the members' children.

• The Homosexual Commune: Currently found in large urban areas, with admission restricted to homophiles. The aim of these communes is to afford individuals who share a common way of life an opportunity to live and communicate together and to benefit from the economies of a communal living arrangement. Some of the communes subscribe to the principles of the homophile liberation movement. From a recent ad in *Kaliflower,* the bi-weekly information journal for communes in the San Francisco Bay Area: " OUR GAY COMMUNE HAS ROOM FOR TWO MORE. CALL AND RAP."

• The Growth-centered Commune: The main focus is on helping members to grow as persons, to actualize their potential. There are ongoing group sessions; sometimes professionals are asked to lead these. The commune continues to seek out new experiences and methods designed to develop the potentialities of its members.

• The Mobile, or Gypsy, Commune: This is a caravan, usually on the move. Cars, buses, and trucks provide both transportation and living quarters. Members usually include artists, a rock group, or a light-show staff. The mobile commune often obtains contributions from "happenings" or performances given in communities or on college campuses.

• The Street, or Neighborhood, Commune: Several of these communes often are on the same street or in the same neighborhood. Ownership of property is in the hands of commune members or friendly and sympathetic neighbors. Basically the idea is of a free enclave or free community. For example, in a recent *New*

York Times article, Albert Solnit, chief of advance planning for California's Marin County, was reported at work "on a city of 20,000 for those who wish to live communally." Several neighborhood or city communes are in the planning stage, but none to my knowledge has as yet been established.

Among the major problems faced by all communes are those involving authority and structure. Ideally, there is no one telling anyone else what to do; directions are given by those best qualified to do a job. In practice, strong personalities in the communes assume responsibility for what happens, and there is a tendency toward the emergence of mother and father figures. There are, however, a clear awareness of this problem and continuing efforts toward resolution. At present, opposition to any form of structure, including organizational structure, is still so strong that communes have found it almost impossible to cooperate with each other in joint undertakings of a major nature. Interestingly enough, communes with transcendent or spiritual values are the most stable and have the highest survival quotient. It is my conclusion that the weekly or periodic meetings of all commune members, which are often run as encounter groups, have a limited effectiveness in the resolution of interpersonal problems and issues. Although trained encounter leaders may be present as facilitators, their effectiveness is often considerably curtailed due to their own deep involvement in the issues that are the subject of confrontation. One answer to this dilemma might be to bring in a trained facilitator or for communes to exchange facilitators.

It is difficult to determine to what extent narcotics represent a problem for communes precisely because their consumption is as casual, widespread, and accepted as is the downing of alcoholic beverages in the business community. Marijuana and hashish are widely enjoyed, while use of such hard drugs as heroin is seldom encountered, especially in the nonurban communes. In a number of communes where drug use was extensive, I noticed a general air of lassitude and a lack of vitality. I also had the distinct impression that "dropping acid" (LSD) was on the decline; among commune members there seemed to be a general awareness of the danger of "speed," or methedrine. A number of communes are totally opposed to the use of narcotics, especially those with members who were former drug addicts. In most communes the subject of drugs periodically comes up for discussion so that changes in the viewpoint of the commune flow from the experience of the members. Similarly, problems of sexual possessiveness and jealousy appear to be less critical and are also handled by open group discussion. I noticed a tendency toward the maintenance of traditional sex roles, with the women doing the cooking and sewing, the men cutting lumber, etc. Upon questioning this, I repeatedly received the same answer: "Everyone does what they enjoy doing."

Another major problem in most communes is overcrowding and the consequent lack of privacy and alone-time. Rarely does a member enjoy the opportunity of having a room to himself for any length of time. The common practice is to walk off into the woods or fields, but this is an inadequate substitute for real privacy.

Community relations remains a major and critical problem since many communes are "hassled" by authorities or are located amid unfriendly neighbors. As one member described it, the emotional climate in a hassled commune is "full of not-so-good vibes—you don't know what they will try next, and you keep looking over your shoulder. That takes energy." Today's commune members generally have a clear awareness of the importance of establishing good community relations.

Many of the communes that have got under way this past year or are now being organized are beginning on a sound financial basis. This trend appears to be related to the strong influx of people in their mid-twenties, early or mid-thirties, and beyond. These individuals have financial reserves or savings and are, for the most part, successful professionals and businessmen with families.

One example is the Morehouse Commune, which now consists of thirteen houses in the San Francisco Bay Area, two in Hawaii, and another in Los Angeles; total assets are in excess of $2 million. Morehouse was founded a year and a half ago by Victor Baranco, a former attorney who is now head of the Institute of Human Abilities, in Oakland, California. There are several categories of membership or involvement in this commune. Members who belong to "the family" give all their assets to the commune, which then "takes care of them," although family members are expected to continue to make a productive contribution within their chosen fields. All income from family members goes into a general fund, but if a family member wishes to withdraw, his assets are returned, including a standard rate of interest for their having been used. Each Morehouse commune in effect makes its own arrangements with members, who may be paid a salary or placed on an allowance system. All communes have a house manager, who assigns tasks or work on a rotating basis. In some Morehouse communes, certain categories of members pay in a fixed monthly sum (as much as $200) toward expenses.

About a third of the Morehouse couples are married and have children. According to one member, "There is no pressure to be married or unmarried. Nobody cares who lives with whom." Morehouse is a teaching commune built around a philosophy and way of life often described by group members as "responsible hedonism." The commune trains its own teachers and offers a considerable number of courses, such as Basic Sensuality, Advanced Sensuality, and Basic Communication.

The aim and credo of this group are taken from a description of the Institute of Human Abilities published in the commune journal *Aquarius:* "We offer the tools of deliberate living; we offer the techniques of successful communication on any level. We offer the knowledge of the human body and its sensual potential. And we offer love to a world that holds love to be suspect."

The rapid growth of the Morehouse communes is by no means an isolated example. A minister in Los Angeles founded a social-service and action-type commune that within a year grew to seven houses. Other instances can be cited. An unprecedented number of people want to join communes. In all but a few instances I was asked to conceal the name and location of the commune to make identification impossible. "We don't know what to do with all the people who come knocking on our door now," I was told repeatedly. In every commune, I heard of people who had recently left either to start a new commune or to join in the founding of one.

There is considerable mobility in communes, which is symptomatic of an endemic wanderlust and search. If people have to leave for any reason, once they have been exposed to communal living, they tend to return. They like the deep involvement with others in a climate of freedom, openness, and commitment. This feeling of belonging has been described as both "a new tribalism" and "a new sense of brotherhood." One young woman with whom I spoke had this to say about her commune experience: "When a white man walks into a room full of other whites, he doesn't feel he is among brothers like the black man does. In the communes, we are now beginning to feel that man has many brothers. . . . There is a new sense of honesty. You can say things to each other and share things like you never could in the family. I never had so much love in my whole life—not even in my own family." She also indicated, however, that commune living is highly intense and possibly not for everyone: "In the commune, there is nothing you can hide. Some people can't take it. They get sick or they leave."

Alvin Toffler in his recent book *Future Shock* notes that

> most of today's "intentional communities" reveal a powerful preference for the past, . . . but society as a whole would be better served by utopian experiments based on super- rather than pre-industrial forms. . . . In short, we can use utopianism as a tool rather than as an escape, if we base our experiments on the technology and society of tomorrow rather than that of the past.

Although Toffler's observation is relevant, we must recognize that the commune movement, as with most other movements, is passing through certain developmental stages. At this stage, there is little readiness for communes to define themselves as laboratories for the exploration of alternative models that might benefit the society of the future. Disenchantment with and opposition to science and technology are other impediments to the adoption of the laboratory concept. With today's communes, faith in the future of mankind appears to be at too low an ebb to produce any sustained interest in what Toffler calls "scientific future-sensing and the techniques of scientific futurism."

Although David Cooper, a colleague and disciple of British psychiatrist Ronald Laing, has sounded a death knell in his new book *The Death of the Family,* I believe we are far from writing the epitaph. The traditional nuclear family will continue, although its form, to some extent, may change; in the years to come, possibly as high as 20 percent of the population will explore alternative models of social living.

It would be a mistake to characterize the commune movement as a collection of dropouts who are content to exist like lilies in the field. A considerable number of successful people from all walks of life are now involved; they have merely shifted their sphere of interest and the nature of their creative contribution. We are dealing with a massive awakening of the awareness that life holds multiple options other than going from school to job to retirement. The commune movement has opened a new and wide range of alternative life-styles and offers another frontier to those who have the courage for adventure. It is the test tube for the growth of a new type of social relatedness, for the development of an organization having a structure that appears, disappears, and reappears as it chooses and as it is needed. Communes may well serve as a laboratory for the study of the processes involved in the regeneration of our social institutions. They have become the symbol of man's new freedom to explore alternative life-styles and to develop deep and fulfilling human relationships through the rebirth and extension of our capacity for familial togetherness.

LEONARD SWIDLER

jesus was a feminist _____

Thesis: *Jesus was a feminist.*
Definition of terms: By *Jesus* is meant the historical person who lived in Palestine two thousand years ago, whom Christians traditionally acknowledge as Lord and Savior, and whom they should "imitate" as much as possible. By a *feminist* is meant a person who is in favor of, and who promotes, the equality of women with men, a person who advocates and practices treating women primarily as human persons (as men are so treated) and willingly contravenes social customs in so acting.

To prove the thesis it must be demonstrated that, so far as we can tell, Jesus neither said nor did anything which would indicate that he advocated treating women as intrinsically inferior to men, but that on the contrary he said and did things which indicated that he thought of women as the equals of men, and that in the process he willingly violated pertinent social mores.

The negative portion of the argument can be documented quite simply by reading through the four Gospels. Nowhere does Jesus treat women as "inferior beings." In fact, Jesus clearly felt especially sent to the typical classes of "in-

From "Jesus Was a Feminist," *Catholic World,* Volume 212, 1971, page 177.

ferior beings," such as the poor, the lame, the sinner—and women—to call them all to the freedom and equality of the Kingdom of God. But there are two factors which raise this negative result exponentially in its significance: the status of women in Palestine at the time of Jesus, and the nature of the Gospels. Both need to be recalled here in some detail, particularly the former.

the status of women in palestine

The status of women in Palestine during the time of Jesus was very decidedly that of inferiors. Despite the fact that there were several heroines recorded in the Scriptures, according to most rabbinic customs of Jesus' time—and long after— women were not allowed to study the Scriptures (Torah). One first-century rabbi, Eliezer, put the point sharply: "Rather should the words of the Torah be burned than entrusted to a woman. . . . Whoever teaches his daughter the Torah is like one who teaches her lasciviousness."

In the vitally religious area of prayer, women were so little thought of as not to be given obligations of the same seriousness as men. For example, women, along with children and slaves, were not obliged to recite the *Shema,* the morning prayer, nor prayers at meals. In fact, the Talmud states: "Let a curse come upon the man who [must needs have] his wife or children say grace for him." Moreover, in the daily prayers of Jews there was a threefold thanksgiving: "Praised be God that he has not created me a gentile; praised be God that he has not created me a woman; praised be God that he has not created me an ignorant man." (It was obviously a version of this rabbinic prayer that Paul controverted in his letter to the Galatians: "There is neither Jew nor Greek, there is neither slave nor free, there is neither male nor female; for you are all one in Christ Jesus.")

Women were also grossly restricted in public prayer. It was (is) not even possible for them to be counted toward the number necessary for a quorum to form a congregation to worship communally—they were again classified with children and slaves, who similarly did not qualify. . . . In the great temple at Jerusalem they were limited to one outer portion, the women's court, which was five steps below the court for the men. In the synagogues the women were also separated from the men, and of course were not allowed to read aloud or take any leading function. . . .

Besides the disabilities women suffered in the areas of prayer and worship there were many others in the private and public forums of society. As one Scripture scholar, Peter Ketter, noted: "A rabbi regarded it as beneath his dignity, as indeed positively disreputable, to speak to a woman in public. The 'Proverbs of the Fathers' contain the injunction: 'Speak not much with a woman.' Since a man's own wife is meant here, how much more does not this apply to the wife of another? The wise men say: 'Who speaks much with a woman draws down misfortune on himself, neglects the words of the law, and finally earns hell. . . .' If it were merely the too free intercourse of the sexes which was being warned against, this would signify nothing derogatory to woman. But since the rabbi may not speak even to his own wife, daughter or sister in the street, then only male arrogance can be the motive." Intercourse with uneducated company is warned against in exactly the same terms. "One is not so much as to greet a woman." In addition, save in the rarest instances, women were not allowed to bear witness in a court of law. Some Jewish thinkers, as for example, Philo, a contemporary of Jesus, thought women ought not leave their households except to go to the synagogue (and that only at a time when most of the other people would be at home); girls ought even not cross the threshold that separated the male and female apartments of the household.

In general, the attitude toward women was epitomized in the institutions and customs surrounding marriage. For the most part the function of women was thought rather exclusively in terms of childbearing and rearing; women were almost always under the tutelage of a man, either the father or husband, or if a widow, the dead husband's brother. Polygamy—in the sense of having several wives, but *not* in the sense of having several husbands—was legal among Jews at the time of Jesus, although probably not heavily practiced. Moreover, divorce of a wife was very easily obtained by the husband—he merely had to give her a writ of divorce; women in Palestine, on the other hand, were not allowed to divorce their husbands.

Rabbinic sayings about women also provide an insight into the attitude toward women: "It is well for those whose children are male, but ill for those whose children are female. . . . At the birth of a boy all are joyful, but at the birth of a girl all are sad. . . . When a boy comes into the world, peace comes into the world: when a girl comes, nothing comes. . . . Even the most virtuous of women is a witch. . . . Our teachers have said: Four qualities are evident in women: They are greedy at their food, eager to gossip, lazy and jealous."

The condition of women in Palestinian Judaism was bleak.

the nature of the gospels

The Gospels, of course, are not the straight factual reports of eyewitnesses of the events in the life of Jesus of Nazareth as one might find in the columns of the *New York Times* or the pages of a critical biography. Rather, they are four different faith statements reflecting at least four primitive Christian communities who believed that Jesus was the Messiah, the Lord, and Savior of the world. They were composed from a variety of sources, written and oral, over a period of time and in response to certain needs felt in the communities and individuals at the time; consequently they are many-layered. Since the Gospel writer-editors were not twentieth-century critical historians they were not particularly intent on recording *ipsissima verba Christi,* nor were they concerned to winnow out all of their own cultural biases and assumptions. Indeed, it is doubtful they were particularly conscious of them.

This modern critical understanding of the Gospels, of course, does not impugn the historical character of the Gospels; it merely describes the type of historical documents they are so their historical significance can more accurately be evaluated. Its religious value lies in the fact that modern Christians are thereby helped to know much more precisely what Jesus meant by certain statements and actions as they are reported by the first Christian communities in the Gospels. With this new knowledge of the nature of the Gospels it is easier to make the vital distinction between the religious truth that is to be handed on and the time-conditioned categories and customs involved in expressing it.

When the fact that no negative attitudes by Jesus toward women are portrayed in the Gospels is set side by side with the recently discerned "communal faith-statement" understanding of the nature of the Gospels, the importance of the former is vastly enhanced. For whatever Jesus said or did comes to us only through the lens of the first Christians. If there were no very special religious significance in a particular concept or custom we would expect that current concept or custom to be reflected by Jesus. The fact that the overwhelmingly negative attitude toward women in Palestine did not come through the primitive Christian communal lens by itself underscores the clearly great religious importance Jesus attached to his positive attitude—his feminist attitude—toward women: feminism, that is, personalism extended to women, is a constitutive part of the Gospel, the Good News, of Jesus.

women disciples of jesus

One of the first things noticed in the Gospels about Jesus' attitude toward women is that he taught them the Gospel, the meaning of the Scriptures, and religious truths in general. When it is recalled that in Judaism it was considered improper, and even "obscene," to teach women the Scriptures, this action of Jesus was an extraordinary, deliberate decision to break with a custom invidious to women. Moreover, women became disciples of Jesus not only in the sense of learning from Him, but also in the sense of following Him in His travels and ministering to Him. A number of women, married and unmarried, were regular followers of Jesus. In Luke 8:1 ff. several are mentioned by name in the same sentence with the Twelve: "He made his way through towns and villages preaching and proclaiming the Good News of the kingdom of God. With him went the Twelve, as well as certain women . . . who provided for them out of their own resources." (Cf. Mark 15:40 f. The Greek word translated here as "provided for" and in Mark as "ministered to" is *diekonoun,* the same basic word as "deacon"; indeed apparently the tasks of the deacons in early Christianity were much the same as these women undertook.) The significance of this phenomenon of women following Jesus about, learning from and ministering to Him, can be properly appreciated when it is recalled that not only were women not to read or study the Scriptures, but in the more observant settings they were not even to leave their household, whether as a daughter, a sole wife, or a member of a harem.

women and resurrection from the dead

Within this context of women being disciples and ministers, Jesus quite deliberately broke another custom disadvantageous to women. Jesus' first appearance
after his resurrection to any of his followers was to a woman (or women), who
was then commissioned by him to bear witness of the risen Jesus to the Eleven
(John 20:11 ff.; Matt. 28:9 f.; Mark 16:9 ff.). In typical male Palestinian style,
the Eleven refused to believe the woman since, according to Judaic law, women
were not allowed to bear legal witness. As one learned in the Law, Jesus obviously was aware of this stricture. His first appearing to and commissioning women
to bear witness to the most important event of his career could not have been
anything but deliberate: it was clearly a dramatic linking of a very clear rejection
of the second-class status of women with the center of His Gospel, His resurrection. The effort of Jesus to centrally connect these two points is so obvious that
it is an overwhelming tribute to man's intellectual myopia not to have discerned
it effectively in two thousand years.

The intimate connection of women with resurrection from the dead is not
limited in the Gospels to that of Jesus. There are accounts of three other resur-
rections in the Gospels—all closely involving a woman. The most obvious connection of a woman with a resurrection account is that of the raising of a woman,
Jairus' daughter (Matt. 9:18 ff.; Mark 5:22 ff.; Luke 8:41 ff.). A second resurrection Jesus performed was that of the only son of the widow of Nain: "And
when the Lord saw her, he had compassion on her and he said to her, 'Do not
weep' " (cf. Luke 7:11 ff.). The third resurrection Jesus performed was Lazarus',
at the request of his sisters Martha and Mary (cf. John 11). From the first it was
Martha and Mary who sent for Jesus because of Lazarus' illness. But when Jesus
finally came Lazarus was four days dead. Martha met Jesus and pleaded for his
resurrection: "Lord, if you had been here, my brother would not have died. And
even now I know that whatever you ask from God, God will give you." Later
Mary came to Jesus and said much the same. "When Jesus saw her weeping, and
the Jews who came with her also weeping, he was deeply moved in spirit and
troubled; and he said, 'Where have you laid him?' They said to him, 'Lord, come
and see.' Jesus wept." Then followed the raising from the dead. Thus, Jesus
raised one woman from the dead, and raised two other persons largely because
of women.

There are two further details that should be noted in these three resurrection
stories. The first is that only in the case of Jairus' daughter did Jesus touch the
corpse—which made him ritually unclean. In the cases of the two men Jesus did
not touch them, but merely said, "Young man, I say to you, arise," or, "Lazarus, come out." One must at least wonder why Jesus chose to violate the laws
for ritual purity in order to help a woman, but not a man. The second detail is in
Jesus' conversation with Martha after she pleaded for the resurrection of Lazarus. Jesus declared himself to be the resurrection ("I am the resurrection and the
life"), the only time he did so that is recorded in the Gospels. Jesus here again

revealed the central event, the central message, in the Gospel—the resurrection, His resurrection, His being the resurrection—to a woman.

women as sex objects

There are of course numerous occasions recorded in the Gospels, where women are treated by various men as second-class citizens. There are also situations where women were treated by others not at all as persons but as sex objects, and it was expected that Jesus would do the same. The expectations were disappointed. One such occasion occurred when Jesus was invited to dinner at the house of a skeptical Pharisee (Luke 7:36 ff.) and a woman of ill repute entered and washed Jesus' feet with her tears, wiped them with her hair and anointed them. The Pharisee saw her solely as an evil sexual creature: "The Pharisee . . . said to himself, 'If this man were a prophet, he would know who this woman is who is touching him and what a bad name she has.' " But Jesus deliberately rejected this approach to the woman as a sex object. He rebuked the Pharisee and spoke solely of the woman's human, spiritual actions; He spoke of her love, her unlove, that is, her sins, of her being forgiven, and her faith. Jesus then addressed her (it was not "proper" to speak to women in public, especially "improper" women) as a human person: "Your sins are forgiven. . . . Your faith has saved you; go in peace."

A similar situation occurred when the scribes and Pharisees used a woman reduced entirely to a sex object to set a legal trap for Jesus. It is difficult to imagine a more callous use of a human person than the "adulterous" woman was put to by the enemies of Jesus. First, she was surprised in the intimate act of sexual intercourse (quite possibly a trap was set up ahead of time by the suspicious husband), and then dragged before the scribes and Pharisees, and then by them before an even larger crowd that Jesus was instructing: "making her stand in full view of everybody." They told Jesus that she had been caught in the very act of committing adultery and that Moses had commanded that such women be stoned to death (Deut. 22:22 ff.). "What have you to say?" The trap was partly that if Jesus said Yes to the stoning He would be violating the Roman law, which restricted capital punishment, and if He said No, He would appear to contravene Mosaic law. It could also partly have been to place Jesus' reputation for kindness toward, and championing the cause of, women in opposition to the law and the condemnation of sin. Jesus of course eluded their snares by refusing to become entangled in legalisms and abstractions. Rather, he dealt with both the accusers and the accused directly as spiritual, ethical, human persons. He spoke directly to the accusers in the context of their own personal ethical conduct: "If there is one of you who has not sinned, let him be the first to throw a stone at her." To the accused woman he likewise spoke directly with compassion, but without approving her conduct: " 'Woman, where are they? Has no one condemned you?' She said, 'No one, Lord.' And Jesus said, 'Neither do I condemn you; go, and do not sin again.' "

· · ·

jesus' rejection of the blood taboo

All three of the synoptic Gospels insert into the middle of the account of raising Jairus' daughter from the dead the story of the curing of the woman who had an issue of blood for twelve years (Matt. 9:20 ff.; Mark 5:25 ff.; Luke 8:43 ff.). Especially touching about this story is that the affected woman was so reluctant to project herself into public attention that she, "said to herself, 'If I only touch his garment, I shall be made well.' " Her shyness was not because she came from the poor, lower classes, for Mark pointed out that over the twelve years she had been to many physicians—with no success—on whom she had spent all her money. It was probably because for twelve years, as a woman with a flow of blood, she was constantly ritually unclean (Lev. 15:19 ff.), which not only made her incapable of participating in any cultic action and made her in some sense "displeasing to God," but also rendered anyone and anything she touched (or anyone who touched what she had touched!) similarly unclean. . . . The sense of degradation and contagion that her "womanly weakness" worked upon her over the twelve years doubtless was oppressive in the extreme. This would have been especially so when a religious teacher, a rabbi, was involved. But not only does Jesus' power heal her, in one of His many acts of compassion on the downtrodden and afflicted, including women, but Jesus also makes a great to-do about the event, calling extraordinary attention to the publicity-shy woman: "And Jesus, perceiving in himself that power had gone forth from him, immediately turned about in the crowd, and said, 'Who touched my garments?' And his disciples said to him, 'You see the crowd pressing around you, and yet you say, 'Who touched me?' And he looked around to see who had done it. But the woman, knowing what had been done to her, came in fear and trembling and fell down before Him and told Him the whole truth. And He said to her, 'Daughter, your faith has made you well; go in peace, and be healed of your disease.' " It seems clear that Jesus wanted to call attention to the fact that He did not shrink from the ritual uncleanness incurred by being touched by the "unclean" woman (on several occasions Jesus rejected the notion of ritual uncleanness), and by immediate implication rejected the "uncleanness" of a woman who had a flow of blood, menstruous or continual. Jesus apparently placed a greater importance on the dramatic making of this point, both to the afflicted woman herself and the crowd, than He did on avoiding the temporary psychological discomfort of the embarrassed woman, which in light of Jesus' extraordinary concern to alleviate the pain of the afflicted, meant He placed a great weight on the teaching this lesson about the dignity of women.

jesus and the samaritan woman

On another occasion Jesus again deliberately violated the then common code concerning men's relationship to women. It is recorded in the story of the Samaritan woman at the well of Jacob (John 4:5 ff.). Jesus was waiting at the well outside the village while His disciples were getting food. A Samaritan woman approached the well to draw water. Normally a Jew would not address a Samaritan, as the woman pointed out: "Jews, in fact, do not associate with Samaritans." But also normally a man would not speak to a woman in public (doubly so in the case of a rabbi). However, Jesus startled the woman by initiating a conversation. The woman was aware that on both counts, her being a Samaritan and being a woman, Jesus' action was out of the ordinary for she replied: "How is it that you, a Jew, ask a drink of me, a woman of Samaria?" As hated as the Samaritans were by the Jews, it is nevertheless clear that Jesus' speaking with a woman was considered a much more flagrant breach of conduct than His speaking with a Samaritan, for John related: "His disciples returned, and were surprised to find him speaking to a woman, though none of them asked, 'What do you want from her?' or, 'Why are you talking to her?' " However, Jesus' bridging of the gap of inequality between men and women continued further, for in the conversation with the woman He revealed himself in a straightforward fashion as the Messiah for the first time: "The woman said to him, 'I know that Messiah is coming.' . . . Jesus said to her, 'I who speak to you am he.' "

Just as when Jesus revealed Himself to Martha as "the resurrection," and to Mary as the "risen one" and bade her to bear witness to the apostles, Jesus here also revealed Himself in one of his key roles, as Messiah, to a woman—who immediately bore witness of the fact to her fellow villagers.

● ● ●

marriage and the dignity of woman
One of the most important stands of Jesus in relation to the dignity of women was His position on marriage. His unpopular attitude toward marriage (cf. Matt. 19:10: "The disciples said to him, 'If such is the case of a man with his wife, it is not expedient to marry.' ") presupposed a feminist view of women; they had rights and responsibilities equal to men.

● ● ●

the intellectual life for women
However, Jesus clearly did not think of woman's role in . . . restricted terms; she was not to be limited to being *only* a housekeeper. Jesus quite directly rejected the stereotype that the proper place of all women is "in the home," during a visit to the house of Martha and Mary (Luke 10:38 ff.). Martha took the typical woman's role: "Martha was distracted with much serving." Mary, however, took the supposedly "male" role: she "sat at the Lord's feet and listened to his teaching." Martha apparently thought Mary was out of place in choosing the role of the "intellectual," for she complained to Jesus. But Jesus' response was a refusal to force all women into the stereotype; he treated Mary first of all as a person . . . who was allowed to set her own priorities, and in this instance had "chosen the better part." And Jesus applauded her: "It is not to be taken from her." Again, when one recalls the Palestinian restriction on women studying the Scriptures or studying with rabbis, that is, engaging in the intellectual life or acquiring any "religious authority," it is difficult to imagine how Jesus could

possibly have been clearer in his insistence that women were called to the intellectual, the spiritual life just as were men.

There is at least one other instance recorded in the Gospels when Jesus uttered much the same message (Luke 11:27 f.). One day as Jesus was preaching a woman from the crowd apparently was very deeply impressed and, perhaps imagining how happy she would be to have such a son, raised her voice to pay Jesus a compliment. She did so by referring to His mother, and did so in a way that was probably not untypical at that time and place. But her image of a woman was sexually reductionist in the extreme (one that largely persists to the present): female genitals and breasts. "Blessed is the womb that bore you, and the breasts that you sucked!" Although this was obviously meant as a compliment, and although it was even uttered by a woman, Jesus clearly felt it necessary to reject this "baby-machine" image of women and insist again on the personhood, the intellectual and moral faculties, being primary for all: "But he said, 'Blessed rather are those who hear the word of God and keep it!' " Looking at this text it is difficult to see how the primary point could be anything substantially other than this. Luke and the tradition and Christian communities he depended on must also have been quite clear about the sexual significance of this event. Otherwise, why would he (and they) have kept and included such a small event from all the years of Jesus' public life? It was not retained *merely* because Jesus said blessed are those who hear and keep God's word, but because that was stressed by Jesus as being primary in comparison to a woman's sexuality.

. . .

god as a woman

In many ways Jesus strove to communicate the notion of the equal dignity of women. In one sense that effort was capped by his parable of the woman who found the lost coin (Luke 15:8 ff.), for here Jesus projected God in the image of a woman! Luke recorded that the despised tax-collectors and sinners were gathering around Jesus, and consequently the Pharisees and scribes complained. Jesus, therefore, related three parables in a row, all of which depicted God's being deeply concerned for that which was lost. The first story was of the shepherd who left the ninety-nine sheep to seek the one lost—the shepherd is God. The third parable is of the prodigal son—the father is God. The second story is of the woman who sought the lost coin—the woman is God! Jesus did not shrink from the notion of God as feminine. In fact, it would appear that Jesus included this womanly image of God quite deliberately at this point for the scribes and Pharisees were among those who most of all denigrated women—just as they did the "tax-collectors and sinners."

. . .

conclusion

From this evidence it should be clear that Jesus vigorously promoted the dignity and equality of women in the midst of a very male-dominated society: Jesus was a feminist, and a very radical one.

JANE HOWARD

the groovy christians
of rye, n.y. ⎯⎯⎯⎯⎯⎯⎯⎯⎯⎯⎯⎯⎯⎯⎯⎯⎯⎯

A good many parents in Rye, N.Y. are bewildered. The sociology professor is bewildered, and the businessman, and the Sunday school teacher, and the banker, and the editor, and the travel agency lady, and a number of others. They are bewildered because their children have become Christians.

The Christianity that obsesses these hundred or so kids in and near Rye, and many thousands elsewhere, has little to do with nativity pageants, bake sales or other sidelights of religion familiar to their parents. Jesus, to these kids, is not the stained-glass embodiment of remote virtue, nor do they regard the Bible as a majestic collection of myths. They feel Christ as an immediate presence, and see the Bible as the irrefutably accurate word of God, containing no contradictions and solving all their problems from the cosmic to the trivial. "For them," as one father observes, "it's the ultimate how-to book, like the very ambitious manual of an automobile mechanic."

Kris Skedgell, a converted ninth-grader, used to hang around stables a lot. "But I'm not so much into riding anymore," she says. "Psalm 33:17 blew my mind. It showed me that horses won't get me eternal life. I'll only get eternal life from the Lord."

Another girl used to be afraid to hitchhike to school, "but the Word gives us authority over all sickness, all evil, all danger. As long as Dad's looking after me, I will fear no evil." By Dad she did not mean her earthly father.

"It's so neat!" the kids say of their new Christianity. "It's out of sight! It's a gas! It frees you from fear! It's super-edifying!"

Their kind of Christianity may look and sound at times like the label-grabbing fundamentalism one thinks of in terms of old-time southern evangelists, but there's much more to it than that. It fuses the threats and promises of the Bible Belt with the subtle, nonverbal vibrations of the subculture of drugs and rock music. It transforms its converts, attacks the premises by which they were raised and unsettles every household it touches. Parents aren't sure whether they should be enchanted or appalled.

"If you'd told me a year ago," says the businessman, "that I'd have a son who'd carry a Bible wherever he went, who'd drop out of college to become a Christian missionary, who'd argue on the wrong side of the Scopes trial issue, I'd never have believed you. And neither would he."

"But I guess we should have known this might happen," says his wife. "These kids had already bugged us with every kind of classic adolescent rebellion. We'd been through long hair, peace marches, macrobiotic diets, meditation. . . . Drugs, too, of course."

⎯⎯⎯⎯⎯⎯⎯⎯
"The Groovy Christians of Rye, N.Y.," *Life*, May 14, 1971.

"Sometimes I almost wish they would go back to something simple like smoking a little grass," says Mrs. Lynn Seiffer, a travel agent who is getting her master's in library science. "Drugs I can try to understand, but this? This is creepy."

Rye, a Westchester County town of 16,000, is set on the Long Island Sound only 45 minutes by car from Manhattan. Rye has big, spacious houses with cozy two-digit addresses on well-kept streets under big old trees. Rye has six churches, four country clubs and stores where you can buy brook trout fresh from Idaho and Brie cheese fresh from France. Rye has orthodontists, psychiatrists, sensitivity trainers, advocates of women's liberation and a high school that sends 80 percent of its graduates to college. Rye citizens have well-stocked wine cellars and libraries, and consciences that impel them to do a lot of volunteer work.

> My sweet Lord, I really want to know you,
> I really want to be with you.
> —GEORGE HARRISON
> "My Sweet Lord"

At 7:45 on weekday mornings the new Christians of the town assemble in a circle for prayer meetings outside the Rye high school, which many of them attend. Inside, later, they pass each other notes that read "SMILE! GOD LOVES YOU!" and do their best to convert nonbelieving classmates and teachers. After school they do odd jobs, race through their homework and beamingly help their mothers make supper. Their fathers, returning home by commuter train, are greeted with joyous hugs.

"Radiant" is the word everybody keeps using to describe these kids, with reason. Their hair and clothes look like those of any privileged Aquarian adolescents, but the nonstop smiles on their faces are singular. No squad of cheerleaders was ever more unbeat. Ask any of the Rye kids, any time, how he feels and he'll answer "TerRIFic!" or "Perfect" and mean it. Remark that a slush storm seems a bit unseasonal, and he'll say, "But it's always a beautiful day when you're walking with the Lord!" and mean that, too.

Many of these kids say detailed graces before all meals. The talk at dinner, heavily laced with references to Ephesians and Leviticus, never strays far from biblical matters.

"But how about your grandmother?" Mrs. Joseph Lagey, the librarian wife of a sociology professor, asked her daughter Barbara over sukiyaki one recent evening. "Why, if God is so gracious, did he let her suffer so long? Wasn't she a good woman?"

"Sure," Barbara explained patiently. "But if she'd believed in the Word, she wouldn't have had to die painfully."

"What about all the Buddhists and Shintos and Hindus? Will they burn in hell because they didn't accept Christ?"

"The Father," answered Barbara, "is merciful." And then, leaving the kitchen spotless, she rushed off—as her brother Christopher already had—to spend the evening "witnessing and fellowshipping" at a Dunkin' Donuts in a neighboring town.

Some rather good paintings young Christopher did last year hang in the Lageys' living room. He doesn't paint anymore, though. None of the new Christians of Rye has much time anymore for painting, or skiing, or mountain-climbing, or any of the old "Satanic" things. This troubles their parents.

Many things trouble them. For all its radiance, the new faith can seem humorless, condescending and vastly oversimplified. When parents suggest that the Koran might also merit study, or that crusades for peace, clean air and birth control might better the world, kids argue that nothing matters but saving individual souls.

"When I was their age," Mrs. John Ranyak says, "it never occurred to me that I could find the answer to anything. I still don't feel I need to."

"I have this Vonnegut sort of view that life's all a big joke," Mrs. Lagey says. "It isn't very comforting, but I'm used to it. My husband and I could never make the leap of faith these kids have, from 'sense knowledge,' as they call it, to 'spirit knowledge.'

"I guess," she says, "that we're what you'd call 'Pediatric Christians.' I stopped being Catholic a long time ago, but we had the kids baptized—you know, 'just in case,'—and then sent them to Unitarian Sunday school, where the first hymn they learned was 'Shalom Chevarim.' We took them to see the mosque in Washington and made sure they learned about *all* religions. Maybe we overdid it, giving them such a rational, eclectic upbringing. I guess the only way they could rebel, from that, was to deep fundamentalism."

Her children, and their friends, disagree. They don't see their new faith in terms of rebellion, or of fundamentalism, but as the dazzlingly simple cure for a "hunger" for absolute truth—a famine, to hear them talk of it, more desperate than that of Biafra, a famine as acute in Westchester County as anywhere else. In Westchester, as in most other places, people have seemed more inclined of late to look backward, or inward, than ahead. In Rye, and in surrounding towns, the growing band of new Christians have been looking intently backward, all the way back to the first century A.D., and are clearly transfixed by what they find.

Sunday is the big night for the new Christians of Rye. They crowd together in a borrowed church room for a special prayer-and-fellowship meeting. They flip through their dog-eared Bibles like graduate seminary students, underlining with yellow Magic Markers passages that hadn't struck them before. Their leader at these meetings is Steve Heefner, a 33-year-old former disc jockey for CBS who was "reborn in Christ" four and a half years ago.

"We're on a conveyor belt called Sin going toward a place called Death," Heefner tells the kids, "unless we're safe in the comforting arms of the Word of God." His scriptural teaching lasts well over an hour, but only the visitors squirm. There are hymns: a couple of original ones composed and led, on guitars, by Tim Bishop and Chuck Remington, and maybe a few choruses of the old favorite "Amazing Grace," lately exalted to national popularity by the recordings of Judy Collins and Arlo Guthrie. There are announcements: believers reported recently on their "witnessing" at nearby towns and Cornell University, and told of "heavy, tight fellowship" they found at "advances" (not retreats) in North Carolina and California. "Praise the Lord!" said Heefner. "Far out!" said the kids.

Speaking in tongues—an ancient practice technically called "glossolalia" and recently voguish in many new Christian circles—is always a feature of the Sunday night meetings. At Heefner's bidding a worshiper will rise to utter a divinely inspired message that sounds, to an unsaved ear, like: "Alokar shamalsh frolaniuk asapolikaj shantih. . . ." The prompt translation, by the same speaker, is usually along the lines of "Be bold, my children, in spreading the Word. Thus saith the Lord."

All eyes are closed during prayers. "Wow, Lord," one boy recently began, "it's really out of sight the way you've brought us together here tonight, and we just want to thank you, Father, for letting us be worthy to be the stewards of your Word, through Jesus Christ our big brother. Old Satan won't know what hit him when we get going. We might have to hassle with him some, but we won't have to worry about *anything* ever, Father, so long as we're walking on your rightly-divided Word."

These children feel invincible. "So long as we keep our shield of believing up," as they say, their cars won't crash, they won't get cancer, and if they're drafted and sent to Vietnam "we won't be killed or even scratched." But why get uptight about the draft? "Jesus," as they say, "might be back before breakfast!"

Poverty, spiritual or otherwise, will never vex these believers, because "if you believe, you'll receive *abundantly,* and not just spiritual abundance. The Father wants his people to be prosperous. That's why He tells us to tithe; we give Him a tenth of our money or more, as love offerings, and it's mind-blowing the way it comes back, just like it says in Malachi. Poverty, see, is just Satanic stuff. Poor people are poor because they don't know how to pray."

The vast underground of Christian revival of which this Rye group is one small outpost strikes different places in different styles. Many factions have already arisen. "New Testament Prayer Groups" in Texas and Minnesota attract members with street-witnessing and youth rallies. Christian communes serve as crash pads or relatively permanent lodging for new believers in San Francisco and Toronto. On the Sunset Strip of Los Angeles, free-lance evangelists have had spectacular success in persuading spaced-out acid heads that a "higher high" is available through Christ, and in holding mass baptisms in the Pacific.

To Rye, thus far afflicted less with a hard-drug problem than with ennui, the salvation message has come in the plainer, tougher form of a $45 class called "Power for Abundant Living." The class consists of 36 hours of tape-recorded lessons "guaranteed to answer 95 percent of your questions about the Bible and about everything else."

The tapes, along with films and much printed matter, are sent out by a rural Ohio organization called The Way Biblical Research Center. The Rye kids, who have converted many of their peers and several adults elsewhere in Westchester and on Long Island call themselves The Way East.

The Way, they make clear, is not a church or a denomination. "Denominations," Steve Heefner tells them, "have failed. They tried to water down the Gospel to make it more palatable, but they tried too hard. Peter, John, James and those dudes had the right idea."

> Christ you know I love you—
> did you see I waved?
> > *Jesus Christ Superstar*

For "Jesus Freaks," as these new Christians are used to being called, the message of glory is best passed not from ordained grownups in pulpits but between kids, by word of mouth, or from radio rock stations or phonograph headsets. One striking gauge of this movement's growth potential is the success of the hit album *Jesus Christ Superstar* and any number of other popular songs alluding to the Lord. This music, the kids say, also can help them lure people away from drugs and toward the New Testament. "If you've ever been stoned," one new convert says, "you know how you can become the music you're listening to—and when the songs have to do with Jesus, you're ready for a heavy Christian trip."

It was Tina Ranyak, now 18, who brought The Way to Rye last August, when she came home from the Midwest. She had gone off to art school in Kansas City and been converted to Christianity there by a classmate who had discovered The Way. "I'd never given any thought to religion before," says Tina. "I'd hardly been inside a church in all my life. But what I heard about Christ seemed to make so much sense. I decided I'd accept Him as my personal Lord and Savior, the way it says in Romans 10:9. It wasn't all that melodramatic; I mean I didn't get any big rushes or anything. I just said the words one night and right away I knew they were true."

After she quit art school, Tina went to live in a Way communal house in Wichita where, a Way leader says, "We've saved souls by the *barrelful*." By the time she came home to Rye last summer, with a Way friend as her houseguest, her faith was clearly contagious and her old friends and classmates were ripe for infection.

Tina's friends—"ex-flesh freaks," they now call themselves—were hip and bright and avant-garde, and had been showered all their lives with all the material "advantages" their parents could afford. "But," says Tina's father, John Ranyak, whose two sons have also joined The Way, "they were thoroughly starved for faith and something they could build a life around." That, perhaps, is why they had made an art form of sulking and moping.

"Some of us," says one 20-year-old boy, "had been through incredible garbage." What kinds of garbage? "What does it matter? There's no difference between seeing how fast you can run a mile or how much acid you can take."

"None of that stuff ever worked," says another believer. "I tried it all and quit each thing whenever I heard of something else that might be a little more groovy, but it never was."

"I'd just graduated from Yale and come back from hitchhiking around Europe, doing what I supposedly always wanted to do, but not feeling particularly happy about it," says Brian Heaney, the one college graduate in the Rye group.

"I was getting ready to go to California," says Tim Bishop, "to see what kind of a flesh trip I could get into."

But the disaffected kids didn't go to California, or get into flesh trips. Premarital sex, like drug use, is discouraged by The Way. So is indolence; the kids are urged to work. So is reading newspapers "because, shoot, newspapers lead to negative thoughts, which poison the mind. We just feed our minds by imbibing the great truth of the Word, so we can be positively positive." Nor is the women's liberation movement in good favor. "My daughter," one mother remembers, "suddenly accused me of bringing her up too leniently, instead of teaching her to be an efficient homemaker."

The Way Word spread fast after Tina came home. So many recruits turned up that Heefner, for several years a parttime Way disciple, felt called to quit his CBS job and move to Rye with his wife and son to set up a fulltime ministry.

Parents of one convert, returning from a long vacation away from their children, expected anything but what they found at home. "I knew the house would be turned into some sort of commune," the father says. "I wouldn't have been surprised to find a marijuana patch in the backyard, or a spate of sudden marriages. The one thing I never thought I'd see was 45 Bibles in the living room, and the maxims of J. Christ taped to all the mirrors."

By last fall The Way had burgeoned enough to merit a visit to Rye by its 53-year-old founder and president, Dr. Victor Paul Wierwille. He came in glory, all the way from New Knoxville, Ohio, on a raspberry-and-white Harley Davidson 74 motorcycle. He called Rye "a very dark town in a very dark county," but held forth hope.

"As long as I'm here," he assured his audience, "nothing bad can happen to you folks, because I'm not *believing* for it to happen. Oh, people, isn't it a beauty-full trip to live and just *ooze* goodness wherever you go? Isn't it tremendous to be able to say I know that I know that I know that I know?"

And then, for about three hours, he explained The Way to the youth and such of their parents as could be persuaded to attend. A dashing dresser, with Holy Spirit doves on his cufflinks, tie clasp, lapel pin and ring, Dr. Wierwille urged the parents to sign up for the course. He told them how he had devoted 30 years to developing "the first pure and correct interpretation of the Word since the first century A.D.," and how "Jesus Christ, the favorite cussword of the United States of America, is the same King of Kings and Lord of Lords who walked on water and fellowshipped with believers. He's alive today as He was in the Book of Acts, and anybody who doesn't accept Him as personal Lord and Savior is absolutely stupid."

As the Beatles and their followers once trooped to the Maharishi's ashram in

India, several Rye kids have already made joyous pilgrimages to The Way headquarters, on Dr. Wierwille's 150-acre ancestral Ohio farm. Many plan to spend much of this summer there, living in trailers or dormitories and enrolling in such studies as "How to Deal with Satan," "Speaking in Tongues, Interpretation and Prophecy," "Christian Family Life and Sex," "Christian Etiquette" and "Biblical Aramaic."

In New Knoxville, a 19th-century town of 800 people who say "shucks" a lot, where men call their wives "Mother" and other women "Ma'am" or "Girl," the kids from Rye will hear how The Way is growing in Samoa, California, Sweden and Alaska and through special courses for inmates of at least two prisons. They may observe, too, the proven success of Dr. Wierwille's policy on tithing. In his remodeled farmhouse are such amenities as a sunken mosaic bathtub, and plans are afoot for a $3.5 million building program, to keep up with the expansion of The Way.

> Won't you look down upon me, Jesus—
> You've got to help me make a stand.
> —James Taylor
> "Fire and Rain"

In Rye, meanwhile, parents are learning to live with The Way, with varying degrees of grace. They're getting used to the fact that when birthdays approach the gift kids request is Young's *Concordance to the Bible*.

A few share their children's delight in The Way. "I wept for joy," the Reverend Joseph Bishop recalls, "when Tim told me he'd found the Lord Jesus Christ." Reverend Bishop's Presbyterian church, unlike most in Rye or anywhere, has given the new movement hospitality and support.

But many parents remain dubious. "We treat our son," one mother says, "as if he were recovering from a dangerous illness."

"It's embarrassing and awkward," says a father, "to have my own children greet me by saying, 'God bless you.' "

"Especially," puts in an irreverent mother, "if you didn't even sneeze."

"I feel like saying to my daughter," says Mrs. Ralph Skedgell, a publishing house editor, " 'Wait till *you* have children.' But I don't mean it the way *my* mother meant it when she said it to me."

John Seiffer, who astounded his mother by spending an entire evening sewing a Bible-sized pocket inside his coat, has decided there isn't much point in talking to her about The Way. That's all right with her. "Arguing with them," Mrs. Seiffer says, "is like arguing with the Communists in the 1950s. They have all the answers. Besides, who can object to their knowing so much about the Bible?"

"In my generation," says Mrs. Skedgell, "we wore our skepticism and cynicism as a badge of honor. We were reacting to our rigid, old-fashioned, unprogressive grandparents. Now these kids are reacting to our habit of saying 'Well, let's see now, there's another whole side of the question.' "

"Every so often," says Joseph Lagey, "I wonder, 'Is this all a charade? When will reality smash down?' But I guess it's no wonder this has happened in Rye.

Brought up in homogenized suburbs sealed off from death, disease, morons, the ugly, the crippled and the poor, these kids can see how deficient are the pseudo-communities around them. They want symbols that define them more honestly.

"I've committed myself," Lagey goes on, "to the hope that rationalism will save humanity, but for all my doubts about The Way, I secretly hope it won't wither away like the flower children and the peace movement and the hippie movement did."

"Their scholarship seems smug and oddly intellectual," one mother says. "But they *do* claim that they've found eternal life and happiness, and I guess that can't *hurt* them."

She sounded, among other things, a little envious.

FREDERICK FRANCK

the exploding church

I was not exactly in condition and climbed the mountain once more on unsteady legs, but I wanted to sit down and take a last look at Angelo Roncalli's village. It was bathed in the afternoon sun that makes even ugly villages beautiful. I wanted to think here about this inquiry, which was now nearly completed.

I saw the faces of the more than fifty people with whom I had struggled through the questions. I was exhausted. "What does the Church mean to you?" "What does the Church mean to me?" I have learned a lot of course, but what? I have been changed through it all, but how? . . . Why on earth had I started all this? What would the man of Sotto il Monte have thought of it? And the others? Would they be able to do something with it? Or would they just say: "That fellow made it all up!" or "Well, if you ask *that* kind of people!" I am as tired as Montini after a long speech. Actually it is all finished. What have I got to add? . . .

In November 1966 Pope Paul VI had said: "We have to be convinced that one cannot demolish the Church of yesterday in order to build a new one for today." I wonder: Does one want to build a new church at all? Is a new structure being born in the midst of the old one? Or is it only the disintegration of old structures we witness, an exploding church?

On the mountain behind Sotto il Monte I tried to sum up what I had gleaned from the answers of the avant-garde, what I had found in the turmoil and ferment of the minds and the hearts of these Catholics.

First of all, the traditional concept of a Providence in the old sense of the word, a Providence that guaranteed the status quo, a concept that assumes that we men do not determine our future, seemed to have become antiquated. Pope Pius XII could still have said that we are not responsible for the way in which our grandchildren will live; Providence will take care of them. This, by now, seems a primitive if not barbarous statement. People, not Providence, make a society, build, in their wisdom or folly, a future in which they shall reap what they have sowed.

The entire concept of sin also seemed modified beyond recognition. A micro-ethic with a detailed catalogue of sins, especially if not integrated into a macro-ethic, was being rejected as hypocritical and irrelevant. It had become complete-ly unacceptable, this "sin," which in practice was limited to sexual behavior quite normal in our culture, and to the sundry forms of dereliction in churchly duties. The emphasis on the hereafter, certainly on an anthropomorphically de-tailed hereafter, had disappeared. Life on earth—now—was being affirmed, a life which only becomes fully human in growth, integration, and conscious accep-tance.

The guilt-machine had been stalled. Hell was either being declared empty or transferred to the earth's surface, where people were slowly becoming conscious that it is of their own making. Of purgatory, all that was left was a vague time concept instead of a space concept. The less said about heaven, the wiser. The idea of the absolute, exclusive perfection of the Church had been replaced by the concept of the "People of God on pilgrimage." The concept had been ex-tended to embrace all mankind. The repetition of the expression "People of God" was already becoming not a little embarrassing to many. All transmitted taboos were being examined and dismissed where they were felt to be irrelevant to contemporary life and culture. It was now recognized that the layman could be regarded as an adult. The institution had started to take him seriously at ex-actly the moment the layman stopped to take the institution so seriously. Co-incidence?

The practice of confession had been undergoing radical change or was dis-appearing. Priests no longer read their breviary and didn't keep this a secret. In-stead, they read psalms, gospels, Robinson, Altizer, Tillich. The right to a per-sonal conscience had been axiomatically accepted; *Kadavergehorsam,* unques-tioning obedience, had become inadmissible, being called "Byzantinism." En-cyclicals and allocutions were read critically, if at all, and all types of ecclesias-tical rhetoric and pseudo-poetry were quoted as jokes, as examples of the eva-sion of real problems. The life and the word of Jesus, his "value system," how-ever, were taken with a new, high seriousness in all their simplicity, incorrupti-bility and eternal youthfulness, and without any need for complex theological virtuosity and acrobatics.

In this time of the suffering—the crucifixion—of innumerable human beings, Jesus is once more being experienced as utterly relevant to our condition. Cruci-fixion and resurrection are seen as the existential elements of every life con-sciously lived. The values Jesus lived by are recognized as the key to the mystery of human meaning. With him there is hope of resurrection for man, for humanity. In this realization, deeply religious people are liberating themselves from their isolation, from their subjection to taboos and imposed duties and bylaws, from their fear of one another, of life and, perhaps, even of death.

I had heard the conviction expressed that Jesus of Nazareth could not have wished to burden people with a new "religion," with new and complex ceremonies, laws, and self-satisfied authorities, but that he initiated a new way of "being human," based on his insight of identity, of equivalence with the humblest of his fellow creatures as well as with that given Reality he calls his Father: To testify to your conviction you do not kill others, you sacrifice yourself. This human Jesus has been recognized as the way and the pointing to the way, as the incarnation of the central truth about what constitutes the mysterious core and meaning of human life. He had been totally de-idolized. He had been rediscovered as that central, that "divine" humanity that makes its appeal to our own humanity. He had been acknowledged also, therefore, as the one who *is* the very criterion for the fullness of being human, individually and in the community of men: "Defend the defenseless," "Judge not," "Feed the hungry." He still demonstrates precisely where humanity, insight, courage, and love begin and where blindness, corruption, cowardice, hypocrisy, exploitation, and cruelty end. He does not judge. He is the judgment, on us as well as on the Church. He is no longer an idol, yet if there is the divine in human life, he shows what exactly it is. He is very much alive! Whether he is technically God or not is not what interests us so much, but rather that our deepest identity with this divine and central humanity is acknowledged anew and intensely. The statement of St. Augustine that what is called Christian religion has existed from the beginning of the human race "until Christ came in the flesh," and until that true religion which had always existed began to be called Christianity, remains valid also in our so-called post-Christian era, which might turn out to be the last pre-Christian one. The rebirth from the unconscious man to the "new," "religious" man, the man of insight into the Reality of which the Christian Gospels, Buddhist scripture, the Upanishads, and the Greek mysteries all speak, still remains the vocation of Everyman.

To follow Christ is to discover him in the depth of one's total authenticity. To believe in him is to apprehend his presence in one's enemy.

The institutional Church, which as Holy Mother had made her children dependent on her, who fed them the forever fixed formula, is losing her authority. Her most gifted children have decided to try to lead adult lives. They have burst out of the nursery, astonished to see themselves as belonging to a community of people as wide as the world, let loose in a universe. While insisting on their human dignity, they are realizing ever more clearly that those who manipulate them, claiming superior status as shepherds, are all too often their inferiors in the awareness of the relationship of man to himself and to the others, of the individual to the community. These shepherds seem merely to continue justifying their compulsive juggling with canon law and with the formalistic theologisms which leave people of today ice cold. It is as if now people do not so much seek definitive answers, certainly not pat answers, to their questions as that they claim the right to ask the ultimate questions. They constantly question themselves and question each other. I ask again: Could this questioning be today's form of prayer?

If one speaks of the crisis of faith in our time, it might well be that "crisis" is the very form contemporary religious awareness takes. The religious crisis seems to be a crisis in awareness.

There is also, of course, a crisis in the religious institutions. This consists essentially in the merciless unmasking of all pseudo-authority, all sanctimoniousness, rhetoric, role playing, and in the rejection of all forms of spiritual terrorism and paternalism.

Religious man, as a vital contemporary type, seems quite aware that he does not know, but he has noticed that "authority" does not know either, because it has forgotten that the shepherds are at least as ignorant as he, who does not regard himself as a sheep. Nevertheless, authority is always ready to repeat the all too easy counsels of a ready-made phraseology. Neither does the religious man know exactly what he wants, but he knows at any rate and very well what he does not want, what he does no longer want.

It is, of course, impossible to define this contemporary religious man, but he can be met everywhere. Negatively, one can say of him that he utterly distrusts religion understood as an objective authoritarian system of unquestioned taboos, duties, and articles of faith. He has recognized the many dehumanizing results of institutionalized religion just as he is beginning to recognize the dehumanizing effect of institutionalized scientism. Paradoxically, however, he does not reject wholesale the norms and values of religious traditions, but on the contrary wishes to maintain and even confirm these norms and values on condition that they are liberated from the petrifactions of the historical institutions and their paternalism. Neither does he reject the norms of the scientific method, but he has begun to have grave doubts about his redemption by scientism, by the Gadget. Nothing, however, could fit his mentality less well than the medieval idea of a specific text interpreted by a central authority as the key to the mystery of his existence.

Paul Tillich's definition of religion as "ultimate concern" expresses this stirring, this urge to find the ultimate depths of one's being, this compulsion to make contact with that "ground of being," with that which we are ourselves in our deepest, most naked reality. It is this search for meaning, for awareness, for integration in our lives, and for a community based on what Michael Polanyi calls "a consensus of conscience" in which contemporary men feel, with Bonhoeffer, that God is the Reality not somewhere beyond the borders of their lives, but one that must be found exactly at their very center.

This new type of religious man seems to have little interest in organizing himself into large groups, closed off to the outside, or, insofar as he is a Catholic, to step out of the Church. He considers it futile to found a new church, but is resolved to find his *communio* within the remains of the old structure. He does not wish to leave it and join other denominations because the denominational approach has demonstrated its fruitlessness. On the contrary, he is after something universal, something catholic. He has done with the old concept of a church as a gap-filler, as a consoler which has little to offer by way of concrete assistance in his problems. The too rigid institutional aspect of religion has become actually repulsive to him. It is too tainted, too identified with obsolete, tribal, and cultural forms and semantics. He can do without church; what he seeks is *communio*.

Listening carefully to the respondents from all the countries I visited, it is very noticeable that insights and concepts from non-Judeo-Christian religions and philosophies and from the sciences of man have been absorbed by all and that the respondents' struggle is, to a great extent, the inevitable struggle for the synthesis and integration of these insights.

. . .

"The Wholly Other," says this new intuition, is to be discovered in "the other" and is our very ground. This is not just Tillich's view; it is also Eckhart's and Boehme's, to speak only of the Christians. All the horrified cries of indifferentism, modernism, syncretism, and pantheism cannot nullify this development. They are merely the cries of a discredited Un-Roman Affairs Committee. Within the ancient forms of Catholicism a new view of man, a new "religion" seems to be synthesizing itself which might well have universal, transcultural validity. The Eucharist as I had experienced it in Holland and in the American underground is the celebration of Unity, grandiose in its utter simplicity, in which the individual participants experience their identity and equivalence with one another and thus—taking in the whole community of mankind, the living and the dead—become identified with the central humanity of Jesus and, through it, with the Reality in which all are one. In it the infinite preciousness of the material world—as bread and wine—is celebrated, made convertible into the Stuff of God. The split between Matter and Spirit is healed. In this awareness I could join them as one of their *communio*. If being a Christian means living according to the insight that every human life, my own and all those surrounding me, has at its core Crucifixion—in the pain of loss, frustration, illness, separation, and death—and Resurrection and Transfiguration—in flashes of realization of life's most central reality—if the embodiment of that central reality in its total acceptance of and identity with the inescapable structure of Reality, addressed as Father, is seen in Jesus of Nazareth, then I am a Christian.

But then the knowledge that Mahaprajna—the "great" knowing insight—and Mahakaruna—the "great" compassion—are one and inseparable, makes me also a Buddhist. Whatever the contrasts in philosophical assumptions and superstructures, the basic insights are parallel. It is a Buddhist, not a Christian, who said:

I am going alone all by myself
And whatever I may be, I meet him.
He is no other than myself
Yet now I am not he.
    —DOSAN, 807–869 A.D.

I also cannot help but recognize the Hindu and Chinese intuitions of a continuum between the depths of my human reality and that of the universe. The deepest experience of my humanity in some way is congruent with Reality itself. In other words, the intuition of my relatedness, if not my identity, with all that is in and around me is possible. Contact can be made with What Matters!

Is it not all too facile to label smugly these direct intuitions of Reality, which men of all cultures and all times have perceived, as "syncretism," etc., and then to retire indignantly into one's shell of concepts?

What is certain is that all attempts at reestablishing an orthodoxy, an obscurantism, are doomed as Philistinism. The avant-garde of the "new Church" no longer sees itself as an embattled clan one is born into. This "People of God" is anything but a tribe on the move. It is a community one joins consciously and voluntarily by a resolve renewed each day, a community no longer introverted, bent on self-preservation, but one that becomes recognizable to the extent that it is devoted to and serves human life every day. It is an organism, not an organization. At this point it even is a nonorganization and, as such, invulnerable to massive counter-attack.

Father Schillebeeckx said: "Tradition is made by the community, while the hierarchy creates and defends its self-sacralization." Or, as I often heard it said in Holland: "The function of Rome never was to inspire, but to organize and to tame or to kill inspiration."

When in April 1967, immediately after his proclamation of *Populorum Progressio,* the pope was heard to speak about the theologians to the gathered Italian bishops, "Even among those who know and study the word of God the faith of the Church is violated, the most radical attacks on the holiest truths of our doctrine are applauded," it was as if one heard a voice from the distant past.

It must indeed be unbearably sad for the pope and his entourage, who have given their lives to the institution so wholeheartedly that they have become the institution, to feel, after the loss of secular power, the spiritual power slip from their hands as well, for pluriformity is here in fact and cannot be undone. Although he deplored, in this same speech, that theologians are reaching embarrassing conclusions without even first asking their bishops' permission to reach them, he cannot easily contemplate massive condemnations and excommunications without condemning his church to decimation. The official Church is caught in an apparently insoluble dilemma: the "conservatives" have caused the estrangement of contemporary humanity and are doomed to aggravate it; the "progressives," with their concessions, undermine the institutional intactness irrevocably. A council of the bishops of the Church can still be manipulated to a certain extent, although even here the manipulation can no longer be completely hidden, and what was intended to be kept secret is all the more sensationally reported by the press. Outside the Città del Vaticano, however, direct manipulation is becoming more hazardous all the time, as was recently shown by the resistance to Pope Paul VI's intervention in the debate on Italian divorce legislation—in reality an atavistic attempt to apply the emphatically renounced secular power just once more.

Pope and Magisterium, now, can expect to be really respected as authority only where they prove themselves more humane, more enlightened than all others. That happens to be where they also represent Christ and his spirit. Pope John XXIII has proved and Pope Paul VI is proving this, each in his own way. As a Dutch priest expressed it: "If Pope Paul insists on changing all the time from third gear into reverse, he might well ruin the car!"

Returning to the Dutch scene, we find the fundamental self-interrogation in Catholicism, the often tormented struggle for self-awareness without subterfuge, obviously demonstrated in the answers of this survey. These answers never pretend to completeness; they are but expressions of a refusal to submit to what the person feels as false. Even should there be no adequate verbal answers, there remains the insight in relationship between me and the other, between me and my time that passes. And there is an orientation point in relationship called Jesus of Nazareth.

In this self-examination, a language is being forged that has emancipated itself from conventional Catholic or even Christian usage, and is becoming catholic, that is, universally understandable. This new language makes it possible to speak at the same time perceptively and understandably about the most fundamental values to partners who may be Catholics, Jews, or Protestants, ministers, monks, or laymen, humanists or Marxists. The frontiers have been crossed and communication has been established on the common ground and experience of a shared human destiny and vocation. Contact has been established, in which men experience, perceive, and affirm their faith, whatever others may say, whatever invective others may use.

. . .

The rapidity of the spread of this new mentality, however, may perhaps be less enigmatic than it seems. For this "spontaneous generation" may well be an optical illusion; the seed must have been germinating under the snow during long winters of discontent and of vaguely felt malaise. If one should want to describe it as an epidemic (but then it is an epidemic of self-recognition, of shedding what is existentially meaningless), the incubation period has been prolonged by fear, a fear that has now disappeared. Devil and priest have been recognized as oneself and the boy next door in disguise. The disguises have been dropped, to everyone's relief.

People have not chosen merely between something old-fashioned and something new; they have recognized themselves and arrived at insights that cannot be reversed. All warnings from above are doomed to fail therefore; they sound increasingly pathetic and self-serving, full of ever more indigestible rhetoric.

A new kind of spirituality seems to be associated with these new insights, a spirituality of the here-and-now, which deserves close study, for it implies a *discretio*, a separation of the spirits, which may have social effects of the greatest importance.

. . .

More and more clearly the avant-garde everywhere asks itself soberly and pragmatically: "What meaning has Christianity for us *now?*" In answering this question, it is ready to declare its solidarity with contemporary man-in-the-concrete above its solidarity with the history of the Church. And so, in Holland, after four centuries of estrangement, Catholics have started to communicate with this "modern man," a man who often is neither a Catholic nor even a Christian, who finds the Catholic vocabulary meaningless, a block to communication, something that repels him, that he is allergic to.

Christians are usually quite in the dark as to the meaning the word "Christian"—used with such confidence by the in-group—has for innumerable non-Christians. It is time they knew! What stereotypes does it evoke? I have asked a number of non-churchgoers in America and Europe: "What does the word 'Christian' make you think of?" From the answers I cull these shocking associations: hypocritical; moralistic; witchhunt; narrow; church-mouse; dull; holier-than-thou; unctuous; self-satisfied; conversion-happy; genteel; clannish; Inquisition; superstition; exclusive; square; self-righteous; bourgeois; formalistic; reactionary; backward; intolerant; divided.

This is not a pretty list, but in one's holy indignation one must remember that great numbers of people who cannot detach themselves from these associations and prejudices (so understandable in view of so much that is inhuman and yet has presented itself as "Christian" through the ages and often still presents itself as such) are nevertheless committed to realize the very same Christian value system, even if unconsciously, in themselves and in the world community. They may even assent to the central image of man presented by Jesus of Nazareth, violently allergic as they may have become to his name, tainted by the institutions which have acted so inhumanly in his name.

It appears that the Dutch avant-garde has accommodated itself to these facts of life, that it is consistently asking itself why and where Christianity could have gone so wrong, and that it is seeking fresh means of communication. Hence the ever-returning question: "What is the meaning of Christianity for us *now?*" In this radical reevaluation, much is thrown overboard, much that is dear also to those who cannot carry it along out of concern for what they understand to be the vital, contemporary mission of Christianity. Nothing is important to them but the living implementation of this mission in the new, developing world culture.

More openly than elsewhere for the time being, the Church of Holland is mirroring the mutations of a period of history which is characterized not only by the revolutions, the wars, and the dictatorships that torture us, but also by that inevitable interaction of all cultures of the world which offers a distant hope of a new civilization based, let us hope, on their equivalence in diversity, and in which their cultural, national, and religious differentiations are valued as contributions to a unity in plurality. Unity conceived as imposed uniformity has been the pipe dream of all the conquerors who have perished by the violence they unchained.

Human unity encompassing all differences is not the unity of wish-fulfillment, is not a moral precept, neither an ideal nor an eschatological expectation, but it is the correct diagnosis of our reality *now*. The denial of this reality is the very delusion that causes our unspeakable catastrophes *now*. It is the reality of our unity on this small globe and in the "ground of our being," which at the same time is that bottomless abyss in which we are, in all our individuality and distinctiveness, identical with one another, which must now be acknowledged. Pluralism in and outside of the Church is a cultural fact. One has either to recognize it or to refuse it recognition as if it were Red China. This is likely to make for greater instead of lesser problems.

The Catholic avant-garde is no longer much interested in a fusion of churches or even in salvaging religious systems. What matters is not salvaging a religious form, but the very rehabilitation of a religious attitude toward life itself, so that life on earth may remain possible. It is not coincidental that the youngest people I questioned were the most vocal in their rejection of the claim of the Church to be the "only true Church." They demonstrated this spreading intuition that pretensions of superiority and exclusiveness are delusional and that, where the spirit of truth reigns, there is human unity. "Where truth reigns, charity is law," said Pope John XXIII, a prophet of human solidarity and compassion.

Much that belongs so organically to an old Latin culture and that was assimilated so thoroughly in northern Europe that it seemed indigenous, is suddenly falling away, abandoned and despised. The writer, who in his childhood had been penetrated by this cultural atmosphere, if only by osmosis, who bore it great love and is still attached to it by emotional and aesthetic bonds, can share the pain this causes, the anxiety and the sense of loss. Yet precisely this enabled him to recognize fully the leap into this new phase of awareness, which to those who do not share it is bound to look like mere foolhardiness, arrogance, a rash vandalism based on a lack of historical sense.

The avant-garde, which feels a greater solidarity with the living and suffering men of today than with the historical past, regards its attitude as firmly rooted in the evangelical tradition. Insofar as one can speak of demolition, this might be the demolition of self-emptying, of *kenosis*. These men have relinquished the security of the womb of the Church, the warmth of the clan, the shelter of authority, the familiarity of clusters of words. They have emerged into the fresh air and the shrill light of ordinary, hard, precious life, the life "that is the light of man." All delusions of superiority, all apartheids, are recognized as forms of insanity.

The body of this book is neither more nor less than a snapshot of this new degree of awareness taken in its phase of catharsis, where a man stretches out, speaks out, spits his gall, tactlessly and brutally. He has burst out of the gothic and baroque shells and shouts: "Look brothers, we have joined the human race!"

Holland is living its moment of truth now.

•   •   •

In this time of anxiety, alienation, and possible sudden extinction, many are becoming aware that we can escape at best only temporarily by regression into the womb of the unconscious, by regression into violence, by drugging ourselves with pharmaceutical magic, alcohol, fun, acquisition, or by withdrawing into "old-fashioned religion." We have no alternative, then, but to accept our adulthood in responsibility, awareness, and integration. Our art, our science, and our technology have to be integrated with that which we discern as the meaning of human life or our game is finished. About that meaning, Christianity—or just Christ and the Gospel—has a message, a mission: "What does Christianity mean to us, *now?*"

In the answers, and especially in those to the question dealing with Christ, the core answer of the avant-garde is given.

The only really lethal heresies, truly mortal sins, that remain are the adoration and idolization of a technical and economic and political development which, torn loose from its moorings in the meaning of human life, menaces us with futility and final decline. The other heresy is group paranoia, whether it uses political, religious, or racist pretexts. Both heresies combined may indeed prove fatal to our race in our own generation. That God has been declared dead and atheism is speaking inside and outside the churches, does not point at spiritual decay or decadence. It only means that false images already in decay for centuries have been finally rejected. We are at the point where committed men as aware adults seek to achieve the humanization the Gospel teaches, the human contact, the social justice, in which God may be rediscovered as the Reality in which the material and the spiritual aspects interpenetrate one another, becoming one.

B. F. SKINNER

beyond freedom and dignity _____

In trying to solve today's terrifying problems of war, over-population and pollution, we naturally play from strength, and our strength is science and technology. But while we have made many advances, things grow steadily worse, and it is disheartening to find that technology itself is increasingly at fault. War has acquired a new horror with the invention of nuclear weapons; sanitation and medicine have made the problems of population more acute, and the affluent pursuit of happiness is largely responsible for pollution.

Man must repair the damage or all is lost. And he can do so if he will recognize the nature of the difficulty. The application of the physical and biological sciences alone will not solve our problems because the solutions lie in another field.

From *Beyond Freedom and Dignity,* ch. 1, "A Technology of Behavior," New York, Knopf, 1971, as abridged in *Psychology Today,* August, 1971.

What we need is a technology of behavior. We could solve our problems quickly enough if we could adjust the growth of the world's population as precisely as we adjust the course of a spaceship, or move toward a peaceful world with something like the steady progress with which physics has approached absolute zero (even though both presumably remain out of reach). But we do not have a behavioral technology comparable in power and precision to physical and biological technology, and those who do not find the very possibility ridiculous are more likely to be frightened by it than reassured.

Twenty-five hundred years ago man probably understood himself as well as he understood any other part of his world. Today he is the thing he understands least. Physics and biology have come a long way, but there has been no comparable development of anything like a science of human behavior. Greek physics and biology are now of historical interest only, but the dialogues of Plato are still assigned to students and cited as if they threw light on human behavior.

One can always argue that human behavior is a particularly difficult field. It is, and we are especially likely to think so just because we are so inept in dealing with it.

But modern physics and biology successfully treat subjects that are certainly no simpler than many aspects of human behavior. The difference is that the instruments and methods they use are of commensurate complexity. That equally powerful instruments and methods are not available in the field of human behavior is not an explanation; it is only part of the puzzle.

It is easy to conclude that there must be something about human behavior that makes a scientific analysis, and hence an effective technology, impossible. But we have by no means exhausted the possibilities. In a sense, we have scarcely applied the methods of science to human behavior. We have used the instruments of science: we have counted and measured and compared, but something essential to scientific practice is missing in practically all current discussions of human behavior. It has to do with our treatment of the causes of behavior.

Man's first experience with causes probably came from his own behavior: things moved because he moved them. If other things moved, it was because someone else was moving them; if the mover could not be seen, it was because he was invisible. Gods and demons served in this way as the causes of physical phenomena.

Physics and biology soon abandoned such explanations and turned to more useful kinds of causes, but the step has not been taken decisively in the field of human behavior. Intelligent people no longer believe that men are possessed by demons (although the daimonic has reappeared in the writings of psychotherapists), but they still commonly attribute human behavior to indwelling agents. They say, for example, that a juvenile delinquent suffers from a disturbed personality. There would be no point in saying it if the personality were not somehow distinct from the body that got itself into trouble. The distinction is clear when people say that one body contains several personalities that control it in different ways at different times. Psychoanalysts have identified three of these personalities—the ego, superego and id—and say that interactions among them are responsible for the behavior of the man in whom they dwell. And almost everyone still attributes human behavior to intentions, purposes, aims and goals.

Most persons concerned with human affairs—as political scientist, philosopher, man of letters, economist, psychologist, linguist, sociologist, theologian, anthropologist, educator, or psychotherapist—continue to talk about human behavior in this prescientific way. They tell us that to control the number of people in the world we need to change *attitudes* toward children, overcome *pride* in size of family or in sexual potency, and build some *sense of responsibility* toward offspring. To work for peace we must deal with the *will to power* or the *paranoid delusions* of leaders; we must remember that wars begin in the *minds* of men, that there is something suicidal in man—a *death instinct,* perhaps—that leads to war, and that man is aggressive by *nature.* This is staple fare. Almost no one questions it. Yet there is nothing like it in physics or most of biology, and that fact may well explain why a science and a technology of behavior have been so long delayed.

The important objection to mentalism is that the world of the mind steals the show. Behavior is not recognized as a subject in its own right. Psychotherapists, for example, almost always regard the disturbing things a person does or says as merely symptoms, and compared with the fascinating dramas staged in the depths of the mind, behavior itself seems superficial indeed. Linguists and literary critics almost always treat what a man says as the expression of ideas or feelings. Political scientists, theologians and economists usually regard behavior as the material from which one infers attitudes, intentions, needs and so on. For more than 2,500 years close attention has been paid to mental life, but only recently have we made any effort to study human behavior as something more than a mere by-product.

We also neglect the conditions of which behavior is a function. The mental explanation brings curiosity to an end. We see the effect in casual discourse. If we ask someone, "Why did you go to the theater?" and he says, "Because I felt like going," we are apt to take his reply as a kind of explanation. It would be much more to the point to know what happened when he went to the theater in the past, what he heard or read about the play he went to see, and what other things in his past or present environments might have induced him to go or to do something else.

The professional psychologist often stops at the same point. A long time ago William James corrected a prevailing view of the relation between feelings and action by asserting that we do not run away because we are afraid but are afraid because we run away. In other words, what we feel when we feel afraid is our behavior—the very behavior that in the traditional view expresses the feeling and is explained by it. But how many of those who have considered James's argument have noted that no antecedent event has in fact been pointed out? Neither "because" should be taken seriously. No explanation has been given as to why we run away *and* feel afraid.

Unable to understand how or why the person we see behaves as he does, we attribute his behavior to a person we cannot see, whose behavior we cannot explain either, but about whom we are not inclined to ask questions. We probably adopt this strategy not so much because of any lack of interest or power but because of a long-standing conviction that for much of human behavior there *are* no relevant antecedents. The function of the inner man is to provide an explanation that will not be explained in turn. Explanation stops with him. He is not a mediator between past history and current behavior; he is a *center* from which behavior emanates. He initiates, originates and creates, and in doing so, he remains, as he was for the Greeks, divine. We say that he is autonomous—and so far as a science of behavior is concerned, that means miraculous.

The position is, of course, vulnerable. Autonomous man serves to explain only the things we are not yet able to explain in other ways. Autonomous man's existence depends upon our ignorance and he naturally loses status as we come to know more about behavior.

The task of a scientific analysis is to explain how the behavior of a person as a physical system relates to the conditions under which the human species evolved and the conditions under which the individual lives. Unless there is indeed some capricious or creative intervention, these events must be related, and no intervention is in fact needed. The contingencies of survival responsible for man's genetic endowment would produce tendencies to *act* aggressively, not feelings of aggression. The punishment of sexual behavior changes sexual *behavior,* and any feelings that may arise are at best by-products. Our age is not suffering from anxiety but from the accidents, crimes, wars and other dangerous and painful things to which people are so often exposed. The fact that young people drop out of school, refuse to get jobs and associate only with others of their own age is not due to feelings of alienation but to defective social environments in homes, schools, factories and elsewhere.

We can follow the path taken by physics and biology by turning directly to the relation between behavior and the environment and neglecting states of mind. We do not need to try to discover what personalities, states of mind, feelings, traits of character, plans, purposes, intentions or other perquisites of autonomous man really are in order to get on with a scientific analysis of behavior.

There are reasons why it has taken us so long to reach this point. The outer man whose behavior is to be explained could be very much like the inner man whose behavior is said to explain it. We have created the inner man in the image of the outer.

A more important reason is that we seem at times to observe the inner man directly. Indeed, we do feel things inside our own skin, but we do not feel the things we have invented to explain behavior. We feel certain states of our bodies associated with behavior, particularly with strong behavior, but as Freud pointed out, we behave in the same way when we do not feel them; they are by-products and not to be mistaken for causes.

A yet more important reason why we have been so slow in discarding mentalistic explanations: it has been hard to find alternatives. Presumably we must look for them in the external environment, but the role of the environment is by no means clear. The history of the theory of evolution illustrates the problem. Before the nineteenth century, people thought of the environment as simply a passive setting in which many different kinds of organisms were born, reproduced themselves and died. No one saw that the environment was responsible for the fact that there *were* many different kinds (and that fact, significantly enough, was attributed to a creative mind). The trouble was that the environment acts in an inconspicuous way: it does not push or pull, it *selects*. For thousands of years in the history of human thought the process of natural selection went unseen in spite of its extraordinary importance. When it was eventually discovered, it became, of course, the key to evolutionary theory.

The effect of the environment on behavior remained obscure for an even longer time. We can see what organisms do to the world around them, as they take from it what they need and ward off its dangers, but it is much harder to see what the world does to *them*.

The triggering action of the environment came to be called a "stimulus"—the Latin for goad—and the effect on an organism a "response," and together they were said to compose a "reflex." Reflexes were first demonstrated in small decapitated animals, and it is significant that people challenged the principle throughout the nineteenth century because it seemed to deny the existence of an autonomous agent to which they had attributed the movement of a decapitated body.

When Ivan Pavlov showed how to build up new reflexes through conditioning, he created a full-fledged stimulus-response psychology that regarded all behavior as reaction to stimuli. The stimulus-response model was never very convincing, however, and it did not solve the basic problem because something like an inner man had to be invented to convert a stimulus into a response.

It is now clear that we must take into account what the environment does to an organism not only before but *after* it responds. Behavior is shaped and maintained by its *consequences*. Once we recognize this fact we can formulate the interaction between organism and environment in a much more comprehensive way.

There are two important results. One concerns the basic analysis. We can study behavior that operates upon the environment to produce consequences ("operant behavior") by arranging environments in which specific consequences are contingent upon behavior. The contingencies have become steadily more complex, and one by one they are taking over the explanatory functions previously assigned to personalities, states of mind, feelings, traits of character, purposes and intentions.

The second result is practical: we can manipulate the environment. Though man's genetic endowment can be changed only very slowly, changes in the environment of the individual have quick and dramatic effects. A technology of operant behavior is already well advanced and it may prove to be commensurate with our problems. However, that possibility raises another problem that we must solve if we are to take advantage of our gains.

We have dispossessed autonomous man, but he has not departed gracefully. He is conducting a sort of rear-guard action in which, unfortunately, he can marshal formidable support. He is still an important figure in political science, law, religion, economics, anthropology, sociology, psychotherapy, philosophy, ethics, history, education, child care, linguistics, architecture, city planning and family life. These fields have their specialists, every specialist has a theory, and almost every theory accepts the autonomy of the individual unquestioningly. Data obtained through casual observation or from studies of the structure of behavior do not seriously threaten the inner man, and many of these fields deal only with groups of people, where statistical or actuarial data impose few restraints upon the individual. The result is a tremendous weight of traditional "knowledge" that a scientific analysis must correct or displace.

Two features of autonomous man—his freedom and dignity—are particularly troublesome. In the traditional view, a person is free. He is autonomous in the sense that his behavior is uncaused. We therefore can hold him responsible for what he does and justly punish him if he offends. We must reexamine that view, together with its associated practices, when a scientific analysis reveals unsuspected controlling relations between behavior and the environment.

Of course, people can tolerate a certain amount of external control. Theologians have accepted the idea that man must be predestined to do what an omniscient God knows he will do, and the Greek dramatist took inexorable fate as his favorite theme. Folk wisdom and the insights of essayists like Michel de Montaigne and Francis Bacon imply some kind of predictability in human conduct, and the statistical and actuarial evidences of the social sciences point in the same direction.

Autonomous man survives in the face of all this because he is the happy exception. Theologians have reconciled predestination with free will, and the Greek audience, moved by the portrayal of an inescapable destiny, walked out of the theater free men. Very little behavioral science raises "the specter of predictable man." On the contrary, many anthropologists, sociologists and psychologists have used their expert knowledge to prove that man is free, purposeful and responsible. Freud was a determinist—on faith, if not on the evidence—but many Freudians have no hesitation in assuring their patients that they are free to choose among different courses of action and are in the long run the architects of their own destinies.

This escape route slowly closes as we discover new evidences of the predictability of human behavior. Personal exemption from a complete determinism is revoked as a scientific analysis progresses, particularly in accounting for the behavior of the individual.

By questioning the control exercised by autonomous man and demonstrating the control exercised by the environment, a science of behavior also seems to question dignity or worth. A person is responsible for his behavior, not only in the sense that he may be justly blamed or punished when he behaves badly, but also in the sense that he is to be given credit and admired for his achievements. A scientific analysis shifts the credit as well as the blame to the environment, and traditional practices can then no longer be justified. These are sweeping changes and persons committed to traditional theories and practices naturally resist them.

There is a third source of trouble. As the emphasis shifts to the environment, the individual seems to face a new kind of danger. Who is to construct the controlling environment, and to what end? Autonomous man presumably controls himself in accordance with a built-in set of values; he works for what he finds good. But what will the putative controller find good and will it be good for those he controls? Answers to questions of this sort are said, of course, to call for value judgment.

Freedom, dignity and value are major issues and unfortunately become more crucial as the power of a technology of behavior becomes more nearly commensurate with the problems we must solve. The very change that has brought some hope of a solution is responsible for a growing opposition to the kind of solution proposed. This conflict is itself a problem in human behavior and we may approach it as such. A science of behavior is by no means as far advanced as physics or biology, but it has an advantage in that it may throw some light on its own difficulties. Science *is* human behavior, and so is the opposition to science. What has happened in man's struggle for freedom and dignity, and what problems arise when scientific knowledge begins to be relevant in that struggle? Answers to these questions may help to clear the way for the technology we so badly need.

FREDERICK S. PERLS

gestalt therapy verbatim _____

I want to talk about the present development of humanistic psychology. It took us a long time to debunk the whole Freudian crap, and now we are entering a new and more dangerous phase. We are entering the phase of the turner-onners: turn on to instant cure, instant joy, instant sensory-awareness. We are entering the phase of the quacks and the con-men, who think if you get some breakthrough, you are cured—disregarding any growth requirements, disregarding any of the real potential, the inborn genius in all of you. If this is becoming a faddism, it is as dangerous to psychology as the year-decade-century-long lying on the couch. At least the damage we suffered under psychoanalysis does little to the patient except for making him deader and deader. This is not as obnoxious as this quick-quick-quick thing. The psychoanalysts at least bring good will with them. I must say I am *very* concerned with what's going on right now.

One of the objections I have against anyone calling himself a Gestalt Thera-

---

From *Gestalt Therapy Verbatim,* ed. John O. Stevens, Moab, Utah, Real People Press, 1969.

pist is that he uses technique. A technique is a gimmick. A gimmick should be used only in the extreme case. We've got enough people running around collecting gimmicks, more gimmicks, and abusing them. These techniques, these tools, are quite useful in some seminar on sensory awareness or joy, just to give you some idea that you are still alive, that the myth that the American is a corpse is not true, that he *can* be alive. But the sad fact is that this jazzing-up more often becomes a dangerous substitute activity, another phony therapy that *prevents* growth.

Now the problem is not so much with the turner-onners but with the whole American culture. We have made a 180-degree turn from puritanism and moralism to hedonism. Suddenly everything has to be fun, pleasure, and any sincere involvement, any really *being here,* is discouraged.

A thousand plastic flowers
Don't make a desert bloom
A thousand empty faces
Don't fill an empty room

In Gestalt Therapy, we are working for something else. We are here to promote the growth process and develop the human potential. We do not talk of instant joy, instant sensory awareness, instant cure. The growth process is a process that takes time. We can't just snap our fingers and say, "Come on, let's be gay! Let's do this!" You can turn on if you want to with LSD, and jazz it up, but that has nothing to do with the sincere work of that approach to psychiatry which I call Gestalt Therapy. In therapy, we have not only to get through the role-playing. We also have to fill in the holes in the personality to make the person whole and complete again. And again, as before, this can't be done by the turner-onners. In Gestalt Therapy we have a better way, but it is no magic shortcut. You don't have to be on a couch or in a Zendo for twenty or thirty years, but you have to invest yourself, and it takes time to grow.

The conditioners also start out with a false assumption. Their basic premise that behavior is "law" is a lot of crap. That is: we learn to breathe, to eat, we learn to walk. "Life is nothing but whatever conditions into which it has been born." *If,* in the behaviorist reorganization of our behavior, we get a modification towards better self-support, and throw away all the artificial social roles we have learned, then I am on the side of the behaviorists. The stopping block seems to be anxiety. Always anxiety. Of course you are anxious if you have to learn a new way of behavior, and the psychiatrists usually are afraid of anxiety. They don't know what anxiety *is.* Anxiety is the excitement, the *élan vital* which we carry with us, and which becomes stagnated if we are unsure about the role we have to play. If we don't know if we will get applause or tomatoes, we hesitate, so the heart begins to race and all the excitement can't flow into activity, and we have stage fright. So the formula of anxiety is very simple: anxiety is the gap between the *now* and the *then.* If you are in the now, you can't be anxious, because the excitement flows immediately into ongoing spontaneous activity. If you are in the now, you are creative, you are inventive. If you have your senses ready, if you have your eyes and ears open, like every small child, you find a solution.

A release to spontaneity, to the support of our total personality—yes, yes, yes. The pseudo-spontaneity of the turner-onners as they become hedonistic—just, let's do something, let's take LSD, let's have instant joy, instant sensory-awareness—No. So between the Scylla of conditioning, and the Charybdis of turning on, there is something—a person that is real, a person who takes a stand.

As you know, there is a rebellion on in the United States. We discover that producing things, and living for things, and the exchange of things, is not the ultimate meaning of life. We discover that the meaning of life is that it is to be lived, and it is not to be traded and conceptualized and squeezed into a pattern of systems. We realize that manipulation and control are not the ultimate joy of life.

But we must also realize that so far we only have a rebellion. We don't have a revolution yet. There is still much of substance missing. There is a race on between fascism and humanism. At this moment it seems to me that the race is about lost to the fascists. And the wild, hedonistic, unrealistic, jazz-it-up, turner-onners have nothing to do with humanism. It is protest, it's a rebelliousness, which is fine as such, but it's not an end. I've got plenty of contact with the youngsters of our generation who are in despair. They see all the militarism and the atomic bomb in the background. They want to get something out of life. They want to become real and exist. If there is any chance of interrupting the rise and fall of the United States, it's up to our youth and it's up to you in supporting this youth. To be able to do this, there is only one way through: to become real, to learn to take a stand, to develop one's center, to understand the basis of existentialism: a rose is a rose is a rose. I am what I am, and at this moment I cannot possibly be different from what I am.

I give you the Gestalt prayer, maybe as a direction. The prayer in Gestalt Therapy is:

I do my thing, and you do your thing.
I am not in this world to live up to your expectations
And you are not in this world to live up to mine.
You are you and I am I,
And if by *chance* we find each other, it's beautiful.
If not, it can't be helped.

• • •

I would like to start out with very simple ideas which, as always, are difficult to grasp because they are so simple. I would like to start out with the question of control. There are two kinds of control: One is the control that comes from outside—I am being controlled by others, by orders, by the environment, and so on—and the other is the control that is built in, in every organism—my own nature.

What is an organism? We call an organism any living being, any living being that has organs, has an organization, that is self-regulating within itself. An organism is not independent from its environment. Every organism needs an environment to exchange essential substances, and so on. We need the physical environment to exchange air, food, etc.; we need the social environment to exchange friendship, love, anger. But within the organism there is a system of unbelievable subtlety—every cell of the millions of cells which we *are,* has built-in messages that it sends to the total organism, and the total organism then takes care of the needs of the cells and whatever must be done for different parts of the organism.

Now what is first to be considered is that the organism always works as a whole. We *have* not a liver or a heart. We *are* liver and heart and brain and so on, and even this is wrong. We are not a summation of parts, but a *coordination*—a very subtle coordination of all these different bits that go into the making of the organism. The old philosophy always thought that the world consisted of the sum of particles. You know yourself it's not true. We consist originally out of one cell. This cell differentiates into several cells, and they differentiate into other organs that have special functions which are diversified and yet needed for each other.

So, we come to the definition of health. Health is an appropriate balance of the coordination of all of what we *are.* You notice that I emphasized a few times the word *are,* because the very moment we say we *have* an organism or we *have* the body, we introduce a split—as if there's an *I* that is in possession of the body or the organism. We *are* a body, we *are* somebody—"I *am* somebody," "I *am* nobody." So it's the question of being rather than *having.* This is why we call our approach the existential approach: We exist *as* an organism—as an organism like a clam, like an animal, and so on, and we relate to the external world just like any other organism of nature. Kurt Goldstein first introduced the concept of the *organism as a whole,* and broke with the tradition in medicine that we *have* a liver, that we have a this/that, that all these organs can be studied separately. He got pretty close to the actuality, but the actuality is what is called the ecological aspect. You cannot even separate the organism and the environment. A plant taken out of its environment can't survive, and neither can a human being if you take him out of his environment, deprive him of oxygen and food, and so on. So we have to consider always the segment of the world in which we live as part of ourselves. Wherever we go, we take a kind of world with us.

Now if this is so, then we begin slowly to understand that people and organisms *can* communicate with each other, and we call it the *Mitwelt*—the common world which you have and the other person has. You speak a certain language, you have certain attitudes, certain behavior, and the two worlds somewhere overlap. And in this overlapping area, communication is possible. You notice if people meet, they begin the gambit of meeting—one says, "How are you?" "It's nice weather," and the other answers something else. So they go into the search for the common interest, or the common world, where they have a possible interest, communication, and togetherness, where we get suddenly from the *I* and *You* to the *We.* So there is a new phenomenon coming, the *We* which is different from the I *and* You, is an everchanging boundary where two people meet. And when we meet there, then I change and you change, through the process of encountering each other, except—and we have to talk a lot about this—except if the two people have character. Once you have a character, you have developed a rigid system. Your behavior becomes petrified, predictable, and you lose your ability to cope freely with the world with all your resources. You are predetermined just to cope with events in one way, namely, as your character prescribes it to be. So it seems a paradox when I say that the richest person, the most productive, creative person, is a person who has no character. In our society, we *demand* a person to have a character, and especially a *good* character, because then you are predictable, and you can be pigeonholed, and so on.

Now, let's talk a bit more about the relationship of the organism to its environment, and here we introduce the notion of the *ego boundary*. A boundary defines a thing. Now a thing has its boundaries, is defined by its boundaries in relation to the environment. In itself a thing occupies a certain amount of space. Maybe not much. Maybe it wants to be bigger, or wants to be smaller—maybe it's not satisfied with its size. We introduce now a new concept again, the wish to change based upon the phenomenon of dissatisfaction. Every time you want to change yourself, or you want to change the environment, the basis always is *dis*-satisfaction.

· · ·

Basically, we call the ego boundary the differentiation between the self and the otherness, and in Gestalt Therapy we write the self with a lower case s. I know that many psychologists like to write the self with a capital S, as if the self would be something precious, something extraordinarily valuable. They go at the discovery of the self like a treasure-digging. The self means nothing but this thing as it is defined by *otherness*. "I do it myself" means that nobody else is doing it, it is this organism that does it.

Now the two phenomena of the ego boundary are *identification* and *alienation*. I identify with my movement: I say that *I* move my arm. When I see *you* sit there in a certain posture, I don't say, "*I* sit there," I say, "*You* sit there." I differentiate between the experience here and the experience there, and this identification experience has several aspects. The *I* seems to be more precious than the otherness. If I identify with, let's say, my profession, then this identification may become so strong that if my profession is then taken away, I feel I don't exist any more, so I might just as well commit suicide.

· · ·

There is always a polarity going on, and inside the boundary we have the feeling of familiarity, of right; outside is strangeness, and wrong. Inside is good, outside is bad. The own God is the right God. The other God is the strange God. My political conviction is sacred, is mine; the other political conviction is bad. If a state is at war, its own soldiers are angels, and the enemy are all devils. Our own soldiers take care of the poor families; the enemy rapes them. So the whole idea of good and bad, right and wrong, is always a matter of boundary, of which side of the fence I am on.

. . .

A living organism is an organism which consists of thousands and thousands of processes that require interchange with other media outside the boundary of the organism. There are processes here in the ashtray, too. There are electronic processes, atomic processes, but for our purpose, these processes are not visible, not relevant to its existence for us here. But in a living organism, the ego boundary has to be negotiated by us because there is something outside that is needed. There is food outside: I want this food; I want to make it mine, *like me*. So, I have to like this food. If I don't like it, if it is un-like me, I wouldn't touch it, I leave it outside the boundary. So something has to happen to get through the boundary and this is what we call *contact*. We touch, we get in contact, we stretch our boundary out to the thing in question. If we are rigid and can't move, then it remains there. When we live, we spend energies, we need energies to maintain this machine. This process of exchange is called the metabolism. Both the metabolism of the exchange of our organism with the environment, and the metabolism within our organism, is going on continually, day and night.

Now what are the laws of this metabolism? They are very strict laws. Let's assume that I walk through the desert, and it's very hot. I lose, let's say, eight ounces of fluid. Now how do I know that I lost this? First, through self-awareness of the phenomenon, in this case called "thirst." Second, suddenly in this undifferentiated general world something emerges as a gestalt, as a foreground, namely, let's say, a well with water, or a pump—or anything that would have plus eight ounces. This minus eight ounces of our organism and the plus eight ounces in the world can balance each other. The very moment this eight ounces goes into the system, we get a plus/minus water which brings balance. We come to rest as the situation is finished, the gestalt is closed. The urge that drives us to do something to walk so and so many miles to get to that place, has fulfilled its purpose.

. . .

The third philosophy I call existentialism. Existentialism wants to do away with concepts, and to work on the awareness principle, on phenomenology. The setback with the present existentialist philosophies is that they need their support from somewhere else. If you look at the existentialists, they say that they are nonconceptual, but if you look at the people, they all borrow concepts from other sources. Buber from Judaism, Tillich from Protestantism, Sartre from Socialism, Heidegger from language, Binswanger from psychoanalysis, and so on. Gestalt Therapy is a philosophy that tries to be in harmony, in alignment with everything else, with medicine, with science, with the universe, with what *is*. Gestalt Therapy has its support in its own formation because the gestalt formation, the emergence of the needs, is a primary biological phenomenon.

So we are doing away with the whole instinct theory and simply consider the organism as a system that is in balance and that has to function properly. Any imbalance is experienced as a need to correct this imbalance. Now, practically, we have hundreds of unfinished situations in us. How come that we are not completely confused and want to go out in all directions? And that's another law which I have discovered, that from the survival point of view, the most urgent situation becomes the controller, the director, and takes over. The most urgent situation emerges, and in any case of emergency, you realize that this has to take precedent over any other activity. If there would be suddenly a fire here, the fire would be more important than our talks. If you rush and rush, and run from the fire, suddenly you will be out of breath, your oxygen supply is more important than the fire. You stop and take a breath because this is now the most important thing.

So, we come now to the most important, interesting phenomenon in all pathology: self-regulation versus external regulation. The anarchy which is usually feared by the controllers is not an anarchy which is without meaning. On the contrary, it means the organism is left alone to take care of itself, without being meddled with from outside. And I believe that this is the great thing to understand: *that awareness per se—by and of itself—can be curative.* Because with full awareness you become aware of this organismic self-regulation, you can let the organism take over without interfering, without interrupting; we can rely on the wisdom of the organism. And the contrast to this is the whole pathology of self-manipulation, environmental control, and so on, that interferes with this subtle organismic self-control.

. . .

Every external control, even *internalized* external control—"you should"—interferes with the healthy working of the organism. There is only one thing that should control: the *situation.* If you understand the situation which you are in, and let the situation which you are in control your actions, then you learn how to cope with life.

. . .

So let's look upon maturing once more. My formulation is that *maturing is the transcendence from environmental support to self-support.* Look upon the unborn baby. It gets all its support from the mother—oxygen, food, warmth, everything. As soon as the baby is born, it has already to do its own breathing. And then we find often the first symptom of what plays a very decisive part in Gestalt Therapy. We find the *impasse.* Please note the word. The *impasse* is the crucial point in therapy, the crucial point in growth. The impasse is called by the Russians "the sick point," a point which the Russians never managed to lick and which other types of psychotherapy so far have not succeeded in licking. The impasse is the position where environmental support or obsolete inner support is not forthcoming any more, and authentic self-support has not yet been achieved. The baby cannot breathe by itself. It doesn't get the oxygen supply through the placenta any more. We can't say that the baby has a choice, because there is no deliberate attempt of thinking out what to do, but the baby either has to die or to learn to breathe. There might be some environmental support forthcoming—

being slapped, or oxygen might be supplied. The "blue baby" is the prototype of the impasse which we find in every neurosis.

Now, the baby begins to grow up. It still has to be carried. After awhile it learns to give some kind of communication—first crying, then it learns to speak, learns to crawl, to walk, and so, step by step, it mobilizes more and more of its potential, its inner resources. He discovers—or learns—more and more to make use of his muscles, his senses, his wits, and so on. So, from this I make the definition that the process of maturation is the transformation from environmental support to self-support, and the aim of therapy is to make the patient *not* depend upon others, but to make the patient discover from the very first moment that he can do many things, *much* more than he thinks he can do.

The average person of our time, believe it or not, lives only 5 percent to 15 percent of his potential at the highest. A person who has even 25 percent of his potential available is already considered to be a genius. So 85 percent to 95 percent of our potential is lost, is unused, is not at our disposal. Sounds tragic, doesn't it? And the reason for this is very simple: we live in clichés. We live in patterned behavior. We are playing the same roles over and over again. So if you find out how you prevent yourself from growing, from using your potential, you have a way of increasing this, making life richer, making you more and more capable of mobilizing yourself. And our potential is based upon a very peculiar attitude: to live and review every second afresh.

The "trouble" with people who are capable of reviewing every second what the situation is like, is that we are not predictable. The role of the good citizen requires that he be predictable, because our hankering for security, for not taking risks, our fear to be authentic, our fear to stand on our own feet, especially on our own intelligence—this fear is just horrifying. So what do we do? We *adjust,* and in most kinds of therapy you find that adjustment to society is the high goal. If you don't adjust, you are either a criminal, or psychopath, or loony, or beatnik or something like that. Anyhow, you are undesirable and have to be thrown out of the boundary of that society.

Most other therapies try to adjust the person to society. This was maybe not too bad in previous years, when society was relatively stable, but now with the rapid changes going on, it is getting more and more difficult to adjust to society. Also, more and more people are not willing to adjust to society—they think that this society stinks, or have other objections. I consider that the basic personality in our time is a neurotic personality. This is a preconceived idea of mine, because I believe we are living in an insane society and that you only have the choice either to participate in this collective psychosis or to take risks and become healthy and perhaps also crucified.

If you are centered in yourself, then you don't adjust any more—then, whatever happens becomes a passing parade and you assimilate, you understand, you are related to whatever happens. In this happening, the symptom of anxiety is very very important, because the more the society changes, the more it produces anxiety. Now the psychiatrist is very afraid of anxiety. I am not. My definition of anxiety is the gap between the now and the later. Whenever you leave the sure basis of the now and become preoccupied with the future, you experience anxiety. And if the future represents a performance, then this anxiety is nothing but stage fright. You are full of catastrophic expectations of the bad things that will happen, or anastrophic expectations about the wonderful things that will happen. And we fill this gap between the now and the later—with insurance policies, planning, fixed jobs, and so on. In other words, we are not willing to see the fertile void, the possibility of the future—we have no future if we fill this void, we only have sameness.

But how can you have sameness in this rapid-changing world? So of course anybody who wants to hold onto the status quo will get more and more panicky and afraid. Usually, the anxiety is not so deeply existential. It is just concerned with the role we want to play, it's just stage fright. "Will my role come off?" "Will I be called a good boy?" "Will I get my approval?" "Will I get applause, or will I get rotten eggs?" So that's not an existential choice, just a choice of inconvenience. But to *realize* that it's just an inconvenience, that it's not a catastrophe, but just an unpleasantness, is part of coming into your own, part of waking up.

So we come to our basic conflict and the basic conflict is this: Every individual, every plant, every animal has only one inborn goal—to actualize itself as it is. A rose is a rose is a rose. A rose is not intent to actualize itself as a kangaroo. An elephant is not intent to actualize itself as a bird. In nature—except for the human being—constitution, and healthiness, potential, growth, is all one unified *something*.

• • •

So where do we find ourselves? We find ourselves on the one hand as individuals who want to actualize themselves; we find ourselves also embedded in a society, in our case the progressive American society, and this society might make demands different from the individual demands. So there is the basic clash. Now this individual society is represented in our development by our parents, nurses, teachers, and so forth. Rather than to facilitate the development of authentic growth, they often intrude into the natural development.

They work with two tools to falsify our existence. One tool is the stick, which then is encountered again in therapy as the *catastrophic expectation*. The catastrophic expectation sounds like this: "If I take the risk, I will not be loved any more. I will be lonely. I'll die." That's the stick. And then there is the hypnosis. Right now, I am hypnotizing you. I am hypnotizing you into believing what I say. I don't give you the chance to digest, to assimilate, to taste what I say. You hear from my voice that I try to cast a spell on you, to slip my "wisdom" into your guts until you either assimilate it or puke, or feed it into your computer and say: "That's an interesting concept." Normally, as you know if you are students, you are only allowed to puke on the examination paper. You swallow all the information and you puke it up and you are free again and you have got a degree. Sometimes, though, I must say, in the process you might have learned something, either discovered something of value, or some experience about your teachers, or about your friends, but the basic dead information is not easy to assimilate.

Now let's go back to the maturation process. In the process of growing up, there are two choices. The child either grows up and learns to overcome frustration, or it is spoiled. It might be spoiled by the parents answering all the questions, rightly or wrongly. It might be spoiled so that as soon as it wants something, it gets it—because the child "should have everything because papa never had it," or because the parents don't know how to frustrate children—don't know how to use frustration. You will probably be amazed that I am using the word frustration so positively. Without frustration there is no need, no reason to mobilize your resources, to discover that you might be able to do something on your own, and in order not to be frustrated, which is a pretty painful experience, the child learns to manipulate the environment.

Now, any time the child, in his development, is prevented from growth by the adult world, any time the child is being spoiled by not being given enough frustration, the child is stuck. So instead of using his potential to grow, he now uses his potential to control the adults, to control the world. Instead of mobilizing his own resources, he creates dependencies. He invests his energy in manipulating the environment for support. He controls the adults by starting to manipulate them, by discerning their weak spots. As the child begins to develop the means of manipulation, he acquires what is called character. The more character a person has, the less potential he has. That sounds paradoxical, but a character is a person that is predictable, that has only a number of fixed responses, or as T. S. Eliot said in *The Cocktail Party,* "You are nothing but a set of obsolete responses."

THOMAS W. OGELTREE

openings
for marxist-christian dialogue _____

That Christian theologians and Marxist philosophers should have anything to do with each other is unthinkable for countless numbers of people, both Communists and Christians. For many Christians, especially in America, communism means quite simply: Stalinist tyranny, totalitarianism, the cynical disregard for human dignity and for basic human values, an international conspiracy to subvert or destroy liberal democratic institutions, a fanatical commitment to gain dominion over the whole world either by deceit or by force. In short, communism is viewed as one of the principal threats to the well-being of men. By the same token, Christianity for many Communists means: the Inquisition, witch hunts, the suppression of free scientific inquiry, the cynical use of religious beliefs and practices both to justify the existence of oppressive social systems and to lull the oppressed into an acceptance of that oppression. In short, Christianity is identified as one of the principal barriers to human progress.

As long as Christians and Communists perceive each other in terms of these stereotypes—and both portraits have a real basis in fact—it is scarcely tolerable even to consider coexistence, let alone genuine dialogue. Dialogue requires an openness to the other, a readiness to learn from the other, to be changed by the other. It stems from a desire on the part of the dialogue partners to grow through mutual interaction, to develop a deeper self-understanding in community with each other. Movements which see each other as unmitigated evils cannot in good faith entertain the prospect of dialogue. They must oppose each other to the bitter end. Yet significant new opportunities are opening up at the present time for a joint exploration of the basic convictions and vital concerns of both Christianity and Marxism, a fact that reflects not a surrender of integrity, but a willingness on the part of some Marxist philosophers and Christian theologians to look behind the sinister mask of the other to the creative sources of value and commitment.

It is scarcely necessary to note that a positive and constructive encounter between Christianity and Marxism is not new. From the beginning Karl Marx and Friedrich Engels drew much of the inspiration for the humanitarian thrust of their work from Christianity. Engels seems to have maintained his fascination with Christianity throughout his life, for he continued to study and analyze theological writings, particularly those dealing with primitive Christianity, long after the basic elements in an essentially negative assessment of religion were well established.

. . .

By the same token, Christians have been repeatedly drawn to the writings of Marx, Engels, Lenin, and other Marxist thinkers, because their own commitments sensitized them to the social problems these men were seeking to understand and overcome. Actually, the Christian interest in various forms of socialism antedates Marx. Quite apart from experiments in communal living by religious orders, there have been Christians since the beginnings of the industrial revolution who have seen in socialism the only practical solution to the human misery precipitated by a new social order.

. . .

In spite of these precedents, we have just passed through a period in which little or no fruitful interaction between Marxists and Christians was possible. That new openings for the Marxist-Christian encounter are developing at the present time is largely a consequence of changing conditions both within communism and within the church. Sidney Lens points to some of the changes taking place within the communist world which have created a situation for dialogue. Chairman Khrushchev's speech denouncing Stalinist excesses at the Twentieth Congress of the Communist Party can appropriately serve as a symbolic event to represent these changes. The essential point is that the present situation both within the socialist block of nations and within the various national Communist Parties allows for the possibility that Marxist thought can be liberated from the shackles of dogmatism and restored to a significant critical function. A critical form of Marxist thought can interact constructively with alternative perspectives on man in a common quest for creative ways to deal with new developments in human society. In this setting a number of distinguished Marxist philosophers, most notably Roger Garaudy, Ernst Bloch, and Milan Machovec, have opened up fresh lines of inquiry that constitute invitations to Christian theologians to engage in dialogue.

If we seek to identify major happenings within the church that manifest a new openness to dialogue, we can point most appropriately to the proceedings of the Second Vatican Council and to the Geneva Conference on Church and Society sponsored by the World Council of Churches (Summer, 1966). The former embodied a drive within Roman Catholicism to bring the Church up to date, primarily by calling it to grapple in a fresh way with the problems and concerns of the contemporary world. The latter represented a growing conviction within Protestantism that the meaning of Christian existence must be expressed in relation to the technical and social revolutions of our times. This common orientation to the contemporary world is the most promising feature of the current stage of the ecumenical movement, for in centering attention on the Christian promise to the worldly concerns of men, it renders obsolete many of the issues which have previously divided Christians. At the same time, the renewed determination to address the modern world in its concreteness can only have a hollow sound if it does not include genuine openness to contemporary forms of the Marxist challenge. . . .

Serious dialogue between Marxists and Christians is presently concentrated in a number of European centers and in certain countries of Latin America. The European discussion is the more theoretical, involving a critical exploration of basic philosophical and theological questions. . . .

However, pressing practical issues are much closer to the surface in Latin America. Many Christians in Latin America see no meaningful hope of progress for their countries apart from violent revolution. This conviction thrusts them into interaction with Marxists and Communists as they seek to clarify their own role and the role of the church in the historical struggles of men.

The impact of the dialogue is just beginning to be felt in the United States. Here it is providing a stimulus for a fresh analysis and assessment of Marxist writings in light of the situation that currently prevails both within our society and within the life of the world at large. It gains its urgency from the necessity of understanding and responding creatively to the emergent black revolution in America's cities, and from the importance of examining critically the present stance of the United States in world affairs, politically, economically, and militarily. It can nourish the quest for a life style that faithfully expresses the Christian promise to the world in the context of the upheavals and uncertainties of our age.

•   •   •

marxist openings to christianity

The understanding of Christianity that became characteristic of the mature thought of both Marx and Engels took its starting point in the work of Ludwig Feuerbach. For Feuerbach, Christianity is an expression of man's alienation from himself, the objectification of the human essence in a supernatural realm. Man takes those qualities of human nature which he regards as intrinsically good and projects them outward in such a way that they are taken to be the qualities of a Divine Subject who exists independently of man.

•   •   •

Marx endorsed Feuerbach's contention that man makes religion, including God and the entire realm of the supernatural. He also appropriated and developed Feuerbach's analysis of the alienation involved in religious projection. However, he did not seek to replace theistic religion with a religion of humanity. In his judgment, religion is inescapably a form of "mystification." It obscures man's perception of the realities of his situation and hinders his effective action in the world to bring about humanizing social change. Consequently, man's liberation from religious alienation finally depends upon his liberation from religion as such. More important, Marx sharply criticized Feuerbach for ending up with a highly abstract notion of humanity, one that interpreted the being of man in isolation from the concrete social and historical conditions which shape his life. Such an interpretation is itself a form of self-alienation. In contrast, Marx emphasized the fact that man is a producer, a maker, and an agent of historical change. To gain an adequate understanding of man, including his religious life, it is necessary to attend to the factors that determine the concrete conditions under which man acts, that set the possibilities and limits for such action.

By emphasizing the concrete conditions that shape man's being, Marx, more than Feuerbach, was able to account for the emergence of religion in human experience. Religion, he noted, expresses both a real distress and a protest against that distress. It represents man's attempt to cope with the forces of nature and history that threaten to overwhelm him. As such, the questions and concerns it embodies are in no sense illusory. The difficulty is that the religious man creates a fantasy world for interpreting and dealing with the actualities of the real world. In this connection Marx speaks of religion as an "inverted world-consciousness." It compensates in an illusory way for the suffering and anguish of life in this world. As a result, genuine understanding, the kind that can lead to real solutions to real human problems, is hindered or even rendered impossible.

Engels picked up Marx's contention that religion stems from genuine human distress. He sought to show that vital religious movements are fundamentally the struggles of oppressed and exploited peoples to realize a new life. In spite of their religious forms, they mask a tangible, earthly interest. He once suggested that the closest thing in the modern world to primitive Christianity is the working-class movement. He spelled out some of the similarities: (1) Christianity was a movement of oppressed peoples, a "slave religion"; (2) it preached salvation from bondage and misery; (3) though it believed itself to be engaged in a bitter struggle with the most powerful forces in the world, it was confident of total victory; and (4) though its adherents were persecuted and baited as enemies not only of the state but of the whole human race, it continued to forge ahead. Unfortunately, however, its revolutionary import was dissipated by the fact that it located man's hope of salvation not in a historic and this-worldly future, but in a heavenly world to come. In this respect it differed sharply from the emerging class consciousness of the modern worker.

•   •   •

While religion has on occasion been associated with genuine revolutionary movements, Marx and Engels still considered it to be primarily a barrier to human progress. On the one hand, it causes the downtrodden to acquiesce in the face of oppression and exploitation, to seek the fulfillment of life not in a real struggle for historical change, but in an illusory world created by the religious imagination. "Religion is the opium of the people." Engels noted how frequently the European bourgeoisie, following the uprisings of 1848, insisted that "religion must be kept alive for the masses." Experience had taught them that religion has a strong stabilizing influence on workers and peasants. The British industrialists went so far as to cover the expenses for a Moody-Sankey revival in order to turn the attention of British workers away from their grievances to more spiritual matters. On the other hand, religion provides a sacral legitimation for the established order, no matter how just or unjust it may be. Paul's own words quite aptly illustrate Marx's point: "Let every person be subject to the governing authorities. For there is no authority except from God, and those that exist have been instituted by God. Therefore, he who resists the authorities resists what God has appointed" (Rom. 13:1-2 RSV). Because religion is characteristically allied with the present order, an attack on social evils necessarily involves an attack on religious authority as well. Marx once observed that the criticism of religion is the beginning of all criticism. His point is that once we are free to challenge sacral authority, we are free to challenge any kind of social arrangement which oppresses or alienates men. Under these circumstances, the final liberation of man from economic exploitation and political oppression requires his liberation from religion itself.

Marx and Engels rejoiced in the developments within Western civilization that were bringing about man's emancipation from religion: the emergence of modern science, the historical-critical study of both the Bible and the traditions of the church, and, most especially, the increasing self-consciousness of revolutionary social movements. . . . The developing proletarian revolution likewise held the promise of being guided by a clearheaded, purely secular assessment of the real factors operative in advanced capitalist nations and of the revolutionary role of the workers in that situation.

Given their understanding of the essentially regressive role of religion, Marx and Engels would have found little sense in a dialogue with Christian theologians. Even if such a dialogue produced no harmful results, it would at least be a diversion from the business at hand. At best, religion is a useless encumbrance destined to pass away with man's "coming of age." At worst, it is a barrier to human progress which must be vigorously opposed. In any case, Marx increasingly concerned himself not with philosophical and theological questions, but with problems of political economy. Likewise, the subsequent impact of his work centered in economic and political theory and in political programs seeking to utilize that theory both in revolutionary action and in the reconstruction of the basic institutions of human society. Generally speaking, there is little evidence that either Marx or his disciples were aware of the latent theological content which is invariably present in the theoretical and practical treatment of social processes. This oversight is not surprising, since Christianity is not in the first instance a social theory, even though it cannot legitimately be separated from social questions. The significance of the current readiness of Marxist philosophers to dialogue with Christian theologians is that it constitutes an acknowledgment of the presence of theological considerations in Marxist thought and a recognition that Marxism has in part functioned in a manner that is equivalent to a religious perspective.

Doubtless many factors have contributed to the current openness to Christianity exhibited by some Marxist philosophers. For one thing, modern developments in scientific and social thinking have not brought about the demise of religion as Marx and Engels anticipated. Especially noteworthy has been the ability of Christian theologians to reformulate the themes of faith in a way that is compatible with modern scientific thinking. Unquestionably Christianity has been significantly altered by the emergence of science, by biblical criticism, and by the epochal changes that have taken place in human society during the past one hundred years. At the same time, it has in some of its expressions manifested considerable capacity to respond creatively to these new developments. Indeed, for many persons the new forms of Christian life and thought represent a revitalization of faith. The realistic Marxist thinker finds it necessary to reflect critically on the fact that religion may have an enduring role in human experience, a fact that necessitates a revision of the traditional Marxist analysis of religion. The "Testament" of Palmiero Togliatti, the late General Secretary of the Italian Communist Party, reflects such a reappraisal:

> The old atheistic propaganda is of no use. The very problem of religious conscience, its content, its roots among the masses, and the way of overcoming it must be presented in a different manner from that adopted in the past if we wish to reach the Catholic masses and be understood by them. Otherwise our outstretched hand to the Catholics would be regarded as pure expediency and almost as hypocrisy.

More important, from the standpoint of the central Marxist concern, is the recognition that religion is not necessarily an opiate, that in some circumstances it may even be a leaven. Roger Garaudy has put the point strongly: "The thesis that religion always and everywhere turns men away from struggle and from work is in flagrant contradiction to the facts of history." In one sense, Garaudy's statement departs in no way from the view of Marx and Engels. As we have noted, Engels knew that religion could be associated with active efforts at social change. Besides, Garaudy himself is firm in his insistence that religion is still allied for the most part with the oppressors rather than the oppressed. Even so, his suggestion that religion may be a leaven of change does move beyond the traditional Marxist critique of religion. It does not simply say that religion sometimes functions as a *disguise* for tangible, earthly interests in a revolutionary struggle; it suggests that religion may be a *contributing factor,* an enabler, in that struggle.

Ernst Bloch and Roger Garaudy have both taken fresh looks at the roots of Christian faith in order to identify the source of its potential as a leaven of change. Their judgment is that the eschatological expectation of Christianity introduced a new factor in man's consciousness of himself and his possibilities in the world which converges with the Marxist understanding of man as an agent of revolutionary change. Indeed, Bloch acknowledges that the Marxist understanding itself derives from the eschatological thrust of biblical faith.

In classical culture man was viewed as a part of a cosmic order that is essentially fixed and unchanging. In this frame of reference an expectation of the genuinely new, which can provide a basis for historical initiative, can scarcely arise. The changes that do occur in human history are experienced as purely contingent, as directionless and without purpose. In some contexts change is even experienced as the deterioration of the cosmic order, leading inexorably to its total disintegration. Under those circumstances man's only hope is that a decaying universe can be reconstituted and restored to its primal form. Biblical eschatology, in contrast, points toward the emergence of a qualitatively new future that breaks through the limits of the present evil age. It holds out the promise that the present age can be negated for the sake of a "new heaven and a new earth." This expectation leads man to understand himself as a man of hope, as a man open to the promise of a qualitatively new future. In that understanding, he is empowered both to struggle with his present world, even to contradict it, and to participate as a subject of historical initiative in the creation of a new world. The point of this analysis is that it suggests to both Bloch and Garaudy that biblical eschatology contains the root of a revolutionary stance toward reality, a stance that is basic to the Marxist vision of man.

Admittedly, Christianity's radical historical orientation was soon neutralized. Intellectually, this development occurred when Christian theologians appropriated Greek thought as the basic framework for interpreting the Christian message. Practically speaking, it occurred as the church, beginning with the Emperor Constantine (fourth century), allied itself with the ruling classes of society. However, as Greek modes of thought give way to pragmatic and developmental ways of thinking, and as the church loses its favored position in society through the process of secularization, Christianity has the possibility of recovering and giving contemporary expression to the radical orientation that characterized its origins. It is this possibility that makes Christianity interesting to Marxist thinkers.

Under the present circumstances, Marxist participants in the dialogue with Christian theologians are not preoccupied with abolishing Christianity or even with merely learning to coexist with the Christian church, which may in any case manage to survive. They are interested in discovering what Christianity can contribute to the continuing development of Marxist thought. Garaudy identifies two themes in regard to which Christianity can supplement and enrich Marxism: transcendence and subjectivity. The first of these is closely related to the notion that man is an agent of change in the historical process. Garaudy speaks of Marxism as a "methodology of historical initiative." By that he means that the theoretical and scientific activity of Marx and his successors is oriented toward the concern to find realistic and practical ways to change the world. Marx expressed this concern succinctly: "The philosophers have only *interpreted* the world in various ways; the point, however, is to *change* it!" Interestingly enough, though Marx's writings assume at many points that man is the subject of historical initiative, he never gives an account of the being of man that clarifies how he can be such a subject. The weight of his effort was directed toward identifying the laws of historical development, the factors that determine the direction of change. As a result, Marxism is characteristically understood as a deterministic system of thought in which everything that happens occurs necessarily and inevitably. In my judgment Garaudy rightly rejects this interpretation of Marx. Marx frequently states that man in any case makes history. The problem is that his acts continually have consequences he neither anticipates nor desires. If he is to act effectively in history, he must have a good grasp of the factors operative in the dynamics of social change. Only by understanding those factors can he utilize them for his own ends. Only by knowing the realistic possibilities for action by means of a critical-empirical analysis of society can he make the active investment of his being count for his own projects.

Still, Marxism is deficient in its failure to show concretely the structures in the being of man that enable him to exercise initiative in relation to the factors that shape and condition his life. Garaudy is sensitive to this deficiency and suggests that the understanding of transcendence in Christian theology can help to overcome it. Transcendence is a category that is usually associated in the first instance with the being of God. Yet it always includes a notion of human transcendence as well—man's ability to transcend himself outward in relation to the presence of the transcendent God in human experience. Broadly speaking, the divine transcendence is understood in two fundamentally different ways: (1) the transcendence of that which is eternal and immutable over the transiency and frailty of finite existence; and (2) the transcendence of the future over the limits, even distortions, of the present. In the former, man's capacity for self-transcendence finds expression in his ability to discern and be governed by his intellectual grasp of the eternal and necessary structures of being. It issues in the contemplative life. In the latter, man's ability to transcend himself involves the imaginative projection of a future that surpasses qualitatively the constrictions of the present. It calls forth the active life. It is the latter form of transcendence that is most characteristic of biblical faith. In the words of Karl Rahner, Christianity is the religion of the absolute future. The Christian understanding of transcendence provides a stimulus for the Marxist to explore the way in which man's openness to the future enables him to play a creative role in the historical process. In this frame of reference man is constituted as much by his orientation to new possibilities as by the social and historical factors that shape and condition his being.

Ernst Bloch in particular has furnished significant new insights into the interpretation of man by his reflections on the openness of the future, or, in his terminology, on the "principle of hope." Bloch's category of the "not-yet-being" (Noch-Nicht-Sein) points to the creative impact of the pressure of new possibility on the self's concrete struggle to realize itself in relation to the world in which it has its being. It is the promise of the future that enables man to exercise historical initiative in the midst of the world. Bloch's aim is to unite real objective possibilities in the historical process—possibilities that become manifest through a critical-empirical analysis of society—with the unconditional passion for the coming of freedom—a passion that stems from the vision of what is "still not yet."

Both Bloch and Garaudy interpret the promise of the future in a strictly humanistic rather than theistic fashion. They express concern lest Christians fill up the future with God, closing off its openness. Where there is a world ruler, Bloch notes, there is no freedom. He advocates a secularized version of the kingdom of God in which "God" becomes the kingdom of God without God, the messianic openness of the "end-space" that draws man to creative historical activity. In the same vein Garaudy speaks of how the Marxist lives with a "never-satisfied exigency of totality and absoluteness, of omnipotence as to nature and of perfect loving reciprocity of consciousness." He rejects the name of God because it implies a presence, a reality, whereas man lives only toward an exigency, an absence. Nevertheless, both thinkers acknowledge that the sensitivity to the "end-space" or to the "never-satisfied exigency" became an important feature in the consciousness of Western man through the impact of the eschatological expectation of biblical faith.

Garaudy also indicates that Christian theology can deepen the Marxist understanding of subjectivity. This motif is itself connected with the discussion of transcendence, since that discussion is primarily significant for its clarification of how man can be a *subject* of historical initiative, a creator as well as a creature of history. Yet subjectivity also relates to those problems in the struggle for humanness which stem not so much from social factors as from the more intensely personal dimensions of selfhood. Marxism has so emphasized the fact that man is a creature constituted by social relationships that it has tended to assume all human difficulties of any consequence would be removed by a reordering of the structures of society. While no societies embody Marx's hopes for society sufficiently to test his expectations, the experience of socialist societies dramatizes the fact that man's alienation from himself cannot be wholly traced to social factors. Particularly pressing is man's contemporary quest for significant meanings in terms of which he can order and interpret his experience. Issues of this kind have been a major concern of twentieth-century Christian theology and of much contemporary philosophy and literature as well. At this point, therefore, Marxists are open to fresh insights and perspectives on man in his struggles to realize his humanness in the context of modern society.

• • •

christian openings to marxism

Generally speaking, Christians have not been as much in agreement in assessing Marxism as Marxists have been in assessing Christianity. Responses have ranged from a bitter denunciation of Marxism as an unmitigated evil to an advocacy of its economic and political tenets as the most adequate expression of the social message of Christianity. This diversity in part reflects variations in the circumstances of the Communist-Christian encounter, but it also indicates that Christians have some unfinished business in seeking to come to terms with the Marxist challenge.

A number of the developments within Christian theology that equip it for dialogue with Marxist thought have no special relation to the Marxist challenge. They are reflections of the more general concern of Christian theologians to interpret Christianity in a manner that is relevant to the contemporary world. For example, any adequate theology for our time must be able to deal openly and creatively with the revolutionary impact of modern scientific thinking on man's intellectual life. It is not sufficient merely to make grudging concessions to scientific advances where concessions are unavoidable, while attempting at the same time to preserve everything else virtually unchanged. What is called for is boldness in reformulating the basic themes of faith in a manner that is compatible with the role scientific thinking currently plays in man's perception of himself and his world. Major Protestant thinkers have for some time been engaged in this undertaking. The extraordinary influence of the efforts of Pierre Teilhard de Chardin to interpret Christian faith in relation to the evolutionary theory of the life sciences suggests a new readiness within Roman Catholicism to respond positively to the scientific consciousness of contemporary man. The continuing vitality of Christianity depends in part upon its ability to clarify its place in a modern, scientific age.

If openness to science is an essential feature of contemporary expressions of Christianity, it is also a necessary part of any fruitful dialogue with Marxist thinkers. Marxism prides itself on its scientific character and condemns the role religion has played in interfering with scientific research and development. Marxists cannot recognize Christians as serious dialogue partners unless a constructive relationship between the life of faith and scientific activity can be established. To be sure, Marxists have themselves distorted the meaning of science, at times claiming scientific proof for views that are in fact based on ideological considerations. Some important Marxist convictions, e.g., the perfectibility of the human spirit or the progressive character of history, are hardly amenable to scientific demonstration at all. Still, Christians cannot effectively challenge the pseudoscience that finds its way into Marxist writings unless it is also prepared to reject the defensiveness that has characterized the history of its own relation to science.

In like manner, recent interpretations of Christianity have given increasing attention to the contributions Christian faith can make to man's quest for fullness of life in *this world*. Otherworldly concerns have diminished in importance, in many cases disappearing altogether. This shift in focus reflects the efforts of Christian theologians to exhibit the significance of faith for modern, secular men. At the same time, it helps to bring about a situation of dialogue with Marxist thinkers. Unlike most secular men, Marxists are not simply uninterested in religious beliefs about the "other" world; they see such beliefs as a positive threat to the humanization of men in this world. Insofar as Christianity maintains its otherworldly hopes, it finds itself challenged to show not only that these hopes do not hinder the worldly progress of the human pilgrimage, but also that they strengthen man in that pilgrimage. Roger Garaudy quotes Teilhard with approval on this point: "In my opinion the world will not be converted to the heavenly promises of Christianity unless Christianity has previously been converted to the promises of the earth."

It must be emphasized that the worldly orientation of Christian theology has been chiefly concentrated on matters that are highly personal, such as death, guilt, or the struggle of each man to make sense of his own life. In their analysis of these matters, Christian theologians have frequently abstracted the being of man from the concrete social, economic, and political factors that shape and condition his life. Dietrich Bonhoeffer has aptly criticized such theology as merely a secularized version of the old pietistic concern for individual salvation in the world to come. With regard to social questions this abstraction has the effect of providing an indirect religious sanction for the status quo. That contemporary Marxist philosophers have become interested in these more personal matters has already been noted. In fact, their readiness to discuss issues such as subjectivity and transcendence may present a temptation to Christian theologians to restrict the agenda of the dialogue to questions with which they are already familiar. Yet Christianity cannot effectively address the situation of contemporary man unless it seeks to come to grips with basic social questions.

The most crucial precondition for Christian openness to dialogue with Marxism is not simply that Christians be oriented to worldly concerns, but that they be committed to explore the meaning of Christian faith in relation to the *social* character of those concerns. It is in regard to these questions that Marxism has made and can continue to make the greatest contribution to the development of Christian thought.

For Christians to become vitally interested in social questions is an important achievement in itself. Yet much is at stake in how these questions are approached. For example, Christian theologians sometimes deal with social questions solely in terms of the *ethical implications* of Christian faith, as if the basic issues of faith were only indirectly related to man's life in society. In contrast Marx located the root of the human problem in a certain ordering of human society and saw the hope of human fulfillment in action aimed at bringing about fundamental changes in that form of social organization. If Marx's thought was too simplistic in linking both man's suffering and his hope to the economic and political structures of human society, Christianity has not given sufficient attention to the way in which the central thrust of the Christian message confronts men in the midst of the social and political struggles of life.

•   •   •

Christian theologians have sometimes dealt with social questions in a purely utopian manner, projecting ideal forms of human social life in the hope that such ideals might lure men to make the needed reforms in society. The social gospel characteristically took this form, failing to appreciate the relative impotence of moral ideals for influencing human behavior. In contrast, Marx sought to gain theoretical competence in the interpretation of the dynamics of social change in order that he might identify effective means for overcoming oppression and exploitation in human society. If the Christian promise is relevant to man's life in society, then Christian theology must also seek to develop or utilize a theoretical understanding of society that can make more effective the concrete efforts of men to give actuality to that promise. Alfred North Whitehead once suggested that Christianity is a religion in search of a metaphysic. In our time it may be more urgent for it to be a religion in search of a social theory, one that will enable it to call men to enter into the redemptive possibilities that are present in the historical process.

A recognition by Christian theologians of the need for a theoretical understanding of social processes inevitably points toward an openness to Marxist thought. Marxism has a number of features that commend it to Christians. For one thing, Marx's serious study of political economy was not motivated by a purely academic interest, but by a concern to bring about humanizing changes in society. In this respect, it has a profoundly moral content. Second, Marx's study embodied a deep emotional identification with the sufferings and needs of oppressed peoples. He was seeking to find means of social change and forms of social organization which at least held the promise of a fundamental alteration in the situation of oppression. His aims must be contrasted with the aims of those who seek only the minimal changes necessary to preserve with some measure of stability the present distribution of power and privilege in society. Marx's central thesis seems to be that there is no way to assure meaningful participation by the masses of people in the determination of their own future unless all men share in the ownership of the means of production. The formal guarantees of freedom provided by the liberal democratic state fail to give adequate protection for the people as long as a minority is able to monopolize the means of production in that society. Christians concerned about human dignity, freedom, and equality of opportunity—not simply as ideals, but as concrete actualities in human life and experience—cannot legitimately disregard the questions Marx raises about the effects economic factors have on the social and political well-being of man.

Through the leadership of Reinhold Niebuhr, disciplined social thinking has in recent decades played a much larger role in American theology than in continental theology. By the mid-fifties something of a Christian consensus regarding Marxism had developed in American theology. This consensus was sympathetic, yet critical, toward Marxism. It endorsed the Marxist attack on the exploitation of wage labor in advanced capitalist societies, but denied the contention that the best way to overcome this exploitation is by a proletarian revolution. It appropriated the Marxist concern for the alienation of the human spirit in modern industrial society, but refused to trace that alienation solely to a certain manner of ordering the productive relations of society. In part, it treated alienation as the inescapable accompaniment of modern technology; in part it located the problem of alienation in the finite freedom of the individual, removing it from an exclusive connection with social questions. In like manner, the American consensus about Marxism conceded an important role to economic factors in determining the course of historical development, but it also emphasized the importance of noneconomic factors—including the value content of human culture—in shaping the quality of human life. Finally, it acknowledged that the Marxist critique of religion had much to commend it, but it denied that this critique provided an adequate interpretation of the significance of religion in the human pilgrimage. Indeed, it contended that communism itself functions as a secular religion in spite of its attempts to dissociate itself from everything religious. Moreover, because it lacks the dimension of transcendence which provides the possibility for radical self-criticism, it is a religion ever subject to the idolatrous perversion of elevating the finite and the relative to a status of ultimacy.

The sharpest criticisms of Marxism in this American "consensus" were directed not against the Marxist analysis of society, but against the Marxist prescriptions for society, especially as these found expression in communist practice. In Niebuhr's writings, these criticisms centered on the moral pretensions of communism. In his view, the primary difficulty with Marxism is that it locates the source of evil exclusively in the structures of society, principally in the relations of production. As a result, one class—the bourgeoisie—is identified as the oppressor class, the sole bearer of social evil, and another class—the proletariat—is identified as the liberator class, the sole bearer of the conscience of civilization. In this frame of reference, a just society could presumably be assured by the complete triumph of the proletariat. When a class is viewed as messianic and endowed with every virtue, Niebuhr charged, it is inevitably blind to the moral ambiguities of its own acts. It continually falls prey to a demonic self-righteousness.

The current stage of the Marxist-Christian dialogue is emerging in a context not significantly influenced by Niebuhr or the consensus which developed around his thought. Theologically, it gives greater weight to the redemptive possibilities of the historical process than to the moral ambiguities of history. Because of this emphasis, it is more able to correct against the opportunistic tendencies of men to accommodate themselves to the injustices of the prevailing society. It frees them to struggle with the destructive features of society, to contradict them, in order that new possibilities might be brought into being. The problem of man's moral pretensions has not been a prominent part of this dialogue, in large measure because the Marxist participants have themselves been more cautious in stating their actual expectations for the future. . . .

Attempts to interpret Christian faith in relation to social processes, particularly those involved in the struggles of oppressed peoples to bring into being a more fulfilling social order, have important implications for theological method. They call into question methodologies that view theology as a self-contained intellectual discipline, perhaps committed to the exegesis of Scripture or to the systematic explication of the meaning of the biblical message for contemporary man. They point instead to a way of doing theology that is shaped and conditioned by the concrete commitment of a community of faith to play a healing, reconciling role in the social and political struggles of men. Biblical exegesis and systematic thinking are not omitted from the latter understanding. Still, they enter most directly into the theological enterprise as activities aimed at helping the struggling community gain insight into the meaning of its own involvements. The crucial tests for this way of doing theology are its power in illuminating the anguish and the promise of the human situation, and its faithfulness in attesting the healing, liberating, and enabling presence of God to men in that situation. Where it does its work well, theology can be the means through which men are empowered to lay hold of the possibilities presented to them for the realization of a new quality of human life.

. . .

One final matter requires at least brief mention: the meaning of God in human experience. It is well known that Marxism from the beginning has been militantly atheistic. Its atheism deserves profound respect, since it is an atheism "for the sake of man." If Marxism is to be open to dialogue with Christianity, it must reexamine the question of God, attending more carefully to what contemporary theologians mean by God and to the positive possibilities the reality of God brings to human life. We have seen the readiness of some Marxists to explore these matters in connection with the notion of transcendence, particularly a transcendence that moves toward the future. A Christian readiness to dialogue with Marxists likewise requires an openness to the problematic nature of belief in God, including its possible demonic consequences in human experience. Once again, the urgency of this issue in contemporary Christian theology does not stem solely from the encounter with Marxism, as the recent "death of God" discussion makes perfectly clear. Still, this dialogue does provide a context in which fresh thinking on the meaning of God has begun to unfold. The important point to be kept in mind is that the problem of atheism is inherent in the Christian understanding of God. As Moltmann has so aptly put it, we must be atheists not simply for the sake of man, but also for the sake of God. This means that

Christian theology is constantly charged with the task of exposing false gods—the gods that impoverish and enslave the being of man. Because of the threats and uncertainties that assail his being, man is constantly tempted to create a cosmic excuse upon which he can project his anxieties and fears and so relieve himself of responsibility for a realistic grappling with the limits and possibilities of his own situation. Christian theology must make it unmistakably clear that the god who is an excuse, a barrier to responsibility, is an impostor god from whom man has been liberated. On the other side of this Christian atheism it is called to witness to the God who is present to man not to control him or overpower him, but to liberate him, empower him, and open up new possibilities by means of which man himself can enter into the struggle for the fulfillment of all the promises of God.

The dialogue between Marxists and Christians is only beginning. It is not possible at this time to predict where it will lead, but it promises to make a contribution not only to greater mutual understanding, but also to the continued development and enrichment of both perspectives.

WILLIAM JOHNSTON

buddhist-christian dialogue

One of the beautiful things of our age—which, alas, has all kinds of ugly things also—is that we have learned to talk to one another. Slowly we are mastering the art of dialogue. And the religions of the world, after centuries of rivalry and quarreling, are learning to wipe the blood off their hands, beat their swords into plowshares, and exchange the kiss of peace. Truly an interesting and exciting age.

Since I myself hail from such a bigoted and intolerant corner of the earth, I have always felt that dialogue with other religions is something of a sacred duty. Somehow I ought to make amends. That is why I have been so glad to attend meetings between Christians and Zen Buddhists that have taken place in various parts of Japan. Most of these meetings have been more or less unofficial (that is to say, the people present were not officially appointed by central religious authorities) and have been conducted in a spirit of the utmost cordiality and friendship. We meet on terms of equality—no attempt, of course, is made at proselytizing—in the belief that none of us possess the totality of the truth. To us Catholic Christians the Vatican Council brought the refreshing news that we are still seekers, members of a pilgrim Church, and so we can join hands with other searchers, whether they be Buddhist, Hindu, Muslim, or anything else, in our common quest for truth. Needless to say, we have Christ, who I believe spoke of God as no man ever spoke; but I do not think we can claim to understand the revelation of Christ in all its fullness. Perhaps we are still at the beginning. Moreover I also believe that in sundry times and in diverse ways God spoke to our fathers through the prophets, and these include prophets whose voices echo beautifully in the *Gita*, the *Lotus Sutra*, and the *Tao Teh Ching*.

I am aware that it sounds awfully patronizing to give Christianity the plum of Divine Sonship and throw a few crumbs of prophethood to Buddhists and Hindus, but I have found that Buddhists, at least those I have met and know, do not take this amiss. They want to know what we think without camouflage or dilution, and in the same way we want to know what they think. None of the Christians are particularly disturbed to hear that they possess the Buddha nature. The fact is, however, that we are only now advancing from the backwoods of intolerance and have not yet found a formula that will keep everyone happy. Perhaps we never will.

The dialogue with Zen owes much to the initiative and enterprise of the Quakers, to whom we are all eternally grateful. No doubt the great similarity between Quaker meditation and Zen (though there are great differences too) was instrumental in prompting their ecumenical interest. The first meeting was held in Oiso, near Tokyo, and the participants talked frankly about their personal religious experience, searching for a link that might bind them together. Conducted in a spirit of great charity, it revealed that the interior life of Buddhists and Christians has much in common; they can be united at the deepest part of their being, at the level of psychic life which Eliot calls the still point of the turning world. But the participants were unable to enunciate any theological or philosophical statement all could agree upon.

When the time came round for the next meeting, this time to be held in Kyoto, it seemed to me that we should leave the subjective realm of religious experience and get down to something objective. Perhaps the whole discussion could center around the problem of ultimate reality—we Christians could explain what we meant by "God," pointing out that we did not believe in an anthropomorphic being "out there" but in the supreme source of existence in whom we live, move, and are. The Buddhists, on the other hand, could explain what they mean by nothingness, emptiness, the void, and so on. In this way a lot of misunderstanding might vanish like smoke; we might discover that we had something in common after all, and what a break-through this would be in religious thinking! Now I realize that I was naive. Or a victim of my Hellenistic education.

Anyhow, with this in mind I spoke to a Buddhist friend who was to be a participant. He listened kindly, and his answer, typically Buddhist and deeply interesting, was more or less as follows. "Do you really think that you can talk about nothingness, emptiness, or the void? Do you really think you can talk about God? Of course you can't. You are part of the void; you are part of nothingness; you are part of God. All is one."

And here I found clearly and directly expressed something that runs all through Zen, whether it be in the thinking of the simplest Master or the most sophisticated scholar: that is to say, there is no duality, no "I and Thou" (alas for Martin Buber), no "God and myself." All is one. This is the so-called monism that underlies all Mahayana Buddhism. Let me illustrate it further with a story about the great Dr. Suzuki.

One time the old philosopher gave a talk on Zen to Western people in Tokyo. He spoke of the silence, the emptiness, the nothingness, and all the rest, together with the deep wisdom that comes from *satori*. When he had finished, one of his audience rose to his feet and, not without a touch of irritation, exclaimed, "But Dr. Suzuki, what about society? What about other people? What about the other?"

Whereupon Suzuki paused for a moment, looked up with a smile, and remarked, "But there is no other!"

There is no other, and there is no self. This is the answer he had to give, and this basically was the answer of my Buddhist friend. What they meant by it (for it is by no means as simple or as terrible as it sounds) I would like to discuss later; for the present, let us return to the dialogue.

We met in Kyoto, where we spent a wonderful week, fifteen of us. The atmosphere was permeated with good will and deep religious faith. Not only did we talk together, we also sat together in a wordless dialogue of silent communication. The meeting was highlighted by a talk from an eminent *roshi* who described with great enthusiasm the experience of enlightenment that had made him wild with ecstatic joy. His head seemed to be shattered and for several days he did not know where he was or what he was doing. *Satori* could never be described or explained, he said, but there was undoubtedly enlightenment in the words of Jesus:

Before Abraham was, I am.

This, he said, was perfect enlightenment—no object, no duality, just "I am."

Here I might digress to say that I have been impressed and moved by the respect and reverence with which Buddhists have always spoken of Christ in my presence. However dim a view they may take of us, and I suppose they have reason on occasion, they have not concealed their admiration for the founder of Christianity. In this case his words gave me food for thought. I had heard it said before that "I am" is an expression of perfect *satori*. It should be noted, however, that when the words "I am" rise up in the depth of the enlightened being, this "I" is not the empirical ego; it is not the little self that is compounded of desires and does not really exist in Zen. This "I" is the very ground of being, the heart of the universe, the true self which rises in the depths and overwhelms everything. It is the voice of the "big self" which drowns all consciousness of the "little self" because it is all that is. I saw then clearly that when Jesus said "I am," the "I" that spoke was not the "I" of a man, but that of the eternal Word that was in the beginning and through whom all things were made. Jesus, I believe, was so filled with God that he no longer had a human personality—within him was only the personality of the eternal Son. That is why that "I" that cried out within him was the same as that which spoke to Moses saying, "I am who I am."

Be that as it may, our talk has gone on over cups of coffee and green tea, while at other times it has been more formal, with tape recorders and press correspondents. Perhaps the reader will ask where it is all going and what we are getting out of it. Yet this is, perhaps, a question no one can answer. In some ways dialogue is a dangerous and tricky business. At one meeting a Buddhist professor humorously made the remark that we all feel the cultural and religious danger. After all, if you leave yourself open, if you recognize the other's position, if you treat with others on terms of equality—then God alone knows what might happen. But the risk is worth taking, and progress will be made. As for myself, my principal preoccupation at present is with learning from Buddhism. I can't help feeling that Western Christianity (like Western everything else) is badly in need of a blood transfusion. Somehow or other we have become effete—is this the old theory about the decline of the West?—and we need new perspectives. Just as a whole new era opened up for Christianity when Thomas introduced Aristotle in the thirteenth century, so a new era, an even bigger one, could be opened up by the assimilation of some Buddhist ideas and attitudes. And the time is particularly ripe for this now that we see Christianity as an open-ended religion, a religion on the march, a religion that has taken things from Hellenism and communism and will only reach something like completion when it sees the truth through the eyes of all cultures. Indeed, it is precisely because of its claim to universality that Christianity needs the insights of other religions. And here I might add that many Buddhists I have met are also on the march, happy and willing to learn from Christianity.

But now about the blood transfusion. What can Christians learn from Zen? Or in a book like this it might be better to ask what I have learned, or am in the process of learning, from Zen. And first of all it seems to me that Zen can teach us a methodology in prayer. Let me explain what I mean.

Every religion that is worth its salt has taught people how to pray. Some religions are poor in theology and organization; but if they have prayer or meditation we can respect them and recognize that they are trying to do their job. In Buddhism and Hinduism there have always been people—gurus and *roshi*—who have so mastered the art of meditation that they can lead their disciples through the tortuous paths of the mind to a high level of concentration. Now Christianity, too, has a similar tradition (how could it otherwise have survived?), as also has Judaism. Recall how the disciples said to Jesus, "Teach us to pray, as John taught his disciples to pray." They expected Jesus to be a Master of prayer, as were John and the other rabbis who moved around the countryside. The fathers of the Church, too, taught prayer; and later on we find men like Ignatius of Loyola wandering around Paris simply instructing people in the ways of meditation. Ignatius had a method—it is outlined in his *Spiritual Exercises*—and he aimed at bringing people to something like *satori*. His method continues and flourishes even today.

Yet the method of Ignatius was grossly misunderstood, and became tied up with rationalism, with reasoning and thinking and a so-called "discursive prayer" that appeals little to modern man, who wants mysticism. Modern people, like Hamlet, have had too many words, words, words. Perhaps it is that they are wrung out and exhausted by television, radio, advertising, and all the stuff that McLuhan calls the extension of man's nervous system throughout our planet. What they want is deep interior silence. And this can be found through Zen, as it could be found through Ignatius' method if it were properly understood. Zen has simple techniques, however, for introducing people to inner peace and even to the so-called Christian "infused contemplation." The Japanese, as is well known in the world of economics, are an eminently practical people, and they have perfected the Zen method that came to birth in China: the sitting, the breathing, the control of the mind.

But the key thing in Zen is not just sitting in the lotus posture. The key (or so it seems to me) is detachment, the art of which is highly developed in Zen. It should be remembered that all forms of Buddhism are built on detachment and that the roots of Zen are here.

"What then is the Holy Truth of the Origination of Ill? It is that craving which leads to rebirth, accompanied by delight and greed, seeking its delight now here, now there, i.e., craving for sensuous experience, craving to perpetuate oneself, craving for extinction.

"What then is the Holy Truth of the Stopping of Ill? It is the complete stopping of that craving, the withdrawal from it, the renouncing of it, throwing it back, liberation from it, nonattachment to it."

True to these principles, Zen inculcates a renunciation or asceticism that is truly extraordinary. One must be detached from everything, even from oneself. Nor does Zen detachment simply mean doing without alcohol and tobacco (this is the usual Christian understanding of the word); it goes much deeper to include detachment from the very process of thinking, from the images and ideas and conceptualization that are so dear to Western man. And through this detachment one is introduced to a deep and beautiful realm of psychic life. One goes down, down to the depths of one's being—or, if you want a Zen physiological explanation, to the pit of one's stomach. As the process continues, one becomes detached even in those subliminal regions in which are found infantile fixations, unconscious drives, and all the rest. When detachment sets in here, Zen has something in common with psychoanalysis and can even be therapeutic for those who are able and willing to take the medicine. But I have written about this in my little book *The Still Point* and need not repeat it here. All I want to say is that so far as detachment is concerned it resembles greatly the Christian contemplative path of John of the Cross. So striking indeed is the similarity that some scholars hold that John of the Cross received Buddhist influence through Neoplatonism. But this is by no means certain.

Anyhow, detachment is only one side of the coin. One becomes detached in order that something else may shine forth. In the Buddhist this is his Buddha nature. For, contrary to what is often said, true Zen is based on a very great faith—faith in the presence of the Buddha nature in the deepest recesses of the personality; faith that, as the Four Noble Truths point out, there is a way out of the morass of suffering and that man can be transformed through enlightenment. I believe this point is worth stressing for one frequently hears that there are in Zen no faith, no presuppositions, "no dependence on words and letters." In one sense this is all true. It is true that no conceptualized system can be present in the mind in time of *zazen;* it is also true that one cannot point to any one sutra and say, "Here is the essence of Zen." But in spite of this the fact remains that the whole thing is penetrated with the spirit of Buddhism, the spirit of the patriarchs, the spirit of the sutras. If one speaks to Zen people one finds this immediately; if one listens to the talks in the temples it is quite clear. There is a great faith here.

In Christian Zen this faith may take the form of a conviction that God is present in the depth of my being or, put in other words, that I am made in the image of God. Or it may express itself in the Pauline words, "I live, now not I; but Christ lives in me." The deepest and truest thing within me is not myself but God. As Christian Zen develops, self disappears (here is the Christian *muga* or nonself situation), and God lives and acts within me; my activity is no longer my own but the activity of God who is all in all. In the last analysis there is nothing except God. Paul says that there is nothing except Christ. "There is no such thing as Jew and Greek, slave and freeman, male and female; for you are all one in Christ." This is how Christian Zen will develop. The point I have tried to make here, for I consider it important, is that some kind of faith is necessary in a practice like Zen, and that one is not floating in the air as much as some people have said. This is true of all forms of deep meditation, and it is probably for this reason that a man like Aldous Huxley, who had great interest in meditation but no particular belief in anything, just didn't get anywhere. You can't go on detaching yourself indefinitely in the hope that something may or may not turn up inside. One may of course begin meditation without much faith, and many of the people who come to our place in Tokyo do just that, but the time comes when faith is necessary, and without it no one goes through to the end.

In short, it seems to me that Christians can profit greatly from Zen methodology to deepen their Christian faith, and here in Japan an increasing number of Christians, both Japanese and Western, are discovering this. A growing number of Catholic Japanese nuns, for example, are quietly practicing Zen, and I believe it has a future within the Church. Surely it would be a good idea to take up this methodology and start once again teaching people how to pray. For the sad fact is that, while Catholic monks and nuns are teaching all kinds of things from botany to business English, not many are teaching people how to pray.

There is, of course, more to the methodology than the couple of points I have mentioned; but I think it better to leave the discussion of the *roshi* and the *koan* to a later chapter. What I want to say here is that impoverished Western man is greatly in need of something like this, because the contemplative life is fantastically underdeveloped in the developed and affluent nations. Western civilization has become horribly one-sided and unbalanced, so much so that serious people cannot see the distinction between a computer and a man. When this happens, and when the contemplative dimension existing in every man becomes starved, then people go berserk and do crazy things. And this is what is happening. Moreover it is ghastly to think that it is happening even among some monks and nuns. Here are people whose lives are geared to *satori,* yet they feel that all is meaningless unless they are moving around the place making noise in the name of Christian charity.

If young people look to Hinduism and Buddhism for the contemplative education that they instinctively long for, may this not be because modern Christianity has projected the image of a churchgoing religion rather than a mystical one? May it not have too much bingo and too little mysticism? Too much theological chatter and not enough subliminal silence? Words, words, words! Perhaps this is why we need the blood transfusion from the East.

CARL JUNG

jung on the chinese
book of changes _____

The Chinese mind, as I see it at work in the *I Ching,* seems to be exclusively preoccupied with the chance aspect of events. What we call coincidence seems to be the chief concern of this peculiar mind, and what we worship as causality passes almost unnoticed. We must admit that there is something to be said for the immense importance of chance. An incalculable amount of human effort is directed to combating and restricting the nuisance or danger represented by chance. Theoretical considerations of cause and effect often look pale and dusty in comparison to the practical results of chance. It is all very well to say that the crystal of quartz is a hexagonal prism. The statement is quite true in so far as an ideal crystal is envisaged. But in nature one finds no two crystals exactly alike, although all are unmistakably hexagonal. The actual form, however, seems to appeal more to the Chinese sage than the ideal one. The jumble of natural laws constituting empirical reality holds more significance for him than a causal explanation of events that, moreover, must usually be separated from one another in order to be properly dealt with.

The manner in which the *I Ching* tends to look upon reality seems to disfavor our causalistic procedures. The moment under actual observation appears to the

The I Ching: or Book of Changes, trans. Richard Wilhelm, rendered into English by Cary F. Baynes, Foreword by C. G. Jung, Bollingen Series XIX (copyright © 1950, 1967 by Bollingen Foundation), reprinted by permission of Princeton University Press.

ancient Chinese view more of a chance hit than a clearly defined result of con-
curring causal chain processes. The matter of interest seems to be the configuration formed by chance events in the moment of observation, and not at all the
hypothetical reasons that seemingly account for the coincidence. While the Western mind carefully sifts, weighs, selects, classifies, isolates, the Chinese picture of
the moment encompasses everything down to the minutest nonsensical detail,
because all of the ingredients make up the observed moment.

Thus it happens that when one throws the three coins, or counts through the
forty-nine yarrow stalks, these chance details enter into the picture of the moment of observation and form a part of it—a part that is insignificant to us, yet
most meaningful to the Chinese mind. With us it would be a banal and almost
meaningless statement (at least on the face of it) to say that whatever happens in
a given moment possesses inevitably the quality peculiar to that moment. This is
not an abstract argument but a very practical one.

· · ·

In other words, whoever invented the *I Ching* was convinced that the hexagram worked out in a certain moment coincided with the latter in quality no less
than in time. To him the hexagram was the exponent of the moment in which it
was cast—even more so than the hours of the clock or the divisions of the calen-
dar could be—inasmuch as the hexagram was understood to be an indicator of
the essential situation prevailing in the moment of its origin.

This assumption involves a certain curious principle that I have termed synchronicity, a concept that formulates a point of view diametrically opposed to
that of causality. Since the latter is a merely statistical truth and not absolute, it
is a sort of working hypothesis of how events evolve one out of another, whereas
synchronicity takes the coincidence of events in space and time as meaning
something more than mere chance, namely, a peculiar interdependence of objective events among themselves as well as with the subjective (psychic) states of
the observer or observers.

The ancient Chinese mind contemplates the cosmos in a way comparable to
that of the modern physicist, who cannot deny that his model of the world is a
decidedly psychophysical structure. The microphysical event includes the observer just as much as the reality underlying the *I Ching* comprises subjective, i.e.,
psychic conditions in the totality of the momentary situation. Just as causality
describes the sequence of events, so synchronicity to the Chinese mind deals
with the coincidence of events.

· · ·

Now the sixty-four hexagrams of the *I Ching* are the instrument by which the
meaning of sixty-four different yet typical situations can be determined. These
interpretations are equivalent to causal explanations. Causal connection is statis-
tically necessary and can therefore be subjected to experiment. Inasmuch as situations are unique and cannot be repeated, experimenting with synchronicity
seems to be impossible under ordinary conditions. In the *I Ching,* the only criterion of the validity of synchronicity is the observer's opinion that the text of a

hexagram amounts to a true rendering of his psychic condition. It is assumed that the fall of the coins or the result of the division of the bundle of yarrow stalks is what it necessarily must be in a given "situation," inasmuch as anything happening in that moment belongs to it as an indispensable part of the picture. If a handful of matches is thrown to the floor, they form the pattern characteristic of that moment. But such an obvious truth as this reveals its meaningful nature only if it is possible to read the pattern and to verify its interpretation, partly by the observer's knowledge of the subjective and objective situation, partly by the character of subsequent events. It is obviously not a procedure that appeals to a critical mind used to experimental verification of facts or to factual evidence. But for someone who likes to look at the world at the angle from which ancient China saw it, the *I Ching* may have some attraction.

. . . Thus it occurred to me that it might interest the uninitiated reader to see the *I Ching* at work. For this purpose I made an experiment strictly in accordance with the Chinese conception: I personified the book in a sense, asking its judgment about its present situation, i.e., my intention to present it to the Western mind.

•   •   •

Why not venture a dialogue with an ancient book that purports to be animated? There can be no harm in it, and the reader may watch a psychological procedure that has been carried out time and again throughout the millennia of Chinese civilization, representing to a Confucius or a Laotse both a supreme expression of spiritual authority and a philosophical enigma. I made use of the coin method, and the answer obtained was hexagram 50, Ting, THE CALDRON.

In accordance with the way my question was phrased, the text of the hexagram must be regarded as though the *I Ching* itself were the speaking person. Thus it describes itself as a caldron, that is, as a ritual vessel containing cooked food. Here the food is to be understood as spiritual nourishment. Wilhelm says about this:

> The *ting,* as a utensil pertaining to a refined civilization, suggests the fostering and nourishing of able men, which redounded to the benefit of the state. . . . The supreme revelation of God appears in prophets and holy men. To venerate them is true veneration of God. The will of God, as revealed through them, should be accepted in humility.

Keeping to our hypothesis, we must conclude that the *I Ching* is here testifying concerning itself.

When any of the lines of a given hexagram have the value of six or nine, it means that they are specially emphasized and hence important in the interpretation. In my hexagram the "spiritual agencies" have given the emphasis of a nine to the lines in the second and in the third place. The text says:

> Nine in the second place means:
> There is food in the *ting.*
> My comrades are envious,

But they cannot harm me.
Good fortune.

Thus the *I Ching* says of itself: "I contain (spiritual) nourishment." Since a share in something great always arouses envy, the chorus of the envious is part of the picture. The envious want to rob the *I Ching* of its great possession, that is, they seek to rob it of meaning, or to destroy its meaning. But their enmity is in vain. Its richness of meaning is assured; that is, it is convinced of its positive achievements, which no one can take away. The text continues:

Nine in the third place means:
The handle of the *ting* is altered.
One is impeded in his way of life.
The fat of the pheasant is not eaten.
Once rain falls, remorse is spent.
Good fortune comes in the end.

The handle (German *Griff*) is the part by which the *ting* can be grasped (*gegriffen*). Thus it signifies the concept (*Begriff*) one has of the *I Ching* (the *ting*). In the course of time this concept has apparently changed, so that today we can no longer grasp (*begreifen*) the *I Ching*. Thus "one is impeded in his way of life." We are no longer supported by the wise counsel and deep insight of the oracle; therefore we no longer find our way through the mazes of fate and the obscurities of our own natures. The fat of the pheasant, that is, the best and richest part of a good dish, is no longer eaten. But when the thirsty earth finally receives rain again, that is, when this state of want has been overcome, "remorse," that is, sorrow over the loss of wisdom, is ended, and then comes the longed-for opportunity. Wilhelm comments: "This describes a man who, in a highly evolved civilization, finds himself in a place where no one notices or recognizes him. This is a severe block to his effectiveness." The *I Ching* is complaining, as it were, that its excellent qualities go unrecognized and hence lie fallow. It comforts itself with the hope that it is about to regain recognition.

The answer given in these two salient lines to the question I put to the *I Ching* requires no particular subtlety of interpretation, no artifices, no unusual knowledge. Anyone with a little common sense can understand the meaning of the answer; it is the answer of one who has a good opinion of himself, but whose value is neither generally recognized nor even widely known. The answering subject has an interesting notion of itself: it looks upon itself as a vessel in which sacrificial offerings are brought to the gods, ritual food for their nourishment. It conceives of itself as a cult utensil serving to provide spiritual nourishment for the unconscious elements or forces ("spiritual agencies") that have been projected as gods—in other words, to give these forces the attention they need in order to play their part in the life of the individual. Indeed, this is the original meaning of the word *religio*—a careful observation and taking account of (from *relegere*) the numinous.

The method of the *I Ching* does indeed take into account the hidden individual quality in things and men, and in one's own unconscious self as well. I have

questioned the *I Ching* as one questions a person whom one is about to introduce to friends: one asks whether or not it will be agreeable to him. In answer
the *I Ching* tells me of its religious significance, of the fact that at present it is
unknown and misjudged, of its hope of being restored to a place of honor—this
last obviously with a sidelong glance at my as yet unwritten foreword, and above
all at the English translation. This seems a perfectly understandable reaction,
such as one could expect also from a person in a similar situation.

I agree with Western thinking that any number of answers to my question
were possible, and I certainly cannot assert that another answer would not have
been equally significant. However, the answer received was the first and only
one; we know nothing of other possible answers. It pleased and satisfied me.
To ask the same question a second time would have been tactless and so I did
not do it: "the master speaks but once." The heavy-handed pedagogic approach
that attempts to fit irrational phenomena into a preconceived rational pattern is
anathema to me. Indeed, such things as this answer should remain as they were
when they first emerged to view, for only then do we know what nature does
when left to herself undisturbed by the meddlesomeness of man. One ought not
to go to cadavers to study life. Moreover, a repetition of the experiment is impossible, for the simple reason that the original situation cannot be recon-
structed. Therefore in each instance there is only a first and single answer.

To return to the hexagram itself. There is nothing strange in the fact that all
of Ting, THE CALDRON, amplifies the themes announced by the two salient
lines. The first line of the hexagram says:

A *ting* with legs upturned.
Furthers removal of stagnating stuff.
One takes a concubine for the sake of her son.
No blame.

A *ting* that is turned upside down is not in use. Hence the *I Ching* is like an
unused caldron. Turning it over serves to remove stagnating matter, as the line
says. Just as a man takes a concubine when his wife has no son, so the *I Ching* is
called upon when one sees no other way out. Despite the quasi-legal status of the
concubine in China, she is in reality only a somewhat awkward makeshift; so
likewise the magic procedure of the oracle is an expedient that may be utilized
for a higher purpose. There is no blame, although it is an exceptional recourse.
The second and third lines have already been discussed. The fourth line says:

The legs of the *ting* are broken.
The prince's meal is spilled
And his person is soiled.
Misfortune.

Here the *ting* has been put to use, but evidently in a very clumsy manner, that
is, the oracle has been abused or misinterpreted. In this way the divine food is
lost, and one puts oneself to shame. Legge translates as follows: "Its subject will
be made to blush for shame." Abuse of a cult utensil such as the *ting* (i.e., the *I*

Ching) is a gross profanation. The *I Ching* is evidently insisting here on its dignity as a ritual vessel and protesting against being profanely used.

The fifth line says:

> The *ting* has yellow handles, golden carrying rings.
> Perseverance furthers.

The *I Ching* has, it seems, met with a new, correct (yellow) understanding, that is, a new concept (*Begriff*) by which it can be grasped. This concept is valuable (golden). There is indeed a new edition in English, making the book more accessible to the Western world than before.

The sixth line says:

> The *ting* has rings of jade.
> Great good fortune.
> Nothing that would not act to further.

Jade is distinguished for its beauty and soft sheen. If the carrying rings are of jade, the whole vessel is enhanced in beauty, honor, and value. The *I Ching* expresses itself here as being not only well satisfied but indeed very optimistic. One can only await further events and in the meantime remain content with the pleasant conclusion that the *I Ching* approves of the new edition.

I have shown in this example as objectively as I can how the oracle proceeds in a given case. Of course the procedure varies somewhat according to the way the question is put. If for instance a person finds himself in a confusing situation, he may himself appear in the oracle as the speaker. Or, if the question concerns a relationship with another person, that person may appear as the speaker.

·   ·   ·

To come back once more to our hexagram. Though the *I Ching* not only seems to be satisfied with its new edition, but even expresses emphatic optimism, this still does not foretell anything about the effect it will have on the public it is intended to reach. Since we have in our hexagram two yang lines stressed by the numerical value nine, we are in a position to find out what sort of prognosis the *I Ching* makes for itself. Lines designated by a six or a nine have, according to the ancient conception, an inner tension so great as to cause them to change into their opposites, that is, yang into yin, and vice versa. Through this change we obtain in the present instance hexagram 35, Chin, PROGRESS.

The subject of this hexagram is someone who meets with all sorts of vicissitudes of fortune in his climb upward, and the text describes how he should behave. The *I Ching* is in this same situation: it rises like the sun and declares itself, but it is rebuffed and finds no confidence—it is "progressing, but in sorrow." However, "one obtains great happiness from one's ancestress." Psychology can help us to elucidate this obscure passage. In dreams and fairy tales the grandmother, or ancestress, often represents the unconscious, because the latter in a man contains the feminine component of the psyche. If the *I Ching* is not accepted by the conscious, at least the unconscious meets it halfway, and the *I*

Ching is more closely connected with the unconscious than with the rational attitude of consciousness. Since the unconscious is often represented in dreams by a feminine figure, this may be the explanation here. The feminine person might be the translator, who has given the book her maternal care, and this might easily appear to the *I Ching* as a "great happiness." It anticipates general understanding, but is afraid of misuse—"Progress like a hamster." But it is mindful of the admonition, "Take not gain and loss to heart." It remains free of "partisan motives." It does not thrust itself on anyone.

The *I Ching* therefore faces its future on the American book market calmly and expresses itself here just about as any reasonable person would in regard to the fate of so controversial a work. This prediction is so very reasonable and full of common sense that it would be hard to think of a more fitting answer.

The *I Ching* insists upon self-knowledge throughout. The method by which this is to be achieved is open to every kind of misuse, and is therefore not for the frivolous-minded and immature; nor is it for intellectualists and rationalists. It is appropriate only for thoughtful and reflective people who like to think about what they do and what happens to them—a predilection not to be confused with the morbid brooding of the hypochondriac. As I have indicated above, I have no answer to the multitude of problems that arise when we seek to harmonize the oracle of the *I Ching* with our accepted scientific canons. But needless to say, nothing "occult" is to be inferred. My position in these matters is pragmatic, and the great disciplines that have taught me the practical usefulness of this viewpoint are psychotherapy and medical psychology. . . .
The irrational fullness of life has taught me never to discard anything, even when it goes against all our theories (so short-lived at best) or otherwise admits of no immediate explanation. It is of course disquieting, and one is not certain whether the compass is pointing true or not; but security, certitude, and peace do not lead to discoveries. It is the same with this Chinese mode of divination. Clearly the method aims at self-knowledge, though at all times it has also been put to superstitious use.

I of course am thoroughly convinced of the value of self-knowledge, but is there any use in recommending such insight, when the wisest of men throughout the ages have preached the need of it without success? Even to the most biased eye it is obvious that this book represents one long admonition to careful scrutiny of one's own character, attitude, and motives. This attitude appeals to me and has induced me to undertake the foreword. Only once before have I expressed myself in regard to the problem of the *I Ching:* this was in a memorial address in tribute to Richard Wilhelm. For the rest I have maintained a discreet silence. It is by no means easy to feel one's way into such a remote and mysterious mentality as that underlying the *I Ching*. One cannot easily disregard such great minds as Confucius and Laotse, if one is at all able to appreciate the quality of the thoughts they represent; much less can one overlook the fact that the *I Ching* was their main source of inspiration. I know that previously I would not have dared to express myself so explicitly about so uncertain a matter. I can take this risk because I am now in my eighth decade, and the changing opinions of men scarcely impress me any more; the thoughts of the old masters are of greater value to me than the philosophical prejudices of the Western mind.

I do not like to burden my reader with these personal considerations; but, as already indicated, one's own personality is very often implicated in the answer of the oracle. Indeed, in formulating my question I even invited the oracle to comment directly on my action. The answer was hexagram 29, K'an, THE ABYSMAL. Special emphasis is given to the third place by the fact that the line is designated by a six. This line says:

> Forward and backward, abyss on abyss.
> In danger like this, pause at first and wait,
> Otherwise you will fall into a pit in the abyss.
> Do not act in this way.

Formerly I would have accepted unconditionally the advice, "Do not act in this way," and would have refused to give my opinion of the *I Ching*, for the sole reason that I had none. But now the counsel may serve as an example of the way in which the *I Ching* functions. It is a fact that if one begins to think about it, the problems of the *I Ching* do represent "abyss on abyss," and unavoidably one must "pause at first and wait" in the midst of the dangers of limitless and uncritical speculation; otherwise one really will lose his way in the darkness. Could there be a more uncomfortable position intellectually than that of floating in the thin air of unproved possibilities, not knowing whether what one sees is truth or illusion? This is the dreamlike atmosphere of the *I Ching*, and in it one has nothing to rely upon except one's own so fallible subjective judgment. I cannot but admit that this line represents very appropriately the feelings with which I wrote the foregoing passages. Equally fitting is the comforting beginning of this hexagram—"If you are sincere, you have success in your heart"—for it indicates that the decisive thing here is not the outer danger but the subjective condition, that is, whether one believes oneself to be "sincere" or not.

The hexagram compares the dynamic action in this situation to the behavior of flowing water, which is not afraid of any dangerous place but plunges over cliffs and fills up the pits that lie in its course (K'an also stands for water). This is the way in which the "superior man" acts and "carries on the business of teaching."

K'an is definitely one of the less agreeable hexagrams. It describes a situation in which the subject seems in grave danger of being caught in all sorts of pitfalls. Just as in interpreting a dream one must follow the dream text with utmost exactitude, so in consulting the oracle one must hold in mind the form of the question put, for this sets a definite limit to the interpretation of the answer. The first line of the hexagram notes the presence of the danger: "In the abyss one falls into a pit." The second line does the same, then adds the counsel: "One should strive to attain small things only." I apparently anticipated this advice by limiting myself in this foreword to a demonstration of how the *I Ching* functions in the Chinese mind, and by renouncing the more ambitious project of writing a psychological commentary on the whole book.

The fourth line says:

A jug of wine, a bowl of rice with it;
Earthen vessels
Simply handed in through the window.
There is certainly no blame in this.

Wilhelm makes the following comment here:

Although as a rule it is customary for an official to present certain introductory gifts and recommendations before he is appointed, here everything is simplified to the utmost. The gifts are insignificant, there is no one to sponsor him, he introduces himself; yet all this need not be humiliating if only there is the honest intention of mutual help in danger.

It looks as if the book were to some degree the subject of this line.

The fifth line continues the theme of limitation. If one studies the nature of water, one sees that it fills a pit only to the rim and then flows on. It does not stay caught there:

The abyss is not filled to overflowing,
It is filled only to the rim.

But if, tempted by the danger, and just because of the uncertainty, one were to insist on forcing conviction by special efforts, such as elaborate commentaries and the like, one would only be mired in the difficulty, which the top line describes very accurately as a tied-up and caged-in condition. Indeed, the last line often shows the consequences that result when one does not take the meaning of the hexagram to heart.

In our hexagram we have a six in the third place. This yin line of mounting tension changes into a yang line and thus produces a new hexagram showing a new possibility or tendency. We now have hexagram 48, Ching, THE WELL. The water hole no longer means danger, however, but rather something beneficial, a well:

Thus the superior man encourages the people at
    their work,
And exhorts them to help one another.

The image of people helping one another would seem to refer to the reconstruction of the well, for it is broken down and full of mud. Not even animals drink from it. There are fishes living in it, and one can shoot these, but the well is not used for drinking, that is, for human needs. This description is reminiscent of the overturned and unused *ting* that is to receive a new handle. Moreover, this well, like the *ting,* is cleaned. But no one drinks from it:

This is my heart's sorrow,
For one might draw from it.

The dangerous water hole or abyss pointed to the *I Ching,* and so does the well, but the latter has a positive meaning: it contains the waters of life. It should be restored to use. But one has no concept (*Begriff*) of it, no utensil with which to carry the water; the jug is broken and leaks. The *ting* needs new handles and carrying rings by which to grasp it, and so also the well must be newly lined, for it contains "a clear, cold spring from which one can drink." One may draw water from it, because "it is dependable."

It is clear that in this prognosis the speaking subject is again the *I Ching,* representing itself as a spring of living water. The preceding hexagram described in detail the danger confronting the person who accidentally falls into the pit within the abyss. He must work his way out of it, in order to discover that it is an old, ruined well, buried in mud, but capable of being restored to use again.

I submitted two questions to the method of chance represented by the coin oracle, the second question being put after I had written my analysis of the answer to the first. The first question was directed, as it were, to the *I Ching:* what had it to say about my intention to write a foreword? The second question concerned my own action, or rather the situation in which I was the acting subject who had discussed the first hexagram. To the first question the *I Ching* replied by comparing itself to a caldron, a ritual vessel in need of renovation, a vessel that was finding only doubtful favor with the public. To the second question the reply was that I had fallen into a difficulty, for the *I Ching* represented a deep and dangerous water hole in which one might easily be mired. However, the water hole proved to be an old well that needed only to be renovated in order to be put to useful purposes once more.

These four hexagrams are in the main consistent as regards theme (vessel, pit, well); and as regards intellectual content, they seem to be meaningful. Had a human being made such replies, I should, as a psychiatrist, have had to pronounce him of sound mind, at least on the basis of the material presented. Indeed, I should not have been able to discover anything delirious, idiotic, or schizophrenic in the four answers. In view of the *I Ching's* extreme age and its Chinese origin, I cannot consider its archaic, symbolic, and flowery language abnormal. On the contrary, I should have had to congratulate this hypothetical person on the extent of his insight into my unexpressed state of doubt. On the other hand, any person of clever and versatile mind can turn the whole thing around and show how I have projected my subjective contents into the symbolism of the hexagrams. Such a critique, though catastrophic from the standpoint of Western rationality, does no harm to the function of the *I Ching.* On the contrary, the Chinese sage would smilingly tell me: "Don't you see how useful the *I Ching* is in making you project your hitherto unrealized thoughts into its abstruse symbolism? You could have written your foreword without ever realizing what an avalanche of misunderstanding might be released by it."

The Chinese standpoint does not concern itself as to the attitude one takes toward the performance of the oracle. It is only we who are puzzled, because we trip time and again over our prejudice, viz., the notion of causality. The ancient wisdom of the East lays stress upon the fact that the intelligent individual realizes his own thoughts, but not in the least upon the way in which he does it. The less one thinks about the theory of the *I Ching,* the more soundly one sleeps.

It would seem to me that on the basis of this example an unprejudiced reader would now be in a position to form at least a tentative judgment on the operation of the *I Ching.* More cannot be expected from a simple introduction. If by means of this demonstration I have succeeded in elucidating the psychological phenomenology of the *I Ching,* I shall have carried out my purpose. As to the thousands of questions, doubts, and criticisms that this singular book stirs up—I cannot answer these. The *I Ching* does not offer itself with proofs and results; it does not vaunt itself, nor is it easy to approach. Like a part of nature, it waits until it is discovered. It offers neither facts nor power, but for lovers of self-knowledge, of wisdom—if there be such—it seems to be the right book. To one person its spirit appears as clear as day; to another, shadowy as twilight; to a third, dark as night. He who is not pleased by it does not have to use it, and he who is against it is not obliged to find it true. Let it go forth into the world for the benefit of those who can discern its meaning.

the beauty of the lord _____

The voice of my beloved!
    Behold, he comes,
leaping upon the mountains,
    bounding over the hills.
My beloved is like a gazelle,
    or a young stag.
Behold, there he stands
    behind our wall,
gazing in at the windows,
looking through the lattice.
My beloved speaks and says to me:
"Arise, my love, my fair one,
    and come away;
for lo, the winter is past.
    the rain is over and gone.
The flowers appear on the earth,
    the time of singing has come,
and the voice of the turtledove
    is heard in our land.

_____

Song of Solomon 2:8–17, RSV.

The fig tree puts forth its figs,
    and the vines are in blossom;
    they give forth fragrance.
Arise, my love, my fair one,
    and come away.
O my dove, in the clefts of the rock,
    in the covert of the cliff,
let me see your face,
    let me hear your voice,
for your voice is sweet,
    and your face is comely.
Catch us the foxes,
    the little foxes,
that spoil the vineyards,
    for our vineyards are in blossom."

My beloved is mine and I am his,
    he pastures his flock among the
        lilies.
Until the day breathes
    and the shadows flee,
turn, my beloved, be like a gazelle,
    or a young stag upon rugged
        mountains.

ST. JOHN OF THE CROSS

upon an obscure night

    Upon an obscure night
    Fevered with Love's anxiety
    (O hapless, happy plight!)
    I went, none seeing me,
Forth from my house, where all things quiet be.

    By night, secure from sight
    And by a secret stair, disguisedly,
    (O hapless, happy plight!)
    By night, and privily
Forth from my house, where all things quiet be.

Translation by John Addington Symonds to be found in vol. ii of his *Collected Poems*.

Blest night of wandering
In secret, when by none might I be spied,
Nor I see anything;
Without a light to guide
Save that which in my heart burnt in my side.

That light did lead me on,
More surely than the shining of noontide
Where well I knew that One
Did for my coming bide;
Where He abode might none but He abide.

O night that didst lead thus,
O night more lovely than the dawn of light;
O night that broughtest us,
Lover to lover's sight,
Lover to loved, in marriage of delight!

Upon my flowery breast
Wholly for Him and save Himself for none,
There did I give sweet rest
To my beloved one:
The fanning of the cedars breathed thereon.

VERNON KATZ

transcendental meditation _____

some basic insights of the present revival

In this article I want to review in very broad terms just a few of those simple,
luminous insights which constitute Maharishi Mahesh Yogi's revival of what he
calls "the understanding about life." One could be forgiven for thinking that
everything worth saying on this subject had been said, and that a long time ago.
But Maharishi has succeeded in making green once again a very parched field
where it seemed no new grass would ever grow again. He himself insists that his
reversal of accepted ideas about the life of the spirit is a revival and not a revolution, and he has made a good case for this view in his commentary on the *Bhagavad-Gita*.[1] But in the context of current understanding his is a completely
fresh vision. . . .

Maharishi's insights are all simple, even obvious, once one has seen their
point, but somehow they have been overlooked in recent times. When "the understanding about life" is lost[2] life itself deteriorates; when it is revived, life too

___

From *Creative Intelligence*, Number 1, n.d.

revives. I hold that it is his clear discernment of principle which has enabled
Maharishi to formulate such an effective practical method of realization or, as he
would say, of enjoying the fullness of life. For this reason I would like to center
my examination of Maharishi's thought around a short and by no means complete definition of transcendental meditation. . . . My definition runs as follows:

> Transcendental meditation is a simple, natural process which involves the
> progressive refinement of the nervous system through the regular alternation
> of deep rest and activity.

a simple, natural process

Maharishi looks around him and finds that everything in the universe is trying to
move towards more fulfillment. One aspect of this general principle is the natural tendency of the mind—the attention, if you like, though I shall use the
broader, common-sense term "mind" here—to move in the direction of greater
satisfaction. Maharishi sees this as a kind of code written into the very nature of
the mind by the force of evolution. It is often observed by writers on matters
spiritual that the mind is like a monkey jumping aimlessly from branch to
branch, never for a moment still. Maharishi likes to compare it with a honey bee
which certainly moves from flower to flower but does so for the sake of the nectar. The mind's nature is to enjoy and wandering is a means towards that end.

Now juxtapose this fact of everyday experience with the age-old Indian
knowledge—also expressed in other traditions in such terms as "the kingdom of
heaven within you"—that fulfillment lies in one's inmost nature, one's Self,
which is all bliss, and you arrive at the obvious, but apparently novel, conclusion
that the inward march of the mind is a perfectly natural, simple, effortless process for it is in the direction of bliss. This is just what Maharishi has concluded
and he has proved his point in practical terms to those many thousands who
practice his method of transcendental meditation. Briefly, this technique involves a specially chosen word, or *mantra,* which is used for its sound value only,
in a way which is just sufficient to keep the attention lively but, because the
mind is not burdened with any meaning, is insufficient to deflect it from its natural flow in the direction of greater satisfaction. Quite automatically, without
any doing, the mantra becomes increasingly refined—in the sense that a whisper
is more refined than a shout—for the finer its state the less will it overshadow the
bliss of the Self. If the process continues to its conclusion the mantra refines
itself out of existence—is transcended—and the mind, not having gone to sleep,
rests in a state of inner wakefulness. This state of transcendental consciousness,
or pure awareness without any object of awareness, is equated with Self-realization, in that all things extraneous to the knower, all percepts, all thoughts, have
disappeared, while only knowingness, or inner wakefulness, remains. It is not a
state of doing, or of thinking, but a state of just being—blissful, completely fulfilled in itself. The mind remains in its own nature, the experiencer finds himself.
So long as images are projected on to a white screen they hide the nature of the

screen; when the images have disappeared the whiteness of the screen becomes apparent.

The important point about the whole process is its completely automatic nature, each more concrete, or gross, state of the mantra withdrawing itself in favor of a more refined, or blissful, one. Maharishi likens it to diving—one takes a correct angle and lets go. The force of gravity (evolution) does the rest. The consequences of this teaching are very far-reaching, and I shall examine just a few of them here.

The whole field of spiritual practice has been bedeviled by the idea that meditation is only for those who are naturally introspective or devotional, for those who have no interest in things of the world, for those who can "sit still"; it is not for ordinary, worldly, pleasure-loving, successful people. The field of the Unconditioned has been hedged about with all kinds of conditions. Maharishi throws the life of the spirit wide open. Transcendental meditation is not something which goes against the grain of the mind; it is completely natural. It is also of universal application, that is, completely independent of the quirks of personality or the variations of psychological type, in that both the natural tendency of the mind to move towards more satisfaction and its inner blissful nature are universally given. No special abilities are required and there are no preconditions. It is certainly not necessary to be able to sit still, because there is no restlessness when the mind is on the path to greater bliss. Nor is it necessary to have given up desires, for the very impulse which makes the mind move from object to object in search for fulfillment in the world is also the motive force in transcendental meditation.

This line of reasoning leads to an important conclusion about accepted techniques of mind control. When one applies effort to achieve something which the force of evolution is trying to bring about naturally the result can only be counter-productive. These techniques are based on the mistaken idea that because transcendental consciousness is a state without thoughts the mind has to be stilled by force, whereas it is only possible to lead the mind to a state of wakeful no-thought by allowing it to experience gradually more and more refined and blissful states of thought. Techniques of concentration which involve stilling the mind or keeping it on one point are hindrances or at best roundabout ways to Self-realization, just because they restrict the movement of the mind towards bliss. They succeed only when they fail; that is, when the mind, tired of the straitjackets which they impose, frees itself to follow its natural path.

• • •

which involves the progressive refinement of the nervous system

What Krishnamurti and most other teachers fail to take into account is the physiological substructure of realization. In Krishnamurti's case this may possibly be because he is one of those rare souls born with a very pure, or "refined," nervous system who was suddenly "there," he knew not how. Such people tend to think

that Self-realization demands a complete mental turnabout, a sudden change
from doing to being. But for the man whose nervous system has not been refined
so as to be capable of sustaining transcendental consciousness, any such attempt
to reverse his usual way of existing will only be a mental construct—it will have
no basis in reality. "Any state of consciousness is the expression of a corresponding state of the nervous system. Transcendental consciousness corresponds to a
certain specific state of the nervous system which transcends any activity and is
therefore completely different from the state of consciousness which corresponds to the waking state of consciousness."

Maharishi shows in great detail and with great clarity how the practice of
transcendental meditation provides a physical basis for realization. I can only
touch upon a few points here. The amount of oxygen intake depends upon the
degree of our activity; when a man is taking a stroll he consumes less oxygen
than when he is running, and when he is sitting and thinking about some problem he consumes less than when he is walking. Similarly, for the very refined
mental activity involved in transcendental meditation less oxygen is required than
for the kind of thinking which is on the level of meaning. Remarkable experiments have shown that both rate and volume of breathing are greatly reduced
during transcendental meditation. The decrease in metabolic rate is found to be
greater than that which occurs in deep sleep. A number of other co-related physiological changes during transcendental meditation have also been measured, all
of them indicative of a state of deep rest and relaxation.

· · ·

No amount of mental gymnastics can bring about the physiological changes
necessary to sustain transcendental consciousness because no techniques which
function on the level of meaning can give the system the deep rest which is required. This applies not only to teachings designed to bring about a sudden and
complete reversal of mental attitudes, but also to those which require prolonged
contemplation of a particular idea. These latter, if Indian-derived, may ask the
aspirant to dwell on such ideas as "I am Brahman," "all this is *maya*" (lit., that
which is not), "I am not a doer," "I am a witness only," "there is no permanent
self, only an aggregate of changing elements" (Buddhist). The ideas in themselves
may be valid and profound, but without a fundamental modification of the nervous system—which they are powerless to bring about—the practices based on
such ideas must remain on the level of moods of the mind, pleasant or unpleasant according to whether one likes or does not like the ideas in question.

· · ·

The case is rather different with physical practices working directly on the
nervous system—the techniques of *hatha yoga*. These obviously do effect physiological changes rather than mere changes of mood and simple hatha yoga exercises form a useful adjunct to the practice of transcendental meditation. However, apart from not producing certain beneficial effects which a suitable mantra,
properly used, will bring in its wake—a point into which I will not enter here—
hatha yoga takes a longer time to be effective and, in its advanced stages, is diffi-

cult, and dangerous to body and mind without the constant supervision of a qualified teacher. The great point about transcendental meditation is its "innocence," in that none of the changes which it effects are in any way sought or willed; they are no more than the automatic byproducts of the experience of refined states of the mantra and of transcendental consciousness. It is for this reason that I used the word "involves" in my definition of transcendental meditation.

· · ·

through the regular alternation of deep rest and activity

Although the physiological effects of transcendental meditation are immediate it will obviously take time to effect that degree of purification, or refinement of the nervous system, which will enable it to sustain the state of transcendental consciousness at all times. Unless this is sustained outside as well as during meditation realization cannot be complete. The pearl is of little value when enjoyed at the bottom of the ocean. The aim must be to liberate the Self from being as it were imprisoned in the depths of meditation and bring it out to be lived in daily life. One can then live what Maharishi calls 200 percent of life. The experiences of life will continue to be enjoyed, but they will no longer be able to hide, or overshadow, one's true nature.

The state where transcendental consciousness is maintained at all times, in waking, dreaming or deep sleep, Maharishi calls "cosmic consciousness." On the level of the nervous system this state requires a seemingly impossible combination of rest and activity, and in order to establish how this comes about it is necessary to examine the process of meditation in more detail.

We have seen that it is the nature of the mind to go to a field of greater satisfaction, but if it is offered a free path to the state of greatest satisfaction why does it not stay there all the time? The answer is quite simple—after a certain point the body calls it back. Not having been accustomed to more refined levels of functioning the body can only sustain the refinement of the breath and the other physiological changes which accompany meditation to a certain extent and for a certain time. Whatever the depth and duration of the "dive"—and these depend basically on the amount of "strain" which the nervous system has accumulated in the past—at a certain point the diver has to surface. Transcendental meditation consists of these inward and outward strokes of lesser and greater activity. The profound rest given by the inward stroke dissolves areas of tension which were preventing the nervous system from functioning on a finer level. This release manifests as the outward stroke during which the nervous system becomes more active again. The outward stroke serves in turn as the basis for another dive within—probably from a slightly "lower" platform than before.

· · ·

In relation to life as a whole, meditation morning and evening is the inward stroke and activity during the day the outward. It is the balanced alternation of meditation and activity which results in the refinement of the nervous system necessary to sustain cosmic consciousness.

In his commentary on the *Bhagavad-Gita,* Maharishi explains how the seemingly impossible becomes possible; "how, in the state of cosmic consciousness . . . the eternal silence of transcendental Self-consciousness becomes compatible with the incessant activity of the waking state of consciousness." For this "it is necessary that the two states of the nervous system corresponding to these two states of consciousness should co-exist. This is brought about by the mind gaining alternately transcendental consciousness and the waking state of consciousness, passing from one to the other. This gradual and systematic culture of the physical nervous system creates a physiological situation in which the two states of consciousness exist together simultaneously. It is well known that there exist in the nervous system many autonomous levels of function, between which a system of coordination also exists. In the state of cosmic consciousness, two different levels of organization in the nervous system function simultaneously while maintaining their separate identities. By virtue of this anatomical separation of function, it becomes possible for transcendental consciousness to co-exist with the waking state of consciousness and with the dreaming and sleeping states of consciousness.

"In the early stages of the practice of transcendental meditation, these two levels of function in the nervous system are unable to occur at the same time; the function of the one inhibits the function of the other. That is why, at this stage, either transcendental consciousness or the waking state of consciousness is experienced. The practice of the mind in passing from one to another gradually overcomes this physiological inhibition, and the two levels begin to function perfectly at the same time, without inhibiting each other and still maintaining their separate identities. The function of each is independent of the other, and that is why this state of the nervous system corresponds to cosmic consciousness, in which Self-awareness exists as separate from activity. Silence is experienced along with activity and yet as separate from it."

The consequences of this analysis are again very far-reaching. Maharishi is unique in showing that it is not the *quality* of thought or action during the outward stroke of meditation which stabilizes realization; it is the mere fact of alternating greater with lesser activity. The state of pure awareness must be exposed to the fire of action if it is to be made fast. His idea of *karma yoga,* or the yoga of action, is therefore completely different from that extant today, which sees the quality of thought during activity as all-important. One is asked to act with equanimity, with detachment, without wishing the fruit of the action for oneself, trying to be completely without desire. Or one may act, thinking the thoughts about not being a doer and about pure, inactive witness-consciousness mentioned above, adding perhaps for good measure from the *Bhagavad-Gita* that "it is the gunas (strands of nature) which act upon the gunas." Such thoughts will again in no way alter the reality of an unpurified nervous system. However, it is one thing to occupy oneself with them in the privacy of one's chamber and quite another to carry them over into one's daily activities. They divide the attention which should be fully upon what one is doing, and therefore make action weak and ineffective. Maharishi holds such practices as largely responsible for the disrepute into which "spiritual life" has fallen among active and successful people who, seeing those who lead such a life becoming unpractical and unsuccessful have no intention of following suit. In so far as they succeed in interposing an artificial idea of the self between perceiver and object of perception these practices may even interfere with the proper coordination of mind and body, as well as stripping life of all the joys of immediate and innocent perception. Maharishi discourages any such "mood-making" among meditators. To those who want to carry over the experiences of meditation into daily life by dwelling on them, he says that thinking about something is not the same as being it. He compares meditation to taking a bath. One takes it and forgets about it— one does not spend the day wondering whether one is clean.

• • •

It is really rather strange that this connection between deep rest and effective action should have been ignored in teachings about the yoga of action. It is, after all, an everyday experience that even after resting deeply in the night one's activity during the day improves. . . . It was not until Maharishi showed the state of Being to be concomitant with the deepest form of physical rest that spiritual awareness could be recognized as something that would support outer activity rather than oppose it.

Here one may object that not every action is worthy of support because not every action springs from a worthy motive. But Maharishi points out that the best way to make one's desires, and therefore one's actions, more life-supporting is through a change in one's level of awareness of the kind effected through the deep rest which transcendental meditation provides. Based as it is on a real modification of the nervous system such a change will transform one's desires in a natural way, while merely trying to change them by emulating the realized man will have little practical effect. When one has not gained the means to live on the level to which one aspires, one has sooner or later to revert to one's former indigence. Maharishi is always concerned to emphasize the right order of priorities: seek ye first the kingdom of heaven. . . .

With characteristic clarity Maharishi has determined the basic reason for the misleading ideas and practices outlined above. "The state of Reality, as described by the enlightened, cannot become a path for the seeker, any more than the description of a destination can replace the road that leads to it. When the understanding of the basic principles of realization is lost the effect is mistaken for the cause, and the path to realization is no longer found. People come to regard what are essentially attributes of realization as the means of gaining it. They read in the *Bhagavad-Gita* of the realized man as 'having abandoned attachment and having become balanced in success and failure' and feel that they must follow his example at all costs." They do not realize that you cannot detach yourself from things but that things will detach themselves from you once you are established in your own Self—in the sense that Self-realization excludes from the domain of Self all that is not Self. They do not see that balance in success and failure is the result of inner contentment rather than a means to it. Similarly, when the realized man is said to be without any selfish desires, this is not the result of practicing desirelessness but the consequence of the complete fulfillment found in the state of realization. "What shall we do with offspring," ask the sages of old, "we who have this Self, this world?" By the same token, the sense of not being an agent, witness-consciousness, maya and so on are explanations of the experience of the realized man; they describe a state that is already established. For the unrealized man to dwell contemplatively on these ideas will not give him even a pale imitation of the reality on which they are based. How can maya, or that which is not, be understood except on the basis of the experience of that which is?

My aim has been to show that Maharishi's clear grasp of principle and consequent insight into the mechanics of spiritual life has enabled him to strip the way to realization of everything that is not intrinsic to it and so to formulate a method unique in its directness, simplicity and effectiveness. I do not exclude the possibility of other, more roundabout ways, but these can be effective only in so far as they contain the elements which make transcendental meditation effective—they must be able to lead man from the gross, or surface, levels of the mind, through more refined levels until the finest is transcended, and then they must find ways of making transcendental consciousness a permanent reality.

NOTES AND REFERENCES
1. Maharishi Mahesh Yogi, *On the Bhagavad-Gita,* Baltimore: Penguin, 1969, commentary on IV, 38.
2. In a concluding passage the author points out that "cosmic consciousness is only a halfway house to complete fulfillment."

PART 5
religious experience

This section is reserved chiefly for testimonies of a wide variety of religious experiences. Donne's poem that heads the section sprang from his own practice of the disciplined meditation that was the fruit of the Catholic Counter-Reformation. Pascal, also the offspring of that reformation, recorded his own ecstatic experience on a small scrap of paper and carried it about for the rest of his life. It represents something immediate that happened to him, not something that he was told about or reasoned himself into.

Similarly Swami Nikhilananda has recorded the experiences of his Master, Sri Ramakrishna, who was in himself a veritable laboratory of religious experiences. The Eastern mystical tradition has been well represented in other parts of the text, so we have here let Ramakrishna speak for that tradition. We have included for comparison some testimonies of Western mystics like Juliana of Norwich and Evelyn Underhill.

Biblical experiences are included since today we may not assume familiarity with them. Contemporary biblical type experiences are to be found in Hammarskjöld's journal *Markings* and Rabbi Abraham Heschel's essay on "Prayer." Other biblical material from earlier sections will expand these examples.

Abraham Maslow's essay is interesting because he insists that mystical experiences can be, and, in fact, are very common. His exploration of what he calls "peak experiences" or religious illumination represents a psychologist's approach to a difficult research topic.

We cannot claim to have made a complete survey of such a protean topic as religious experience, but the selections are representative of a wide range and should give ample substance for reflection. We have included not only the drug-induced experiences of John Addington Symonds but also an instance of his more natural and spontaneous experience. Whether these experiences are really the same as those of the great mystics who labored for years in the practice of meditation and contemplation is an unsettled question.

The final essay by Mahatma Gandhi, "Through Love to God," reminds us of an old theme. If we are not inclined to mystical practices, he assures us that love of this universal order will in itself bring us to what is ultimately real. And, after all, the greatest saints and mystics have all insisted that compassion is the best test of genuine religious experience.

batter my heart, three person'd god

Batter my heart, three person'd God; for, you
As yet but knocke, breathe, shine, and seeke to mend;
That I may rise, and stand, o'erthrow mee, and bend
Your force, to breake, blowe, burn and make me new.
I, like an usurpt towne, to another due,
Labour to admit you, but Oh, to no end,
Reason your viceroy in mee, mee should defend,
But is captiv'd, and proves weake or untrue.
Yet dearely I love you, and would be loved faine,
But am betroth'd unto your enemie:
Divorce mee, untie, or breake that knot againe,
Take mee to you, imprison mee, for I
Except you enthrall mee, never shall be free,
Nor ever chast[e], except you ravish mee.

pascal's memorial

Whatever the influences leading up to it may be, we can date the turning point in
Pascal's life precisely, for he wrote a record of it which he kept sewn inside his
jacket and which was discovered only after his death. Actually two papers were
found: one an ordinary sheet which may contain the notes he wrote down immediately after his mystical experience. The second was a copy on parchment
including a few additional lines. At the top of the paper stands a cross, and then
follows:

> The year of grace 1654,
> Monday, 23 November, day of Saint Clement, pope and martyr, and of
> others in the martyrology.
> Eve of Saint Chrysogonus, martyr, and others,
> From about half past ten in the evening until about half past twelve,
> .... FIRE ....
> God of Abraham, God of Isaac, God of Jacob, not of the philosophers and
> scholars.

From *Existentialism and Religious Belief* by David E. Roberts. New York, copyright © 1957
by Oxford University Press, Inc. Reprinted by permission.

Certitude, certitude, feeling, joy, peace.
God of Jesus Christ.
Deum meum et Deum vestrum.
Thy God will be my God.
Forgetfulness of the world and of everything, except GOD.
He is to be found only by the ways taught in the Gospel. *Greatness* of the human soul.
O righteous Father, the world hath not known thee, but I have known thee.
Joy, joy, joy, tears of joy.
I have been separated from him.
Dereliquerunt me fontem aquae vivae.
My God, wilt thou forsake me?
Let me not be separated from him eternally.
This is the eternal life, that they know thee as the only true God, and the one whom thou has sent, Jesus Christ.
Jesus Christ,
Jesus Christ.
I have been separated from him; I have fled him, renounced him, crucified him,
Let me never be separated from him.
He is preserved only by the ways taught in the Gospel.
Renunciation, total and sweet.
[The parchment adds:]
Total submission to Jesus Christ and to my director.
Eternally in joy for a day's trial on earth.
Non obliviscar sermones tuos. Amen.

We know from a letter of Jacqueline to Gilberte that in the period immediately preceding this event Pascal had been living in solitude and in a condition of spiritual emptiness. He had already been seized by "a great scorn of the world and an unbearable disgust for all the people who are in it"; he had been rereading volumes already familiar to him by Montaigne and Epictetus, but had found no solace in the skepticism of the one or the stoicism of the other; he felt remote from God and could not overcome the feeling, no matter how sincerely he tried.

The association of the Memorial with the third chapter of Exodus is unmistakable, although of course we cannot recapture precisely what the experience meant to Pascal at the time. It is the God of the burning bush, I AM THAT I AM, Who reveals Himself with the promise to lead him out of bondage. Here, in direct encounter, Pascal experiences the difference between reason and the heart. The efforts of his own mind to solve the problem of human existence have left him in a bondage like that of the children of Israel in Egypt. The pathway of philosophy and science has led to a dead end, and the pathway of worldly ambition has brought only misery. But now, through no effort of his own, certainty and joy are given to him. Henceforth Pascal will never forget the misery of man when separated from God, and the grandeur of the human soul when it receives the knowledge and forgiveness of God. It is in Jesus Christ that he finds assurance. God did not forsake Pascal even though he had forsaken God. By a total renunciation of the world and of self, he now finds release from misery and comes to know the joy of certitude.

SWAMI NIKHILANANDA

the experiences
of sri ramakrishna

the first vision of kāli

And, indeed, he soon discovered what a strange Goddess he had chosen to serve. He became gradually enmeshed in the web of Her all-prevading presence. To the ignorant She is, to be sure, the image of destruction; but he found in Her the benign, all-loving Mother. Her neck is encircled with a garland of beads and Her waist with a girdle of human arms, and two of Her hands hold weapons of death, and Her eyes dart a glance of fire; but, strangely enough, Ramakrishna felt in Her breath the soothing touch of tender love and saw in Her the Seed of Immortality. She stands on the bosom of Her Consort, Śiva; it is because She is the Śakti, the Power inseparable from the Absolute. She is surrounded by jackals and other unholy creatures, the denizens of the cremation ground. But is not the Ultimate Reality above holiness and unholiness? She appears to be reeling under the spell of wine. But who would create this mad world unless under the influence of a divine drunkenness? She is the highest symbol of all the forces of nature, the synthesis of their antinomies, the Ultimate Divine in the form of woman. She now became to Sri Ramakrishna the only Reality, and the world became an unsubstantial shadow. Into Her worship he poured his soul. Before him She stood as the transparent portal to the shrine of Ineffable Reality.

The worship in the temple intensified Sri Ramakrishna's yearning for a living vision of the Mother of the Universe. He began to spend in meditation the time not actually employed in the temple service; and for this purpose he selected an extremely solitary place. A deep jungle, thick with underbrush and prickly plants, lay to the north of the temples. Used at one time as a burial ground, it was shunned by people even during the daytime for fear of ghosts. There Sri Ramakrishna began to spend the whole night in meditation, returning to his room only in the morning with eyes swollen as though from much weeping. While meditating, he would lay aside his cloth and his brāhminical thread. Explaining this strange conduct, he once said to Hriday: "Don't you know that

From Introduction to *The Gospel of Sri Ramakrishna,* trans. and ed. Swami Nikhilananda, New York, Ramakrishna-Vivekananda Center, 1942.

when one thinks of God one should be freed from all ties? From our very birth we have the eight fetters of hatred, shame, lineage, pride of good conduct, fear, secretiveness, caste, and grief. The sacred thread reminds me that I am a brāhmin and therefore superior to all. When calling on the Mother one has to set aside all such ideas." Hriday thought his uncle was becoming insane.

As his love for God deepened, he began either to forget or to drop the formalities of worship. Sitting before the image, he would spend hours singing the devotional songs of great devotees of the Mother, such as Kamalākānta and Rāmprasād. Those rhapsodical songs, describing the direct vision of God, only intensified Sri Ramakrishna's longing. He felt the pangs of a child separated from its mother. Sometimes, in agony, he would rub his face against the ground and weep so bitterly that people, thinking he had lost his earthly mother, would sympathize with him in his grief. Sometimes, in moments of skepticism, he would cry: "Art Thou true, Mother, or is it all fiction—mere poetry without any reality? If Thou dost exist, why do I not see Thee? Is religion a mere fantasy and art Thou only a figment of man's imagination?" Sometimes he would sit on the prayer carpet for two hours like an inert object. He began to behave in an abnormal manner, most of the time unconscious of the world. He almost gave up food; and sleep left him altogether.

But he did not have to wait very long. He has thus described his first vision of the Mother: "I felt as if my heart were being squeezed like a wet towel. I was overpowered with a great restlessness and a fear that it might not be my lot to realize Her in this life. I could not bear the separation from Her any longer. Life seemed to be not worth living. Suddenly my glance fell on the sword that was kept in the Mother's temple. I determined to put an end to my life. When I jumped up like a madman and seized it, suddenly the blessed Mother revealed Herself. The buildings with their different parts, the temple, and everything else vanished from my sight, leaving no trace whatsoever, and in their stead I saw a limitless, infinite, effulgent Ocean of Consciousness. As far as the eye could see, the shining billows were madly rushing at me from all sides with a terrific noise, to swallow me up! I was panting for breath. I was caught in the rush and collapsed, unconscious. What was happening in the outside world I did not know; but within me there was a steady flow of undiluted bliss, altogether new, and I felt the presence of the Divine Mother." On his lips when he regained consciousness of the world was the word "Mother."

god-intoxicated state

Yet this was only a foretaste of the intense experiences to come. The first glimpse of the Divine Mother made him the more eager for Her uninterrupted vision. He wanted to see Her both in meditation and with eyes open. But the Mother began to play a teasing game of hide-and-seek with him, intensifying both his joy and his suffering. Weeping bitterly during the moments of separation from Her, he would pass into a trance and then find Her standing before him, smiling, talking, consoling, bidding him be of good cheer, and instructing him. During this period of spiritual practice he had many uncommon experiences. When he sat to meditate, he would hear strange clicking sounds in the joints of his legs, as if someone were locking them up, one after the other, to keep him motionless; and at the conclusion of his meditation he would again hear the same sounds, this time unlocking them and leaving him free to move about. He would see flashes like a swarm of fire-flies floating before his eyes, or a sea of deep mist around him, with luminous waves of molten silver. Again, from a sea of translucent mist he would behold the Mother rising, first Her feet, then Her waist, body, face, and head, finally Her whole person; he would feel Her breath and hear Her voice. Worshipping in the temple, sometimes he would become exalted, sometimes he would remain motionless as stone, sometimes he would almost collapse from excessive emotion. Many of his actions, contrary to all tradition, seemed sacrilegious to the people. He would take a flower and touch it to his own head, body, and feet, and then offer it to the Goddess. Or, like a drunkard, he would reel to the throne of the Mother, touch Her chin by way of showing his affection for Her, and sing, talk, joke, laugh, and dance. Or he would take a morsel of food from the plate and hold it to Her mouth, begging Her to eat it, and would not be satisfied till he was convinced that She had really eaten. After the Mother had been put to sleep at night, from his own room he would hear Her ascending to the upper story of the temple with the light steps of a happy girl, Her anklets jingling. Then he would discover Her standing with flowing hair, Her black form silhouetted against the sky of the night, looking at the Ganges or at the distant lights of Calcutta.

• • •

It is said that samādhi, or trance, no more than opens the portal of the spiritual realm. Sri Ramakrishna felt an unquenchable desire to enjoy God in various ways. For his meditation he built a place in the northern wooded section of the temple garden. With Hriday's help he planted there five sacred trees. The spot, known as the Panchavati, became the scene of many of his visions.

As his spiritual mood deepened he more and more felt himself to be a child of the Divine Mother. He learnt to surrender himself completely to Her will and let Her direct him.

"O Mother," he would constantly pray, "I have taken refuge in Thee. Teach me what to do and what to say. Thy will is paramount everywhere and is for the good of Thy children. Merge my will in Thy will and make me Thy instrument."

His visions became deeper and more intimate. He no longer had to meditate to behold the Divine Mother. Even while retaining consciousness of the outer world, he would see Her as tangibly as the temples, the trees, the river, and the men around him.

On a certain occasion Mathur Babu stealthily entered the temple to watch the worship. He was profoundly moved by the young priest's devotion and sincerity. He realized that Sri Ramakrishna had transformed the stone image into the living Goddess.

Sri Ramakrishna one day fed a cat with the food that was to be offered to

Kāli. This was too much for the manager of the temple garden, who considered himself responsible for the proper conduct of the worship. He reported Sri Ramakrishna's insane behavior to Mathur Babu.

Sri Ramakrishna has described the incident: "The Divine Mother revealed to me in the Kāli temple that it was She who had become everything. She showed me that everything was full of Consciousness. The image was Consciousness, the altar was Consciousness, the water-vessels were Consciousness, the door-sill was Consciousness, the marble floor was Consciousness—all was Consciousness. I found everything inside the room soaked, as it were, in Bliss—the Bliss of God. I saw a wicked man in front of the Kāli temple; but in him also I saw the power of the Divine Mother vibrating. That was why I fed a cat with the food that was to be offered to the Divine Mother. I clearly perceived that all this was the Divine Mother—even the cat. The manager of the temple garden wrote to Mathur Babu saying that I was feeding the cat with the offering intended for the Divine Mother. But Mathur Babu had insight into the state of my mind. He wrote back to the manager: 'Let him do whatever he likes. You must not say anything to him.' "

One of the painful ailments from which Sri Ramakrishna suffered at this time was a burning sensation in his body, and he was cured by a strange vision. During worship in the temple, following the scriptural injunctions, he would imagine the presence of the "sinner" in himself and the destruction of this "sinner." One day he was meditating in the Panchavati, when he saw come out of him a red-eyed man of black complexion, reeling like a drunkard. Soon there emerged from him another person, of serene countenance, wearing the ochre cloth of a sannyāsi and carrying in his hand a trident. The second person attacked the first and killed him with the trident. Thereafter Sri Ramakrishna was free of his pain.

About this time he began to worship God by assuming the attitude of a servant toward his master. He imitated the mood of Hanumān, the monkey chieftain of the *Rāmāyana,* the ideal servant of Rāma and traditional model for this self-effacing form of devotion. When he meditated on Hanumān his movements and his way of life began to resemble those of a monkey. His eyes became restless. He lived on fruits and roots. With his cloth tied around his waist, a portion of it hanging in the form of a tail, he jumped from place to place instead of walking. And after a short while he was blessed with a vision of Sitā, the divine consort of Rāma, who entered his body and disappeared there with the words, "I bequeath to you my smile."

. . .

Hardly had he crossed the threshold of the Kāli temple when he found himself again in the whirlwind. His madness reappeared tenfold. The same meditation and prayer, the same ecstatic moods, the same burning sensation, the same weeping, the same sleeplessness, the same indifference to the body and the outside world, the same divine delirium. He subjected himself to fresh disciplines in order to eradicate greed and lust, the two great impediments to spiritual progress. With a rupee in one hand and some earth in the other, he would reflect on the comparative value of these two for the realization of God, and finding them equally worthless he would toss them, with equal indifference, into the Ganges. Women he regarded as the manifestations of the Divine Mother. Never even in a dream did he feel the impulses of lust. And to root out of his mind the idea of caste superiority, he cleaned a pariah's house with his long and neglected hair. When he would sit in meditation, birds would perch on his head and peck in his hair for grains of food. Snakes would crawl over his body, and neither would be aware of the other. Sleep left him altogether. Day and night, visions flitted before him. He saw the sannyāsi who had previously killed the "sinner" in him again coming out of his body, threatening him with the trident, and ordering him to concentrate on God. Or the same sannyāsi would visit distant places, following a luminous path, and bring him reports of what was happening there. Sri Ramakrishna used to say later that in the case of an advanced devotee the mind itself becomes the guru, living and moving like an embodied being.

• • •

the brāhmani

There came to Dakshineswar at this time a brāhmin woman who was to play an important part in Sri Ramakrishna's spiritual unfoldment. Born in East Bengal, she was an adept in the Tāntrik and Vaishnava methods of worship. She was slightly over fifty years of age, handsome, and garbed in the orange robe of a nun. Her sole possessions were a few books and two pieces of wearing-cloth.

Sri Ramakrishna welcomed the visitor with great respect, described to her his experiences and visions, and told her of people's belief that these were symptoms of madness. She listened to him attentively and said: "My son, everyone in this world is mad. Some are mad for money, some for creature comforts, some for name and fame; and you are mad for God." She assured him that he was passing through the almost unknown spiritual experience described in the scriptures as mahābhāva, the most exalted rapture of divine love. She told him that this extreme exaltation had been described as manifesting itself through nineteen physical symptoms, including the shedding of tears, a tremor of the body, horripilation, perspiration, and a burning sensation. The Bhakti scriptures, she declared, had recorded only two instances of the experience, namely, those of Sri Rādhā and Sri Chaitanya.

Very soon a tender relationship sprang up between Sri Ramakrishna and the Brāhmani, she looking upon him as the Baby Krishna, and he upon her as mother. Day after day she watched his ecstasy during the kirtan and meditation, his samādhi, his mad yearning; and she recognized in him a power to transmit spirituality to others. She came to the conclusion that such things were not possible for an ordinary devotee, not even for a highly developed soul. Only an Incarnation of God was capable of such spiritual manifestations. She proclaimed openly that Sri Ramakrishna, like Sri Chaitanya was an Incarnation of God.

• • •

When the excitement created by the Brāhmani's declaration was over, he set himself to the task of practicing spiritual disciplines according to the traditional methods laid down in the Tantra and Vaishnava scriptures. Hitherto he had pursued his spiritual ideal according to the promptings of his own mind and heart. Now he accepted the Brāhmani as his guru and set foot on the traditional highways.

tantra

According to the Tantra, the Ultimate Reality is Chit, or Consciousness, which is identical with Sat, or Being, and with Ānanda, or Bliss. This Ultimate Reality, Satchidānanda. Existence-Knowledge-Bliss Absolute, is identical with the Reality preached in the Vedas. And man is identical with this Reality; but under the influence of māyā, or illusion, he has forgotten his true nature. He takes to be real a merely apparent world of subject and object, and this error is the cause of his bondage and suffering. The goal of spiritual discipline is the rediscovery of his true identity with the divine Reality.

For the achievement of this goal the Vedānta prescribes an austere negative method of discrimination and renunciation, which can be followed by only a few individuals endowed with sharp intelligence and unshakable will-power. But Tantra takes into consideration the natural weakness of human beings, their lower appetites, and their love for the concrete. It combines philosophy with rituals, meditation with ceremonies, renunciation with enjoyment. The underlying purpose is gradually to train the aspirant to meditate on his identity with the Ultimate.

The average man wishes to enjoy the material objects of the world. Tantra bids him enjoy these, but at the same time discover in them the presence of God. Mystical rites are prescribed by which, slowly, the sense-objects become spiritualized and sense attraction is transformed into a love of God. So the very "bonds" of man are turned into "releasers." The very poison that kills is transmuted into the elixir of life. Outward renunciation is not necessary. Thus the aim of Tantra is to sublimate bhoga, or enjoyment, into yoga, or union with Consciousness. For, according to this philosophy, the world with all its manifestations is nothing but the sport of Śiva and Śakti, the Absolute and Its inscrutable Power.

The disciplines of Tantra are graded to suit aspirants of all degrees. Exercises are prescribed for people with "animal," "heroic," and "divine" outlooks. Certain of the rites require the presence of members of the opposite sex. Here the aspirant learns to look on woman as the embodiment of the Goddess Kāli, the Mother of the Universe. The very basis of Tantra is the Motherhood of God and the glorification of woman. Every part of a woman's body is to be regarded as incarnate Divinity. But the rites are extremely dangerous. The help of a qualified guru is absolutely necessary. An unwary devotee may lose his foothold and fall into a pit of depravity.

According to the Tantra, Śakti is the active creative force in the universe. Śiva, the Absolute, is a more or less passive principle. Further, Śakti is as inseparable from Śiva as fire's power to burn is from fire itself. Śakti, the Creative Power, contains in Its womb the universe, and therefore is the Divine Mother. All women are Her symbols. Kāli is one of Her several forms. The meditation on Kāli, the Creative Power, is the central discipline of the Tantra. While meditating, the aspirant at first regards himself as one with the Absolute and then thinks that out of that Impersonal Consciousness emerge two entities, namely, his own self and the living form of the Goddess. He then projects the Goddess into the tangible image before him and worships it as the Divine Mother.

Sri Ramakrishna set himself to the task of practicing the disciplines of Tantra; and at the bidding of the Divine Mother Herself he accepted the Brāhmani as his guru. He performed profound and delicate ceremonies in the Panchavati and under the bel-tree at the northern extremity of the temple compound. He practiced all the disciplines of the sixty-four principal Tantra books, and it took him never more than three days to achieve the result promised in any one of them. After the observance of a few preliminary rites, he would be overwhelmed with a strange divine fervor and would go into samādhi, where his mind would dwell in exaltation. Evil ceased to exist for him. The word "carnal" lost its meaning. The whole world and everything in it appeared as the līlā, the sport, of Śiva and Śakti. He beheld everywhere manifest the power and beauty of the Mother; the whole world, animate and inanimate, appeared to him as pervaded with Chit, Consciousness, and with Ānanda, Bliss.

He saw in a vision the Ultimate Cause of the universe as a huge luminous triangle giving birth every moment to an infinite number of worlds. He heard the Anāhata Śabda, the great sound Om, of which the innumerable sounds of the universe are only so many echoes. He acquired the eight supernatural powers of yoga, which make a man almost omnipotent, and these he spurned as of no value whatsoever to the Spirit. He had a vision of the divine Māyā, the inscrutable Power of God, by which the universe is created and sustained, and into which it is finally absorbed. In this vision he saw a woman of exquisite beauty, about to become a mother, emerging from the Ganges and slowly approaching the Panchavati. Presently she gave birth to a child and began to nurse it tenderly. A moment later she assumed a terrible aspect, seized the child with her grim jaws, and crushed it. Swallowing it, she re-entered the waters of the Ganges.

But the most remarkable experience during this period was the awakening of the Kundalini Śakti, the "Serpent Power." He actually saw the Power, at first lying asleep at the bottom of the spinal column, then waking up and ascending along the mystic Sushumnā canal and through its six centers, or lotuses, to the Sahasrāra, the thousand-petaled lotus in the top of the head. He further saw that as the Kundalini went upward the different lotuses bloomed. And this phenomenon was accompanied by visions and trances. Later on he described to his disciples and devotees the various movements of the Kundalini: the fishlike, birdlike, monkeylike, and so on. The awakening of the Kundalini is the beginning of spiritual consciousness, and its union with Śiva in the Sahasrāra, ending in samādhi, is the consummation of the Tāntrik disciplines.

About this time it was revealed to him that in a short while many devotees would seek his guidance.

vaishnava disciplines

After completing the Tāntrik sādhanā Sri Ramakrishna followed the Brāhmani in the disciplines of Vaishnavism. The Vaishnavas are worshippers of Vishnu, the "All-pervading," the Supreme God, who is also known as Hari and Nārāyana. Of Vishnu's various Incarnations the two with the largest number of followers are Rāma and Krishna.

Vaishnavism is exclusively a religion of bhakti. Bhakti is intense love of God, attachment to Him alone; it is of the nature of bliss and bestows upon the lover immortality and liberation. God, according to Vaishnavism, cannot be realized through logic or reason; and, without bhakti, all penances, austerities, and rites are futile. Man cannot realize God by self-exertion alone. For the vision of God His grace is absolutely necessary, and this grace if felt by the pure of heart. The mind is to be purified through bhakti. The pure mind then remains for ever immersed in the ecstasy of God-vision. It is the cultivation of this divine love that is the chief concern of the Vaishnava religion.

There are three kinds of formal devotion: tāmasic, rājasic, and sāttvic. If a person, while showing devotion to God, is actuated by malevolence, arrogance, jealousy, or anger, then his devotion is tāmasic, since it is influenced by tamas, the quality of inertia. If he worships God from a desire for fame or wealth, or from any other worldly ambition, then his devotion is rājasic, since it is influenced by rajas, the quality of activity. But if a person loves God without any thought of material gain, if he performs his duties to please God alone and maintains toward all created beings the attitude of friendship, then his devotion is called sāttvic, since it is influenced by sattva, the quality of harmony. But the highest devotion transcends the three gunas, or qualities, being a spontaneous, uninterrupted inclination of the mind toward God, the Inner Soul of all beings; and it wells up in the heart of a true devotee as soon as he hears the name of God or mention of God's attributes. A devotee possessed of this love would not accept the happiness of heaven if it were offered him. His one desire is to love God under all conditions—in pleasure and pain, life and death, honor and dishonor, prosperity and adversity.

There are two stages of bhakti. The first is known as vaidhi-bhakti, or love of God qualified by scriptural injunctions. For the devotees of this stage are prescribed regular and methodical worship, hymns, prayers, the repetition of God's name, and the chanting of His glories. This lower bhakti in course of time matures into parā-bhakti, or supreme devotion, known also as prema, the most intense form of divine love. Divine love is an end in itself. It exists potentially in all human hearts, but in the case of bound creatures it is misdirected to earthly objects.

To develop the devotee's love for God, Vaishnavism humanizes God. God is to be regarded as the devotee's Parent, Master, Friend, Child, Husband, or Sweetheart, each succeeding relationship representing an intensification of love. These bhāvas, or attitudes toward God, are known as śānta, dāsya, sakhya, vātsalya, and madhur. The rishis of the Vedas, Hanumān, the cowherd boys of Vrindāvan, Rāma's mother Kausalyā, and Rādhikā, Krishna's sweetheart, exhibited, respectively, the most perfect examples of these forms. In the ascending scale the glories of God are gradually forgotten and the devotee realizes more and more the intimacy of divine communion. Finally he regards himself as the mistress of his Beloved, and no artificial barrier remains to separate him from his Ideal. No social or moral obligation can bind to the earth his soaring spirit. He experiences perfect union with the Godhead. Unlike the Vedāntist, who strives to transcend all varieties of the subject-object relationship, a devotee of the Vaishnava path wishes to retain both his own individuality and the personality of God. To him God is not an intangible Absolute, but the Purushottama, the Supreme Person.

While practicing the discipline of the madhur bhāva, the male devotee often regards himself as a woman, in order to develop the most intense form of love for Sri Krishna, the only purusha, or man, in the universe. This assumption of the attitude of the opposite sex has a deep psychological significance. It is a matter of common experience that an idea may be cultivated to such an intense degree that every idea alien to it is driven from the mind. This peculiarity of the mind may be utilized for the subjugation of the lower desires and the development of the spiritual nature. Now, the idea which is the basis of all desires and passions in a man is the conviction of his indissoluble association with a male body. If he can inoculate himself thoroughly with the idea that he is a woman, he can get rid of the desires peculiar to his male body. Again, the idea that he is a woman may in turn be made to give way to another higher idea, namely, that he is neither man nor woman, but the Impersonal Spirit. The Impersonal Spirit alone can enjoy real communion with the Impersonal God. Hence the highest realization of the Vaishnava draws close to the transcendental experience of the Vedāntist.

A beautiful expression of the Vaishnava worship of God through love is to be found in the Vrindāvan episode of the *Bhāgavata*. The gopis, or milkmaids, of Vrindāvan regarded the six-year-old Krishna as their Beloved. They sought no personal gain or happiness from this love. They surrendered to Krishna their bodies, minds, and souls. Of all the gopis, Rādhikā, or Rādhā, because of her intense love for Him, was the closest to Krishna. She manifested mahābhāva and was united with her Beloved. This union represents, through sensuous language, a supersensuous experience.

Sri Chaitanya, also known as Gaurānga, Gorā, or Nimāi, born in Bengal in 1485 and regarded as an Incarnation of God, is a great prophet of the Vaishnava religion. Chaitanya declared the chanting of God's name to be the most efficacious spiritual discipline for the Kaliyuga.

Sri Ramakrishna, as the monkey Hanumān, had already worshipped God as his Master. Through his devotion to Kāli he had worshipped God as his Mother. He was now to take up the other relationships prescribed by the Vaishnava scriptures.

rāmlālā

About the year 1864 there came to Dakshineswar a wandering Vaishnava monk, Jatadhari, whose Ideal Deity was Rāma. He always carried with him a small metal image of the Deity, which he called by the endearing name of Rāmlālā, the Boy Rāma. Toward this little image he displayed the tender affection of Kausalyā for her divine Son, Rāma. As a result of lifelong spiritual practice he had actually found in the metal image the presence of his Ideal. Rāmlālā was no longer for him a metal image, but the living God. He devoted himself to nursing Rāma, feeding Rāma, playing with Rāma, taking Rāma for a walk, and bathing Rāma. And he found that the image responded to his love.

Sri Ramakrishna, much impressed with his devotion, requested Jatadhari to spend a few days at Dakshineswar. Soon Rāmlālā became the favorite companion of Sri Ramakrishna too. Later on he described to the devotees how the little image would dance gracefully before him, jump on his back, insist on being taken in his arms, run to the fields in the sun, pluck flowers from the bushes, and play pranks like a naughty boy. A very sweet relationship sprang up between him and Rāmlālā, for whom he felt the love of a mother.

One day Jatadhari requested Sri Ramakrishna to keep the image and bade him adieu with tearful eyes. He declared that Rāmlālā had fulfilled his innermost prayer and that he now had no more need of formal worship. A few days later Sri Ramakrishna was blessed through Rāmlālā with a vision of Rāmachandra, whereby he realized that the Rāma of the *Rāmāyana*, the son of Daśaratha, pervades the whole universe as Spirit and Consciousness; that He is its Creator, Sustainer, and Destroyer, that, in still another aspect, He is the transcendental Brahman, without form, attribute, or name.

While worshipping Rāmlālā as the Divine Child, Sri Ramakrishna's heart became filled with motherly tenderness, and he began to regard himself as a woman. His speech and gestures changed. He began to move freely with ladies of Mathur's family, who now looked upon him as one of their own sex. During this time he worshipped the Divine Mother as Her companion or handmaid.

in communion with the divine beloved

Sri Ramakrishna now devoted himself to scaling the most inaccessible and dizzy heights of dualistic worship, namely, the complete union with Sri Krishna as the Beloved of the heart. He regarded himself as one of the gopis of Vrindāvan, mad with longing for her divine Sweetheart. At his request Mathur provided him with woman's dress and jewelry. In this love-pursuit, food and drink were forgotten. Day and night he wept bitterly. The yearning turned into a mad frenzy; for the divine Krishna began to play with him the old tricks He had played with the gopis. He would tease and taunt, now and then revealing Himself, but always keeping at a distance. Sri Ramakrishna's anguish brought on a return of the old physical symptoms: the burning sensation, an oozing of blood through the pores, a loosening of the joints, and the stopping of physiological functions.

The Vaishnava scriptures advise one to propitiate Rādhā and obtain her grace in order to realize Sri Krishna. So the tortured devotee now turned his prayer to her. Within a short time he enjoyed her blessed vision. He saw and felt the figure of Rādhā disappearing into his own body.

He said later on: "It is impossible to describe the heavenly beauty and sweetness of Rādhā. Her very appearance showed that she had completely forgotten herself in her passionate attachment to Krishna. Her complexion was a light yellow."

Now one with Rādhā, he manifested the great ecstatic love, the mahābhāva, which had found in her its fullest expression. Later Sri Ramakrishna said: "The manifestation in the same individual of the nineteen different kinds of emotion for God is called, in the books on bhakti, mahābhāva. An ordinary man takes a whole lifetime to express even a single one of these. But in this body [meaning himself] there has been a complete manifestation of all nineteen."

The love of Rādhā is the precursor of the resplendent vision of Sri Krishna, and Sri Ramakrishna soon experienced that vision. The enchanting form of Krishna appeared to him and merged in his person. He became Krishna; he totally forgot his own individuality and the world; he saw Krishna in himself and in the universe. Thus he attained to the fulfillment of the worship of the Personal God. He drank from the fountain of Immortal Bliss. The agony of his heart vanished forever. He realized Amrita, Immortality, beyond the shadow of death.

One day, listening to a recitation of the *Bhāgavata* on the verandah of the Rādhākānta temple, he fell into a divine mood and saw the enchanting form of Krishna. He perceived the luminous rays issuing from Krishna's Lotus Feet in the form of a stout rope, which touched first the *Bhāgavata* and then his own chest, connecting all three—God, the scripture, and the devotee. "After this vision," he used to say, "I came to realize that Bhagavān, Bhakta, and *Bhāgavata*—God, Devotee, and Scripture—are in reality one and the same."

· · ·

totapuri

Totapuri arrived at the Dakshineswar temple garden toward the end of 1864. Perhaps born in the Punjab, he was the head of a monastery in that province of India and claimed leadership of seven hundred sannyāsis. Trained from early youth in the disciplines of the Advaita Vedānta, he looked upon the world as an illusion. The gods and goddesses of the dualistic worship were to him mere fantasies of the deluded mind. Prayers, ceremonies, rites, and rituals had nothing to do with true religion, and about these he was utterly indifferent. Exercising self-exertion and unshakable will-power, he had liberated himself from attachment to the sense-objects of the relative universe. For forty years he had practiced austere discipline on the bank of the sacred Narmadā and had finally realized his identity with the Absolute. Thenceforward he roamed in the world as an unfettered soul, a lion free from the cage. Clad in a loin-cloth, he spent his days under the canopy of the sky alike in storm and sunshine, feeding his body on the slender pittance of alms. He had been visiting the estuary of the Ganges. On his return journey along the bank of the sacred river, led by the inscrutable Divine Will, he stopped at Dakshineswar.

Totapuri, discovering at once that Sri Ramakrishna was prepared to be a student of Vedānta, asked to initiate him into its mysteries. With the permission of the Divine Mother, Sri Ramakrishna agreed to the proposal. But Totapuri explained that only a sannyāsi could receive the teaching of Vedānta. Sri Ramakrishna agreed to renounce the world, but with the stipulation that the ceremony of his initiation into the monastic order be performed in secret, to spare the feelings of his old mother, who had been living with him at Dakshineswar.

On the appointed day, in the small hours of the morning, a fire was lighted in the Panchavati. Totapuri and Sri Ramakrishna sat before it. The flame played on their faces. "Ramakrishna was a small brown man with a short beard and beautiful eyes, long dark eyes, full of light, obliquely set and slightly veiled, never very wide open, but seeing half-closed a great distance both outwardly and inwardly. His mouth was open over his white teeth in a bewitching smile, at once affectionate and mischievous. Of medium height, he was thin to emaciation and extremely delicate. His temperament was high-strung, for he was supersensitive to all the winds of joy and sorrow, both moral and physical. He was indeed a living reflection of all that happened before the mirror of his eyes, a two-sided mirror, turned both out and in." Facing him, the other rose like a rock. He was very tall and robust, a sturdy and tough oak. His constitution and mind were of iron. He was the strong leader of men.

In the burning flame before him Sri Ramakrishna performed the rituals of destroying his attachment to relatives, friends, body, mind, sense-organs, ego, and the world. The leaping flame swallowed it all, making the initiate free and pure. The sacred thread and the tuft of hair were consigned to the fire, completing his serverance from caste, sex, and society. Last of all he burnt in that fire, with all that is holy as his witness, his desire for enjoyment here and hereafter. He uttered the sacred mantras giving assurance of safety and fearlessness to all beings, who were only manifestations of his own Self. The rites completed, the disciple received from the guru the loincloth and ochre robe, the emblems of his new life.

The teacher and the disciple repaired to the meditation room near by. Totapuri began to impart to Sri Ramakrishna the great truths of Vedānta.

"Brahman," he said, "is the only Reality, ever pure, ever illumined, ever free, beyond the limits of time, space, and causation. Though apparently divided by names and forms through the inscrutable power of māyā, that enchantress who makes the impossible possible, Brahman is really One and undivided. When a seeker merges in the beatitude of samādhi, he does not perceive time and space or name and form, the offspring of māyā. Whatever is within the domain of māyā is unreal. Give it up. Destroy the prisonhouse of name and form and rush out of it with the strength of a lion. Dive deep in search of the Self and realize It through samādhi. You will find the world of name and form vanishing into void, and the puny ego dissolving in Brahman-Consciousness. You will realize your identity with Brahman, Existence-Knowledge-Bliss Absolute." Quoting the Upanishad, Totapuri said: "That knowledge is shallow by which one sees or hears or knows another. What is shallow is worthless and can never give real felicity. But the Knowledge by which one does not see another or hear another or know another, which is beyond duality, is great, and through such Knowledge one attains the Infinite Bliss. How can the mind and senses grasp That which shines in the heart of all as the Eternal Subject?

Totapuri asked the disciple to withdraw his mind from all objects of the relative world, including the gods and goddesses, and to concentrate on the Absolute. But the task was not easy even for Sri Ramakrishna. He found it impossible to take his mind beyond Kāli, the Divine Mother of the Universe. "After the initiation," Sri Ramakrishna once said, describing the event, "Nangtā began to teach me the various conclusions of the Advaita Vedānta and asked me to withdraw the mind completely from all objects and dive deep into the Ātman. But in spite of all my attempts I could not altogether cross the realm of name and form and bring my mind to the unconditioned state. I had no difficulty in taking the mind from all the objects of the world. But the radiant and too familiar figure of the Blissful Mother, the Embodiment of the essence of Pure Consciousness, appeared before me as a living reality. Her bewitching smile prevented me from passing into the Great Beyond. Again and again I tried, but She stood in my way every time. In despair I said to Nangtā: 'It is hopeless. I cannot raise my mind to the unconditioned state and come face to face with Ātman.' He grew excited and sharply said: 'What? You can't do it? But you have to.' He cast his eyes around. Finding a piece of glass he took it up and stuck it between my eyebrows. 'Concentrate the mind on this point,' he thundered. Then with stern determination I again sat to meditate. As soon as the gracious form of the Divine Mother appeared before me, I used my discrimination as a sword and with it clove Her in two. The last barrier fell. My spirit at once soared beyond the relative plane and I lost myself in samādhi."

Sri Ramakrishna remained completely absorbed in samādhi for three days. "Is it really true?" Totapuri cried out in astonishment. "Is it possible that he has attained in a single day what it took me forty years of strenuous practice to achieve? Great God. It is nothing short of a miracle." With the help of Totapuri, Sri Ramakrishna's mind finally came down to the relative plane.

a vision
of vishnu-krishna _____

arjuna:
By your grace, you have taught me the truth about the Atman. Your words are
    mystic and sublime. They have dispelled my ignorance.
From you, whose eyes are like the lotus-flowers, I have learnt in detail of the

From *The Song of God: Bhagavad-Gita*, New York, New American Library, Inc., 1957, Vedanta Society of Southern California, copyright holder.

origin and dissolution of creatures, and of your own infinite glory.
O Supreme Lord, you are as you describe yourself to be: I do not doubt that.
Nevertheless, I long to behold your divine Form.
If you find me worthy of that vision, then reveal to me, O Master of yogis, your
changeless Atman.

sri krishna:

Behold, O Prince, my divine forms, hundreds upon thousands, various in kind,
various in color and in shape.
Behold the Adityas, and the Vasus, and the Rudras, and the Aswins, and the
Maruts. Behold many wonders, O Descendant of Bharata, that no man has
seen before.
O conqueror of sloth, this very day you shall behold the whole universe with all
things animate and inert made one within this body of mine. And whatever else you desire to see, that you shall see also.
But you cannot see me thus with those human eyes. Therefore, I give you divine
sight. Behold—this is my yoga power.

sanjaya:

Then, O King, when he had spoken these words, Sri Krishna, Master of all yogis,
revealed to Arjuna his transcendent, divine Form, speaking from innumerable mouths, seeing with a myriad eyes, of many marvelous aspects,
adorned with countless divine ornaments, brandishing all kinds of heavenly
weapons, wearing celestial garments and the raiment of paradise, anointed
with perfumes of heavenly fragrance, full of revelations, resplendent,
boundless, of ubiquitous regard.
Suppose a thousand suns should rise together into the sky: such is the glory of
the Shape of Infinite God.
Then the son of Pandu beheld the entire universe, in all its multitudinous diversity, lodged as one being within the body of the God of gods.
Then was Arjuna, that lord of mighty riches, overcome with wonder. His hair
stood erect. He bowed low before God in adoration, and clasped his hands,
and spoke:

arjuna:

Ah, my God, I see all gods within your body;
Each in his degree, the multitude of creatures;
See Lord Brahma throned upon the lotus;
See all the sages, and the holy serpents.

Universal Form, I see you without limit,
Infinite of arms, eyes, mouths and bellies—
See, and find no end, midst, or beginning.

Crowned with diadems, you wield the mace and discus,
Shining every way—the eyes shrink from your splendor
Brilliant like the sun; like fire, blazing, boundless.

You are all we know, supreme, beyond man's measure,
This world's sure-set plinth and refuge never shaken,
Guardian of eternal law, life's Soul undying.
Birthless, deathless; yours the strength titanic,
Million-armed, the sun and moon your eyeballs,
Fiery-faced, you blast the world to ashes,

Fill the sky's four corners, span the chasm
Sundering heaven from earth. Superb and awful
Is your Form that makes the three worlds tremble.

Into you, the companies of devas
Enter with clasped hands, in dread and wonder.
Crying "Peace," the Rishis and the Siddhas
Sing your praise with hymns of adoration.

Adityas and Rudras, Sadhyas, Viswas, Aswins,
Maruts and Vasus, the hosts of the Gandharvas,
Yakshas, Asuras, Ushmapas and Siddhas—
All of them gaze upon you in amazement.

At the sight of this, your shape stupendous
Full of mouths and eyes, feet, thighs and bellies,
Terrible with fangs, O mighty master,
All the worlds are fear-struck, even as I am.

When I see you, Vishnu, omnipresent,
Shouldering the sky, in hues of rainbow,
With your mouths agape and flame-eyes staring—
All my peace is gone; my heart is troubled.

Now with frightful tusks your mouths are gnashing,
Flaring like the fires of Doomsday morning—
North, south, east and west seem all confounded—
Lord of devas, world's abode, have mercy!

Dhritarashtra's offspring, many a monarch,
Bhisma, Drona, and the son of Karna,
There they go—with our own warriors also—
Hurrying to your jaws, wide-fanged and hideous—
See where mangled heads lie crushed between them!

Swift as many rivers streaming to the ocean,
Rush the heroes to your fiery gullets:
Mothlike, to meet the flame of their destruction,
Headlong these plunge into you, and perish.

Licking with your burning tongues, devouring
All the worlds, you probe the heights of heaven
With intolerable beams, O Vishnu.

Tell me who you are, and were from the beginning,
You of aspect grim, O God of gods, be gracious.
Take my homage, Lord. From me your ways are hidden,

sri krishna:

I am come as Time, the waster of the peoples,
Ready for that hour that ripens to their ruin.
All these hosts must die; strike, stay your hand—no matter.

Therefore, strike. Win kingdom, wealth and glory.
Arjuna, arise, O ambidextrous bowman.
Seem to slay. By me these men are slain already.

You but smite the dead, the doom-devoted heroes,
Jayadrtha, Drona, Bhisma, Karna.
Fight, and have no fear. The Foe is yours to conquer.

sanjaya:

After Arjuna had heard these words of the Lord Krishna, he folded his palms
and bowed down, trembling. Prostrating himself, with great fear, he addressed Krishna once more, in a choking voice:

arjuna:

Well it is the world delights to do you honor!
At the sight of you, O master of the senses,
Demons scatter every way in terror,
And the hosts of Siddhas bow adoring.

Mightiest, how should they indeed withhold their homage?
O Prime Cause of all, even Brahma the Beginner—
Deathless, world's abode, the Lord of devas,
You are what is not, what is, and what transcends them.

You are first and highest in heaven, O ancient Spirit.
It is within you the cosmos rests in safety.
You are known and knower, goal of all our striving.
Endless in your change, you body forth creation.

Lord of fire and death, of wind and moon and waters,
Father of the born, and this world's father's Father.
Hail, all hail to you—a thousand salutations.

Take our salutations, Lord, from every quarter,
Infinite of might and boundless in your glory,
You are all that is, since everywhere we find you.

Carelessly I called you "Krishna" and "my comrade,"
Took undying God for friend and fellow-mortal,
Overbold with love, unconscious of your greatness.

Often I would jest, familiar, as we feasted
Midst the throng, or walked, or lay at rest together:
Did my words offend? Forgive me, Lord Eternal.

Author of this world, the unmoved and the moving,
You alone are fit for worship, you the highest.
Where in the three worlds shall any find your equal?

Therefore I bow down, prostrate and ask for pardon:
Now forgive me, God, as friend forgives his comrade,
Father forgives son, and man his dearest lover.

I have seen what no man ever saw before me:
Deep is my delight, but still my dread is greater.
Show me now your other Form, O Lord, be gracious.

Thousand-membered, Universal Being,
Show me now the Shape I knew of old, the four-armed,
With your diadem and mace, the discus-bearer.

sri krishna:
This my Form of fire, world-wide, supreme, primeval,
Manifest by yoga power, alone of all men,
Arjuna, I showed to you because I love you.

Neither through sacrifice, nor study of the Vedas,
Nor strict austerities, nor alms, nor rituals,
Shall this my Shape be viewed by any mortal,
Other than you, O hero of the Pandus.

Now you need fear no more, nor be bewildered,
Seeing me so terrible. Be glad, take courage.
Look, here am I, transformed, as first you knew me.

sanjaya:
Having spoken thus to Arjuna, Krishna appeared in his own shape. The Great-
Souled One, assuming once more his mild and pleasing form, brought
peace to him in his terror.

arjuna:
O Krishna, now I see your pleasant human form, I am myself again.

sri krishna:
That Shape of mine which you have seen is very difficult to behold. Even the
devas themselves are always longing to see it. Neither by study of the

Vedas, nor by austeries, nor by alms-giving, nor by rituals can I be seen as you have seen me. But by single-minded and intense devotion, that Form of mine may be completely known, and seen, and entered into, O Consumer of the foe.

Whosoever works for me alone, makes me his only goal and is devoted to me, free from attachment, and without hatred toward any creature—that man, O Prince, shall enter into me.

god appears to moses

Now Moses was keeping the flock of his father-in-law, Jĕthrō, the priest of Mĭd'-iăn; and he led his flock to the west side of the wilderness, and came to Horeb, the mountain of God. And the angel of the Lord appeared to him in a flame of fire out of the midst of a bush; and he looked, and lo, the bush was burning, yet it was not consumed. And Moses said, "I will turn aside and see this great sight, why the bush is not burnt." When the Lord saw that he turned aside to see, God called to him out of the bush, "Moses, Moses!" And he said, "Here am I." Then he said, "Do not come near; put off your shoes from your feet, for the place on which you are standing is holy ground." And he said, "I am the God of your father, the God of Abraham, the God of Isaac, and the God of Jacob." And Moses hid his face, for he was afraid to look at God.

Then the Lord said, "I have seen the affliction of my people who are in Egypt, and have heard their cry because of their taskmasters; I know their sufferings, and I have come down to deliver them out of the hand of the Egyptians, and to bring them up out of that land to a good and broad land, a land flowing with milk and honey, to the place of the Cā'naănites, the Hĭttĭtes, the Ăm'ŏrites, the Pĕr'izzĭtes, the Hĭvĭtes, and the Jĕb'ūsites. And now, behold, the cry of the people of Israel has come to me, and I have seen the oppression with which the Egyptians oppress them. Come, I will send you to Pharaōh that you may bring forth my people, the sons of Israel, out of Egypt." But Moses said to God, "Who am I that I should go to Pharaōh, and bring the sons of Israel out of Egypt?" He said, "But I will be with you; and this shall be the sign for you, that I have sent you: when you have brought forth the people out of Egypt, you shall serve God upon this mountain."

Then Moses said to God, "If I come to the people of Israel and say to them, 'The God of your fathers has sent me to you,' and they ask me, 'What is his name?' what shall I say to them?" God said to Moses, "I AM WHO I AM." And he said, "Say this to the people of Israel, 'I AM has sent me to you.' " God also

Exodus 3:1–15, RSV.

said to Moses, "Say this to the people of Israel, 'The Lord, the God of your fathers, the God of Abraham, the God of Isaac, and the God of Jacob, has sent me to you': this is my name for ever, and thus I am to be remembered throughout all generations."

god speaks to job
out of the whirlwind ───────────────────────────

Then God answered Job out of the whirlwind:
"Gird up your loins like a man: I will question you and you declare to me.
Will you even put me in the wrong? Will you condemn me that you may be justified?
Have you an arm like God, and can you thunder with a voice like his?
Deck yourself with majesty and dignity; clothe yourself with glory and splendor.
Pour forth the overflowings of your anger, and look on every one that is proud, and abase him.
Look on every one that is proud, and bring him low; and tread down the wicked where they stand.
Hide them all in the dust together; bind their faces in the world below.
Then will I also acknowledge to you, that your own right hand can give you victory.
Behold, Behemoth, which I made as I made you; he eats grass like an ox.
Behold, his strength in his loins, and his power in the muscles of his belly.
He makes his tail stiff like a cedar; the sinews of his thighs are knit together.
His bones are tubes of bronze, his limbs like bars of iron.
He is the first of the works of God; let him who made him bring near his sword!
For the mountains yield food for him where all the wild beasts play.
Under the lotus plants he lies, in the covert of the reeds and in the marsh.
For his shade the lotus trees cover him; the willows of the brook surround him.
Behold, if the river is turbulent he is not frightened; he is confident though Jordan rushes against his mouth.
Can one take him with hooks, or pierce his nose with a snare?

Can you draw out Leviathan with a fishhook, or press down his tongue with a cord?
Can you put a rope in his nose, or pierce his jaw with a hook?
Will he make many supplications to you? Will he speak to you soft words?
Will he make a covenant with you to take him for your servant for ever?
Will you play with him as with a bird, or will you put him on leash for your maidens?

Job 40:6 to 42:6, RSV.

Will traders bargain over him? Will they divide him up among the merchants?
Can you fill his skin with harpoons, or his head with fishing spears?
Lay hands on him; think of the battle; you will not do it again!
Behold, the hope of a man is disappointed; he is laid low even at the sight of
  him.
No one is so fierce that he dares to stir him up. Who then is he that can stand
  before me?
Who has given to me, that I should repay him? Whatever is under the whole
  heaven is mine.
I will not keep silence concerning his limbs, or his mighty strength, or his goodly
  frame.
Who can strip off his outer garment? Who can penetrate his double coat of mail?
Who can open the doors of his face? Round about his teeth is terror.
His back is made of rows of shields, shut up closely as with a seal.
One is so near to another that no air can come between them.
They are joined one to another; they clasp each other and cannot be separated.
His sneezings flash forth light, and his eyes are like the eyelids of the dawn.
Out of his mouth go flaming torches; sparks of fire leap forth.
Out of his nostrils comes forth smoke, as from a boiling pot and burning rushes.
His breath kindles coals, and a flame comes forth from his mouth.
In his neck abides strength, and terror dances before him.
The folds of his flesh cleave together, firmly cast upon him and immovable.
His heart is hard as a stone, hard as the nether millstone.
When he raises himself up the mighty are afraid; at the crashing they are beside
  themselves.
Though the sword reaches him, it does not avail; nor the spear, the dart, or the
  javelin.
He counts iron as straw, and bronze as rotten wood.
The arrow cannot make him flee; for him slingstones are turned to stubble.
Clubs are counted as stubble; he laughs at the rattle of javelins.
His underparts are like sharp potsherds; he spreads himself like a threshing
  sledge on the mire.
He makes the deep boil like a pot; he makes the sea like a pot of ointment.
Behind him he leaves a shining wake; one would think the deep to be hoary.
Upon earth there is not his like, a creature without fear.
He beholds everything that is high; he is king over all the sons of pride."
Then Job answered the Lord:
"I know that thou canst do all things, and that no purpose of thine can be
  thwarted.
'Who is this that hides counsel without knowledge?' Therefore I have uttered
  what I did not understand, things too wonderful for me, which I did not
  know.
'Hear, and I will speak; I will question you, and you declare to me.'
I had heard of thee by the hearing of the ear, but now my eye sees thee;
therefore I despise myself, and repent in dust and ashes."

isaiah's vision of god

1. god's holiness revealed
In the year that King Ùzzi'ah died I saw the Lord sitting upon a throne, high and lifted up; and his train filled the temple. Above him stood the seraphim; each had six wings: with two he covered his face, and with two he covered his feet, and with two he flew. And one called to another and said:

"Holy, holy, holy is the Lord of hosts; the whole earth is full of his glory."

And the foundations of the thresholds shook at the voice of him who called, and the house was filled with smoke. And I said:

2. isaiah's repentance, confession, and cleansing
"Woe is me! For I am lost; for I am a man of unclean lips, and I dwell in the midst of a people of unclean lips; for my eyes have seen the King, the Lord of hosts!"

Then flew one of the seraphim to me, having in his hand a burning coal which he had taken with tongs from the altar. And he touched my mouth, and said: "Behold, this has touched your lips; your guilt is taken away, and your sin forgiven." And I

3. his commission to preach
heard the voice of the Lord saying, "Whom shall I send, and who will go for us?" Then I said, "Here am I! Send me."

Isaiah 6:1–8, RSV.

a singer meditates
on the presence of god

Thou searchest me, Eternal One, thou knowest me,
thou knowest me sitting or rising, my very thoughts thou readest from afar;
walking or resting, I am scanned by thee, and all my life to thee lies open;
ere ever a word comes to my tongue, O thou Eternal, 'tis well known to thee;
thou art on every side, behind me and before, laying thy hand on me.
Such knowledge is too wonderful for me; it is far, far beyond me.
Where could I go from thy Spirit, where could I flee from thy face?
I climb to heaven?—but thou art there; I nestle in the netherworld?—and there
thou art!

From *The Bible: A New Translation* by James Moffatt, Psalm 139. Copyright 1954 by James Moffatt. Reprinted by permission of Harper & Row Publishers, Inc.

If I darted swift to the dawn, to the verge of ocean afar, thy hand even there
    would fall on me, thy right hand would reach me.
If I say, "The dark will screen me, night will hide me in its curtains,"
yet darkness is not dark to thee, the night is clear as daylight.

O God, what mysteries I find in thee! How vast the number of thy purposes!
I try to count them?—they are more than the sand; I wake from my reverie, and
    I am still lost in thee.

Search me, O God, and know my heart, test me and try my thoughts;
see if I am taking a wrong course, and do thou lead me on the lines of life eter-
    nal.

matthew hears god's call _____

Noticing the big crowd around him, Jesus planned to withdraw to the other side.
And along the way this theologian said to him, "Doctor, I'll share your life, regardless of where it takes me!" Then Jesus said to him, "Foxes have dens, and
the birds have nests, but the son of man has nowhere to hang his hat." Someone
else—one of the students—said, "Sir, let me first take care of my family obligations." But Jesus told him, "*You* live my life, and let the uncommitted care for
the uncommitted."

•   •   •

    Jesus left there and saw a man named Matthew sitting behind his desk at the
Internal Revenue office. And he says to him, "Live my life." So Matthew quit
his job and started living his life.

From *The Cotton Patch Version of Matthew and John* by Clarence Jordan, New York, Association Press, 1969.

jesus is transfigured
on a mountain _____

And after six days Jesus took with him Peter and James and John his brother,
and led them up a high mountain apart. And he was transfigured before them,
and his face shone like the sun, and his garments became white as light. And
behold, there appeared to them Moses and Elijah, talking with him. And Peter

Matthew 17:1–18, RSV.

said to Jesus, "Lord, it is well that we are here; if you wish, I will make three booths here, one for you and one for Moses and one for Elijah." He was still speaking, when lo, a bright cloud overshadowed them, and a voice from the cloud said, "This is my beloved Son, with whom I am well pleased; listen to him." When the disciples heard this, they fell on their faces, and were filled with awe. But Jesus came and touched them, saying, "Rise, and have no fear." And when they lifted up their eyes, they saw no one but Jesus only.

And as they were coming down the mountain, Jesus commanded them, "Tell no one the vision, until the Son of man is raised from the dead." And the disciples asked him, "Then why do the scribes say that first Elijah must come?" He replied, "Elijah does come, and he is to restore all things; but I tell you that Elijah has already come, and they did not know him, but did to him whatever they pleased. So also the Son of man will suffer at their hands." Then the disciples understood that he was speaking to them of John the Baptist.

And when they came to the crowd, a man came up to him and kneeling before him said, "Lord, have mercy on my son, for he is an epileptic and he suffers terribly; for often he falls into the fire, and often into the water. And I brought him to your disciples, and they could not heal him." And Jesus answered, "O faithless and perverse generation, how long am I to be with you? How long am I to bear with you? Bring him here to me." And Jesus rebuked him, and the demon came out of him, and the boy was cured instantly.

jesus tells his followers about true happiness ————————————————————————

When Jesus saw the large crowd, he went up the hill and sat down. His students gathered around him, and he began teaching them. This is what he said:

"The spiritually humble are God's people, for they are citizens of his new order.

"They who are deeply concerned are God's people, for they will see their ideas become reality.

"They who are gentle are his people, for they will be his partners across the land.

"They who have an unsatisfied appetite for the right are God's people, for they will be given plenty to chew on.

"The generous are God's people, for they will be treated generously.

"Those whose motives are pure are God's people, for they will have spiritual insight.

From *The Cotton Patch Version of Matthew and John* by Clarence Jordan, New York, Association Press, 1969.

"Men of peace and good will are God's people, for they will be known throughout the land as his children.

"Those who have endured much for what's right are God's people; they are citizens of his new order.

"You all are God's people when others call you names, and harass you and tell all kinds of false tales on you just because you follow me. Be cheerful and good-humored, because your spiritual advantage is great. For that's the way they treated men of conscience in the past.

st. paul sees the light of god in the face of christ _____

Therefore, having this ministry by the mercy of God, we do not lose heart. We have renounced disgraceful, underhanded ways; we refuse to practice cunning or to tamper with God's word, but by the open statement of the truth we would commend ourselves to every man's conscience in the sight of God. And even if our gospel is veiled, it is veiled only to those who are perishing. In their case the god of this world has blinded the minds of the unbelievers, to keep them from seeing the light of the gospel of the glory of Christ, who is the likeness of God. For what we preach is not ourselves, but Jesus Christ as Lord, with ourselves as your servants for Jesus' sake. For it is the God who said, "Let light shine out of darkness," who has shone in our hearts to give the light of the knowledge of the glory of God in the face of Christ.

But we have this treasure in earthen vessels, to show that the transcendent power belongs to God and not to us. We are afflicted in every way, but not crushed; perplexed, but not driven to despair; persecuted, but not forsaken; struck down, but not destroyed; always carrying in the body the death of Jesus, so that the life of Jesus may also be manifested in our bodies. For while we live we are always being given up to death for Jesus' sake, so that the life of Jesus may be manifested in our mortal flesh. So death is at work in us, but life in you.

Since we have the same spirit of faith as he had who wrote, "I believed, and so I spoke," we too believe, and so we speak, knowing that he who raised the Lord Jesus will raise us also with Jesus and bring us with you into his presence. For it is all for your sake, so that as grace extends to more and more people it may increase thanksgiving, to the glory of God.

So we do not lose heart. Though our outer nature is wasting away, our inner nature is being renewed every day. For this slight momentary affliction is preparing for us an eternal weight of glory beyond all comparison, because we look not to the things that are seen but to the things that are unseen; for the things that are seen are transient, but the things that are unseen are eternal.

_____

II Corinthians 3:17 to 4:4–18, RSV.

st. paul writes
of weakness and vision _____

I repeat, let no one think me foolish; but even if you do, accept me as a fool, so
that I too may boast a little. (What I am saying I say not with the Lord's authority but as a fool, in this boastful confidence; since many boast of worldly things,
I too will boast.) For you gladly bear with fools, being wise yourselves! For you
bear it if a man makes slaves of you, or preys upon you, or takes advantage of
you, or puts on airs, or strikes you in the face. To my shame, I must say, we
were too weak for that.

But whatever any one dares to boast of—I am speaking as a fool—I also dare
to boast of that. Are they Hebrews? So am I. Are they Israelites? So am I. Are
they descendants of Abraham? So am I. Are they servants of Christ? I am a better one—I am talking like a madman—with far greater labors, far more imprison-
ments, with countless beatings, and often near death. Five times I have received
at the hands of the Jews the forty lashes less one. Three times I have been beaten
with rods; once I was stoned. Three times I have been shipwrecked; a night and a
day I have been adrift at sea; on frequent journeys, in danger from rivers, danger
from robbers, danger from my own people, danger from Gentiles, danger in the
city, danger in the wilderness, danger at sea, danger from false brethren; in toil
and hardship, through many a sleepless night, in hunger and thirst, often without
food, in cold and exposure. And, apart from other things, there is the daily pressure upon me of my anxiety of all the churches. Who is weak, and I am not
weak? Who is made to fall, and I am not indignant?

If I must boast, I will boast of the things that show my weakness. The God
and Father of the Lord Jesus, he who is blessed for ever, knows that I do not lie.
At Damascus, the governor under King Ar′étàs guarded the city of Damascus in
order to seize me, but I was let down in a basket through a window in the wall,
and escaped his hands.

I must boast; there is nothing to be gained by it, but I will go on to visions
and revelations of the Lord. I know a man in Christ who fourteen years ago was
caught up to the third heaven—whether in the body or out of the body I do not
know, God knows. And I know that this man was caught up into Paradise—
whether in the body or out of the body I do not know, God knows—and he
heard things that cannot be told, which man may not utter. On behalf of this
man I will boast, but on my own behalf I will not boast, except of my weaknesses. Though if I wish to boast, I shall not be a fool, for I shall be speaking the
truth. But I refrain from it, so that no one may think more of me than he sees in
me or hears from me. And to keep me from being too elated by the abundance
of revelations, a thorn was given me in the flesh, a messenger of Satan, to harass
me, to keep me from being too elated. Three times I besought the Lord about
this, that it should leave me; but he said to me, "My grace is sufficient for you,

_____

II Corinthians 11:16 to 12:12, RSV.

for my power is made perfect in weakness." I will all the more gladly boast of my weaknesses, that the power of Christ may rest upon me. For the sake of Christ, then, I am content with weaknesses, insults, hardships, persecutions, and calamities; for when I am weak, then I am strong.

I have been a fool! You forced me to it, for I ought to have been commended by you. For I am not at all inferior to these superlative apostles, even though I am nothing. The signs of a true apostle were performed among you in all patience, with signs and wonders and mighty works.

the resurrected jesus
appears to mary magdalene ——————————————————————

Now on the first day of the week Mary Mag'dalēne came to the tomb early, while it was still dark, and saw that the stone had been taken away from the tomb. So she ran, and went to Simon Peter and the other disciple, the one whom Jesus loved, and said to them, "They have taken the Lord out of the tomb, and we do not know where they have laid him." Peter then came out with the other disciple, and they went toward the tomb. They both ran, but the other disciple outran Peter and reached the tomb first; and stooping to look in, he saw the linen cloths lying there, but he did not go in. Then Simon Peter came, following him, and went into the tomb; he saw the linen cloths lying, and the napkin, which had been on his head, not lying with the linen cloths but rolled up in a place by itself. Then the other disciple, who reached the tomb first, also went in, and he saw and believed; for as yet they did not know the scripture, that he must rise from the dead. Then the disciples went back to their homes.

But Mary stood weeping outside the tomb, and as she wept she stooped to look into the tomb; and she saw two angels in white, sitting where the body of Jesus had lain, one at the head and one at the feet. They said to her, "Woman, why are you weeping?" She said to them, "Because they have taken away my Lord, and I do not know where they have laid him." Saying this, she turned round and saw Jesus standing, but she did not know that it was Jesus. Jesus said to her, "Woman, why are you weeping? Whom do you seek?" Supposing him to be the gardener, she said to him, "Sir, if you have carried him away, tell me where you have laid him, and I will take him away." Jesus said to her, "Mary." She turned and said to him in Hebrew, "Răb-bō'nĭ!" (which means Teacher). Jesus said to her, "Do not hold me, for I have not yet ascended to the Father; but go to my brethren and say to them, I am ascending to my Father and your Father, to my God and your God." Mary Măg'dalēne went and said to the disciples, "I have seen the Lord"; and she told them that he had said these things to her.

———————

From the Gospel of John, chapter 20.

RUDOLF BULTMANN

how does god speak to us through the bible?

"How does God speak to us through the Bible?" Who asks that? Would some one who is certain *that* God speaks through the Bible ask such a question? Why should he want to know *how*? If it were asked as a purely theoretical question, it would be a useless, even a frivolous game. For what God says to us through the Bible is in the form of *address*. It can only be listened to, not examined. The man to whom God really speaks through the Bible hears what God says to him and acts accordingly, and he has just as little time and reason to ponder over the *how*, as has a son to submit the style of his father's words to theoretical examinations. In doing so, he would forget to hear rightly.

Or does the question come from a doubter, who has heard from others that God speaks through the Scriptures and who wants to know how this is possible, how it can be understood? We shall not help him if we think that we must first of all explain *how* God speaks, so that he can convince himself of the *fact*. We cannot first of all prove the *possibility* of God's speaking through the Bible in order that belief in its *reality* may naturally follow.

No! The question of *how* God speaks to us through the Bible has no sense unless we ask at the same time *what* God says to us through the Bible. And we have good reason for putting this question. We have a reason even if we do not doubt the *fact* that he speaks. For the conviction *that* he speaks might be only a theoretical conviction, only a dogma with which we reassure ourselves. And with such a conviction we might be deaf to what God really says to us through the Scriptures. Perhaps we are interested in the Bible and read it, always assuming that it is God's word, but all the same in no other way than we read other serious and devotional books with a view to enriching our spiritual knowledge, with a view to the upbuilding of our philosophy of life and to confirm the thoughts— also the Christian thoughts—that we already have. If this is so, the question: how does God really speak to us through the Bible? should stir us and make us think. If this is so, we are, however, not so much concerned with the "how" of *God's speech,* but with the "how" of *our listening*. How should we listen? Unless we find the true answer we cannot help those who ask in doubt, skeptics or seekers, how God speaks.

How then should we hear? Which is the right way to prepare? The first condition for readiness is this: we must silence all other voices; everything we say to ourselves, everything other people say to us. For we want to hear what *God* says to us. And if we take this seriously, there is room for but one voice. For God's voice sounds from beyond the world. If we wish to hear it, we must be prepared to let it challenge everything in us and everything in the world: our instincts and

Reprinted by permission of The World Publishing Company from *Existence and Faith: Shorter Writings of Rudolf Bultmann,* trans. Schubert M. Ogden. A Meridian Book. Translation copyright © 1960 by Meridian Books, Inc.

desires, our ideals and enterprises, all everyday and ordinary things, but also everything extraordinary and noble. If we wish to hear God, we must give up everything to which we are attached, everything that binds us. If we wish to come before God, we must be prepared to look into nothingness, into death. For God does not grant life except after first having demanded death. His word is the word of creation, creating out of nothingness; before him all that we ourselves are and have must be wiped out. The everlasting life, which God wishes to grant through his word (John 6:63, 6:68), he grants to the *dead* and in doing so wakes them (John 5:24). Are we prepared to realize that without this word we are dead? That through this word we shall be "born again," that we shall be "newly created" (John 3:3ff.; II Cor. 5:17)? Do we want to expose ourselves to this word that is sharper than a two-edged sword (Heb. 4:12f.)?

Those only who are thus ready to hear the word of the Bible will hear it as God's word. Yes, *because* they hear it with this readiness, they hear it already as God's word. For the call to this preparedness is already the call of God through the Bible. The readiness to listen will increase through it; i.e., the word of the Scriptures teaches men to recognize ever more clearly what is the "beyond" and the "here," death and life, flesh and Spirit, God and man. Why does hearing the word make one ever readier to listen to it? Why does hearing it lead to an ever clearer recognition of human nothingness and God's greatness? Because it teaches us to understand that the word of *judgment* is at the same time the word of *grace,* that God demands the death of man in order to grant him life, that God in his mercy sent us Jesus Christ, that his mercy surrounded us before we were aware of it. For God's word teaches us to consider our nothingness and the death in us, as our *sin,* as the revolt against him who is our life, while we, the rebels, wanted to live by and for ourselves. And the radical readiness that we receive through the Scriptures for the Scriptures is the submission to God's word as the word of forgiveness.

Is that possible? Is the promise of the Scriptures that God has forgiven us and received us in his mercy through Jesus Christ a word that we can believe as God's word?

If we still ask these questions, we are obviously not yet rightly prepared. For they indicate that we still consider the Bible as an ordinary book which we may study like other books in order to profit by it. If we ask for plain convincing reasons why God speaks actually here, in the Bible, then we have not yet understood what God's sovereignty means. For it is due to his sovereign will, that he has spoken and speaks here. The Bible does not approach us at all like other books, nor like other "religious voices of the nations," as catering for our interest. It claims from the outset to be God's word. We did not come across the Bible in the course of our cultural studies, as we came across, for example, Plato or the Bhagavad-Gita. We came to know it through the Christian church, which put it before us with its authoritative claim. The church's preaching, founded on the Scriptures, passes on the word of the Scriptures. It says: God speaks to you *here*! In his majesty he has chosen *this* place! We cannot question whether this place is the right one; we must listen to the call that summons us.

Only thus do we rightly understand the word of judgment and grace. For the word does not teach the nothingness of human things and the mercy of God as general and abstract propositions. The realization of the nothingness of human nature can easily go together with human conceit, and the knowledge that God's nature is grace may be combined with desperation. But when in the preaching of the church the word addresses *you*, it shows you *your* nothingness, *your* sin, and tells you that God is merciful to *you* and has loved you from all time.

The Scriptures teach this as God's word addressed to you, ever more clearly, and *again and again*. For no one has ever heard it enough. One does not come to know this in the same way that one grasps an enlightening thought, nor so that one knows it once for all. God's word is not a general truth that can be stored in the treasure-house of human spiritual life. It remains his sovereign word, which we shall never master and which can only be believed as an ever-living miracle, spoken by God, and constantly renewed. How should he who has heard it once not listen and hope, strive and pray, that he may hear it again?

Belief in this word is the surrender of one's whole existence to it; readiness to hear it is readiness to submit one's whole life to its judgment and its grace and, since our life is always trying to evade the word, readiness always to hear it anew. This does not mean that one takes a "biblical philosophy of life" from the Bible, by means of which one can find a reason for one's life, from which one can lay down hard and fast rules of conduct, and which supplies an infallible solution for the riddle of destiny. Nay, far more: if the way of faith leads from glory to glory (II Cor. 3:18), it is so just because it remains a way through perplexity and darkness (II Cor. 6:4 ff.). Glory is that which is granted from beyond—granted to the faith that hears God's word ever anew.

The word of God never becomes our property. The test of whether we have heard it aright is whether we are prepared always to hear it anew, to ask for it in every decision in life; whether we are prepared to let it intervene in the moment of decision; to let it convince us of our nothingness, but also of God's mercy, freeing us from all pride—"and what hast thou that thou didst not receive?" (I Cor. 4:7)—but also from any faint-heartedness—"as having nothing, and yet possessing all things" (II Cor. 6:10)!

We are constantly under the temptation not to listen to God's word any more. It is drowned for us by the noise of the world, by the quiet stream of everyday life with its soothing murmur, by the call of pressing duties and cares, or the stunning fury of fate. Which call sounds the louder, the manifold and varied voices of the world or the voice of God?

Or could a word of God possibly resound out of these many voices of the world, out of our duties and destinies, out of nature that surrounds our lives, out of history that forms them, and could this not complete the word received through the Bible? Yes, God speaks here too—but enigmatically, incomprehensibly. God's voice can be *understood* only by him who lets the word enter into him every time it speaks to him out of the Scriptures. For without the criterion of this word, which has only one interpretation, all these other voices are uncertain in their meaning. If we listen only to them we shall go astray. Are we not constantly being misled by these manifold and varied voices? Do they not constantly tempt us to become the masters of our own lives? We need then to have the word of judgment and grace continually repeated to us.

The readiness to submit one's whole life to God's word, to hear God's word ever again, i.e., to hear it anew each moment, is at the same time the *readiness to love.* When God's word frees us from ourselves and makes us into new beings through his love, it sets us free to love others. We abide in him only if his words abide in us (John 15:7), if we keep his commandments (John 15:10). And his commandment is love (John 15:12).

How does God speak to us through the Bible? As the sovereign Lord, who demands death and brings life, who claims our whole existence for his will, who sets us free to love. Are we ready to hear?

RABBI ABRAHAM J. HESCHEL

for the soul, home is where prayer is

Public worship is an act of the highest importance. However, it tends in our day to become a spectacle, in which the congregation remains passive, inert spectators. But prayer is action, it requires complete mobilization of heart, mind, and soul. What is the worth of attending public worship when mind and soul are not involved? Renewal of liturgy involves renewal of prayer.

There is, in addition, a malady indigenous, or congenital, to liturgy.

Liturgy as an act of prayer is an outcome and distillation of the inner life. Although its purpose is to exalt the life which engenders it, it harbors a tendency to follow a direction and rhythm of its own, independent of and divorced from the energies of life which brought prayer into being. At the beginning, liturgy is intimately related to the life which calls it into being. But as liturgy unfolds, it enters a state of stubborn disconnection, even into a state of opposition. Liturgy is bound to become rigid, to stand by itself, and to take on a measure of imperviousness. It tends to become timeless, transpersonal, liturgy for the sake of liturgy. Personal presence is replaced by mere attendance; instead of erecting a sanctuary of time in the realm of the soul, it attracts masses of people to a sanctuary in the realm of space.

I plead for primacy of prayer in our inner existence. The test of authentic theology is the degree to which it reflects and enhances the power of prayer, the way of worship . . . God is hiding, and man is defying. Every moment God is creating and self-concealing.

From *Tempo,* October 15, 1969.

Prayer is disclosing or at least preventing irreversible concealing. God is ensconced in mystery, hidden in the depths. Prayer is pleading with God to come out of the depths.

Prayer as an episode, as a cursory incident, will not establish a home in the land of oblivion. Prayer must pervade as a climate of living, and all our acts must be carried out as variations on the theme of prayer. A deed of charity, an act of kindness, a ritual moment, it is prayer in the form of a deed.

All things have a home, the bird has a nest, the fox has a hole, the bee has a hive. A soul without prayer is a soul without a home. Weary, sobbing, the soul after roving, roaming through a world pestered with aimlessness, falsehoods, absurdities, seeks a moment in which to gather up its scattered trivialized life, in which to divest itself of enforced pretentions and camouflage; in which to simplify complexities, in which to call for help without being a coward—such a home is prayer. Continuity, permanence, intimacy, authenticity, earnestness are its attributes. For the soul, home is where the prayer is.

Everybody must build his own home; everybody must guard the independence and the privacy of his prayers. It is the source of security for the integrity of conscience, for whatever inkling we attain of eternity.

At home I have a father who judges and cares, who has regard for me, and when I fail and go astray, misses me. I will never give up my home.

What is a soul without prayer? A soul runaway or a soul evicted from its own home.

How marvelous is my home. I enter as a suppliant and emerge as a witness; I enter as a stranger and emerge as next of kin. I may enter spiritually shapeless, inwardly disfigured, and emerge wholly changed. It is in moments of prayer that my image is forged, that my striving is fashioned.

To understand the world you must love your home. It is difficult to perceive luminosity anywhere, if there is no light in my home. It is in the light of prayer's radiance that I find my way in the dark. It is prayer that illumines my way.

Prayer serves many aims. It serves to save the inward life from oblivion. It serves to alleviate anguish. It serves to partake of God's mysterious grace and guidance. Yet, ultimately prayer must not be experienced as an act for the sake of something else. We pray in order to pray. Prayer is a perspective from which to behold, from which to respond to, the challenges we face. Man in prayer does not seek to impose his will upon God; he seeks to impose God's will and mercy upon himself.

To pray is to open a door, where both God and soul may enter. Prayer is arrival, for Him and for us. To pray is to overcome distance, to shatter screens, to render straight obliquities, to heal the break between God and the world. A dreadful oblivion prevails in the world. The world has forgotten what it means to be human. The gap is widening, the abyss is within the self.

Though often I do not know how to pray, I can say: Redeem us from the agony of not knowing what to strive for, from the agony of not knowing how my inner life is falling apart.

A candle of the Lord is the soul of man, but the soul can become a holocaust, a fury, a rage.

The only cure is to discover that over and above the anonymous stillness in the world there is a Name and a waiting.

Many young people suffer from fear of the self. They do not feel at home in their own selves. The inner life is a place of dereliction, a no-man's land, inconsolate, weird. The self has become a place to run away from. The use of narcotic drugs is a search for a home.

Human distress, wretchedness, agony, is a signal of a universal distress. It is a sign of human misery, it also proclaims a divine predicament. God's mercy is too great to permit the innocent to suffer. There are forces that interfere with God's mercy, with God's power.

I pray because God, the Shekinah, is an outcast, I pray because God is in exile, because we all conspire to blur all signs of this presence in the present or in the past. I pray because I refuse to despair, because extreme denials and defiance are refuted in the confrontation of my own presumption and the mystery all around me. I pray because I am unable to pray.

And suddenly I am forced to do what I seem unable to do. Even callousness to the mystery is not immortal. There are moments when the clamor of all sirens dies, presumption is depleted, and even the bricks in the walls are waiting for a song.

The door is closed, the key is lost. Yet the new sadness of my soul is about to open the door.

Some souls are born with a scar, others are endowed with anesthesia. Satisfaction with the world is base and the basic callousness. The remedy to absurdity is still to be revealed. The irreconcilable opposites which agonize human existence are the outcry, the prayer. Every one of us is a cantor, every one of us is called to intone a song, to put into prayer the anguish of all.

God is in captivity in this world, in the oblivion of our lives. God is in search of man, in search of a home in the soul and deeds of man. God is not at home in our world. Our task is to hallow time, to enable Him to enter our moments, to be at home in our time, in what we do with time. . . .

The hour calls for a revision of fundamental religious concerns. The wall of separation between the sacred and the secular has become a wall of separation between the conscience and God. In the Pentateuch, the relation of man to things of space, to money, to property is a fundamental religious problem. In the affluent society sins committed with money may be as grievous as sins committed with our tongue. We will give account for what we have done.

Religion as an establishment must remain separated from the government. Yet prayer as a voice of mercy, as a cry for justice, as a plea for gentleness, must not be kept apart. Let the spirit of prayer dominate the world. Let the spirit of prayer interfere in the affairs of man. Prayer is private, a service of the heart, but let concern and compassion, born out of prayer, dominate public life.

The predicament of prayer is that not only do we not know how to pray; we do not know what to pray for.

We have lost the ability to be shocked.

The malignity of our situation is increasing rapidly, spreading furiously, the magnitude of evil, surpassing our ability to be shocked. The human soul is too limited to experience dismay in proportion to what has happened in Auschwitz, in Hiroshima, for example.

It is with shame and anguish that I recall that it was possible for a Roman Catholic Church adjoining the extermination camp in Auschwitz to offer communion to the officers of the camp, to people who day after day drove thousands of people to be killed in the gas-chambers.

Prayer is meaningless unless it is subversive, unless it seeks to overthrow and to ruin the pyramids of callousness, hatred, opportunism, falsehoods.

The liturgical movement must become a revolutionary movement, seeking to overthrow the forces that continue to destroy the promise, the hope, the vision.

Dark is the world to me, for all its cities and stars. If not for my faith that God in His silence still listens to a cry, who could stand such agony?

The strength of faith is in silence, and in words that hibernate and wait. Uttered faith must come out as a surplus of silence, as the fruit of lived faith, of enduring intimacy.

Prayer will not come about by default. It requires education, training, reflection, contemplation. It is not enough to join others; it is necessary to build a sanctuary within, brick by brick, instants of meditation, moments of devotion. This is particularly true at an age when overwhelming forces seem to conspire at destroying our ability to pray.

The relentless pursuit of our interests makes us oblivious of reality itself. Nothing we experience has value in itself; nothing counts unless it can be turned to our advantage, into a means for serving our self-interests.

The beginning of prayer is praise. The power of worship is song. First we sing, then we understand. First we praise, then we believe. Praise and song open eyes to the grandeur of reality that transcends the self. Song restores the soul; praise repairs spiritual deficiency.

While it is true that being human is gained and verified in relations between man and man, depth and authenticity of existence are disclosed in moments of worship.

Worship is more than paying homage. To worship is to join the cosmos in praising God. The whole cosmos, every living being sings, the Psalmists insist. Neither joy nor sorrow but song is the ground-plan of being. It is the quintessence of life. To praise is to call forth the promise and presence of the divine. We live for the sake of a song. We praise for the privilege of being.

"Choose Life!" is the great legacy of the Hebrew Bible, and the cult of life is affirmed in contemporary theology. However, life is not a thing, static and final.

Life means living, and in living you have to choose a road, direction, goals. Pragmatists who believed that life itself can provide us with the criteria for truth overlook the fact that inherent in life are also forces of suicide and destruction.

Just to be is a blessing. Just to live is holy. And yet, being alive is no answer to the problems of living. To be or not to be is *not* the question. The vital question is: how to be and how not to be?

The tendency to forget this vital question is the tragic disease of contemporary man, a disease that may prove fatal, that may end in disaster. To pray is passionately to recollect the perpetual urgency of this vital question.

Religious commitment is not just an ingredient of the social order, an adjunct or reinforcement of existence, but rather the heart and core of being human, its exultation, its verification being manifest in the social order, in daily deeds.

Religious existence is living in solidarity with God. Yet to maintain such solidarity involves knowing how to cross an abyss. Vested interests are more numerous than locusts, and of solidarity of character there is only a smattering. Too much devotion is really too little. It is grave self-deception to assume that our destiny is to be just human. In order to be human, one must be more than human.

A person must never stand still. He must always rise, he must always climb. Be stronger than you are.

Well-trodden ways lead into swamps. There are no easy ways, there are no simple solutions. What comes easy is not worth a straw. It is a tragic error to assume that the world is flat, that our direction is horizontal. The way is always vertical. It is either up or down; we either climb or fall.

The tragedy of our time is that we have moved out of the dimension of the holy, that we have abandoned the intimacy in which relationship to God can be patiently, honestly, persistently nourished. Intimate inner life is forsaken. Yet the soul can never remain a vacuum. It is either a vessel for grace or it is occupied by demons.

At first men sought mutual understanding by taking counsel with one another, but now we understand one another less and less. There is a gap between the generations. It will soon widen to be an abyss. The only bridge is to pray together, to consult God before seeking council with one another.

Prayer brings down the wall which we have erected between man and man, between man and God.

We of this generation are afflicted with a severe case of dulling or loss of vision. Is it the result of our own intoxication or is it the result of God's deliberate concealment of visible lights?

Spiritual memory of many people is empty, words are diluted, incentives exhausted, inspirations drained.

Is God to be blamed for all this?

Is it not man who has driven them out of our hearts and minds?

This is an age of spiritual blackout, a blackout of God. We have entered not only the dark night of the soul, but also the dark night of society. Together with our efforts to cure the ills of society, we must try to seek out a strong and deep truth of a living God theology in the midst of the Blackout.

For the darkness is neither final nor complete. Our power is first in waiting for the end of darkness, for the defeat of evil, and our power is also in coming upon single, isolated sparks and occasional ways, upon moments full of God's grace and radiance.

We are called to bring together the sparks to preserve and to keep alive in our lives the single moments of radiance, to defy absurdity and despair and to wait for God to say again: Let there be light. And there will be light.

JULIANA OF NORWICH

shewings of divine love _____

I saw that he is to us everything that is good and strengthening for our help. He is our clothing that, for love, wrappeth us up and windeth us about; embraceth us, all becloseth us and hangeth about us, for tender love; so that he can never leave us. And so, in this sight, I saw that he is to us everything that is good, as I understand it.

Also in this he shewed a little thing, the size of a hazelnut, which seemed to lie in the palm of my hand; and it was as round as any ball. I looked upon it with the eye of my understanding, and thought, "What may this be?" I was answered in a general way, thus: "It is all that is made." I wondered how long it could last; for it seemed as though it might suddenly fade away to nothing, it was so small. And I was answered in my understanding: "It lasts, and ever shall last; for God loveth it. And even so hath everything being—by the love of God."

In this little thing I saw three properties. The first is that God made it: the second, that God loveth it: the third, that God keepeth it. And what beheld I in this? Truly, the Maker, the Lover and the Keeper. And until I am substantially oned to him, I can never have full rest nor true bliss; that is to say, until I am so fastened to him that there is no created thing at all between my God and me. And this little thing that is made—it seemed as though it would fade away to nothing, it was so small. We need to have knowledge of this—that we should reckon as naught everything that is made, to love and have God who is unmade. For this is the reason why we are not all in ease of heart and of soul: that we seek here rest in this thing that is so little and where no rest is in; we know not our God that is almighty, all-wise and all-good. For he is very rest. It is his will to

From *Shewings of Divine Love,* ed. Warrock, London, Methuen & Co., Ltd., n.d. Also reprinted in Elmer O'Brien, S.J., *Varieties of Mystic Experience,* New York, Holt, Rinehart, and Winston, 1964.

be known and it is his pleasure that we rest us in him. All that is beneath him sufficeth not to us. And this is the reason why no soul can be in rest until it is naughted of everything that is made. When the soul is willingly naughted, for love, so as to have him who is All, then is she able to receive ghostly rest.

After this, our Lord shewed me concerning prayer. In this shewing I saw two conditions for prayer—as our Lord understandeth it; one is rightfulness, the other is sure trust. For oftentimes our trust is not full; we are not sure that God heareth us, because (so we imagine) of our unworthiness, and the fact that we feel nothing at all—for we are as barren and as dry oftentimes after our prayers as we were before. Thus, in our feelings and in our folly is the cause of this weakness of ours; and this is my own experience.

All this our Lord brought to my mind at once, and shewed these words:

I am the ground of thy beseeching. First, it is my will that thou have it—and seeing that I make thee to desire it, and seeing that I make thee to beseech it and thou beseechest it, how could it then be that thou shouldst not have thy beseeching?

Thus in the first reason, with the three that follow, our Lord shewed a mighty comfort, as may be seen in these same words. In the first reason, where he saith "and thou beseechest it," he there sheweth the exceeding pleasure and endless reward that he willeth to give us for our beseeching. And the sixth reason (where he says "How could it then be?") was given as an impossibility. For nothing is more impossible than that we should seek mercy and grace, and not have it. For all the things that our good Lord himself maketh us to beseech, these he hath ordained to us from without-beginning. Here then may we see that his proper goodness and not our beseeching is the cause of the goodness and the grace that he doeth to us; and that shewed he truly in all these sweet words where he saith "I am the ground." Our good Lord willeth that this be known amongst his lovers on earth; and the more we know it the more shall we beseech, if we understand it wisely—and that is our Lord's intention.

Beseeching is a true and grace-giving, lasting will of the soul which is oned and fastened to the will of our Lord, by the sweet and secret working of the Holy Ghost.

Our Lord willeth us to have true understanding in what belongeth to our prayer, especially in three things. The first is to know by whom and how our prayer beginneth. By whom, he sheweth when he says "I am the ground": and how, by his goodness; for he saith, "First, it is my will." The second is to know in what manner and how we should use our time of prayer; this is that our will be turned to the will of our Lord in joy. This is his meaning when he saith "I make thee to will it." The third is to know the fruit and end of our prayer; which is to be oned and like to our Lord in everything. To this meaning and to this end was all this lovely lesson shewed. He will help us, and he shall bring it about, as he says himself, blessed may he be!

For this is our Lord's will—that our prayer and our trust be alike, large. For if we do not trust as much as we pray, we fail in full worship to our Lord in our prayer; and also we hinder and hurt ourselves. The reason is that we do not know truly that our Lord is the ground from whom our prayer springeth; not do we know that it is given us by his grace and his love. If we knew this, it would make us trust to have of our Lord's gift all that we desire. For I am sure that no man asketh mercy and grace with sincerity, without mercy and grace being given to him first.

ABRAHAM MASLOW

the "core-religious," or "transcendent," experience —————————————————

The very beginning, the intrinsic core, the essence, the universal nucleus of every known high religion (unless Confucianism is also called a religion) has been the private, lonely, personal illumination, revelation, or ecstasy of some acutely sensitive prophet or seer. The high religions call themselves revealed religions and each of them tends to rest its validity, its function, and its right to exist on the codification and the communication of this original mystic experience or revelation from the lonely prophet to the mass of human beings in general.

But it has recently begun to appear that these "revelations" or mystical illuminations can be subsumed under the head of the "peak-experiences" or "ecstasies" or "transcendent" experiences which are now being eagerly investigated by many psychologists. That is to say, it is very likely, indeed almost certain, that these older reports, phrased in terms of supernatural revelation, were, in fact, perfectly natural, human peak-experiences of the kind that can easily be examined today, which, however, were phrased in terms of whatever conceptual, cultural, and linguistic framework the particular seer had available in his time (Laski).

In a word, we can study today what happened in the past and was then explainable in supernatural terms only. By so doing, we are enabled to examine religion in all its facets and in all its meanings in a way that makes it a part of science rather than something outside and exclusive of it.

Also this kind of study leads us to another very plausible hypothesis: to the extent that all mystical or peak-experiences are the same in their essence and have always been the same, all religions are the same in their essence and always have been the same. They should, therefore, come to agree in principle on teach-

From *Religions, Values, and Peak-Experiences,* Columbus, Ohio State University Press, 1964. Used by permission of Kappa Delta Pi, An Honor Society in Education, owners of the copyright.

ing that which is common to all of them, i.e., whatever it is that peak-experiences teach in common (whatever is *different* about these illuminations can fairly be taken to be localisms both in time and space, and are, therefore, peripheral, expendable, not essential). This something common, this something which is left over after we peel away all the localisms, all the accidents of particular languages or particular philosophies, all the ethnocentric phrasings, all those elements which are *not* common, we may call the "core-religious experience" or the "transcendent experience."

To understand this better, we must differentiate the prophets in general from the organizers or legalists in general as (abstracted) types. (I admit that the use of pure, extreme types which do not really exist can come close to the edge of caricature; nevertheless, I think it will help all of us in thinking through the problem we are here concerned with.) The characteristic prophet is a lonely man who has discovered his truth about the world, the cosmos, ethics, God, and his own identity from within, from his own personal experiences, from what he would consider to be a revelation. Usually, perhaps always, the prophets of the high religions have had these experiences when they were alone.

Characteristically the abstraction-type of the legalist-ecclesiastic is the conserving organization man, an officer and arm of the organization, who is loyal to the structure of the organization which has been built up on the basis of the prophet's original revelation in order to make the revelation available to the masses. From everything we know about organizations, we may very well expect that people will become loyal to it, as well as to the original prophet and to his vision; or at least they will become loyal to the organization's version of the prophet's vision. I may go so far as to say that characteristically (and I mean not only the religious organizations but also parallel organizations like the Communist Party or like revolutionary groups) these organizations can be seen as a kind of punch card or IBM version of an original revelation or mystical experience or peak-experience to make it suitable for group use and for administrative convenience.

It will be helpful here to talk about a pilot investigation, still in its beginnings, of the people I have called nonpeakers. In my first investigations, in collaboration with Gene Nameche, I used this word because I thought some people had peak-experiences and others did not. But as I gathered information, and as I became more skillful in asking questions, I found that a higher and higher percentage of my subjects began to report peak-experiences. . . . I finally fell into the habit of expecting everyone to have peak-experiences and of being rather surprised if I ran across somebody who could report none at all. Because of this experience, I finally began to use the word "nonpeaker" to describe, not the person who is unable to have peak-experiences, but rather the person who is afraid of them, who suppresses them, who denies them, who turns away from them, or who "forgets" them. My preliminary investigations of the reasons for these negative reactions to peak-experiences have led me to some (unconfirmed) impressions about why certain kinds of people renounce their peak-experiences.

Any person whose character structure (or *Weltanschauung,* or way of life) forces him to try to be extremely or completely rational or "materialistic" or mechanistic tends to become a nonpeaker. That is, such a view of life tends to make the person regard his peak- and transcendent experiences as a kind of insanity, a complete loss of control, a sense of being overwhelmed by irrational emotions, etc. The person who is afraid of going insane and who is, therefore, desperately hanging on to stability, control, reality, etc., seems to be frightened by peak-experiences and tends to fight them off. For the compulsive-obsessive person, who organizes his life around the denying and the controlling of emotion, the fear of being overwhelmed by an emotion (which is interpreted as a loss of control) is enough for him to mobilize all his stamping-out and defensive activities against the peak-experience. I have one instance of a very convinced Marxian who denied—that is, who turned away from—a legitimate peak-experience, finally classifying it as some kind of peculiar but unimportant thing that had happened but that had best be forgotten because this experience conflicted with her whole materialistic mechanistic philosophy of life. I have found a few nonpeakers who were ultra-scientific, that is, who espoused the nineteenth-century conception of science as an emotional or anti-emotional activity which was ruled entirely by logic and rationality and who thought anything which was not logical and rational had no respectable place in life. (I suspect also that extremely "practical," i.e., exclusively means-oriented, people will turn out to be nonpeakers, since such experiences earn no money, bake no bread, and chop no wood. So also for extremely otherdirected people, who scarcely know what is going on inside themselves. Perhaps also people who are reduced to the concrete à la Goldstein, etc., etc.) Finally, I should add that, in some cases, I could not come to any explanation for nonpeaking.

If you will permit me to use this developing but not yet validated vocabulary, I may then say simply that the relationship between the prophet and the ecclesiastic, between the lonely mystic and the (perfectly extreme) religious-organization man may often be a relationship between peaker and nonpeaker. Much theology, much verbal religion through history and throughout the world, can be considered to be the more or less vain efforts to put into communicable words and formulas, and into symbolic rituals and ceremonies, the original mystical experience of the original prophets. In a word, organized religion can be thought of as an effort to communicate peak-experiences to nonpeakers, to teach them, to apply them, etc. Often, to make it more difficult, this job falls into the hands of nonpeakers. On the whole we now would expect that this would be a vain effort, at least so far as much of mankind is concerned. The peak-experiences and their experiential reality ordinarily are not transmittable to nonpeakers, at least not by words alone, and certainly not by nonpeakers. What happens to many people, especially the ignorant, the uneducated, the naive, is that they simply concretize all of the symbols, all of the words, all of the statues, all of the ceremonies, and by a process of functional autonomy make *them,* rather than the original revelation, into the sacred things and sacred activities. That is to say, this is simply a form of the idolatry (or fetishism) which has been the curse of every large religion. In idolatry the essential original meaning gets so lost in concretizations that these finally become hostile to the original mystical experiences, to mystics, and to prophets in general, that is, to the very people that we might call from our present point of view the truly religious people. Most religions have wound up denying and being antagonistic to the very ground upon which they were originally based.

If you look closely at the internal history of most of the world religions, you will find that each one very soon tends to divide into a left-wing and a right-wing, that is, into the peakers, the mystics, the transcenders, or the privately religious people, on the one hand, and, on the other, into those who concretize the religious symbols and metaphors, who worship little pieces of wood rather than what the objects stand for, those who take verbal formulas literally, forgetting the original meaning of these words, and, perhaps most important, those who take the organization, the church, as primary and as more important than the prophet and his original revelations. These men, like many organization men who tend to rise to the top in any complex bureaucracy, tend to be nonpeakers rather than peakers. Dostoevski's famous Grand Inquisitor passage, in his *Brothers Karamazov,* says this in a classical way.

This cleavage between the mystics and the legalists, if I may call them that, remains at best a kind of mutual tolerance, but it has happened in some churches that the rulers of the organization actually made a heresy out of the mystic experiences and persecuted the mystics themselves. This may be an old story in the history of religion, but I must point out that it is also an old story in other fields. For instance, we can certainly say today that professional philosophers tend to divide themselves into the same kind of characterologically based left-wing and right-wing. Most official, orthodox philosophers today are the equivalent of legalists who reject the problems and the data of transcendence as "meaningless." That is, they are positivists, atomists, analysts, concerned with means rather than with ends. They sharpen tools rather than discovering truths. These people contrast sharply with another group of contemporary philosophers, the existentialists and the phenomenologists. These are the people who tend to fall back on experiencing as the primary datum from which everything starts.

A similar split can be detected in psychology, in anthropology, and, I am quite sure, in other fields as well, perhaps in *all* human enterprises. I often suspect that we are dealing here with a profoundly characterological or constitutional difference in people which may persist far into the future, a human difference which may be universal and may continue to be so. The job then will be to get these two kinds of people to understand each other, to get along well with each other, even to love each other. This problem is paralleled by the relations between men and women who are so different from each other and yet who *have to* live with each other and even to love each other. (I must admit that it would be almost impossible to achieve this with poets and literary critics, composers and music critics, etc.)

To summarize, it looks quite probable that the peak-experience may be the model of the religious revelation or the religious illumination or conversion which has played so great a role in the history of religions. But, because peak-experiences are in the natural world and because we can research with them and investigate them, and because our knowledge of such experiences is growing and may be confidently expected to grow in the future, we may now fairly hope to understand more about the big revelations, conversions, and illuminations upon which the high religions were founded.

(Not only this, but I may add a new possibility for scientific investigation of transcendence. In the last few years it has become quite clear that certain drugs called "psychedelic," especially LSD and psilocybin, give us some possibility of control in this realm of peak-experiences. It looks as if these drugs often produce peak-experiences in the right people under the right circumstances, so that perhaps we needn't wait for them to occur by good fortune. Perhaps we can actually produce a private personal peak-experience under observation and whenever we wish under religious or nonreligious circumstances. We may then be able to study in its moment of birth the experience of illumination or revelation. Even more important, it may be that these drugs, and perhaps also hypnosis, could be used to produce a peak-experience, with core-religious revelation, in non-peakers, thus bridging the chasm between these two separated halves of mankind.)

To approach this whole discussion from another angle, in effect what I have been saying is that the evidence from the peak-experiences permits us to talk about the essential, the intrinsic, the basic, the most fundamental religious or transcendent experience as a totally private and personal one which can hardly be shared (except with other "peakers"). As a consequence, all the paraphernalia of organized religion—buildings and specialized personnel, rituals, dogmas, ceremonials, and the like—are to the "peaker" secondary, peripheral, and of doubtful value in relation to the intrinsic and essential religious or transcendent experience. Perhaps they may even be very harmful in various ways. From the point of view of the peak-experiencer, each person has his own private religion, which he develops out of his own private myths and symbols, rituals and ceremonials, which may be of the profoundest meaning to him personnally and yet completely idiosyncratic, i.e., of no meaning to anyone else. But to say it even more simply, each "peaker" discovers, develops, and retains his own religion.

In addition, what seems to be emerging from this new source of data is that this essential core-religious experience may be embedded either in a theistic, supernatural context or in a nontheistic context. This private religious experience is shared by all the great world religions including the atheistic ones like Buddhism, Taoism, Humanism, or Confucianism. As a matter of fact, I can go so far as to say that this intrinsic core-experience is a meeting ground not only, let us say, for Christians and Jews and Mohammedans but also for priests and atheists, for communists and anti-communists, for conservatives and liberals, for artists and scientists, for men and for women, and for different constitutional types, that is to say, for athletes and for poets, for thinkers and for doers. I say this because our findings indicate that all or almost all people have or can have peak-experiences. Both men and women have peak-experiences, and all kinds of constitutional types have peak-experiences, but, although the content of the peak-experiences is approximately as I have described for all human beings . . . the situation or the trigger which sets off peak-experience, for instance in males and females, can be quite different. These experiences can come from different sources, but their content may be considered to be very similar. To sum it up, from this point of view, the two religions of mankind tend to be the peakers and the nonpeakers, that is to say, those who have private, personal, transcendent, core-religious experiences easily and often and who accept them and make use of them, and, on the other hand, those who have never had them or who repress or suppress them and who, therefore, cannot make use of them for their personal therapy, personal growth, or personal fulfillment.

DAG HAMMARSKJÖLD

markings:
the private journal of a secular man ———————————————

thus it was

I am being driven forward
Into an unknown land.
The pass grows steeper,
The air colder and sharper.
A wind from my unknown goal
Stirs the strings
Of expectation.

Still the question:
Shall I ever get there?
There where life resounds,
A clear pure note
In the silence.

on being under god

Thou who has created us free, Who seest all that happens—yet art confident of
     victory,
Thou who at this time art the one among us who suffereth the uttermost loneli-
     ness,

From *Markings,* trans. Leif Sjöberg and W. H. Auden, New York, Knopf, 1964.

Thou—who art also in me,
May I bear Thy burden, when my hour comes,
May I—

.   .   .

In a dream I walked with God through the deep places of creation; past walls
that receded and gates that opened, through hall after hall of silence, darkness
and refreshment—the dwelling place of souls acquainted with light and warmth—
until, around me, was an infinity into which we all flowed together and lived
anew, like the rings made by raindrops falling upon wide expanses of calm dark
waters.

.   .   .

The "mystical experience." Always *here* and *now*—in that freedom which is one
with distance, in that stillness which is born of silence. But—this is a freedom in
the midst of action, a stillness in the midst of other human beings. The mystery
is a constant reality to him who, in this world, is free from self-concern, a reality
that grows peaceful and mature before the receptive attention of assent.

.   .   .

In our era, the road to holiness necessarily passes through the world of action.

.   .   .

On the field where Ormuzd has challenged Ahriman to battle, he who chases
away the dogs is wasting his time.

.   .   .

faith as self knowledge
On the bookshelf of life, God is a useful work of reference, always at hand but
seldom consulted. In the whitewashed hour of birth, He is a jubilation and a
refreshing wind, too immediate for memory to catch. But when we are compelled to look ourselves in the face—then He rises above us in terrifying reality,
beyond all argument and "feeling," stronger than all self-defensive forgetfulness.

.   .   .

The road to self-knowledge does not pass through faith. But only through the
self-knowledge we gain by pursuing the fleeting light in the depth of our being
do we reach the point where we can grasp what faith is. How many have been
driven into outer darkness by empty talk about faith as something to be rationally comprehended, something "true."

.   .   .

Our secret creative divines its counterpart in others, experiencing its own universality, and this intuition builds a road towards knowledge of the power which is
itself a spark within us.

god does not die
God does not die on the day when we cease to believe in a personal deity, but
we die on the day when our lives cease to be illumined by the steady radiance,
renewed daily, of a wonder, the source of which is beyond all reason.

. . .

How easy Psychology has made it for us to dismiss the perplexing mystery with a label which assigns it a place in the list of common aberrations.

. . .

It is not sufficient to place yourself daily under God. What really matters is to be *only* under God: the slightest division of allegiance opens the door to daydreaming, petty conversation, petty boasting, petty malice—all the petty satellites of the death-instinct.

"But how, then, am I to love God?" "You must love Him as if He were a non-God, a non-Spirit, a non-Person, a non-Substance: love Him simply as the One, the pure and absolute Unity in which is no trace of Duality. And into this One, we must let ourselves fall continually from being into nonbeing. God helps us to do this."

. . .

He broke fresh ground—because, and only because, he had the courage to go ahead without asking whether others were following or even understood. He had no need for the divided responsibility in which others seek to be safe from ridicule, because he had been granted a faith which required no confirmation—a contact with reality, light and intense like the touch of a loved hand: a union in self-surrender without self-destruction, where his heart was lucid and his mind loving. In sun and wind, how near and how remote—how different from what the knowing ones call Mysticism.

. . .

faith

We act in faith—and miracles occur. In consequence, we are tempted to make the miracles the ground for our faith. The cost of such weakness is that we lose the confidence of faith. Faith *is,* faith creates, faith carries. It is not derived from, nor created, nor carried by anything except its own reality.

. . .

2.24.57

We can reach the point where it becomes possible for us to recognize and understand Original Sin, that dark counter-center of evil in our nature—that is to say, though it *is* not our nature, it is *of* it—that something within us which rejoices when disaster befalls the very cause we are trying to serve, or misfortune overtakes even those whom we love.

Life in God is not an escape from this, but the way to gain full insight concerning it. It is not our depravity which forces a fictitious religious explanation upon us, but the experience of religious reality which forces the "Night Side" out into the light.

It is when we stand in the righteous all-seeing light of love that we can dare to look at, admit, and *consciously* suffer under this something in us which wills disaster, misfortune, defeat to everything outside the sphere of our narrowest self-interest. So a living relation to God is the necessary precondition for the

•self-knowledge which enables us to follow a straight path, and so be victorious over ourselves, forgiven by ourselves.

· · ·

4.10.58
In the faith which is "God's marriage to the soul," you are *one* in God, and
   God is wholly in you,
   just as, for you, He is wholly in all you meet.
   With this faith, in prayer you descend into yourself to meet the Other,
   in the steadfastness and light of this union,
   see that all things stand, like yourself, alone before God.
   and that each of your acts is an act of creation, conscious, because you are a human being with human responsibilities, but governed, nevertheless, by the power beyond human consciousness which has created man.
   You are liberated from things, but you encounter in them an experience which has the purity and clarity of revelation.
   In the faith which is "God's marriage to the soul," *everything,* therefore, has a meaning.
   So live, then, that you may use what has been put into your hand. . . .

· · ·

responding
Whitsunday, 1961
I don't know who—or what—put the question, I don't know when it was put. I don't even remember answering. But at some moment I did answer *Yes* to Someone—or Something—and from that hour I was certain that existence is meaningful and that, therefore, my life, in self-surrender, had a goal.

· · ·

July 6, 1961
Tired
And lonely,
So tired
The heart aches.
Meltwater trickles
Down the rocks,
The fingers are numb,
The knees tremble.
It is now,
Now, that you must not give in.

On the path of the others
Are resting places,
Places in the sun
Where they can meet.
But this
Is your path,
And it is now,
Now, that you must not fail.

Weep
If you can,
Weep,
But do not complain.
The way chose you—
And you must be thankful.

a japanese business man experiences satori

Dear Nakagawa-roshi:
Thank you for the happy day I spent at your monastery.

You remember the discussion which arose about Self-realization centering around that American. At that time I hardly imagined that in a few days I would be reporting to you my own experience.

The day after I called on you I was riding home on the train with my wife. I was reading a book on Zen by Son-o, who, you may recall, was a master of Soto Zen living in Sendai during the Genroku period (1688-1703). As the train was nearing Ofuna station I ran across this line: "I came to realize clearly that Mind is no other than mountains and rivers and the great wide earth, the sun and the moon and the stars."

I had read this before, but this time it impressed itself upon me so vividly that I was startled. I said to myself: "After seven or eight years of zazen I have finally perceived the essence of this statement," and couldn't suppress the tears that began to well up. Somewhat ashamed to find myself crying among the crowd, I averted my face and dabbed at my eyes with my handkerchief.

Meanwhile the train had arrived at Kamakura station and my wife and I got off. On the way home I said to her: "In my present exhilarated frame of mind I could rise to the greatest heights." Laughingly she replied: "Then where would I be?" All the while I kept repeating that quotation to myself.

From Philip Kapleau, "A Letter of Mr. K. Y., A Japanese Executive, age 47. November 27, 1953," *The Three Pillars of Zen,* New York, John Weatherhill, Inc., 1965.

It so happened that that day my younger brother and his wife were staying at my home, and I told them about my visit to your monastery and about that American who had come to Japan again only to attain enlightenment. In short, I told them all the stories you had told me, and it was after eleven-thirty before I went to bed.

At midnight I abruptly awakened. At first my mind was foggy, then suddenly that quotation flashed into my consciousness: "I came to realize clearly that Mind is no other than mountains, rivers, and the great wide earth, the sun and the moon and the stars." And I repeated it. Then all at once I was struck as though by lightning, and the next instant heaven and earth crumbled and disappeared. Instantaneously, like surging waves, a tremendous delight welled up in me, a veritable hurricane of delight, as I laughed loudly and wildly: "Ha, ha, ha, ha, ha, ha! There's no reasoning here, no reasoning at all! Ha, ha, ha!" The empty sky split in two, then opened its enormous mouth and began to laugh uproariously: "Ha, ha, ha!" Later one of the members of my family told me that my laughter had sounded inhuman.

I was now lying on my back. Suddenly I sat up and struck the bed with all my might and beat the floor with my feet, as if trying to smash it, all the while laughing riotously. My wife and youngest son, sleeping near me, were now awake and frightened. Covering my mouth with her hand, my wife exclaimed: "What's the matter with you? What's the matter with you?" But I wasn't aware of this until told about it afterwards. My son told me later he thought I had gone mad.

"I've come to enlightenment! Shakyamuni and the Patriarchs haven't deceived me! They haven't deceived me!" I remember crying out. When I calmed down I apologized to the rest of the family, who had come downstairs frightened by the commotion.

Prostrating myself before the photograph of Kannon you had given me, the Diamond sutra, and my volume of the book written by Yasutani-roshi, I lit a stick of incense and did zazen until it was consumed half an hour later, though it seemed only two or three minutes had elapsed.

Even now my skin is quivering as I write.

That morning I went to see Yasutani-roshi and tried to describe to him my experience of the sudden disintegration of heaven and earth. "I am overjoyed, I am overjoyed!" I kept repeating, striking my thigh with vigor. Tears came which I couldn't stop. I tried to relate to him the experience of that night, but my mouth trembled and words wouldn't form themselves. In the end I just put my face in his lap. Patting me on the back he said: "Well, well, it is rare indeed to experience to such a wonderful degree. It is termed 'Attainment of the emptiness of Mind.' You are to be congratulated!"

"Thanks to you," I murmured, and again wept for joy. Repeatedly I told him: "I must continue to apply myself energetically to zazen." He was kind enough to give me detailed advice on how to pursue my practice in the future, after which he again whispered in my ear, "My congratulations!" and escorted me to the foot of the mountain by flashlight.

Although twenty-four hours have elapsed, I still feel the aftermath of that earthquake. My entire body is still shaking. I spent all of today laughing and weeping by myself.

I am writing to report my experience in the hope that it will be of value to your monks, and because Yasutani-roshi urged me to.

Please remember me to that American. Tell him that even I, who am unworthy and lacking in spirit, can grasp such a wonderful experience when time matures. I would like to talk with you at length about many things, but will have to wait for another time.

P.S. That American was asking us whether it is possible for him to attain enlightenment in one week of sesshin. Tell him this for me: don't say days, weeks, years, or even lifetimes. Don't say millions or billions of *kalpa*. Tell him to vow to attain enlightenment though it take the infinite, the boundless, the incalculable future.

Midnight of the 28th / [These diary entries were made during the next two days.] Awoke thinking it 3 or 4 A.M., but clock said it was only 12:30.

Am totally at peace at peace at peace.

Feel numb throughout body, yet hands and feet jumped for joy for almost half an hour.

Am supremely free free free free free.

Should I be so happy?

There is no common man.

The big clock chimes—not the clock but Mind chimes. The universe itself chimes. There is neither Mind nor universe. Dong, dong, dong!

I've totally disappeared. Buddha is!

"Transcending the law of cause and effect, controlled by the law of cause and effect"—such thoughts have gone from my mind.

Oh, you *are*! You laughed, didn't you? This laughter is the sound of your plunging into the world.

The substance of Mind—this is now luminously clear to me.

My concentration in zazen has sharpened and deepened.

Midnight of the 29th / I am at peace at peace at peace. Is this tremendous freedom of mine the Great Cessation described by the ancients? Whoever might question it would surely have to admit that this freedom is extraordinary. If it isn't absolute freedom or the Great Cessation, what is it?

4 A.M. of the 29th / Ding, dong! The clock chimed. This alone *is*! This alone *is*! There's no reasoning here.

Surely the world has changed [with enlightenment]. But in what way?

The ancients said the enlightened mind is comparable to a fish swimming. That's exactly how it is—there's no stagnation. I feel no hindrance. Everything flows smoothly, freely. Everything goes naturally. This limitless freedom is beyond all expression. What a wonderful world!

Dogen, the great teacher of Buddhism, said: "Zen is the wide, all-encompass-ing gate of compassion."

I am grateful, so grateful.

faust exults in nature

forest and cavern

Faust (alone): Exalted Spirit, you gave me, gave me all
  I prayed for. Aye, and it is not in vain
  That you have turned your face in fire upon me.
  You gave me glorious Nature for my kingdom
  With power to feel her and enjoy her. Nor
  Is it a mere cold wondering glance you grant me
  But you allow me to gaze into her depths
  Even as into the bosom of a friend.
  Aye, you parade the ranks of living things
  Before me and you teach me to know my brothers
  In the quiet copse, in the water, in the air.
  And when the storm growls and snarls in the forest
  And the giant pine falls headlong, bearing away
  And crushing its neighbors, bough and bole and all,
  With whose dull fall the hollow hill resounds,
  Then do you carry me off to a sheltered cave
  And show me myself, and wonders of my own breast
  Unveil themselves in their deep mystery.

  And now that the clear moon rises on my eyes
  To soften things, now floating up before me
  From walls of rock and from the dripping covert
  Come silver forms of the past which soothe and temper
  The dour delight I find in contemplation.

  That nothing perfect falls to men, oh now
  I feel that true. In addition to the rapture
  Which brings me near and nearer to the gods
  You gave me that companion whom already
  I cannot do without, though cold and brazen
  He lowers me in my own eyes and with

From *Faust* (Part One), ed. and trans. Stephen Spender, *Great Writings of Goethe*, New York, New American Library, 1958. Reprinted by permission of A. D. Peters and Company.

One whispered word can turn your gifts to nothing.
He is always busily fanning in my breast
A fire of longing for that lovely image.
So do I stagger from desire to enjoyment
And in enjoyment languish for desire.

(Mephistopheles enters)

Mephistopheles: Haven't you yet had enough of this kind of life?
　　How can it still appeal to you?
　　It is all very well to try it once,
　　Then one should switch to something new.
Faust: I wish you had something else to do
　　On my better days than come plaguing me.
Mephistopheles: Now, now! I'd gladly leave you alone;
　　You needn't suggest it seriously.
　　So rude and farouche and mad a friend
　　Would certainly be little loss.
　　One has one's hands full without end!
　　One can never read in the gentleman's face
　　What he likes or what should be left alone.
Faust: That is exactly the right tone!
　　He must be thanked for causing me ennui.
Mephistopheles: Poor son of earth, what sort of life
　　Would you have led were it not for me?
　　The flim-flams of imagination,
　　I have cured you of those for many a day.
　　But for me, this terrestrial ball
　　Would already have seen you flounce away.
　　Why behave as an owl behaves
　　Moping in rocky clefts and caves?
　　Why do you nourish yourself like a toad that sips
　　From moss that oozes, stone that drips?
　　A pretty pastime to contrive!
　　The doctor in you is still alive.
Faust: Do you comprehend what a new and vital power
　　This wandering in the wilderness has given me?
　　Aye, with even an inkling of such joy,
　　You would be devil enough to grudge it me.
Mephistopheles: A supernatural gratification!
　　To lie on the mountaintops in the dark and dew
　　Rapturously embracing earth and heaven,
　　Swelling yourself to a godhead, ferreting through

The marrow of the earth with divination,
To feel in your breast the whole six days of creation
To enjoy I know not what in arrogant might
And then, with the Old Adam discarded quite,
To overflow into all things in ecstacy;
After all which your lofty intuition (he makes a gesture)
Will end—hm—unmentionably.

Faust: Shame on you!

Mephistopheles: Am I to blame?
  You have the right to be moral and cry shame!
  One must not mention to the modest ear
  What the modest heart is ever agog to hear.
  And, in a word, you are welcome to the pleasure
  Of lying to yourself in measure;
  But this last deception will not last.
  Already overdriven again,
  If this goes on you must collapse,
  Mad or tormented or aghast.
  Enough of this! Back there your love is sitting
  And all her world seems sad and small;
  You are never absent from her mind,
  Her love for you is more than all.
  At first your passion came overflowing
  Like a brook that the melted snows have bolstered high;
  You have poured your passion into her heart
  And now your brook once more is dry.
  I think, instead of lording it here above
  In the woods, the great man might think it fit
  In view of that poor ninny's love
  To make her some return of it.
  She finds the time wretchedly long;
  She stands at the window, watches the clouds
  As over the old town walls they roll away.
  "If I had the wings of a dove"—so runs her song
  Half the night and all the day.
  Now she is cheerful, mostly low,
  Now has spent all her tears,
  Now calm again, it appears,
  But always loves you so.

Faust: You snake! You snake!

Mephistopheles (aside): Ha! It begins to take!

Faust: You outcast! Take yourself away
  And do not name that lovely woman.
  Do not bring back the desire for her sweet body

Upon my senses that are half astray.

Mephistopheles: Where's this to end? She thinks you have run off,
    And so you have—about half and half.

Faust: I am still near her and, though far removed,
    Her image must always be in my head;
    I already envy the body of the Lord
    When her lips rest upon the holy bread.

Mephistopheles: Very well, my friend, I have often envied you
    Those two young roes that are twins, I mean her two—

Faust: Pimp! Get away!

Mephistopheles: Fine! So you scold? I must laugh.
    The God who created girl and boy
    Knew very well the high vocation
    Which facilitates their joy.
    But come, this is a fine excuse for gloom!
    You should take the road to your sweetheart's room,
    Rather than that to death, you know.

Faust: What is the joy of heaven in her arms?
    Even when I catch fire upon her breast
    Do I not always sense her woe?
    Am I not the runaway? The man without a home?
    The monster restless and purposeless
    Who roared like a waterfall from rock to rock in foam
    Greedily raging towards the precipice?
    And she on the bank in childlike innocence
    In a little hut on the little alpine plot
    And all her little household world
    Concentrated in that spot.
    And I, the loathed of God,
    I was not satisfied
    To seize and crush to powder
    The rocks on the riverside!
    Her too, her peace, I must undermine as well!
    This was the sacrifice I owed to Hell!
    Help, Devil, to shorten my time of torment!
    What must be, must be; hasten it!
    Let her fate hurtle down with mine,
    Let us go together to the pit!

Mephistopheles: How it glows again, how it boils again!
    Go in and comfort her, my foolish friend!
    When such a blockhead sees no outlet
    He thinks at once it is the end.
    Long live the man who does not flinch!
    But you've a devil in you, somewhere there.

I know of nothing on earth more unattractive
Than your devil who feels despair.

. . .

martha's garden

Gretchen: Promise me, Heinrich!

Faust: If I can!

Gretchen: Tell me: how do you stand in regard to religion?
    You are indeed a good, good man
    But I think you give it scant attention.

Faust: Leave that, my child! You feel what I feel for you;
    For those I love I would give my life and none
    Will I deprive of his sentiments and his church.

Gretchen: That is not right; one must believe thereon.

Faust: Must one?

Gretchen: If only I had some influence!
    Nor do you honor the holy sacraments.

Faust: I honor them.

Gretchen: Yes, but not with any zest.
    When were you last at mass, when were you last confessed?
    Do you believe in God?

Faust: My darling, who dare say:
    I believe in God?
    Ask professor or priest,
    Their answers will make an odd
    Mockery of you.

Gretchen: You don't believe, you mean?

Faust: Do not misunderstand me, my love, my queen!
    Who can name him?
    Admit on the spot:
    I believe in him?
    And who can dare
    To perceive and declare:
    I believe in him not?
    The All-Embracing One,
    All-Upholding One,
    Does he not embrace, uphold,
    You, me, Himself?
    Does not the Heaven vault itself above us?
    Is not the earth established fast below?
    And with their friendly glances do not
    Eternal stars rise over us?
    Do not my eyes look into yours,
    And all things thrust

Into your head, into your heart,
And weave in everlasting mystery
Invisibly, visibly, around you?
Fill your heart with *this,* great as it is,
And when this feeling grants you perfect bliss,
Then call it what you will—
Happiness! Heart! Love! God!
I have no name for it!
Feeling is all;
Name is mere sound and reek
Clouding Heaven's light.

Gretchen: That sounds quite good and right;
And much as the priest might speak,
Only not word for word.

Faust: It is what all hearts have heard
In all the places heavenly day can reach,
Each in his own speech;
Why not I in mine?

Gretchen: I could almost accept it, you make it sound so fine,
Still there is something in it that shouldn't be;
For you have no Christianity.

Faust: Dear child!

Gretchen: It has long been a grief to me
To see you in such company.

Faust: You mean?

Gretchen: The man who goes about with you,
I hate him in my soul, right through and through.
And nothing has given my heart
In my whole life so keen a smart
As that man's face, so dire, so grim.

Faust: Dear poppet, don't be afraid of him!

Gretchen: My blood is troubled by his presence.
All other people, I wish them well;
But much as I may long to see you,
He gives me a horror I cannot tell,
And I think he's a man too none can trust.
God forgive me if I'm unjust.

Faust: Such queer fish too must have room to swim.

Gretchen: I wouldn't live with the like of him!
Whenever that man comes to the door,
He looks in so sarcastically,
Half angrily,
One can see he feels no sympathy;
It is written on his face so clear

There is not a soul he can hold dear.
I feel so cozy in your arms,
So warm and free from all restraint,
And his presence ties me up inside.
Faust: You angel, with your wild alarms!
Gretchen: It makes me feel so ill, so faint,
That, if he merely happens to join us,
I even think I have no more love for you.
Besides, when he's there, I could never pray,
And that is eating my heart away;
You, Heinrich, you must feel it too.
Faust: You suffer from an antipathy.
Gretchen: Now I must go.
Faust: Oh, can I never rest
One little hour hanging upon your breast,
Pressing both breast on breast and soul on soul?
Gretchen: Ah, if I only slept alone!
I'd gladly leave the door unlatched for you tonight;
My mother, however, sleeps so light
And if she found us there, I own
I should fall dead upon the spot.
Faust: You angel, there is no fear of that.
Here's a little flask. Three drops are all
It needs—in her drink—to cover nature
In a deep sleep, a gentle pall.
Gretchen: What would I not do for your sake!
I hope it will do her no injury.
Faust: My love, do you think that of me?
Gretchen: Dearest, I've only to look at you
And I do not know what drives me to meet your will
That little more is left me to fulfill.

(She goes out—and Mephistopheles enters)

Mephistopheles: The monkey! Is she gone?
Faust: Have you been spying again?
Mephistopheles: I have taken pretty good note of it,
The doctor had been catechized—
And much, I hope, to his benefit;
The girls are really keen to be advised
If a man belongs to the old simple-and-pious school.
"If he stand that," they think, "he'll stand *our* rule."
Faust: You, you monster, cannot see

How this true and loving soul
For whom faith is her whole
Being and the only road
To beatitude, must feel a holy horror
Having to count her beloved lost for good.
Mephistopheles: You supersensual, sensual buck,
    Led by the nose by the girl you court!
Faust: O you abortion of fire and muck!
Mephistopheles: And she also has skill in physiognomy;
    In my presence she feels she doesn't know what,
    She reads some hidden sense behind my little mask,
    She feels that I am assuredly a genius—
    Maybe the devil if she dared to ask.
    Now: tonight—
Faust: What is tonight to you?
Mephistopheles: I have my pleasure in it too.

JEAN-PAUL SARTRE

two dark visions

bouville

I watch the grey shimmerings of Bouville at my feet. In the sun they look like
heaps of shells, scales, splinters of bone, and gravel. Lost in the midst of this
debris, tiny glimmers of glass or mica intermittently throw off light flames. In an
hour the ripples, trenches, and thin furrows which run between these shells will
be streets, I shall walk in these streets, between these walls. These little black
men I can just make out in the Rue Boulibet—in an hour I shall be one of them.

I feel so far away from them, on the top of this hill. It seems as though I belong to another species. They come out of their offices after their day of work,
they look at the houses and the squares with satisfaction, they think it is *their*
city, a good, solid, bourgeois city. They aren't afraid, they feel at home. All they
have ever seen is trained water running from taps, light which fills bulbs when
you turn on the switch, half-breed, bastard trees held up with crutches. They
have proof, a hundred times a day, that everything happens mechanically, that
the world obeys fixed, unchangeable laws. In a vacuum all bodies fall at the same
rate of speed, the public park is closed at 4 P.M. in winter, at 6 P.M. in summer,
lead melts at 335 degrees centigrade, the last streetcar leaves the Hotel de Ville

at 11.05 P.M. They are peaceful, a little morose, they think about Tomorrow, that is to say, simply, a new today; cities have only one day at their disposal and every morning it comes back exactly the same. They scarcely doll it up a bit on Sundays. Idiots. It is repugnant to me to think that I am going to see their thick, self-satisfied faces. They make laws, they write popular novels, they get married, they are fools enough to have children. And all this time, great, vague nature has slipped into their city, it has infiltrated everywhere, in their house, in their office, in themselves. It doesn't move, it stays quietly and they are full of it inside, they breathe it, and they don't see it, they imagine it to be outside, twenty miles from the city. I *see* it, I *see* this nature . . . I know that its obedience is idleness, I know it has no laws: what they take for constancy is only habit and it can change tomorrow.

What if something were to happen? What if something suddenly started throbbing? Then they would notice it was there and they'd think their hearts were going to burst. Then what good would their dykes, bulwarks, power houses, furnaces and pile drivers be to them? It can happen any time, perhaps right now: the omens are present. For example, the father of a family might go out for a walk, and, across the street, he'll see something like a red rag, blown towards him by the wind. And when the rag has gotten close to him he'll see that it is a side of rotten meat, grimy with dust, dragging itself along by crawling, skipping, a piece of writhing flesh rolling in the gutter, spasmodically shooting out spurts of blood. Or a mother might look at her child's cheek and ask him: "What's that—a pimple?" and see the flesh puff out a little, split, open, and at the bottom of the split an eye, a laughing eye might appear. Or they might feel things gently brushing against their bodies, like the caresses of reeds to swimmers in a river. And they will realize that their clothing has become living things. And someone else might feel something scratching in his mouth. He goes to the mirror, opens his mouth: and his tongue is an enormous, live centipede, rubbing its legs together and scraping his palate. He'd like to spit it out, but the centipede is a part of him and he will have to tear it out with his own hands. And a crowd of things will appear for which people will have to find new names—stone-eye, great three cornered arm, toe-crutch, spider-jaw. And someone might be sleeping in his comfortable bed, in his quiet, warm room, and wake up naked on a bluish earth, in a forest of rustling birch trees, rising red and white towards the sky like the smokestacks of Jouxtebouville, with big bumps half-way out of the ground, hairy and bulbous like onions. And birds will fly around these birch trees and pick at them with their beaks and make them bleed. Sperm will flow slowly, gently, from these wounds, sperm mixed with blood, warm and glassy with little bubbles. Or else nothing like that will happen, there will be no appreciable change, but one morning people will open their blinds and be surprised by a sort of frightful sixth sense, brooding heavily over things and seeming to pause. Nothing more than that: but for the little time it lasts, there will be hundreds of suicides. Yes! Let it change just a little, just to see, I don't ask for anything better. Then you will see other people, suddenly plunged into solitude. Men all alone, completely alone with horrible monstrosities, will run through the streets, pass heavily in front of me, their eyes staring, fleeing their ills yet carrying them with them, open-mouthed, with their insect-tongue flapping its wings. Then I'll burst out laughing even though my body may be covered with filthy, infected scabs which blossom into flowers of flesh, violets, buttercups. I'll lean against a wall and when they go by I'll shout: "What's the matter with your science? What have you done with your humanism? Where is your dignity?" I will not be afraid—or at least no more than now. Will it not still be existence, variations on existence? . . .

the chestnut tree

So I was in the park just now. The roots of the chestnut tree were sunk in the ground just under my bench. I couldn't remember it was a root any more. The words had vanished and with them the significance of things, their methods of use, and the feeble points of reference which men have traced on their surface. I was sitting, stooping forward, head bowed, alone in front of this black, knotty mass, entirely beastly, which frightened me. Then I had this vision.

It left me breathless. Never, until these last few days, had I understood the meaning of "existence." I was like the others, like the ones walking along the seashore, all dressed in their spring finery. I said, like them, "The ocean *is* green; that white speck up there *is* a seagull," but I didn't feel that it existed or that the seagull was an "existing seagull"; usually existence hides itself. It is there, around us, in us, it is *us*, you can't say two words without mentioning it, but you can never touch it. When I believed I was thinking about it, I must believe that I was thinking nothing, my head was empty, or there was just one word in my head, the word "to be." Or else I was thinking . . . how can I explain it? I was thinking of *belonging,* I was telling myself that the sea belonged to the class of green objects, or that the green was a part of the quality of the sea. Even when I looked at things, I was miles from dreaming that they existed: they looked like scenery to me. I picked them up in my hands, they served me as tools, I foresaw their resistance. But that all happened on the surface. If anyone had asked me what existence was, I would have answered, in good faith, that it was nothing, simply an empty form which was added to external things without changing anything in their nature. And then all of a sudden, there it was, clear as day: existence had suddenly unveiled itself. It had lost the harmless look of an abstract category: it was the very paste of things, this root was kneaded into existence. Or rather the root, the park gates, the bench, the sparse grass, all that had vanished: the diversity of things, their individuality, were only an appearance, a veneer. This veneer had melted, leaving soft, monstrous masses, all in disorder—naked, in a frightful, obscene nakedness.

I kept myself from making the slightest movement, but I didn't need to move in order to see, behind the trees, the blue columns and the lamp-posts of the bandstand and the Velleda, in the midst of a mountain of laurel. All these objects . . . how can I explain? They inconvenienced me: I would have liked them to exist less strongly, more dryly, in a more abstract way, with more reserve. The chestnut tree pressed itself against my eyes. Green rust covered it half-way up; the bark, black and swollen, looked like boiled leather. The sound of the water in the Masqueret Fountain sounded in my ears, made a nest there, filled them with signs; my nostrils overflowed with a green, putrid odor. All things, gently, tenderly, were letting themselves drift into existence like those relaxed women who burst out laughing and say: "'Tis good to laugh," in a wet voice; they were parading, one in front of the other, exchanging abject secrets about their existence. I realized that there was no halfway house between nonexistence and this flaunting abundance. If you existed, you had to *exist all the way*, as far as moldiness, bloatedness, obscenity were concerned. In another world, circles, bars of music keep their pure and rigid lines. But existence is a deflection. Trees, night-blue pillars, the happy bubbling of a fountain, vital smells, little heat-mists floating in the cold air, a red-haired man digesting on a bench: all this somnolence, all these meals digested together, had its comic side. . . . Comic . . . no: it didn't go as far as that, nothing that exists can be comic; it was like a floating analogy, almost entirely elusive, with certain aspects of vaudeville. We were a heap of living creatures, irritated, embarrassed at ourselves, we hadn't the slightest reason to be there, none of us, each one, confused, vaguely alarmed, felt in the way in relation to the others. *In the way*: it was the only relationship I could establish between these trees, these gates, these stones. In vain I tried to *count* the chestnut trees, to *locate* them by their relationship to the Velleda, to compare their height with the height of the plane trees: each of them escaped the relationship in which I tried to enclose it, isolated itself, and overflowed. Of these relations (which I insisted on maintaining in order to delay the crumbling of the human world, measures, quantities, and directions)—I felt myself to be the arbitrator; they no longer had their teeth into things. *In the way,* the chestnut tree there, opposite me, a little to the left. *In the way,* the Velleda. . . .

And I—soft, weak, obscene, digesting, juggling with dismal thoughts—I, too, was *In the way*. Fortunately, I didn't feel it, although I realized it, but I was uncomfortable because I was afraid of feeling it (even now I am afraid—afraid that it might catch me behind my head and lift me up like a wave). I dreamed vaguely of killing myself to wipe out at least one of these superfluous lives. But even my death would have been *In the way*. *In the way,* my corpse, my blood on these stones, between these plants, at the back of this smiling garden. And the decomposed flesh would have been *In the way* in the earth which would receive my bones, at last, cleaned, stripped, peeled, proper and clean as teeth, it would have been *In the way:* I was *In the way* for eternity.

The word absurdity is coming to life under my pen; a little while ago, in the garden, I couldn't find it, but neither was I looking for it, I didn't need it: I thought without words, *on* things, *with* things. Absurdity was not an idea in my head, or the sound of a voice, only this long serpent dead at my feet, this wooden serpent. Serpent or claw or root or vulture's talon, what difference does it make. And without formulating anything clearly, I understood that I had found the key to Existence, the key to my Nauseas, to my own life. In fact, all that I could grasp beyond that returns to this fundamental absurdity.

● ● ●

This moment was extraordinary. I was there, motionless and icy, plunged in a horrible ecstasy. But something fresh had just appeared in the very heart of this ecstasy; I understood the Nausea, I possessed it. . . .

● ● ●

Had I dreamed of this enormous presence? It was there, in the garden, toppled down into the trees, all soft, sticky, soiling everything, all thick, a jelly. And I was inside, I was the garden. I was frightened, furious, I thought it was so stupid, so out of place, I hated this ignoble mess. Mounting up, mounting up as high as the sky, spilling over, filling everything with its gelatinous slither, and I could see depths upon depths of it reaching far beyond the limits of the garden, the houses, and Bouville, as far as the eye could reach. I was no longer in Bouville, I was nowhere, I was floating. I was not surprised, I knew it was the World, the naked World suddenly revealing itself, and I choked with rage at this gross, absurd being. You couldn't even wonder where all that sprang from, or how it was that a world came into existence, rather than nothingness. It didn't make sense, the World was everywhere, in front, behind. There had been nothing *before* it. Nothing. There had never been a moment in which it could not have existed. That was what worried me: of course there was no *reason* for this flowing of larva to exist. *But it was impossible* for it not to exist. It was unthinkable: to imagine nothingness you had to be there already, in the midst of the World, eyes wide open and alive; nothingness was only an idea in my head, an existing idea floating in this immensity: this nothingness had not come *before* existence, it was an existence like any other and appeared after many others. I shouted "filth! what rotten filth!" and shook myself to get rid of this sticky filth, but it held fast and there was so much, tons and tons of existence, endless: I stifled at the depths of this immense weariness. And then suddenly the park emptied as through a great hole, the World disappeared as it had come, or else I woke up—in any case, I saw no more of it; nothing was left but the yellow earth around me, out of which dead branches rose upward.

JOHN ADDINGTON SYMONDS

spontaneous and induced
mystical experience

"Suddenly," writes Symonds, "at church, or in company, or when I was reading, and always, I think, when my muscles were at rest, I felt the approach of the mood. Irresistibly it took possession of my mind and will, lasted what seemed an eternity, and disappeared in a series of rapid sensations which resembled the awakening from anaesthetic influence. One reason why I disliked this kind of trance was that I could not describe it to myself. I cannot even now find words to render it intelligible. It consisted in a gradual but swiftly progressive obliteration of space, time, sensation, and the multitudinous factors of experience which seem to qualify what we are pleased to call our Self. In proportion as these conditions of ordinary consciousness were subtracted, the sense of an underlying or essential consciousness acquired intensity. At last nothing remained but a pure, absolute, abstract Self. The universe became without form and void of content. But Self persisted, formidable in its vivid keenness, feeling the most poignant doubt about reality, ready, as it seemed, to find existence break as breaks a bubble round about it. And what then? The apprehension of a coming dissolution, the grim conviction that this state was the last state of the conscious Self, the sense that I had followed the last thread of being to the verge of the abyss, and had arrived at demonstration of eternal Maya or illusion, stirred or seemed to stir me up again. The return to ordinary conditions of sentient existence began by my first recovering the power of touch, and then by the gradual though rapid influx of familiar impressions and diurnal interests. At last I felt myself once more a human being; and though the riddle of what is meant by life remained unsolved, I was thankful for this return from the abyss—this deliverance from so awful an initiation into the mysteries of skepticism.

"This trance recurred with diminishing frequency until I reached the age of twenty-eight. It served to impress upon my growing nature the phantasmal unreality of all the circumstances which contribute to a merely phenomenal consciousness. Often have I asked myself with anguish, on waking from that formless state of denuded, keenly sentient being, Which is the unreality?—the trance of fiery, vacant, apprehensive, skeptical Self from which I issue, or these surrounding phenomena and habits which veil that inner Self and build a self of flesh-and-blood conventionality? Again, are men the factors of some dream, the dream-like unsubstantiality of which they comprehend at such eventful moments? What would happen if the final stage of the trance were reached?"

under chloroform
"After the choking and stifling had passed away, I seemed at first in a state of utter blankness; then came flashes of intense light, alternating with blackness,

From William James, *Varieties of Religious Experience,* New York and London, Longmans, Green, and Co., 1928.

and with a keen vision of what was going on in the room around me, but no sensation of touch. I thought that I was near death; when, suddenly, my soul became aware of God, who was manifestly dealing with me, handling me, so to speak, in an intense personal present reality. I felt him streaming in like light upon me. . . . I cannot describe the ecstasy I felt. Then, as I gradually awoke from the influence of the anaesthetics, the old sense of my relation to the world began to return, the new sense of my relation to God began to fade. I suddenly leapt to my feet on the chair where I was sitting, and shrieked out, 'It is too horrible, it is too horrible, it is too horrible,' meaning that I could not bear this disillusionment. Then I flung myself on the ground, and at last awoke covered with blood, calling to the two surgeons (who were frightened), 'Why did you not kill me? Why would you not let me die?' Only think of it. To have felt for that long dateless ecstasy of vision the very God, in all purity and tenderness and truth and absolute love, and then to find that I had after all had no revelation, but that I had been tricked by the abnormal excitement of my brain."

ALEXANDER SOLZHENITSYN

prayer _____

How easy it is for me to live with You, Lord! How easy it is for me to believe in You! When my thoughts get stuck or my mind collapses, when the cleverest people see no further than this evening and do not know what must be done tomorrow, You send down to me clear confidence that You exist and that you will ensure that not all the ~~ays~~ of goodness are blocked.

From the summit of earthly fame I look round with wonder at that road through hopelessness to this point, from which even I have been able to shed abroad among men the refulgence of Your glory.

And You will grant me to express this as much as is necessary. And insofar as I am not able to do it, that means You have allotted this to others.

_____

From *Religion in Communist Dominated Areas,* vol. X, nos. 7–8, April 1971.

WILLIAM FAULKNER

the sermon _____

When the visitor rose to speak he sounded like a white man. His voice was level and cold. It sounded too big to have come from him and they listened at first through curiosity, as they would have to a monkey talking. They began to watch him as they would a man on a tight rope. They even forgot his insignificant appearance in the virtuosity with which he ran and poised and swooped upon the cold inflectionless wire of his voice, so that at last, when with a sort of swooping glide he came to rest again beside the reading desk with one arm resting upon it at shoulder height and his monkey body as reft of all motion as a mummy or an emptied vessel, the congregation sighed as if it waked from a collective dream and moved a little in its seats. Behind the pulpit the choir fanned steadily. Dilsey whispered, "Hush, now. Dey fixin to sing in a minute."

Then a voice said, "Brethren."

The preacher had not moved. His arm lay yet across the desk, and he still held that pose while the voice died in sonorous echoes between the walls. It was as different as day and dark from his former tone, with a sad, timbrous quality like an alto horn, sinking into their hearts and speaking there again when it had ceased in fading and cumulate echoes.

"Brethren and sisteren," it said again. The preacher removed his arm and he began to walk back and forth before the desk, his hands clasped behind him, a meager figure, hunched over upon itself like that of one long immured in striving with the implacable earth, "I got the recollection and the blood of the Lamb!" He tramped steadily back and forth beneath the twisted paper and the Christmas bell, hunched, his hands clasped behind him. He was like a worn small rock whelmed by the successive waves of his voice. With his body he seemed to feed the voice that, succubus like, had fleshed its teeth in him. And the congregation seemed to watch with its own eyes while the voice consumed him, until he was nothing and they were nothing and there was not even a voice but instead their hearts were speaking to one another in chanting measures beyond the need for words, so that when he came to rest against the reading desk, his monkey face lifted and his whole attitude that of a serene, tortured crucifix that transcended its shabbiness and insignificance and made it of no moment, a long moaning expulsion of breath rose from them, and a woman's single soprano: "Yes, Jesus!"

As the scudding day passed overhead the dingy windows glowed and faded in ghostly retrograde. A car passed along the road outside, laboring in the sand, died away. Dilsey sat bolt upright, her hand on Ben's knee. Two tears slid down her fallen cheeks, in and out of the myriad coruscations of immolation and abnegation and time.

"Brethren," the minister said in a harsh whisper, without moving.

"Yes, Jesus!" the woman's voice said, hushed yet.

_____

From *The Sound and the Fury,* New York, Vintage Books, 1956.

"Breddren en sistuhn!" His voice rang again, with the horns. He removed his arm and stood erect and raised his hands. "I got de ricklickshun en de blood of de Lamb!" They did not mark just when his intonation, his pronunciation, became negroid, they just sat swaying a little in their seats as the voice took them into itself.

"When de long, cold—Oh, I tells you, breddren, when de long, cold—I sees de light en I sees de word, po sinner! Dey passed away in Egypt, de swingin chariots; de generations passed away. Wus a rich man: whar he now, O breddren? Wus a po man: whar he now, O sistuhn? Oh I tells you, ef you aint got de milk en de dew of de old salvation when de long, cold years rolls away!"

"Yes, Jesus!"

"I tells you, breddren, en I tells you, sistuhn, dey'll come a time. Po sinner sayin Let me lay down wid de Lawd, lemme lay down my load. Den whut Jesus gwine say, O breddren? O sistuhn? Is you got de ricklickshun en de Blood of de Lamb? Case I aint gwine load down heaven!"

He fumbled in his coat and took out a handkerchief and mopped his face. A low concerted sound arose from the congregation: "Mmmmmmmmmmmmm!" The woman's voice said, "Yes, Jesus! Jesus!"

"Breddren! Look at dem little chillen settin dar. Jesus wus like dat once. He mammy suffered de glory en de pangs. Sometimes maybe she helt him at de nightfall, whilst de angels singin him to sleep; maybe she look out de do' en see de Roman po-lice passin." He tramped back and forth, mopping his face. "Listen, breddren! I sees de day. Ma'y settin in de do' wid Jesus on her lap, de little Jesus. Like dem chillen dar, de little Jesus. I hears de angels singin de peaceful songs en de glory; I sees de closin eyes; sees Mary jump up, sees de sojer face: We gwine to kill! We gwine to kill! We gwine to kill yo little Jesus! I hears de weepin en de lamentation of de po mammy widout de salvation en de word of God!"

"Mmmmmmmmmmmmmmmmmm! Jesus! Little Jesus!" and another voice, rising:

"I sees, O Jesus! Oh I sees!" and still another, without words, like bubbles rising in water.

"I sees hit, breddren! I sees hit! Sees de blastin, blindin sight! I sees Calvary, wid de sacred trees, sees de thief en de murderer en de least of dese; I hears de boasting en de braggin: Ef you be Jesus, lif up yo tree en walk! I hears de wailin of women en de evenin lamentations; I hears de weepin en de cryin en de turntaway face of God: dey done kilt Jesus; dey done kilt my son!"

"Mmmmmmmmmmmmmmm. Jesus! I sees, O Jesus!"

"O blind sinner! Breddren, I tells you; sistuhn, I says to you, when de Lawd did turn His mighty face, say, Aint gwine overload heaven! I can see de widowed God shet His do'; I sees de whelmin flood roll between; I sees de darkness en de death everlastin upon de generations. Den, lo! Breddren! Yes, breddren! Whut I see? Whut I see, O sinner? I sees de resurrection en de light; sees de meek Jesus sayin Dey kilt Me dat ye shall live again; I died dat dem whut sees en believes shall never die. Breddren, O breddren! I sees de doom crack en hears de golden horns shoutin down de glory, en de arisen dead whut got de blood en de ricklick-shun of de Lamb!"

In the midst of the voices and the hands Ben sat, rapt in his sweet blue gaze. Dilsey sat bolt upright beside, crying rigidly and quietly in the annealment and the blood of the remembered Lamb.

As they walked through the bright noon, up the sandy road with the dispersing congregation talking easily again group to group, she continued to weep, unmindful of the talk.

"He sho a preacher, mon! He didn't look like much at first, but hush!"

"He seed de power en de glory."

"Yes, suh. He seed hit. Face to face he seed hit."

Dilsey made no sound, her face did not quiver as the tears took their sunken and devious courses, walking with her head up, making no effort to dry them away even.

"Whyn't you quit dat, mammy?" Frony said. "Wid all dese people lookin. We be passin white folks soon."

"I've seed de first en de last," Dilsey said. "Never you mind me."

"First en last whut?" Frony said.

"Never you mind," Dilsey said. "I seed de beginnin, en now I sees de endin."

EVELYN UNDERHILL

contemplation

Contemplation is not, like meditation, one simple state, governed by one set of psychic conditions. It is a general name for a large group of states, partly governed—like all other forms of mystical activity—by the temperament of the subject, and accompanied by feeling-states which vary from the extreme of quietude or "peace in life naughted" to the rapturous and active love in which "thought into song is turned." Some kinds of Contemplation are inextricably entwined with the phenomena of "intellectual vision" and "inward voices." In others we find what seems to be a development of the "Quiet": a state which the subject describes as a blank absorption, a darkness, or "contemplation *in caligine*." Sometimes the contemplative tells us that he passes through this darkness to the light: sometimes it seems to him that he stays for ever in the "beneficent dark." In some cases the soul says that even in the depths of her absorption, she "knows her own bliss": in others she only becomes aware of it when contemplation is over and the surface-intelligence reassumes the reins.

In this welter of personal experiences, it becomes necessary to adopt some

From the book *Mysticism* by Evelyn Underhill. Published 1961 by E. P. Dutton & Co., Inc. and used with their permission.

basis of classification, some rule by which to distinguish true Contemplation from other introversive states. Such a basis is not easy to find. I think, however, that there are two marks of the real condition: (A) The Totality and Givenness of the Object. (B) Self-Mergence of the subject. These we may safely use in our attempt to determine its character.

(A) Whatever terms he may employ to describe it, and however faint or confused his perceptions may be, the mystic's experience in Contemplation is the experience of the All, and this experience seems to him to be *given* rather than attained. It is indeed the Absolute which is revealed to him: not, as in meditation or vision, some partial symbol or aspect thereof.

(B) This revealed Reality is apprehended by way of participation, not by way of observation. The passive receptivity of the Quiet is here developed into an active, outgoing self-donation, which is the self's response to the Divine initiative. By a free act, independent of man's effort, God is self-disclosed to the soul; and that soul rushes out willingly to lose itself in Him. Thus a "give and take"—a divine osmosis—is set up between the finite and the Infinite life. That dreadful consciousness of a narrow and limiting I-hood which dogs our search for freedom and full life, is done away. For a moment, at least, the independent spiritual life is achieved. The contemplative is merged in it "like a bird in the air, like a fish in the sea": loses to find and dies to live.

"We must," says Dionysius the Areopagite, "be transported wholly out of ourselves and given unto God." This is the "passive union" of Contemplation: a temporary condition in which the subject receives a double conviction of ineffable happiness and ultimate reality. He may try to translate this conviction into "something said" or "something seen": but in the end he will be found to confess that he can tell nothing, save by implication. The essential fact is that he was *there*: as the essential fact for the returning exile is neither landscape nor language, but the homely spirit of place.

"To see and to have seen that Vision," says Plotinus in one of his finest passages, "is reason no longer. It is more than reason, before reason, and after reason, as also is the vision which is seen. . . . And perhaps we should not here speak of *sight*: for that which is seen is not discerned by the seer—if indeed it is possible here to distinguish seer and seen as separate things. . . . Therefore this vision is hard to tell of: for how can a man describe as other than himself that which, when he discerned it, seemed not other, but one with himself indeed?"

Ruysbroeck, who continued in the medieval world the best traditions of Neoplatonic mysticism, also describes a condition of supreme insight, a vision of Truth, which is closely related to the Plotinian ecstasy. "Contemplation," he says, "places us in a purity and a radiance which is far above our understanding . . . and none can attain to it by knowledge, by subtlety, or by any exercise whatsoever: but he whom God chooses to unite to Himself, and to illuminate by Himself, he and no other can contemplate God. . . . But few men attain to this divine contemplation, because of our incapacity and of the hiddenness of that light in which one sees. And this is why none by his own knowledge or by subtle consideration will ever really understand these things. For all words and all that one can learn or understand in a creaturely way, are foreign to the truth that I mean and far below it. But he who is united to God, and illumined by this truth—he can understand Truth by Truth.

This final, satisfying knowledge of reality—this understanding of Truth by Truth—is, at bottom, that which all men desire. The saint's thirst for God, the philosopher's passion for the Absolute; these are nothing else than the crying need of the spirit, variously expressed by the intellect and by the heart. The guesses of science, the diagrams of metaphysics, the intuitions of artists; all are pressing towards this. "Adam sinned when he fell from Contemplation. Since then, there has been division in man."

dante has a vision of god

"My vision, becoming purified, entered deeper and deeper into the ray of that Supernal Light which in itself is true. Thenceforth my vision was greater than our language, which fails such a sight; and memory too fails before such excess. As he who sees in a dream, and after the dream is gone the impression or emotion remains, but the rest returns not to the mind, such am I; for nearly the whole of my vision fades, and yet there still wells within my heart the sweetness born therefrom. . . . I think that by the keenness of the living ray which I endured I had been lost, had I once turned my eyes aside. And I remember that for this I was the bolder so long to sustain my gaze, as to unite it with the Power Infinite. . . . Thus did my mind, wholly in suspense, gaze fixedly, immovable and intent, ever enkindled by its gazing. In the presence of that Light one becomes such, that never could one consent to turn from it to any other sight. Because the Good, which is the object of the will, is therein wholly gathered; and outside of this, that is defective which therein is perfect."

From *The Divine Comedy*, Par. xxxiii, trans. Evelyn Underhill.

birds of appetite _____

Where there is carrion lying, meat-eating birds circle and descend. Life and death are two. The living attack the dead, to their own profit. The dead lose nothing by it. They gain too, by being disposed of. Or they seem to, if you must think in terms of gain and loss. Do you then approach the study of Zen with the idea that there is something to be gained by it? This question is not intended as an implicit accusation. But it *is*, nevertheless, a serious question. Where there is a lot of fuss about "spirituality," "enlightenment" or just "turning on," it is often because there are buzzards hovering around a corpse. This hovering, this circling, this descending, this celebration of victory, are not what is meant by the study of Zen—even though they may be a highly useful exercise in other contexts. And they enrich the birds of appetite.

Zen enriches no one. There is no body to be found. The birds may come and circle for a while in the place where it is thought to be. But they soon go elsewhere. When they are gone, the "nothing," the "no-body" that was there, suddenly appears. That is Zen. It was there all the time but the scavengers missed it, because it was not their kind of prey.

through love to god _____

My uniform experience has convinced me that there is no other God than Truth. And if every page of these chapters does not proclaim to the reader that the only means for the realization of Truth is ahimsā, I shall deem all my labor in writing these chapters to have been in vain. And, even though my efforts in this behalf may prove fruitless, let the readers know that the vehicle, not the great principle, is at fault. After all, however sincere my strivings after ahimsā may have been, they have still been imperfect and inadequate. The little fleeting glimpses, therefore, that I have been able to have of Truth can hardly convey an idea of the indescribable luster of Truth, a million times more intense than that of the sun we daily see with our eyes. In fact what I have caught is only the faintest glimmer of that mighty effulgence. But this much I can say with assurance, as a result of all my experiments, that a perfect vision of Truth can only follow a complete realization of ahimsā.

To see the universal and all-pervading Spirit of Truth face to face one must be able to love the meanest of creation as oneself. And a man who aspires after that cannot afford to keep out of any field of life. That is why my devotion to Truth has drawn me into the field of politics; and I can say without the slightest hesitation, and yet in all humility, that those who say that religion has nothing to do with politics do not know what religion means.

Identification with everything that lives is impossible without self-purification; without self-purification the observance of the law of ahimsā must remain an empty dream; God can never be realized by one who is not pure of heart. Self-purification therefore must mean purification in all the walks of life. And purification being highly infectious, purification of oneself necessarily leads to the purification of one's surroundings.

But the path of self-purification is hard and steep. To attain to perfect purity one has to become absolutely passion-free in thought, speech, and action; to rise above the opposing currents of love and hatred, attachment and repulsion. I know that I have not in me as yet that triple purity, in spite of constant ceaseless striving for it. That is why the world's praise fails to move me, indeed it very often stings me. To conquer the subtle passions seems to me to be harder far than the physical conquest of the world by the force of arms. Ever since my return to India I have had experiences of the dormant passions lying hidden within me. The knowledge of them has made me feel humiliated though not defeated. The experiences and experiments have sustained me and given me a great joy. But I know that I have still before me a difficult path to traverse. I must reduce myself to zero. So long as a man does not of his own free will put himself last among his fellow creatures, there is no salvation for him. Ahimsā is the farthest limit of humility.

In bidding farewell to the reader, for the time being at any rate, I ask him to join with me in prayer to the God of Truth that He may grant me the boon of ahimsā in mind, word, and deed.

notes on principal authors

Bankei-Eitaku (1622–1693)—A Master of Rinzai Zen. Independent and very influential. Suzuki published in 1942 a volume entitled *Studies in Bankei Zen*.

Samuel Beckett—Contemporary Nobel Prize-winning Irish writer who has lived most of his productive life in France. He is known for the existential character of his themes.

Norman O. Brown—Contemporary exponent of a Christic-Dionysiac vision of man in protest against static notions of established religious institutions. He became known through his *Life Against Death*. His latest book is *Love's Body*.

Martin Buber (1878–1965)—One of the most celebrated of modern Jewish philosophers. His phrase "I-Thou" has become part of the language. He was for fifteen years on the faculty of Hebrew University in Jerusalem.

Rudolf Bultmann—One of Europe's leading Protestant theologians. He employed existentialism as a basis for the reinterpretation of the Christian faith for modern man.

Albert Camus (1913–1959)—French essayist and novelist who, along with Sartre, is regarded as a founder of modern existentialism. Winner of the Nobel Prize for Literature for his novel *The Plague*.

Robert Farrar Capon—Contemporary Episcopalian Priest whose writings have emphasized the incarnational (embodied) nature of Christian truth.

Teilhard de Chardin (1881–1954)—Jesuit paleontologist whose work on man's evolutionary past and his future destiny, all published posthumously, made him famous within a decade of his death. This work, perhaps more than any other, has made plausible the union of Christian and scientific perspectives on nature.

Chuang Tzu (third century B.C.)—The greatest philosopher of Chinese Taoism, known for his humor and literary genius.

Dante Alighieri (1265–1321)—Italian poet of the Renaissance. Best known for his *Divine Comedy.*

René Descartes (1596–1650)—French philosopher famous for his *Meditations on First Philosophy* which earned him the title of Father of Modern Philosophy.

Emily Dickinson (1830–1886)—One of the most celebrated American poets of the 19th century.

John Donne (1573–1631)—English poet whose conversion in middle life led him to write some of the finest religious poetry in the English language.

Loren Eiseley—Contemporary anthropologist and paleontologist who has the gift of blending scientific knowledge and imaginative vision. One of his recent books is entitled *The Unexpected Universe.*

Mircea Eliade—Widely accepted as an authoritative historian of religion. He is currently Chairman of the Department of the History of Religions at the University of Chicago.

Erik H. Erikson—Contemporary psychologist known for his work on human development and for his application of psychoanalytic insights to historical figures like Martin Luther and Gandhi.

William Faulkner (1897–1962)—American novelist who drew most of his stories out of the American South. He is justly famous for his novels *The Sound and the Fury, Light in August,* and *Intruder in the Dust,* among others. In 1950 he received the Nobel Prize for Literature.

Frederick Franck—Contemporary artist and writer. Known for his *Days with Albert Schweitzer* and his drawings of Vatican Council II. His work *The Exploding Church* is an exploration of the results of the renewal of the Catholic Church in Holland.

Sigmund Freud (1853–1939)—Modern founder of psychoanalysis. His great contribution was to demonstrate the influence of the unconscious on behavior and thought.

Mohandas K. Gandhi (1869–1948)—Indian saint and nationalist leader who sparked the liberation of the sub-continent and introduced to the world the practice of satyagraha (truth force) as an alternative to war.

Johann Wolfgang von Goethe (1749–1832)—One of the greatest German poets and dramatists. Celebrated as the author of *Faust.*

Dag Hammarskjöld (1905–1963)—Secretary-General of the United Nations from 1953 until his death. His inner religious life was completely unknown to his associates until after his death, when his private journal *Markings* was found in his house with an undated letter. He wrote, "These entries provide the only true 'profile' that can be drawn."

Abraham J. Heschel (1907–1972)—One of Judaism's leading American philosophers, he was an outstanding historian of Jewish mysticism.

Gerard Manley Hopkins (1844–1889)—English Jesuit who wrote poetry in the 19th century that many of today's readers find compellingly contemporary.

St. John of the Cross (1542–1591)—Called by Thomas Merton, "the greatest of all mystical theologians." He was also a fine poet. His theology is all the more impressive because it reflects his own personal experience. His most famous work is *The Ascent of Mount Carmel.*

William Johnston—Professor at Sophia University in Tokyo, Japan, where he has lived and worked for many years. He is known for his comparative study of Eastern and Western mysticism *The Still Point. Christian Zen,* from which our selection has been taken, is a further exploration of these themes.

Juliana of Norwich (1343–1416)—One of the greatest of the English mystics, she was visited with mystical openings which are the substance of her *Shewings of Divine Love.*

Carl Jung (1875–1961)—One of the founders, with Freud, of psychoanalysis, he broke early with him and established his own school of psychoanalytic thought. He is famous for his work on archaic symbols as clues to human personality.

Vernon Katz—Studied Indian philosophy at Oxford under Professor Radhakrishnan. He has been associated with transcendental meditation since the earliest days of Maharishi's teaching in Great Britain and assisted him in preparing his translation of the *Bhagavad-Gita.*

Gordon Kaufman—Contemporary theologian on the faculty of Harvard Divinity School.

Sam Keen—Rebel theologian who has become known as an advocate of a more Dionysian view of life in his books *Apology for Wonder* and *To a Dancing God.*

Sören Kierkegaard (1813–1855)—Danish theologian who founded in the 19th century the existential thought of the 20th. He was a bitter critic of established religion and Hegelian philosophy.

Laotzu—Flourished in China during the sixth century before Christ. The fountainhead of pure Taoism, he is a shadowy figure to whom is attributed the famous *Tao Te Ching.*

D. H. Lawrence (1885–1930)—English poet and novelist. Best known for his novel *Sons and Lovers.*

Archibald MacLeish—American poet.

Abraham Maslow—Until his recent death, Professor in the Department of Psychology at Brandeis University. Noted for his explorations into the new possibilities of human development along the self-actualizing lines of the essay we have reprinted in this volume.

Herman Melville (1819–1891)—American poet and novelist, best known for his epic novel *Moby Dick.*

Thomas Merton (1915–1968)—A trappist monk who was also a prolific literary figure, writing on social questions and religion. His later writings on the mysticism of the non-Christian religions are very highly regarded. He died in Bangkok where he was addressing a gathering of Buddhist monks.

Mohammed (570–632)—The prophet and founder of Islam who received in a trance the words of the sacred *Koran.*

James Naylor (1618–1660)—One of the earliest Quakers, joining the movement in 1651 after serving in the English army. He was an associate of George Fox, the founder. This deathbed exaltation of peace was made when he was dying of battle wounds inflicted by his enemies.

Friedrich Nietzsche (1844–1900)—German philosopher who anticipated many of the anxieties of the 20th century. He is popularly known for his prophetic *Thus Spake Zarathustra* and for his concept of the Superman.

Swami Nikhilananda—Presently head of the Ramakrishna-Vivekananda Center in New York City. Editor of the five-volume *Gospel of Sri Ramakrishna.* It is from his extensive biographical introduction to this work that our selection on Sri Ramakrishna has been taken

Thomas W. Ogeltree—Professor of Theology at Chicago Theological Seminary. Author of *Christian Faith and History* and *The Death of God Controversy.* His *Openings for Marxist-Christian Dialogue* is one of the clearest statements of this new development.

Boris Pasternak (1890–1960)—Russian poet and novelist whose Nobel Prize-winning *Doctor Zhivago* made him world-figure.

St. Paul—One of the early Christian apostles whose writings compose the bulk of the New Testament apart from the *Gospels.*

Frederick S. Perls—The originator and developer, until his recent death, of what has become widely known as Gestalt Therapy.

Theodore Roszak—Contemporary essayist on social themes, especially marked by dissent from established views. His reflections on the youthful subculture in *The Making of a Counter Culture* are among the best treatments of this theme.

Bertrand Russell (1872–1970)—Famous English philosopher who wrote on both highly technical themes and on social philosophy. A pacificst during the First World War, he spent his last years attempting to prevent humanity from committing collective suicide through war.

Jean-Paul Sartre—Contemporary French playwright, literary critic, and novelist. He is considered the principal founder of modern existentialism. *Nausea* from which our selections have been taken is thought to be largely autobiographical. After the Castro revolution in Cuba he has worked steadily to produce a synthesis of existentialism and Marxism.

Harold K. Schilling—Physicist, lecturer and writer. He is the author of *Science and Religion, An Interpretation of Two Communities.*

Shankaracharya—Greatest of the Vedantic philosophers of India. He was born around 800 A.D.

B. F. Skinner—Contemporary behavioral psychologist, professor at Harvard University. He is famous for his work on operant conditioning. His theories are presently used widely in education. His *Walden Two* is a utopian novel showing some of the social implications of his theories.

Wilfred Cantwell Smith—Distinguished theologian and scholar, Professor of World Religions and Director of the Center for the Study of World Religions, Harvard University.

Alexander Solzhenitsyn—Russian poet and novelist. Winner of the Nobel Prize for Literature for his novel *One Day in the Life of Ivan Denisovich.* He has recently been the first member of the Russian intelligentsia to criticize the Russian Church for its cooperation with the government in the suppression of religion. He and Pasternak, along with many others, are evidence that atheistic communism in Russia has not succeeded in stamping out religious faith there.

Oswald Spenglar (1880–1936)—German philosopher of history who became known for his cyclical view of civilizations as expounded in his *Decline of the West.*

John Addington Symonds (1840–1893)—English poet and literary critic. Against a critic who said that his mystical experiences had enfeebled him, William James wrote, "Symonds was a perfect monster of many-sided cerebral efficiency, and his critic gives no objective grounds whatever for his strange opinion. . . ."

Rabindranath Tagore (1861–1941)—Hindu poet, associate of Gandhi, and liberator who received the Nobel Prize for Literature in 1931.

Henry David Thoreau (1817–1862)—American naturalist, philosopher, and writer, chiefly remembered for his resistance to the Mexican-American war and for his *Walden Pond.*

Paul Tillich (1886–1965)—One of the most influential philosophical theologians of our time, famous especially for his three-volume *Systematic Theology* and for his extensive writings on the philosophy of culture.

Leo Tolstoy (1828–1910)—Social reformer and one of the greatest of the Russian novelists. Famous for his *War and Peace* and *Anna Karenina,* from which our selection is taken.

Evelyn Underhill (1875–1941)—English mystic and writer on mystical themes. She became known through her authorship of *Mysticism,* from which our selection has been taken.

Alan W. Watts—Contemporary writer and lecturer who has become popular for his interpretations of Eastern religions, especially Zen. Lately he has become an advocate of the use of drugs to induce mystical states.

Walt Whitman (1819–1964)—Known as the poet of American Democracy. His chief work was the collection of poems *Leaves of Grass.*

Simone Weil (1903–1943)—A French mystic and social philosopher who died in exile in England during World War II. She is best known for her *Gravity and Grace* and *Waiting for God.*

Wu Ch'êng-ên (c.1500–1580)—One of the leaders of the classical revival of Chinese literature in his day.

Lewis Yablonsky—Contemporary sociologist whose studies of the youthful subculture have been widely hailed. *The Hippie Trip* is a comprehensive survey of the hippie scene and its implications.

William Butler Yeats (1865–1939)—Irish essayist, poet, and dramatist. He received the Nobel Prize for Literature in 1923.

Heinrich Zimmer—A leading expert on the subject of Indian Philosophy. He died in 1943 while on a lectureship at Columbia University.

73 74 75 76 77 9 8 7 6 5 4 3 2 1

DIMENSIONS OF MAN

EDITED BY
Harold P. Simonson and John B. Magee

This anthology contains
a broad range of perspectives
on religious experience—
literary and theological,
Eastern and Western,
Christian and non-Christian.
Avoiding discussion of religion per se
and of religious institutions,
denominations, and customs,
the readings express important dimensions
of the human experience
that generate religious thought.
Varieties of religious consciousness
from madness and drug experiences
to the highest forms of mysticism
are explored.

SBN 06–046177–2